A history of women's writing in France

This volume is the first historical introduction to women's writing in France from the sixth century to the present day. Specially commissioned essays by leading scholars provide the first introduction in English to the wealth and diversity of French women writers, offering new readings and new perspectives. Each chapter focuses on a given period and a range of writers, taking account of prevailing sexual ideologies and women's activities in, or their relation to, their social, political, economic and cultural surroundings. The volume as a whole offers a cohesive history of women's writing which has sometimes been obscured by the canonization of a small feminine elite. Complemented by an extensive bibliography of primary and secondary works and a biographical guide to more than one hundred and fifty women writers, it represents an invaluable resource for those wishing to discover or extend their knowledge of French literature written by women

SONYA STEPHENS is Senior Lecturer in French at Royal Holloway University of London. She is author of *Baudelaire's Prose Poems: The Practice and Politics of Irony* (1999).

A HISTORY OF WOMEN'S WRITING IN FRANCE

EDITED BY

SONYA STEPHENS

CAMBRIDGE
UNIVERSITY PRESS

PUBLISHED BY THE PRESS SYNDICATE OF THE UNIVERSITY OF CAMBRIDGE
The Pitt Building, Trumpington Street, Cambridge, United Kingdom

CAMBRIDGE UNIVERSITY PRESS
The Edinburgh Building, Cambridge CB2 2RU, UK   www.cup.cam.ac.uk
40 West 20th Street, New York, NY 10011-4211, USA   www.cup.org
10 Stamford Road, Oakleigh, Melbourne 3166, Australia
Ruiz de Alarcón 13, 28014 Madrid, Spain

© Cambridge University Press 2000

First published 2000

Printed in the United Kingdom at the University Press, Cambridge

Typeface Monotype Baskerville 11/12½ pt.   *System* QuarkXPress™ [SE]

A catalogue record for this book is available from the British Library

Library of Congress Cataloguing in Publication Data

A history of women's writing in France / edited by Sonya Stephens.
p.   cm.
Includes bibliographical references.
ISBN 0 521 58167 2 (hardback)   0 521 58844 8 (paperback)
1. French literature – Women authors – History and criticism.
2. Women in literature.   3. Women and literature – France – History.
1. Stephens, Sonya.
PQ149.H57   2000
840.9'9287–dc21   99-43665   CIP

ISBN 0 521 58167 2 hardback
ISBN 0 521 58844 8 paperback

Contents

Notes on contributors

CATHLEEN M. BAUSCHATZ is Associate Professor of French at the University of Maine. She has published numerous articles on Montaigne, Gournay and sixteenth-century French women writers. She is currently at work on a book about women as readers in and of French Renaissance literature.

FAITH E. BEASLEY is Associate Professor of French at Dartmouth College (USA). She is the author of *Revising Memory: Women's Fiction and Memoirs in Seventeenth-Century France* (1990) and of articles on seventeenth-century women writers, the *salons* and the development of literary taste. She co-edited *Approaches to Teaching the Princesse de Clèves* with Katharine Ann Jensen (1998). She is currently completing a book on the *salons* and French national identity

MICHAEL BISHOP is Professor of French at Dalhousie University in Canada. He has published widely in the field of modern and contemporary French literature and culture. He is author of *The Contemporary Poetry of France* (1985), *Michael Deguy* (1988), *René Char: Les Dernières Années* (1990), *Nineteenth-Century French Poetry* (1993), *Contemporary Women Poets* (2 vols., 1995), *Women's Poetry in France 1965–95: A Bilingual Anthology* (1997). A major translation of Salah Stétié and a critical study of Prévert are in press.

JEAN BLOCH is Senior Lecturer in French at Royal Holloway, University of London. The author of *Rousseauism and Education in Eighteenth-Century France* (1995), she has published widely on eighteenth-century French educational theory, particularly in relation to gender and the education of women. She is at present completing a book on pedagogical ideals for girls in eighteenth-century France.

MARTIN HALL is Lecturer in French at King's College, University of London. His interests lie particularly in the field of eighteenth-century French fiction, and he has published work on the historical novel of the period, on Diderot and women novelists such as Tencin and Elie de Beaumont. He is currently working on eighteenth-century novelists in relation to their readers.

LESLIE HILL is Professor of French Studies at the University of Warwick and the author of *Beckett's Fiction* (1990), *Marguerite Duras: Apocalyptic Desires* (1993), and *Blanchot: Extreme Contemporary* (1997). He is currently completing a book on the relationship between literature and philosophy in the writings of Georges Bataille, Maurice Blanchot and Pierre Klossowski.

ALEX HUGHES is Professor of twentieth-century French Literature at the University of Birmingham. She has published widely, including a book on Violette Leduc, *Violette Leduc: Mothers, Lovers and Language* (1994), and a co-edited volume (with Kate Ince) entitled *French Erotic Fiction: Women's Desiring Writing 1880–1990* (1996). Her research interests include autobiography, women's and gay and lesbian writing, as well as the intersections of writing and photography.

ROBERTA L. KRUEGER is Professor of French at Hamilton College. She is the author of *Women Readers and the Ideology of Gender in Old French Verse Romance* (1993) and editor of the forthcoming *Cambridge Companion to Medieval Romance*. A founding editor of the *Medieval Feminist Newsletter*, she has published numerous articles on medieval French literature. She is currently researching a book-length study on late medieval French conduct books written for women, including Christine de Pizan's *Livre des Trois Vertus*.

ROSEMARY LLOYD is Rudy Professor of French at Indiana University. She has published five monographs and six book-length translations, plus numerous articles on subjects ranging from Baudelaire and Mallarmé to childhood and jealousy in French literature. She has long held an interest in women's writing, both in France and Australia, and in 1999 organized an international and multidisciplinary conference on women seeking expression in France 1789–1914. She is currently editing two volumes connected with that conference.

MARY NOONAN lectures in French at University College, Cork. She is currently completing a doctoral thesis of the theatres of Sarraute,

Duras and Cixous in the light of the philosophical work of Irigaray. She has published articles on the plays of Duras and Cixous, as well as on the mother–daughter relationship in contemporary French theatre. She co-edited a volume of *Theatre Research International*, 'Women Give Voice to Women: Feminist Theory in Practice on the French Stage' (1998), an issue based on papers delivered at the 1997 conference of the same title, which she co-organized.

MICHAEL SHERINGHAM is Professor of French at Royal Holloway, University of London. He has written extensively on André Breton and Surrealism, on modern and contemporary French poetry, on autobiography and related genres, and has published essays and monographs on Beckett, Duras, Queneau, Genet, Sartre and many other writers. He is a regular contributor to the *Times Literary Supplement* and is General Editor of Cambridge Studies in French. His most recent books are *French Autobiography: Devices and Desires* (1993) and *Parisian Fields* (1996). He is currently completing a book on theories and practices of everyday life.

SONYA STEPHENS is Senior Lecturer in French at Royal Holloway, University of London. She is author of *Baudelaire's Prose Poems: The Practice and Politics of Irony* (1999) and numerous essays and articles on Baudelaire and nineteenth-century French culture. She has also written on the contemporary French-Canadian writer, Marie-Claire Blais. She is currently at work on a book about the unfinished in nineteenth-century French literature and art.

JUDITH STILL is Professor of French and Critical Theory at the University of Nottingham. She is the author of *Justice and Difference in the Work of Rousseau* (1993) and *Feminine Economies: Thinking Against the Market in the Enlightenment and Late Twentieth Century* (1997). She is also co-editor (with M. Worton) of *Intertextuality* (1990) and *Textuality and Sexuality* (1993); co-editor (with D. Knight) of *Women and Representation* (1995); and co-editor (with S. Ribeiro) of *Brazilian Feminisms* (1999). She has been on the editorial board of *Paragraph* since 1989. She is currently working on a project on masculinity in the late twentieth century.

Introduction

Sonya Stephens

'All history is first chronology', Henri-Jean Martin, the cultural historian, asserts in the opening lines of his *Histoire et pouvoirs de l'écrit*.[1] *A History of Women's Writing in France* is true to this definition of history, since it is, first and foremost, a chronological survey, with contributions ranging from the Middle Ages to the present day. As this organization suggests, traditional categories have been retained within this chronology, despite the fact that feminist historiography has called into question the very notion of 'periodization', implying as it does a common history for both sexes. Such categories, one could argue, can and should be retained in a volume devoted exclusively to women's writing, not least because, both implicitly and explicitly, this History is relational and seeks to reinstate women's distinctive contribution to those periods, even as it excludes the men who history records as shaping them.

Histories such as this one are necessarily selective and exclusive. First, and most obviously, there is the exclusion of male writers, important figures canonized by other sorts of literary history and criticism. This particular exclusion needs no excuses, but it does make this account of writing in France a partial one, in both senses of the word. Only when women's part in the shaping of literary history is fully restored, only when their activities and works are fully re-integrated in the chronology of both history and writing, will it be possible to address this first kind of exclusivism. But, as the title announces, there are two further sorts of selectivity which relate specifically to women. Whilst the notion of women writing *in France* nominally allows the inclusion of women from beyond the hexagon who are working and/or publishing in it – such as Marguerite Yourcenar, who was born in Belgium and spent much of her life in the United States, to name only the most established example – the focus of this volume is almost exclusively French. This is in no way to dismiss the rich and varied body of writing produced by women writing in other Francophone countries, nor its influence on women

writing in mainland France. But, in a history of this length, geographical selections are the first to be made. The second form of selectivity is
more difficult still and is one of the reasons that this is simply *a* history.
The many exclusions and omissions mean that this account of women's
writing is incomplete. To be exhaustive, or to write *the* history of
women's writing would be impossible. Instead, rather like Henri-Jean
Martin contemplating writing the chronology of writing, this history
alternates between the vertigo caused by the scale and scope of women's
writing and the myopia necessary to condense it into any sort of history.

Many of the writers included will be familiar to students of French
and to the general reader, for they are already an established part of the
literary canon. Others will be unknown to both, and perhaps even to
specialists in French literature, despite the fact that their works are
often published by the major French publishing houses. The aim of this
History is to provide an introductory survey to the wealth and diversity
of female literary production in France, whilst offering new readings of
and new perspectives on those writers. The aim is also to venture beyond
the canon required by such an introduction, and whilst there are some
writers one could not – and would not want to – exclude, there are many
others who are just emerging from relative literary and, especially, from
critical obscurity. The reintegration of women in a broader (male inclusive) history and literary history has already been evoked, but more
pressing still is the need to restore cohesion to a history of women's
writing which the canonization of a feminine literary elite militates
against. If this History cannot be comprehensive, what it does strive to
do is to provide a more inclusive overview and to restore a sense of the
collective identity and the continuity expressed in writing by women,
and within what Nancy K. Miller has called a 'poetics of location'.[2]

These preliminary remarks allude, if somewhat covertly, to the central
– and much debated – preoccupations of much feminist theory: femininity, identity and difference. The history of women's writing does not
necessarily demand a feminist approach, but it should be recognized that
the focus on gender that is explicit in this enterprise does require an
understanding of sexual differences. The attempt to explain female literary production in any period must, then, take some account of the prevailing sexual ideologies, and of women's activities in, or their relation
to, the social, political, economic and cultural spheres. These socio-historical factors are brought out clearly by the contributors, so that the literary history of women's writing is interwoven with relevant strands of
other histories influencing and conditioning literary production. As it

will be seen, not all women seek to assert their difference as women and most strive rather to establish their difference as writers, often in a way which is inclusive of their gender (if only, sometimes, because it cannot be exclusive of it). The convergence of literary trends and constraints with social ones, and women's creative engagement with these trends and constraints, brings to the fore the question of established literary forms and feminine experimentation and the highly complex relationships between gender and genre.

This History spans more than fourteen hundred years of women's writing across all the genres. As the diversity revealed in the individual contributions and the bibliographical guide at the end of the volume demonstrate, even in this selective account of women's writing in France the body of work is large and growing. Alongside this, critical activity devoted to women's writing is also growing, developing readings of existing texts and expanding the corpus by retrieving forgotten works from oblivion and restoring them to their place in literary history. And so, the bibliographical guide, whilst it does list works by every author discussed in this account and attempts to classify these, is no more exhaustive than the account itself. Indeed, it is still more selective in the sense that it has not usually included *all* works by any given author. Instead, it lists the major works, and more works by those women who are deemed to be central to an understanding of the period than by those who might be considered more peripheral. This selectivity is reproduced with still greater exclusivism with respect to the further reading recommended. This is often just a fraction of the secondary material available and should be seen as a starting point or points of orientation. Many of the works recommended, both under the headings of individual authors and in the critical works and histories section, themselves offer extensive bibliographies, both of the primary texts under consideration and selected secondary material. Where translations of the primary texts exist, both in original and modern versions, they have been provided in the hope that they will be of benefit to the scholar who does not read French and to the general English-speaking reader wishing to experience something of the wealth of French women's literary production. Where no translations are mentioned, it is because bibliographical searches have not revealed any. New translations are, however, appearing all the time. As works continue to be read and reread, assessed and appreciated, and then included on the reading lists of students across the English-speaking world, so the literary heritage of French women's writing evolves and, in parallel, translations appear to open up new texts for discovery, investigation and interpretation by the non-francophone reader.

A History of Women's Writing in France seeks to do much the same by offering in English both an introduction to and an overview of the whole field. Roberta L. Krueger's chapter spans nine hundred years and demonstrates that, from the very beginnings of French literature, women played a role in the shaping of society and culture, often in ways which are silenced by history, as promoters of an oral tradition, as readers, and as patrons of the arts and education. Despite conditions militating against writing, women did record their voices and, in so doing, established themselves in history as exceptions to their sex. One of the problems with writing in such a climate, however, is that there is often a price to be paid for being an exception and, as a result, many of the extant texts are anonymous. This raises the issue of recognized authorship, central to women's writing well beyond the medieval period. This leads to a number of anonymous texts, or questions raised about historical identity, as well as to hoaxes, ghost-writing and to the adoption of male pseudonyms. As Krueger points out, such anonymity in the medieval period means that one cannot discount the possibility that some texts, to date assumed to be masculine, might have been composed by women.

Much of the writing in the medieval period is composed of letters, songs, courtly narratives, devotional writings and saints' lives. Often, too, it is devoted to questions of moral instruction and spirituality, either by those in religious orders or by noblewomen seeking to play a role in the shaping of society through the education of the next generation. Krueger's chapter explains feminine agency in the period, showing the medieval woman's role in the family, in education and in the oral tradition as a productive and social force. It demonstrates the diversity of writings in the period and explains the role of women in the medieval courtly tradition. Most of all, Krueger shows that in a variety of feminine voices and forms – lyric, romance, didactic and devotional – medieval women writers assert their differences in both gender and genre to make an unquestionable contribution to the processes of change.

As in the medieval period, the conditions for learning that prevailed at court in the Renaissance often benefited women, if not as much as they did men. Cathleen M. Bauschatz's chapter places women's writing in the sixteenth century in the context of important socio-historic changes affecting reading and culture, such as the Protestant Revolution, the invention of print and the influence of the Italian Renaissance. The latter two together brought, in the first half of the century, a literary tradition dominated by Boccaccio and Petrarch, within which women sought to voice their individuality and gender, their relationship to and, most importantly, their difference from the courtly tradition inherited from the Middle Ages and from the prevailing Italian cultural influences. In so doing, the women writing in this period, set out to reveal the masculinist bias of culture and to present a feminine perspective on similar themes. As Bauschatz reveals, much of the writing by women in this period bears witness to the phenomenon described by Harold Bloom as the 'anxiety of influence', so that even when there is a shift away from the Italian cultural model, women strive to define a voice within the conventions of their French predecessors; to affirm an identity which is legitimized by a masculinist tradition even as their writing reworks it. In their development of this tradition, and in their search for an authentic feminine voice in a range of different genres, women writers of the late sixteenth century establish a form of subjective, autobiographical writing which we can trace right through to contemporary fiction.

It is certainly clearly developed in the seventeenth century, as Faith E. Beasley demonstrates, with personalized forms and interiorized accounts reworking perspectives on history, commenting on the contemporary social conditions, recording the details of their lives and so creating themselves in literary form. But, in comparison to the relatively small number of women who participated in the literary history of the sixteenth century, the seventeenth century witnessed a surge in female creativity. Although conditions for learning were not propitious, women could read and sought to enhance their knowledge in ways reflecting contemporary debates. In her chapter on this period, Beasley describes the growth of women's participation in the literary field and the role of the *ruelle* which contributed so dramatically to women's literary influence. The *ruelle*, a form of social gathering which continued to exist in different forms until the Revolution, was an elaborate forum for the exchange of views on a variety of topics: social codes and practices, matters of the human heart, literary works, and perhaps most significantly, women's place in the intellectual sphere. Beasley explains how these collaborative discussions led to similar collaboration on creative projects, at first in minor genres which, in their turn led to the creation of the novel and the fairy tale. These genres allowed women to raise contemporary issues affecting their gender in a carefully constructed historical or marvellous context, and the development of these fictional forms can, therefore, be seen to be engaging in the same assertion of feminine difference as other literary and non-literary forms explored in the period.

The achievements of the seventeenth century were built upon by women writing in the eighteenth, but in this period, with its emphasis on science and knowledge, it was, as Jean Bloch argues, extremely difficult for inadequately educated women to compete in the most valued spheres of writing. Women continued to develop the literary genres which had been prevalent in the previous century: the novel, the fairy tale, the memoir and the letter, often combining their predilection for the first and the last in epistolary fiction. But, as Martin Hall explains, the problem with such writing in an era which favours the non-fictional over works of the imagination, and male creativity over women's, is that the female gender, and the feminine novel, are increasingly marginalized. This fact of literary history is echoed in many of the fictional concerns, where the dominance of men and the constraints of marriage, determine the lives of women in a heterosexual economy. The result of this masculine dominance was that those women who did seek to engage with the ideas of science were so constrained by social circumstance that they either did not write at all, published their work anonymously or kept their writing secret. It was in the scientific sphere of education, however, that women were able to make the boldest political statements and writing by women on pedagogy is, as Jean Bloch demonstrates, one of the most significant contributions to the period. Such pedagogical treatises bring women to a better defined sense of self, enabling them to shape their role as mothers, to articulate their aspirations and to campaign for more equal opportunities in the sphere of knowledge. These concerns are articulated in earlier periods, indeed as early as the Middle Ages, but it is in the eighteenth century that they find their most positive expression.

The Revolution brought about new political activism – for without women there would have been no Revolution – and new narrative possibilities. But most of all, as Rosemary Lloyd argues, it diminished freedom for women, so that whilst they fought with the men for *liberté, égalité, fraternité*, they found themselves without the very rights they had advocated for all. Women in the nineteenth century had a greater sense, then, of the possibilities of emancipation, but their aspirations were at odds with a climate of repression which persisted almost until the end of the century. Despite this, women's writing developed in this period. As Rosemary Lloyd's chapter demonstrates, women seized the opportunities presented by the growth in the press to engage in journalistic writing, developing feminist periodicals which voiced their convictions, as well as other sorts of publications for women. The strong convictions held by feminists of the period also led them to publish book-length statements advocating women's rights. In a parallel quest for a sense of identity and self-definition, women writers also expressed their sense of self by engaging with other cultures in travel writing. Women continued to write on education and to develop the genres of the novel, letters and autobiography, often experimenting with a wider range of genres than their predecessors. Poetry, too, enjoyed a revival in this period and some women even managed to have dramatic works staged. Lloyd shows that the prolific production of many women writers in this period, their sense of literary adventure, and their tenacity and dynamism, contributed not only to the rich cultural diversity of the period, but also established – by building upon the centuries-long struggle in the cultural, political and social spheres – the foundations for much of what was to occur in the twentieth century.

The twentieth century represents, in many ways, a realization of so many of the aspirations articulated by women in earlier periods. If the preceding summary of the nineteenth century seems, to return to the image evoked earlier, more vertiginous in its accumulation of genres and activities of women, it is because of the dizzying energy with which women devoted themselves to a cause, whether political or literary. It is, in part at least, to counteract this effect in a period when women's writing becomes still more prolific and diverse that the organization of the chapters in this part of the volume is slightly different. While retaining a strong sense of the chronology of history, the chapters written by Alex Hughes (1900–69) and Leslie Hill (1970 to the present) concentrate exclusively on fiction, the dominant literary genre of twentieth-century women's writing. These two chapters form a historical and literary backdrop against which Michael Sheringham's chapter on autobiography should be read for, building upon the rich tradition of feminine autobiography that this History reveals, women in the twentieth century engage with the central repositioning of autobiography in French culture in ways which, Michael Sheringham demonstrates, enable them to map their own identities against a broader social reality. The autobiographical experimentation by women since 1975 is testimony to feminine engagement with mainstream culture and their contribution to it. Mary Noonan's chapter on women playwrights, and Michael Bishop's chapter on poetry can also be reintegrated into the historical chronologies, although these forms seem to have more independent trajectories, despite the involvement of women writing across a range of genres.

Alex Hughes argues that the first sixty years of the twentieth century can be characterized as a period both of stasis and change, whereas the period discussed by Leslie Hill is one marked by radical gender-related socio-cultural transformation. Hughes illuminates the ways in which narratives 1900–69 articulate the historical moment and the particular feminine condition associated with that moment, as well as the ways in which they problematize the language available to them. Hill develops this argument in the post-68 period, showing how women's writing developed new strategies and a new language in the wake of new social/sexual freedoms and in a climate of cultural experimentation and theorization. Writing comes to be associated with the body and an explicitly female difference, whilst continuing to engage with past traditions and the implications of the canonic in ways which continually return to the problems and adventures of finding a language in which to narrate that difference. Such is the adventure of the poetry explored by Michael Bishop and of – in different but complementary ways – the dramatization of voice and female subjectivity in the plays by women analysed by Mary Noonan.

Judith Still's chapter on feminist literary theory concludes the volume. One might argue that it should be placed at the heart of the chronology, between the chapters by Hughes and Hill. But, since many of the theorists discussed by Still are not interested in the historical developments of gender relations and focus rather upon language and reading, there is a case for removing it from its chronology and placing it either at the beginning – as a way of reading texts by women – or at the end, where it might suggest to the reader who has reached the end of this history's trajectory new ways of rereading the texts featured here and of approaching others.

In a sense, the role played by 'theory' in the shaping of an *écriture féminine* is historically present in all chapters (as an ongoing *querelle des femmes*), even if recent theoretical writings are specifically and more frequently invoked by contributors writing on twentieth-century women's writing to explain points of contact between literary theory and practice in this period. This chapter, like the others, seeks to offer an overview of an important aspect of women's writing. In so doing, it also offers the reader critical tools, feminist perspectives and a reading strategy which helps us to define what constitutes a feminine text and which, when practised with other reading strategies, can restore the feminine both to literary and other histories.

NOTES

1 Published by Perrin, 1988. Translated by Lydia G. Cochrane as *The History and Power of Writing* (Chicago University Press, 1994).
2 In *Subject to Change: Reading Feminist Writing* (New York: Columbia University Press, 1988), pp. 4–5.

CHAPTER ONE

Female voices in convents, courts and households: the French Middle Ages

Roberta L. Krueger

Women writers and readers have shaped the course of French literature from its inception, although their history is a fragmented one that includes silence and engagement, marginalization and empowerment, convention and originality, fragmentation and continuity. It is, moreover, a history that requires us to re-examine and expand the concepts of language, genre, national identity and authorship often implied in the terms 'French literature' in order to appreciate fully the contribution of literate women who lived in the territory of contemporary France or who wrote in French during the long period extending from the Merovingian dynasty (sixth century) to the Hundred Years' War (1337–1453).

The first Frankish women writers wrote in Latin. The earliest female-authored works in the French vernacular were composed not only in France but also in England, where Anglo-Norman was the language of the elite from the Norman Conquest (1066) until the fourteenth century. Women's writings include not only lyric poetry and courtly narratives, genres recognized as having a strong aesthetic component, but also letters, devotional writing, saints' lives and didactic treatises. Female authorship is not always easily recognizable, given the conditions of manuscript culture. Many texts written in female voices are anonymous.

Other texts name a woman author whose historical identity remains shrouded in mystery. Even when a name can be linked to a historical woman, in certain cases scholars have argued that male clerics have shaped or wholly fabricated women's words. Yet, if scribal intervention is always possible, we should not discount the idea that at least a few of the many manuscripts that have survived as 'anonymous' or with named male authors might well have been written by a woman. Finally, as befits a culture so strongly invested in oral traditions, many more women shaped culture through story-telling, song, performance and speech than through writing. Representations of women as singers, performers and teachers abound in medieval French literature.

During the nine hundred years surveyed within this chapter, Western Europe underwent a series of violent political upheavals as well as more gradual social changes that shaped the conditions for female literacy and women's writing. From the tumultuous internecine strife among the first Frankish kings, there emerged a feudal society organized around a network of familial and interpersonal bonds and, eventually, a more centralized kingship, bolstered by a burgeoning clerical administration. Despite the ravages of the Black Death and the Hundred Years' War in the fourteenth century, by the end of our period urban centres witnessed the growth of an important class of artisans and merchants. During this time, women's literacy expanded in ever-widening spheres, beginning with the protected haven of convents during the Merovingian period, when women read, and sometimes, wrote devotional texts and letters in Latin. Women's Latin learning flourished in royal courts and aristocratic households in the Carolingian era (700s–900s) and, after a tumultuous interlude, resurfaced forcefully in French and English courts and convents of the eleventh and early twelfth century. Beginning in the mid-twelfth century, as French vernacular works became increasingly popular, courtly literature captivated male and female readers, emerging first under the patronage of powerful women such as Eleanor of Aquitaine and Marie de Champagne, and then expanding to courts of the lower aristocracy.

Throughout the thirteenth and fourteenth centuries, the appeal of vernacular fictions as well as hagiography, devotional works and didactic treatises extended from aristocratic circles to bourgeois households. Religious women wrote not only inside convent walls, but also independently, without Church sanction. Indeed, medieval women participated in the emergence of French literature and culture as readers and as writers to such an extent that it is impossible to imagine the course of French literature as we know it without their activity. In every period, women's voices have recounted the efforts of women and men to preserve their families, to seek and offer spiritual guidance, and to shape their communities.

Yet, if elite women throughout the Middle Ages made an indelible mark on literary history, they did so in spite of, rather than because of, the gender roles ascribed to them, in theory, by medieval society. The status of women varied throughout the medieval period according to rank and to region, which makes it impossible to generalize about their relative power and privilege. But women of all classes faced social restrictions and pervasive antifeminism. Although Christian doctrine preached spiritual equality for both sexes, religious women were denied access to the priesthood and to the highest administrative functions from the early days of the Church. Twelfth- and thirteenth-century canon and customary law defined women as the dependents of fathers and husbands, denied them legal autonomy or the right to bear arms, and restricted their ability to dispose of their own property or to rule. The University of Paris, founded in the thirteenth century, formally excluded women from study. Cultural prejudices against lay women *writing*, fed by clerical anti-feminist notions of female inferiority and by fears of women's autonomy beyond the domestic sphere, prevailed well into the Renaissance.

In practice, however, elite women throughout the Middle Ages were often able to expand or transform traditional gender roles and to achieve a degree of agency, if not autonomy, in their roles as queens, regents and counsellors, as managers of estates in their husbands' absence, as patrons of the arts or benefactors of monasteries, convents or schools. Religious women founded and maintained religious orders, which functioned as centres of education. When the Church abolished double monasteries and attempted to limit the establishment of new convents, especially after the Lateran Council of 1215, determined, spiritual women continued to join religious communities or lived as solitary *mulieres religiosae* (religious women), or *béguines*. Noblewomen's role in educating their children was widely sanctioned throughout the Middle Ages, and most moralists stressed the role of reading appropriate materials as a means of acquiring virtue. Women with a taste for literature or thirst for learning could evidently not be restrained from their active cultural participation, as Christine de Pizan attested when she described how her 'natural' inclination for learning rebelled against the limited, domestic role advocated by her mother (*Le Livre de la Cité des dames* (*The Book of the City of Ladies*), Book II, chap. 36). As female literacy extended its domain from the twelfth to the thirteenth century, centres of lay and religious culture in France and England provided contexts where privileged women with literary accomplishments and inspiration could display their knowledge and eloquence. Although the social climate for women's writing in medieval France can hardly be described as favourable, the landscape was far from barren.

The extant works of medieval French female writers may be few in comparison to works to which male authorship is attributed, but they are among the most important works of their respective genres. Until recently, medieval literary history has tended to marginalize or discount the work of women writers, either by questioning female authorship or by focusing attention only on selected works, such as Marie de France's *Lais*, and by neglecting genres such as correspondence or devotional literature where women wrote more extensively. Yet if we consider the totality of medieval French women's literary writings, their extent and their originality become more apparent, as does the commonality of their themes and approaches. Each medieval French woman writer, in her own way, takes a bold stand by writing against the grain of masculine literary traditions. As she establishes her feminine authority through strategies that differ from those of men writing in similar genres, each woman author creates a different voice, provides a new perspective, or, in many cases, participates in a form of social or political engagement.

Writing in the Middle Ages was a public act. Even letters and love poems were read aloud or sung, and copied and read in new surroundings. Viewed chiefly as an art of persuasion, rhetoric was a means by which moral thinking could be influenced and communities could be shaped. The writings of Radegund, Baudonivia, Heloise, Clemence of Barking, Marie de France, the *trobairitz* and female *trouvères*, Marguerite d'Oingt, Marguerite Porete and Christine de Pizan constitute a remarkable body of reflections on women's authority, desire and faith and attest to women's power in forming families and communities. Although it is unlikely, for the most part, that these historical writers had direct knowledge of each other's writings, the recurrence of particular concerns, the strength of authorship in the face of misogyny or calumny, the spirited defence and illustration of women's learning that we read in their texts, all suggest that, as a countercurrent to the 'silences of the Middle Ages' surrounding women's lives, there were lively traditions of female performances and literacies that involved both oral and written practice.

THE EARLY MIDDLE AGES

The Latin letters, epistolary verses and hagiography that surround the celebrated figure Radegund (*ca* 525–87), wife of the Merovingian King Clothar, show how literate women deployed their writing to consolidate bonds of friendship and kin, to seek consolation, to offer spiritual guidance and instruction, and to shape their communities during turbulent times. Taken as a child and forced into marriage as a result of war negotiations, the Thuringian princess, Radegund, finally fled from her husband Clothar after he murdered her brother.[1] She resisted her husband's subsequent attempt to reclaim her and eventually established herself in a monastery endowed by Clothar at Poitiers, the abbey of

Sainte-Croix, probably around 561. The letter that Caesaria of Arles sent to Radegund at her request, which encloses the *Rules* for nuns that her brother, Caesarius of Arles, had written earlier, stresses the importance of study and reading within the convent.[2] Radegund and her sister nun, Agnes, exchanged letters with the poet and hagiographer, Venantius Fortunatus. Although Radegund's replies to Fortunatus are lost, three of her epistolary poems to others survive; two of these – 'The Fall of Thuringia' and 'Letter to Atarchis' – recount the horrors of war and her sorrow at the loss of family members.[3] The author skilfully blends together elements drawn from classical epic, Latin lament, Ovidian elegiac epistles, as well as German lament to produce moving accounts of her struggles that were calculated to elicit sympathy – and perhaps strategic support – from her kin.[4]

Baudonivia's *Life of Saint Radegund*, addressed to Abbess Dedima and to the nuns of Radegund's convent about twenty years after the saint's death, was written as a supplement to a previous *vita*, which Fortunatus had composed. Adopting a humble tone that she describes as more 'rustic' than that of her learned male predecessor, Baudonivia, a nun from Radegund's convent, recounts her mentor's courageous resistance to her husband's plots, her charity, and her sometimes extreme asceticism within the convent, as well as the miracles performed by the saint after her death. Radegund's piety entailed intense literary activity, according to Baudonivia. The saint never ceased meditating upon the Scriptures, day and night; when she momentarily stopped reading, an appointed nun would continue to read to her.[5] Baudonivia also reports that as Queen, writing from her convent, Radegund attempted to persuade kings to refrain from war 'whenever she heard of bitterness arising among them'.[6] Mixing fact and legend in the *Life of Saint Radegund*, Baudonivia seeks to move and improve her audience of nuns by the holy woman's example. Taken together, the early writings of Caesaria, Radegund and Baudonivia reveal how some women in the tumultuous world of sixth century Gaul used their rhetorical skills to consolidate female communities, to strengthen family and political ties, to foster spirituality through literacy, and to attempt to calm the political storms of the day.

Charlemagne's court attached great importance to learning and included women in its programme of lay education. A noblewoman's association with books, through patronage, reading and teaching, might enhance her moral authority within her family. A woman who wrote might try to extend that authority to the next generation and to strengthen her family against future adversity and loss, as the one female-authored work extant from this period makes poignantly clear. In 843, the Frankish noblewoman Dhuoda, wife of Count Bernard of Septimania, completed a book of moral instruction, the *Liber manualis* ('handbook'), for her fifteen-year-old son, William. Dhuoda's situation at the time she composed the book was solitary and precarious. She had been placed at Uzès to safeguard Bernard's southern territories while he navigated troubled political waters in the North following the death of Louis the Pious, Charlemagne's son, in 840. She was bereft of both her sons: William had been taken from his mother and offered as a hostage guaranteeing his father's loyalty to the new king, Charles the Bald; her younger son had been removed from her (probably as a potential hostage) before she had even learned his name.

In the midst of such turmoil, Dhuoda's desire to educate her elder son by means of her book takes on a special urgency. She borrows heavily from biblical and patristic sources, as do all medieval moralists, but tailors her style for a young reader and infuses her advice with maternal concern.[7] Dhuoda offers her book as a 'mirror' so that her son may contemplate her soul from afar and absorb the principles of Christian love, family loyalty and paternal authority that she holds so dear. Her instruction is offered not only for William's moral improvement, but more immediately for his survival since, as she puts it, animals who link together in mutual support and love may hold each other up in safety to struggle against the current (Neel, *Handbook for William*, p. 36). She expects William to convey her precepts to his younger brother and to his entire entourage. Her book is a moving testimony to a Carolingian noblewoman's faith in the benefits of education and piety, and to a Frankish mother's authority within her family. Dhuoda's *Liber manualis* reveals an author who espouses patriarchal values yet is fully cognizant of a mother's primordial influence on her children's moral development. Paradoxically, as it places loyalty to the father even above loyalty to the King, her work attests to the power and the limitations of Frankish women's role within the family (Neel, *Handbook for William*, p. xix). After Dhuoda's time, a widespread eclipse of learning, enduring for several generations, resulted from the collapse of the Carolingian empire and subsequent barbarian invasions.

THE TWELFTH-CENTURY 'RENAISSANCE'

The rebirth of intellectual and cultural activity in Europe during the twelfth century was evidenced or fostered by demographic growth, the cessation of invasions, the rise of court culture, the institution of knight-hood, the reform and expansion of monastic orders and the growth of urban centres, which became sites of learning. Most medieval people remained illiterate, unable to read or write Latin. They encountered Scripture, the liturgy and popular songs, stories or saints' lives through their oral transmission in Church, the manor hall, the household, or the marketplace. But for elite twelfth-century women, the opportunities for learning at court appear to have been at least as good as they were for men and evidence of women as readers and patrons during this period abounds.

Literacy did not necessarily imply writing, which was considered a separate, more specialized skill. Advanced writing was practised chiefly by male clerks, monks and nuns. Most of the female-authored works that survive during this period come from women living in religious orders or with probable religious connections. Nonetheless, the precious female-authored works that have come down to us attest to the vitality of female literary practices and to the originality of their authors' responses.

The three Latin letters that Heloise, abbess of the Paraclete (ca 1100 – ca 1163/4), wrote to her estranged husband, the controversial theolo-gian and teacher, Peter Abelard (1079–1142), brilliantly display their author's learning. They also reveal an independent thinker who used writings as a means of expressing difference. Set against the backdrop of traditional medieval marriage, of church doctrine or of soon-to-be-born 'courtly love,' Heloise's writings describe a love that dramatically opposes theological teachings or conventional morality. Her so-called 'Personal Letters' were written in response to Abelard's harrowing account, in his *Historia calamitatum* (1132), of how he seduced and impreg-nated his brilliant pupil; how their unpublicized marriage did not suffice to calm the wrath of Heloise's guardian and uncle, Fulbert; and how Fulbert had Abelard castrated after Heloise entered the convent at Argenteuil. Although Abelard views his brutally enforced celibacy and monastic solitude as God's fitting punishment for his sins of pride and lust, Heloise's letters tell a different story. She has taken the veil to please Abelard, not God, she insists, and she has never ceased loving and car-nally desiring her husband. Staunchly unrepentant for her actions or desires, Heloise confesses that the title of 'whore' is sweeter to her than that of 'wife', and that, despite the high position in which Abelard has placed her as abbess of the Paraclete, she cannot suppress sexual long-ings as she celebrates Mass.[8] In her third epistle, Heloise agrees to remain silent about her suffering, but begs Abelard to suggest how the Benedictine Rule might be adapted to women's lives in a convent. Abelard replies in a lengthy discourse on daily life in a well-ordered nunnery, and later sends, at her request, hymns, sermons and answers to forty-three Scriptural questions (the 'Problemata'). Heloise thereby succeeded, some argue, in redirecting his attentions toward her and her female community.

Partly because of the nature of Heloise's confessions, partly because of preconceptions about the style or content a woman 'should' have chosen, various scholars since the nineteenth century have questioned the authenticity of the letters, especially those of Heloise, which some claim to be written by Abelard. Scholars today are more likely to point out that Heloise was perfectly capable of holding her own rhetorically; they are more willing to grant her full credit for her subtle arguments, her emotional range and the calculated control of her prose. The female epistolary tradition was well established in Europe, as were correspondences such as that between Radegund and Fortunatus and, in the eleventh-century, between a nun called Constance and Baudri de Borgueil.[9] Readers may disagree, however, about how to evaluate the degree of self-effacement or empowerment, sincerity or performance, in Heloise's 'Personal Letters'. However one reads the correspondence, it is Heloise's voice that transforms Abelard's straightforward exemplum of male lust repented into a vexed account of negotiated gender differences. Heloise's letters established the notoriety of the lovers' legend, which was retold by many translators and adaptors, among them Jean de Meun (thirtheenth century) and Rousseau in his popular novel, *Julie ou la nouvelle Héloïse* (1761).

An equally passionate but different expression of female authority, desire, and community is conveyed by the *Life of Saint Catherine* (late twelfth century), a saints' life composed by Clemence of Barking, who writes from an abbey east of London that was one of the most important centres of female learning in Britain. Clemence's *Saint Catherine* is one of three female-authored Anglo-Norman saints' lives to come down to us; the others are an anonymous *Life of Edward the Confessor* (which some scholars have suggested was written by Clemence) and an anonymous *Life of Saint Audrey*, written by an unknown Marie (whom some have speculated might be Marie de France). Saints' lives were not only written for monks and nuns; they were also compiled along with courtly works in secular manuscripts, which reached audiences of lay men and women in courts and wealthy households.

Catherine's story doubtless held particular attraction for literate nuns and for noblewomen who prized learning. Its heroine, the legendary Saint Catherine of Alexandria, uses her skill as a rhetorician not for personal glory but for God. As a bold attempt to reveal the true faith to the cruel emperor Maxentius, Catherine confronts and brilliantly outwits fifty pagan philosophers in public disputation and inspires them, through her eloquence, to convert and undergo martyrdom. She also converts the Emperor's wife, his most trusted advisor, and two hundred vassals. Empowered by a passionate love of Christ, she resists the amorous advances of Maxentius and submits courageously to his torments. When the tyrant devises a terrible wheel of torture upon which to break the saint, Catherine's prayers bring God's vengeful thunderbolt, which splinters the wheel and kills four thousand pagans. When the saint is finally beheaded, milk flows from her body instead of blood. Although Clemence translates faithfully from her Latin source, her personal engagement manifests itself in many authorial interventions and telling details, such as her use of courtly language and her description of Catherine's effect on the empress and her female attendants.[10]

For a community of nuns, and for the world outside the convent, Clemence's *Life of Saint Catherine* exemplifies the power of a woman's faith, love and eloquence to transform the spiritual values of those around her. The popularity of Saint Catherine's legend throughout the Middle Ages is evidenced by other versions in French and Middle English, as well as pictorial images in wall paintings and manuscript illuminations. Christine de Pizan, for example, features the saint prominently in book III of the *Cité des dames* [*City of Ladies*].

In some respects, Clemence's history of Saint Catherine and Heloise's letters to Abelard seem diametrically opposed. One text extols a woman who has eschewed worldly passions and endures bodily martyrdom as a bride of Christ; in the other text, the subject laments her loss of physical love and professes to serve God only reluctantly. Clemence's subject is a saint; Heloise's an avowedly unrepentant sinner. But both texts inscribe female erudition as defiant and transformative and portray love as embodied suffering. Directly or indirectly, both writers show how female rhetoric can persuade male 'authorities', be they philosophers, husbands or Emperors; both writers describe an uncompromising passion, physically embodied, whether for an unattainable man or for a God with whom union occurs only after death. Heloise's *Letters* and Clemence's *Life of Saint Catherine* might be seen as complementary attempts by women writers to create a discursive space where faith, intellect, and embodied passion can coexist. They serve to remind us of the diversity and the intensity of religious women's writings in Anglo-Norman and French twelfth-century culture.

Perhaps the greatest monument to such diversity of expression in twelfth-century French and Anglo-Norman culture is the work of Marie de France. Sometime around 1160, twelve *Lais*, short narrative poems, were assembled by one 'Marie' and dedicated to '*le noble rei*' (probably Henry II Plantagenet, King of England); one manuscript contains all the *lais* and four others preserve selections. Between 1160 and 1190, 102 moral *Fables* were presented by a 'Marie' who says she is 'de France' to 'Count William' (whose identity is uncertain); there are twenty-three manuscripts. Finally, probably sometime after 1190, one 'Marie' translated Henry of Saltrey's Latin account of a knight's spiritual voyage to the underworld in *Espurgatoire Seint Patriz* [*Saint Patrick's Purgatory*], extant in a single manuscript. The historical identity of these three 'Maries' has not been fixed with certainty, and a few scholars have doubted that the same author wrote all three works, or even that 'Marie' was necessarily a woman. But the more common critical consensus is that Marie de France was a French-born female author who lived in England, probably in religious orders, and that she wrote the *Lais*, the *Fables* and the *Espurgatoire*, all in octosyllabic verse. Many also believe that Marie's direct yet sophisticated style; her artful compilation of stories that examine in diverse yet related ways the vexing problems of love, sexuality, maturation, marriage, family, communities, death; and her depiction of magical, moral and spiritual transformations place her works among the most remarkable vernacular productions in medieval literature. Of all the authors in this chapter, Marie de France has been most widely acclaimed by twentieth-century scholars. The *Lais* have been prized as a gem within the French literary canon and their sources, symbolism and treatment of love have been the object of numerous critical studies. Recent scholarship has drawn particular attention to Marie's bold stance as a female clerkly narrator in the *Lais* and to the many ways her poetic and moral vision diverges from 'courtly' literature by her male contemporaries.

In her Prologue to the *Lais*, Marie's narrator announces her poetic originality: she will *not* do what her contemporaries are doing by translating from Latin but will instead translate Breton *lais* (the *lai* may refer to a popular song and to the traditional story that explained its origins). She further states that a goal of ancient writers was to write 'obscurely' so that others who came after them might add the increment – '*le surplus*'

– of their own wisdom ('Prologue', lines 9–16). The ensuing stories skilfully adapt and blend Celtic, classical and courtly literary materials with
poetic brevity and thematic complexity in a way that invites Marie's
readers to use their own '*sens*' to interpret them.

All the *lais* are about women and men in love, yet the characters, settings, ethical crises and social or magical solutions are diversely presented. The *Lais* foreground the speech and actions of female
protagonists who include unhappy *mal mariées*, a devoted wife, a courageous maiden, a maiden pregnant out of wedlock, sympathetic and
detestable adulteresses. Marie's tales do not spare the wicked, but they
offer the weak a chance of redemption.

Several *lais* allow female characters to voice their desires, to make mis-
takes and yet to retain, rediscover or redefine a sense of female honour
in spite of their errors. (One thinks, inevitably, of Heloise.) Marie does
not advocate sexual transgression, but her narrator displays sympathy
towards women who are trapped in loveless marriages or who are
swayed by youthful passion, like the young maiden who finds herself
pregnant in *Milun*. The stories' marvellous otherworlds and magic interventions sometimes allow their characters to achieve a happy resolution
to their problems that is not possible in the 'real' life of a court or household. At the end of *Lanval* the knight and his lady escape on horseback
to fairyland, leaving the unjust Arthurian court forever. In *Eliduc*, a
betrayed wife who has discovered the comatose body of her husband's
young beloved reacts not with jealousy but with compassion for the girl's
beauty and brings her back to life with a magical flower that a weasel has
used to revive its companion. Not only does Eliduc's wife retire to a
convent so that her former husband may marry his mistress, eventually,
the new wife joins the former wife in religious order and Eliduc, too,
devotes his life to God.

The *Lais* present a multiplicity of perspectives on problems of love
and death, desire and transgression, birth and rediscovery in stories that
are at once similar and different. Throughout the collection, a crisscross-
ing of motifs – birds, flowers, beasts, textiles, marvellous objects, fathers,
mothers, abandoned children, twins and doubles – invites readers to
compare the protagonists' ethical crises and solutions. Poetic regeneration and moral transformation are at the heart of Marie's endeavour;
these processes include the readers in Marie's courtly audience.

Marie's feminocentric *lais* contrast sharply with the dominant current
of later twelfth- and thirteenth-century romance, which recount stories
about chivalry and the Arthurian court. But an important sub-genre of

later romance, the so-called '*roman réaliste*', drew inspiration directly or indirectly from Marie's tales of virtuous or resourceful heroines as their authors spun tales of maidens who set forth on their own to vindicate their honour or to arrange the marriage of their choice (as, for example, does the author of *Galeran de Bretagne* in his rewriting of *Fresne*).[11] By telling the stories of *mal mariées* and single-women from their own perspective, Marie used courtly literature as a means to redefine female *honour* on her own terms, as would the *trobairitz* and Christine de Pizan after her (although there is no evidence that they had direct knowledge of Marie's works).

Possibly even more widely read in the Middle Ages than the *Lais* were Marie's *Fables*, which have survived in twenty-three manuscripts and include forty of the earliest Old French fables of the Aesopic tradition, as well as over sixty fables derived from other sources. Although Marie claims to be translating her fables from an English translation done by a 'King Alfred', neither the text nor Alfred's precise identity have been determined, and it has been suggested that Marie herself may have compiled 'the earliest extant collection of fables in the vernacular of Western Europe'.[12] Comparison with Marie's Latin source, the *Romulus* collection, shows the extent to which she has made the French translation her own book, as evidenced not only by a particular concern for the plight of female animals and characters but also by a sensitivity to injustice and a keen concern with social realities that recall the *Lais*.[13] That such a book may well have served as a 'mirror for princes' intended to instruct the count to whom it was dedicated as well as other courtiers (whose common human foibles would have been amply exemplified in the collection) attests to the active role of counsellor and educator that a learned woman such as Marie may have played in her day.[14] As astutely critical as Marie has been in telling the *Fables*, she by no means disavows moral responsibility for their composition. Indeed, in the Epilogue when she names herself – 'Marie ai num, si sui de France' [My name is Marie and I am from France] – she specifically claims the collection as her own and warns against clerks who may assert authorship ('Epilogue,' *Fables*, lines 1–8).

If the *Espurgatoire Seint Patriz* is by the same Marie, then her last extant work might seem to be her least original, by modern standards. The author translates from a single Latin source rather than from diverse fables or oral and literary tales. But no translation is neutral, and the choice of text is key. Possibly near the end of her life, Marie elects to tell her most harrowing tale of spiritual perdition and salvation, that of the knight Owen's *aventure* to Purgatory, not so that her own reputation may be enhanced but so that the souls of those 'laie gent' [lay people] who hear her translation may be saved. And the *Espurgatoire*'s last *exemplum* seems to return us, full circle, to the enigmatic, sexually troubled world of the *Lais*. It tells how a priest, overwhelmed with desire for a foundling child whom he has raised, castrates himself to avoid temptation and places the girl in religious orders. It is perhaps fitting that in the last extant narrative couplet attributed to Marie de France, an educated young woman finds a haven in God's service from a man who has plotted against her. Marie's last translation recalls the vexed intersection of male and female desires, learning, and faith that we have glimpsed, with different emphases, in the textual accounts of Radegund, Clemence of Barking and Heloise.

WOMEN AT COURT: PATRONS, READERS, PERFORMERS, COMPOSERS

Although Marie de France may well have been a member of a religious order, her audience in the *Lais* and the *Fables* is a specifically courtly one that would have included young noblewomen and married ladies as well as feudal lords, knights and clerics. Women formed an important part of the audience in courts and noble households in England and France and the names of many noblewomen have come down to us as patrons of literary or sacred works from this period – Eleanor of Aquitaine, granddaughter of William IX, the first troubadour; Marie de Champagne, Eleanor's daughter by her first husband, King Louis VII; Marie de Ponthieu; Eleanor of Castille, among others.

After Marie de France, no female signature is attached to another *lai* or full-length romance, although we must not entirely discount the intriguing possibility that one of the more than two hundred extant French romances might be female-authored. Most romances ultimately affirm the conservative values of the aristocratic court and confirm traditional gender roles, but some remarkable romances explore, at least temporarily, a space where gender roles may be critiqued, playfully expanded or even subverted. Male-authored French romances represent women in a great variety of roles – not only as damsels in distress, adulterous queens, seductive temptresses, but also as virtuous maidens, enchanting fairies, resourceful entrepreneurs and – most pertinent for our study – as readers, writers and singers and musical performers. Indeed, romance heroines who sing or perform at court are often those who successfully escape from social confinement and bring events about to a happy resolution – as does Nicolette in *Aucassin et Nicolette*, the heroine Silence in *Le Roman de Silence*, the clever maiden Lienor in *Le Roman de la Rose ou de Guillaume de Dole*, or Marie's textual heir, Fresne, in *Galeran de Bretagne*.

The literary motif of resourceful women who sing in romance resonates with a chorus of female voices that are extant in troubadour and *trouvère* lyric poetry. A modest but significant corpus of lyric poems in female voices survives in medieval *chansonniers*, or collections of songs, both in the *langue d'oc*, or Old Provençal, from southern France and in the *langue d'oïl* of northern France. Southern French women poets are known as *trobairitz*, which is the feminine form of *troubadour*, a term that designates one who 'invents' (*trobar*) or composes verse. Northern French poets are *trouvères*, and the women may be called *troveresses*.

When considering medieval women's songs, critics have distinguished between 'textualité féminine,' female-voiced texts that were not necessarily composed by a female author and 'féminité génétique', the expression of a woman author.[15] But given the paucity or unreliability of information that survives about the circumstances of the songs' composition and about authorial identity, the distinction is not always an easy one to make. Controversy about the gender of authorship haunts the *trobairitz* corpus. Female authorship of certain poems has been disputed and, in an extreme case, it has been argued that all the 'women's poems' are written by men who take up the position of *dame*.[16] Consequently, the number of poems attributed to *trobairitz*, female composers, in different popular and scholarly editions ranges from twenty-three to over twice that many. In the most recent edition of *trobairitz*, which gives thoughtful consideration to questions of authorship, the editors ascribe female authorship to eleven *cansos* (the most refined form of love song); sixteen *tensos*, or debate poems; three *sirventes*, or political satires; one *planh*, or lament; are *alba*, or dawn song; and two fragments.[17] Of the twenty named *trobairitz* who have come down to us, only two, the Comtessa de Dia and Na Castelloza, have more than one song attributed to them, and only one song, La Comtessa de Dia's 'A chantar m'er de so q'ieu no volria,' survives with melody, in a fragment containing one *strophe*, or stanza.

Although the number of surviving *trobairitz* songs may seem small compared to the 2,500 troubadour lyrics that survive from 400 named poets, the poems' generic diversity, the authors' *franchise* [directness] and artistry, and their intriguing mix of convention and originality make the *trobairitz*'s songs a highly distinctive and important body of work. The

voices of the *trobairitz* reveal how some women responded in public performances to a tradition created chiefly by male poets who idealized
female beauty, decried women's inaccessibility, lusted for 'her' physical
presence and, while lamenting the *domna*'s imposing haughtiness, ren-
dered her often a silent object of desire.

Ever since Gaston Paris in 1883 coined the term 'amour courtois', or
courtly love, to refer to the stylized manner in which a submissive male
lover adores a distant, powerful lady,[18] critics and historians have offered
many different explanations of how the gender relations of literary
lovers depicted in hundreds of lyric poems and romances reflected the
social realities of elite men's and women's lives in Occitan and Northern
French society. Early assessments tended to see courtly love as a system
that reflected and fostered noblewomen's real or imagined power. More
recently, many critics have doubted that the idealized lady promoted or
reflected the social advancement of noblewomen and have stressed
instead the masculinist bias of so called 'courtly' love. However one
assesses these literary representations, it is clear that sexually charged,
ambiguous, and often conflicted gender relations are a hallmark of the
courtly tradition. Ongoing historical studies about the social status, marriage practices and inheritance rights of elite men and women in
different regions of Northern and Southern France demonstrate how
difficult it has become to generalize about whether twelfth-century
Southern French women had more political and economic power than
their Northern French counterparts, as has been argued, or whether the
twelfth and thirteenth century in the North and the South marked the
beginning of a significant change in marriage and inheritance practices.
Whatever complex emerging data might tell us about noblewomen's historical powers, the literary evidence shows that questions of gender and
power were a source of continual fascination for courtly audiences and
that literary texts often created a discursive space where gender relations
could be analysed, contested and sometimes subverted. This is nowhere
more evident than in poems of the *trobairitz* who sing with remarkable
directness and presence, yet often reveal the limitations of their feminine
voices within a misogynist culture.

Critics have been fascinated by the ways in which the *trobairitz* adapt,
transform and sometimes subvert the conventions that drive the troubadour lyric and by how the 'women's songs' differ stylistically and thematically from the men's. A frequently asked question is whether the
women's songs display power and agency or whether the women's voices
are ultimately 'contained' by conventions that reflect patriarchal hierar-

chy. Some songs seem to tease self-consciously at this gender tension. For example, in seeming defiance of 'rules' that make the lady remote and inaccessible, the Comtessa de Dia declares in 'Estat ai en greu cossirier' [I have been sorely troubled] that she would like to hold her 'cavallier' . . . 'un ser en mos bratz nut,' [naked in my arms one night] (pp. 10–11, line 10). But when she says that she would like to be his pillow 'cosseillier', she playfully dramatizes physical submission. At the song's end, she reveals her desire to maintain control of the situation even as she voices passionate longings: she boldly declares that she desires to have her 'cavallier' in her husband's place – 'provided you had promised me / to do everything I wished' ['ab so que m'aguessetz plevit / de far tot so qu'eu volria'] (pp. 10–11, lines 24–5).

Acutely aware of issues of status and power, yet seemingly undaunted by gender inequality, Na Castelloza openly argues her case before her knight, using conspicuously legalistic language, even though she knows that others say that it is improper for a lady to plead before a knight in 'Amics, s'ie.us trobes avinen' (pp. 18–21, lines 17–24). Both the Comtessa and Na Castelloza dramatize a variety of subject positions in their poem. Castelloza in particular has elicited a range of responses from her readers. If some would agree with the description of her as a 'dark lady in song' because of her frequent negativity and expressions of hopelessness,[19] other readers find power precisely in her refusal to remain silent about her suffering.[20]

Compared to their male counterparts, the *trobaritz* in the *cansos* eschew complicated rhyme schemes and elaborate metaphors or extended conceits, but their more 'direct' expression is by no means devoid of art. As these few examples have shown, the emotional range of the *trobairitz* is complex and deep in the *cansos*. In the *tensos* and *sirventes*, women's voices take up with firm rhetorical control a variety of issues ranging from the proper duties of a knight in love to the evils of sumptuary legislation. Taken together, the extant songs in a female voice from Southern France provide a fascinating glimpse of the way women's voices intermingled with male lyricism in courtly culture and how those complex voices – forceful, defiant, dramatic, playful, sorrowful, proud and, above all, resourceful – might have contributed to the shaping of gender relations at court.

Northern French lyric poetry also preserves a number of songs composed in female voices, although it is less common to speak of female *trouvères* or ascribe female authorship to these works. This may derive partly from the greater anonymity and the great number of 'popular' women's songs in Northern France, and partly from the bias of modern critics. In contrast to the *trobairitz*, there are fewer named female composers in the North, and there are more songs that spring from a non-courtly (and hence less individuated) setting rather than an aristocratic one. But if we bring together the thirteen female-voiced love songs and the twelve debate poems (*jeux-partis*) that present at least one female speaker, then the Northern French corpus of female *trouvères* compares favourably to the work of the *trobairitz*.[21]

Aside from those songs where 'je' is female, Northern French *chansonniers* and courtly narratives have preserved an intriguing group of poems where a narrator (sometimes identified as male, sometimes anonymous) overhears and recounts the words of women. Such is the case for the *chansons de toile*, or women's sewing songs, a corpus of twenty-one lyrico-narrative compositions that describe the love pangs of maidens or *mal mariées* and that often portray a woman (sometimes accompanied by her mother) engaged in needlework as she laments a crisis in love.[22] Five of these songs have been attributed to a male author, Audefroi le Batard; seven songs are known only from their inclusion in male-authored narratives; a single manuscript, the *chansonnier* of Saint Germain des Prés, contains the anonymous songs. Although there is no evidence that any of these songs were written by women, all the songs evoke a strong tradition of female vocality as they set women's voices into play. Furthermore, unlike the troubadour and *trouvère* aristocratic love songs, where gender relations are often frozen in emotional impasse, a number of the *chansons de toile* portray female characters who find or help to bring about a happy solution to their predicaments. In 'Bele Yolanz en ses chambres seoit' [Beautiful Yolanda was seated in her chambers], Yolande's lover materializes to ease her pain with his kisses just as she is about to send him an embroidered shift (I, pp. 77–9). In 'Bele Amelot soule an chanbre feloit' [Beautiful Amelot was spinning alone in her room], the initially disconsolate heroine ultimately marries her lover, Garin, with her mother's blessing and assistance (IX, pp. 102–6). Whether or not these poems reflect some vestige of popular songs that women sang while they worked, the *chansons de toile* convey the voices of women who openly express their desires and who, in many cases, work to find erotic fulfilment without sacrificing social honour.

The *Lais* of Marie de France, the songs of *trobairitz* and women *trouvères*, and the *chansons de toile* provide compelling examples of women's contributions to courtly culture. These works portray female voices or female characters who respond with conviction, eloquence and imagination to cultural restrictions, clerical misogyny or courtly idealizations. Their female speakers or characters often transform literary or social conventions in a way that redefines female identity or defends woman's honour. Another intriguing example of a female 'author' who responds to a clerical 'courtly' voice by cleverly dismantling his rhetoric is found in the *Response* to Richard de Fournival's *Bestiaire d'Amour* [*Master Richard's Bestiary of Love*], from the mid-thirteenth century. Once again, we cannot know for certain whether or not the *Response* was composed by a historical woman. Whoever the author may be, the *Reponse au bestiaire d'amour*, reveals a female speaker who stands on her own by refusing to fall prey to the clerk's rhetorical games.[23] She cleverly defends her honour by turning against him the animal metaphors he deploys to court her and, in so doing, she provides an example for other women who might be misled by such artful verbal assault and warns readers to be wary of the animal natures and deceptive discourse of men.

THIRTEENTH-CENTURY AND FOURTEENTH-CENTURY RELIGIOUS WOMEN'S WRITING: MARGUERITE D'OINGT AND MARGUERITE PORETE

Religious writings constitute the majority of texts by medieval European women writers, and French women wrote important devotional works. The thirteenth and fourteenth century witnessed a proliferation of new forms of female spirituality, as evidenced by the number of women who lived in established or new orders; a rise in the number of female saints; and the rapid increase of quasi-religious women, called *béguines*, who lived outside convents, either alone, in small households, or in larger communities known as *béguinages*.

Women embraced conventual or religious life for a variety of reasons, not the least of which was a true spiritual calling, but which also included inability or lack of desire to marry, distaste for the traditional female roles of wife and mother, the desire or necessity of their families, the search for a measure of economic security. Although convent life offered women a broader sphere for pious and intellectual pursuits than did most marriages, female religious were more restricted than their male counterparts, upon whom they depended for key functions of spiritual and administrative life. Women were forbidden to preach, to officiate at Mass or administer the sacraments, or to absolve the penitent; writing commentary upon the Scriptures was not permitted. Convent life was structured around prayers for the consecrated nuns and manual labour for those who served them. Although nuns were expected to read devotional texts and many knew how to write (principally for the purposes of copying manuscripts), opportunities for autonomous self-expression were exceptional. Yet, despite or because of such restrictions, some women sought greater freedom of thought and expression through spiritual visions and mystical meditations, which they recorded themselves or recounted to male clerics. A remarkable body of women's devotional literature throughout Europe confirms the vitality of female spirituality and literary practices in a variety of conventual and quasi-religious settings.[24]

Two religious women from late thirteenth-century France have left moving accounts of their visions and teachings in important devotional texts. The distinct character of their work reflects the very different circumstances of their writing. Both Marguerite d'Oingt and Marguerite Porete died in 1310. At the time of their deaths, the former was the respected and beloved prioress of a religious house near Lyons where she had presided for more than twenty years and where she wrote with the approval of Church authorities. The latter was burned at the stake in Paris as a heretic who refused to recant the allegedly heretical beliefs in her book, the *Mirouer des simples ames* (*The Mirror of Simple Souls*).

Marguerite d'Oingt (1240–1310), prioress at the Carthusian charterhouse of Poleteins, in Southern France, received official sanction for her writings from the Carthusian Chapter General in 1294. Marguerite's three major texts, written in Latin, French and Francoprovençal, attest to their author's high degree of literacy, to the intensity of her devotion and asceticism (encouraged by the strict enclosure of the Carthusian order) and, not least, to her role as a spiritual leader who urged others to lead more perfect lives. Her first work, *Pagina meditationum* (*Page of Meditations*), is an extended meditation on a verse of Scripture that recounts Marguerite's spiritual conversion and healing, following her physical and emotional collapse in despair in 1286. As Christ appears to her, and she meditates on His love for her and His suffering, Marguerite effects her own healing, through conversion, confession and contrition. In the second half of the work, she castigates religious men and women who profess religion but act basely, and she urges them to be transformed by Christ's love. Throughout this and all her works, Marguerite describes her relationship with Christ in strongly sensual language typical of the 'bridal mysticism' found in other female mystics.[25] At various moments, she describes Him as lover, father and even as a mother who has suffered the pains of childbirth, although unlike her mother, 'you, my sweet and lovely Lord, were in pain for me not just one day, but you were in labour for me for more than thirty years'.[26]

Her second work, called simply *Speculum* [Mirror], written in Francoprovençal, develops the metaphor of the book as a mirror that displays Christ's body which, mirror-like itself, reflects both her soul and celestial angels. Marguerite's book becomes a space through which souls can commune with a vision of God as they seek to transform darkness into light and their sins into salvation. In *Li Via Seiti Biatrix Virgina de Ornaciu* (*La Vie de Sainte Béatrix d'Ornacieux Vierge*), a vernacular saint's life, she recounts the story of her contemporary, Beatrice of Ornacieux (died 1303), a Carthusian nun from Parmenic. Beatrice struggled against inner torments and she learned to moderate her self-mortification so that she might better perform God's work. Marguerite's *Life of Saint Beatrice* contains vivid descriptions of Eucharistic visions and experiences, including a moment where the saint chokes on the Host, which has become an enlarged mass of flesh in her mouth (*Writings*, p. 56). Several letters penned by Marguerite d'Oingt and other short texts written to or about her attest to the prioress's role as a spiritual leader. In one of these, Marguerite writes in the third person to explain how writing down God's revelation has saved her from madness: 'I firmly believe that if she had not put all this down in writing, she would have died or gone mad . . .' (*Writings*, p. 65). But Marguerite d'Oingt's work transcends personal therapy as it provides examples of piety and salvation for a larger Christian community.

Unlike the Carthusian prioress, who lived and wrote in a close spiritual community that revered her and her work, Marguerite Porete appears to have been something of an outcast whose hermetic writing was controversial. Although Marguerite Porete claims to have received approval from three Church authorities,[27] her book was burned in her presence in 1306 and again condemned in 1309 and 1310. Contemporaries describe Marguerite Porete as a *béguine*, a term which could refer either to a religious woman living in a *béguinage* or living independently. Tacit approval for the extra-mural association of such female religious had been secured from the Pope in the early thirteenth century by Jacques of Vitry, author of *The Life of Marie d'Oignies*, the biography of a courageous *béguine*.[28] In 1264, Louis IX founded a large Parisian *béguinage* that was governed by principles of moderate enclosure, and this community benefited from statutes offering royal protection in 1327 and in 1341.[29] Marguerite, however, may have been a wandering, autonomous *béguine*, for at one point she portrays herself in opposition to '*béguines*, priests, clerics and preachers' who disparage her writing.[30] Whatever her living arrangements, her mystical writings tested the limits of ecclesiastical tolerance for autonomous religious practice.

Le Mirouer des simples ames [The Mirror of Simple Souls] is a lengthy prose dialogue written in vernacular Middle French, which recounts a dialogue between the Soul, Love, Reason, God and other divine voices and which includes lyrical spiritual poems. The *Mirouer* describes the seven stages through which the Soul must journey to attain spiritual perfection. In the Prologue, the author compares her 'mirror', which reflects a distant beloved God, to a portrait made of the 'noble king' Alexander the Great by a faraway princess who loved him (*Mirouer*, pp. 10–12). The language of religious love, as developed by Saint Bernard in his allegory of the Song of Songs, mingles with courtly discourse throughout the *Mirouer*, creating a register that one critic has dubbed '*la mystique courtoise*', or 'courtly mysticism', typical of medieval female visionary writing.[31] As in many a courtly love affair, the lover debases herself in contemplation of her cherished '*Loingpres*', the Far-near Christ, or the Trinity, whose light she desires to fill her soul (*Mirouer*, p. 178). With greater intensity than the most adamant *trobairitz*, Marguerite seeks to become an 'annihilated soul' ['*ame adnientie*'] in order to transcend first reason and nature, followed by desire and finally will, so that her destroyed soul may be completely filled with divine love.

Marguerite Porete's incantatory style, her counterintuitive arguments, her exploration of religious paradox and her probing of divine mysteries all make for a text that is dense and, at times, confounding. She writes not for the common reader but for the spiritual elite, noble souls who would follow her tortuous path to enlightenment. Its combination of intense ratiocination and rhapsodic lyricism makes the *Mirouer des âmes simples* a remarkable spiritual treatise.

The autonomous spiritual path traced by the *Mirouer* was unsettling to Church authorities. Some of Marguerite's mystical language might seem to imply that the soul need not concern itself with good works, that it need not refuse anything that nature asks and that it has no use for prayers, sacraments or religious offices. In the eyes of her inquisitors, such ideas were grounds for heresy, although modern scholars have questioned this judgment. It has been suggested, as well, that Marguerite's case allowed the French crown to garner the favour of clergy in established mendicant orders, who feared solitary mystics like Marguerite (as opposed to enclosed *béguines*), at a time when the King sought the French clergy's support for its suppression of the order of

Templars. But even without such a political motive, Marguerite Porete's inquisitors may have perceived her independent status, her refusal to prevent the dissemination of her book or to recant its controversial ideas and her lack of cooperation during her trial as threatening to the established ecclesiastical and royal order.

On 11 April 1310 the *Mirouer* was condemned by twenty-one theologians in the Church of the Mathurins in Paris. On 9 May 1310, Marguerite Porete was condemned as a relapsed heretic, for she had refused to swear an oath or respond to the inquisitor's questions and had continued to pass her book on to others; she was burned at the stake on the Place de Grève in Paris on 1 June 1310.

Despite attempts to suppress Marguerite's book, the *Mirror of Simple Souls* was disseminated throughout Europe in the later Middle Ages. In addition to the Chantilly French manuscript, there are four Latin manuscripts and two fragments, as well as translations into Italian and Middle English. It has been suggested that Marguerite de Navarre drew inspiration from Marguerite's *Mirror* in her own devotional writings. Marguerite Porete's life and writing stand as a poignant testimony, then, to the opportunities and obstacles encountered by women who dared to blaze alternative spiritual paths.

FROM COURTLY LOVE TO HUMANISM: CHRISTINE DE PIZAN AND THE LATE MIDDLE AGES

Female literacy widened its circle in late medieval France. As women's education continued in courts, wealthy households and convents, town schools instructed girls and boys in letters and numeracy. Aside from its practical uses for artisan and merchant families, reading was meant to impart ethical principles to bourgeois and aristocratic women, which they would in turn pass on to their children as they taught them to read; moralists advocated reading pious and salutary works. Teaching women to write was another matter. In his 1372 book of instruction for his daughters, when the Chevalier de la Tour Landry urged that young children be sent to school so that they might learn read books of wisdom and eschew sin, he remarked that women need not learn to write: '. . . je dy ainsi que, quant d'escrire, n'ay a force que femme en saiche riens; mais, quant à lire, toute femme en vault mieulx de le sçavoir, et cognoist mieulx la foy et les perils de l'ame et son saulvement' [and thus I say, as for writing, a woman need not know anything about it, but as for reading, every woman would be better off knowing how to do it and would know more about faith, and the perils of the soul, and salvation] (178).[32] In such a context, women's writing in the secular domain remained the purview of exceptional women.

Writing at the end of the Middle Ages and at the dawn of the early modern period, Christine de Pizan (1365–1430?) was such an exception. A propitious combination of class privilege, unusual upbringing, family tragedy and notoriety created the conditions of her authorship, which were shaped by a formidable intelligence and moral vision. Christine travelled from Northern Italy as a young child with her family to the Paris court of King Charles V, for whom her father, Thomas de Pizan, was the appointed astrologer. Under Thomas's tutelage, despite her mother's attempts to confine her to the feminine activity of needlework, Christine received an education in French and, to some extent, in Latin; she also may have been introduced at this point to works from the King's impressive library. Her happy marriage at age fifteen to Etienne du Castel, secretary to the King, ended tragically when her husband succumbed to an epidemic in 1389, leaving Christine, at age twenty-five, with three dependent children and a widowed mother in her charge. After spending thirteen years in court defending her modest estate from claims against her husband, Christine turned to writing poetry for the court as her only independent means of support and thereby became France's first professional *femme de lettres*.

From sometime before 1399, when she began to write, until 1418, when she fled civil war in Paris and retired to the convent of Poissy, where her only daughter lived, Christine embarked on an ambitious programme of self-education and produced a remarkable literary corpus. Her collected works stand as a *summa* of the diverse genres produced by medieval French women writers, and their themes and forms also anticipate the writings of women in the early modern period. Continuing in the voice of women who wrote songs and poetry at court, Christine began her literary career by writing lyric poetry in a variety of forms. Many poems in her *Cent Ballades* [Hundred Ballads] lament the death of her beloved husband and decry her solitude with poignant directness, as in the ballade 'Seulete suy et seulete vueil estre' (*Cent Balades* XI, Roy, vol. I, p. 12). Christine's emotive lyricism forms a bridge from writers like the Comtessa de Dia and Na Castelloza to Louise Labé in the sixteenth century.

Like Heloise, Christine was also well versed in the epistolary genre. One of her first *epistres* was a fictional complaint sent to the God of Love about men who defamed women and slandered female nature, which

Christine defended as virtuous (*L'Epistre au Dieu d'Amours* (*The Letter to the God of Love*), May 1399). Among the misogynists Christine criticized were Ovid, whose *Art d'amour* [Art of love] was an art of deceiving women, and Jean de Meun, irreverent continuator of the thirteenth-century *Roman de la Rose*. Two years later, the author found herself arguing similar points in a real-life debate among Parisian intellectuals. Her trenchant critique of misogyny in the *Roman de la Rose* launched the first full-scale literary debate in French letters, the *querelle de la Rose*. When, in 1410, Christine copied the letters in a single volume and 'published' them by sending them to the Queen, she established her reputation as an engaged writer, a spirited defender of women and a courageous moralist. The questions raised about women's reputation in the *Rose* debate gave rise in turn to later disputes about and defences of women, such as Alain Chartier's *Belle dame sans mercy* [Beautiful, Merciless Lady] and Martin le Franc's *Champion des dames* [Defender of Ladies], and thus prefigured the early modern *querelle des femmes*.

The *Rose* debate marked a turning point in Christine's career. Although she continued to produce some works that depicted amorous relations at court in either lyrical or narrative poetry, her criticism of deceptive and slanderous masculine discourse in so-called 'courtly' texts became more pointed. In the lyrico-narrative epistolary romance *Le Livre du Duc des Vrais Amans* (*The Book of the Duke of True Lovers*) (*ca* 1403–5) and in the lyrical sequences *Cent ballades d'amant et de dame* [A Hundred Ballads between Lover and Lady] (1409–10) Christine examines the arguments that men make to compromise women's honour and shows that a man's love talk is often a lady's demise. Her cautious approach to love and her principled concern for female honour will be echoed in the work of Marguerite de Navarre, (who would have had access to Christine's works in the royal library), and in later *ancien régime* literature, such as Madame de Lafayette's *La Princesse de Clèves*.

Christine's defence of women finds its fullest expression in two works published in 1405, *Le Livre de la Cité des dames* (*The Book of the City of Ladies*) and *Le Livre des Trois Vertus* (*The Book of the Three Virtues*). The *Cité des dames* is a compilation of exempla of learned, powerful and virtuous women that significantly revises its male-authored sources, mainly Boccaccio's *De claris mulieribus* (*On Famous Women*), but also the *Decameron*, and other diverse works. Christine not only heightens the agency of her female examples and removes any trace of misogyny from her sources, she also adds virtuous contemporary women and Christian martyrs to the roster. Most important, she sets the compilation within the framework of a feminized Boethian dialogue. Three female allegorical figures – Reason, Rectitude and Justice – console the author, Christine, who has become depressed by the misogynist tenor of almost all literary and philosophical works. The Virtues propose to help Christine lay the architectural foundations – stone by stone, story by story – for a resplendent City of Women (deliberately reminiscent of Augustine's *City of God*) that includes ancient queens and Amazons (e.g., Semiramis, Penthesilea), learned women such as the sibyls, Sappho, Cornificia and Carmentis; virtuous women such as Susanna, Lucretia and Griselda; and finally, virgin martyrs such as Saint Catherine and Saint Christine. Through such female worthies, the Virtues refute absolutely the charges that men throughout history have levied against women's inferior intellectual or moral nature and so pave the way for Christine's contemporaries to find their own place alongside their illustrious foremothers.

Le Livre des Trois Vertus, also called the *Tresor de la Cité des dames*, was conceived as a practical handbook to accompany the *Cité des dames*, a book telling 'how to' enter the illustrious city of female virtue. Dedicated to the twelve-year-old princess Marguerite of Burgundy, who was eleven when she married the young dauphin, Louis de Guyenne, the *Livre des Trois Vertus* offers three books of moral instruction for Princesses (book I), ladies of rank (book II) and, finally, women of all other social stations (book III) – including wives of merchants, farmers and labourers, nuns, widows and even prostitutes and destitute women. Christine's is the first female-authored French conduct book for women and the first to speak to all ranks of women in such detail.

In some senses, *Le Livre des Trois Vertus* is profoundly conservative, for it espouses principles of chastity, marital fidelity and obedience, sartorial moderation and conformity to rank; many of its precepts resemble those advocated by male moralists writing for women. In other ways, however, Christine's lessons are tailored to girls and women who might learn how to work within social restraints to enhance their lives and their communities. She urges women to use prudent speech and thoughtful actions as strategic tools for survival and change. She counsels the princess to persuade her husband to keep peace within the realm. She realizes that young girls must be instructed with kindness and gentle persuasion; she recognizes the important moral and economic contributions of active, resourceful, skilled women in every sphere. Taken together, the utopian *Cité* and the pragmatic *Trois Vertus* offer medieval France's fullest portrait of the constraints and opportunities of medieval women's lives and the most extensive account of women's accomplishments.

Christine never advocates that other women adopt her humanistic programme of studies; she was far too cognizant of the realities of most women's lives to do so. But her own life is a prototype for women's humanism and her work, by appealing to women of different classes, helped to advance the spread of female lay literacy and to establish a taste for books that would enhance their owners' lives.

At the end of the *Livre des Trois Vertus*, the author expressed her desire that her work should be 'multiplied' and disseminated throughout the world in several copies to queens, princesses and noble ladies of diverse realms and that, through them, the work would be passed on to other women. Of all the writers in this chapter, Christine was the only one to state such ambitious plans for the publication of her work and was the first to target such a widespread female public. She supervised the copying of her manuscripts and worked closely with the artists who illuminated them. To judge from the twenty-one extant French manuscripts of the *Livre des Trois Vertus*, and the twenty-five manuscripts of the *Cité des dames* (as well as early printed editions of both these works), to say nothing of the translation of the *Trois Vertus* into Portuguese and of the *Cité* into English, Christine appears to have achieved her goal. Christine's feminist revision of Boccaccio's stories was continued, in another vein, by Marguerite de Navarre in the *Heptaméron*, and her conduct book inspired Anne de France, sister of Charles VIII, to write a book of *Enseignements* ['Teachings'] for her daughter Suzanne.[33] Although Christine's works were not edited beyond the sixteenth century and her name fell out of recognition (as was the case for many medieval authors and works), the questions she raised about the cultural representation of women and the advice she offered for female empowerment were matters that continued to be debated and discussed throughout the early modern period.

Christine's lessons were by no means limited to women's concerns. The *Rose* debate also helped to further Christine's career as a didactic writer for princes and their courts. This had begun with the composition of two collections of proverbs and dicta (*ca* 1400) and with her popular *Epistre d'Othéa à Hector* (*Letter of Othéa to Hector*) (*ca* 1400), dedicated to King Charles VI's brother, Louis d'Orléans. In the latter book, the goddess Othéa serves as a teacher to the fifteen-year-old Hector by presenting him with one hundred exempla drawn from the *Ovide moralisé*, accompanied by a gloss and allegorical interpretation. Since many of Othéa's lessons concern problems of governance and counsel, it is thought that Christine already attempted, in this early work, to provide wise counsel to the rulers of a troubled realm.

Since 1392, King Charles VI had been beset with intermittent periods
of insanity. Influence in matters of the crown was contested between his
brother and uncles; tensions increased with the assassination of Louis
d'Orléans in 1407, with the subsequent warring between the
Burgundians and the Armagnacs, or Orléanistes, with the Cabochian
revolt in 1413, and with resumption of the Hundred Years' War with
England. Throughout this period, Christine wrote historical and didactic works that explored the consequences of human follies and injustices,
praised virtuous rulers of the past, and preached moral probity and spiritual devotion. These were commissioned by, or dedicated to, numerous
royal and ducal patrons, including Charles VI, his wife Queen Isabeau
de Bavière, Philip of Burgundy and Jean, Duke of Berry. Her work
included allegorical dream visions, such as the *Chemin de Long Estude* [The
Long Road of Learning] (1403), the *Livre de la mutacion de fortune* [The
Mutation of Fortune] (1400–3), and the *L'Avision Christine* [Christine's
Vision] (1405), a spiritual autobiography; a biography of the late Charles
V, *Le Livre des faits et bonnes moeurs du roi Charles V le Sage* (1404); treatises
advocating good government such as the *Livre du corps de policie* [The Body
of Policy] (1406–7) and the *Livre de la paix* [Book of Peace] (1412–14); an
epistle to Queen Isabeau imploring her to intervene in the internecine
struggles to preserve the peace (1405); and even a treatise on warfare,
Le Livre des fais d'armes et de chevalerie [The Book of Feats of Arms and
Chivalry] (*ca* 1410).

Christine's didactic work draws heavily from classical and medieval
sources, and her work may not strike modern readers as 'original'. Yet,
as Christine herself explained by comparing her method to the work of
masons, who use manufactured bricks, and embroiderers, who use pre-
made threads and cloth, her task as a writer was to frame and arrange
her 'found' literary materials into a compilation that is '*conforme à ma
pensée*' [suitable to my thinking] (*Charles V*, trans. Hicks, p. 158). Indeed,
Christine's hand as architect and embroiderer are evident in all her
works through the frequent display of 'signature' features such as unique
framing devices; personal dialogue between the author and a mentor, a
sibyl or an allegorical virtue; autobiographical vignettes; principled
selection and compilation of materials; pointed criticism of misogyny or
moral weakness, among other distinctive narratorial interventions. As a
lay moralist, Christine often strikes an ambivalent stance, at once
humbly deferential in her profession of intellectual modesty and bold in
her propensity to attack injustice, sloth, greed, corruption and misogyny
– social flaws that were evident throughout the social hierarchy, but

whose effects were most damaging at the top. Christine never attacked the monarchy or the political system *per se*; she advocated inner moral reform rather than broader political change. But her position as an outsider, a self-educated bourgeois woman who had struggled against personal loss and vicissitudes, had endowed her with particularly strong moral convictions and a belief in the capacity of human beings to amend their world. Like Marie de France in her *Lais* and *Fables*, Christine boldly deployed her position as a writer who had found favour at court to urge her readers to transform themselves and their communities.

A final dimension of Christine's writings that links her to female literary traditions in France is piety. Christine composed religious poetry (*Sept psaumes allegorisés* [Seven Allegorized Psalms] 1409) and her most autobiographical work, *L'Avision Christine*, traces her inner voyage toward a perception of God's providence. Precisely because Christine writes as a lay woman and not as a nun, she reveals the role that devotional texts played in the lives of women: as educational tools, as spiritual 'mirrors', as consolation. When she chooses to tell the stories of the Christian martyrs in book three of the *Cité des dames* (exempla that are absent in Boccaccio), she continues the female hagiographic tradition in which Baudonivia, Clemence, the anonymous authors of *Saint Edouard le Confesseur* and *Sainte Audrée* and Marguerite d'Oingt participated. In the tradition of the female-authored saints' lives that precede Christine, Christine's martyrology evokes the urgency and the difficulty of women who choose to teach the ways of God in a hostile world.

As did Radegund, Dhuoda and other medieval French women writers before her, Christine wrote in difficult times and in spite of great personal misfortunes. Conflict between the Armagnacs and the Burgundians, which had been intermittent throughout Christine's adult life, intensified in the Parisian massacres of 1418 and forced her retreat from Paris, probably to the convent of Poissy. Her extraordinary career as a public intellectual was curtailed by the vicissitudes of history. The years that follow her composition of the *Epistre de la prison de vie humaine* (*The Epistle of the Prison of Human Life*) (1418), a letter consoling Marie de Berry and others who had lost family members during the civil war, left few extant works by this once prolific writer. But Christine's last extant work, dated July 1429, is a fitting tribute to her lifelong defence of female honour and France's moral and political order, which she had tried to restore so often through her writings. *Le Ditié de Jehanne d'Arc* (*The Poem of Joan of Arc*), the first non-anonymous poem written about Joan of Arc in her lifetime, celebrates the Maid's victory over the English at Orléans.

Like so many of her literary foremothers who recorded deeds of courageous, resourceful women, Christine commemorates a heroine who
embodied the power of the powerless to transform the world. We do not
know if she lived to witness Joan's tragic end in May 1431; records indicate that Christine had certainly died by 1434.

Although Christine's texts circulated widely during the first half of the
sixteenth century, her work eventually fell out of vogue, along with most
things medieval, and received mixed reviews during the nineteenth-
century revival of literary studies. Alongside some who honoured her by
editing her works or praising their merit, such as Raimond Thomassy
and Maurice Roy, there were others who disparaged their quality. By
calling her 'the first in that line of insufferable bluestockings whose inde-
fatigable facility was equaled only by her universal mediocrity',[34]
Gustave Lanson proved the bitter truth of Christine's work on misogyny,
which had not ceased in its efforts to stifle women's education and
writing. Happily, twentieth-century scholars, many of them women,
kindled the embers of Christine scholarship with needed critical studies
and editions, until a major resurgence of interest in her work and that
of other medieval women writers occurred in the last quarter of the
twentieth century. A recent spate of editions, translations and critical
studies produced by an international 'city of scholars'[35] attests to
Christine's ultimate success in multiplying her works and her ideas
throughout the intellectual realm.

Writing at the end of the Middle Ages and at the dawn of the
Renaissance, Christine's literary activity as a *femme de lettres* was exceptional for any age. Yet, her textual and intellectual practices are rooted
in medieval French women's literary history. Christine drew her inspiration not only from the male poets and philosophers whose work she critiques and revises, but also from the fertile traditions of women's
correspondence, song, disputation, teaching and devotion that preceded
her. As she breathes new life into lyric, romance, didactic, epistolary,
hagiographic and devotional genres, Christine de Pizan's work epitomizes the diversity and the transformative qualities of medieval women's
writings and beckons towards the many forms in which women's voices
will be heard in Renaissance and early modern French literatures.

NOTES

1   For further details of Radegund's story, see McNamara and Halborg, *Sainted
    Women of the Dark Ages*, pp. 60–105.

2 In 'Cesaria to Radegund and Richild', trans. Thiébaux, *Writings of Medieval Women*, p. 40.

3 Although Radegund's autonomy as author has been questioned, recent translators and editors give major credit to Radegund for these works. See McNamara and Halborg, *Sainted Women of the Dark Ages*, p. 65.

4 See the astute analysis by Cherewatuk, 'Radegund and the Epistolary Tradition', in Cherewatuk and Wiethaus, (eds.), *Dear Sister*, pp. 20–45.

5 'The Life of the Holy Radegund', book II, trans. McNamara and Halborg, *Sainted Women of the Dark Ages*, p. 92.

6 *Ibid*, p. 94.

7 Because Dhuoda remarks at several points that she will have various lessons 'copied' for her son, some critics have seen the hand of a clerk, rather than that of a mere scribe recording Dhuoda's thoughts, in the book's composition. But most readers are struck by the work's distinctive, autobiographical register. See the analysis by Neel, 'Introduction', *Handbook for William*, pp. ix–xxviii.

8 Respectively, letter 1, Heloise to Abelard, *The Letters of Abelard and Heloise*, p. 113 and letter 3, Heloise to Abelard, p. 133.

9 For the epistolary poem written by the nun Constance *ca* 1107 to Baudri de Borgueil, see *Les Œuvres poétiques de Baudri de Borgueil (1046–1130)*, ed. Phyllis Abraham (Paris: Champion, 1926), pp. 344–9.

10 See Robertson, 'Writing in the Textual Community'.

11 *Galeran de Bretagne*, ed. Lucien Foulet (Paris: Champion, 1975). Foulet's attribution of the work to Jean Renart has been since dismissed.

12 Harriet Spiegel, 'Introduction', *Fables*, p. 7.

13 See Harriet Spiegel, 'The Woman's Voice in the *Fables* of Marie de France', in Maréchal (ed.), *In Quest of Marie de France*.

14 See Karen C. Jambeck, 'The Fables of Marie de France: A Mirror of Princes', in Maréchal (ed.), *In Quest of Marie de france*, pp. 59–106.

15 Pierre Bec, '*Trobairitz* et chansons de femme: contribution à la connaissance du lyrisme féminin au moyen âge', *Cahiers de civilisation médiévale* 22: 3 (1979), 253–62.

16 Jean-Charles Huchet, 'Les femmes troubadours ou la voix critique', *Littérature* 51 (1983), 59–90.

17 Bruckner, Shepard and White (eds.), *Songs of the Women Troubadours*. The introduction to this edition provides an outstanding general presentation of the *trobairitz*. All examples will be cited from this edition, with page and line numbers indicated in parentheses.

18 Gaston Paris, 'Etudes sur les romans de la Table Ronde, Lancelot du Lac: II: *Le conte de la charrette*', *Romania* 12 (1883), 459–534.

19 See William D. Paden Jr *et al.*, 'The Poems of the *Trobairitz* Na Castelloza', *Romance Philology* 35: 1 (1981), 158–82.

20 E.g., Jay H. Siskin and Julie A. Storm, 'Suffering Love: The Reversed Order in the Poetry of Na Castelloza', in Paden (ed.), *The Voice of the Trobairitz*, pp. 157–82.

21 See Medeline Tyssens, 'Voix de femmes dans la lyrique d'oïl', in Rita Lejeune *et al.* (eds.), *Femmes-Mariages-Lignages, XIIᵉ–XIVᵉ siècles, mélanges offerts à Georges Duby* (Brussels: De Boeck-Wesmael, 1992), 372–87. Examples can be found in *Songs of the Troubadours and Trouvères*, ed. Rosenberg, Switten and Le Vot, pp. 210–215. As this volume goes to press so does an edition and translation of over seventy lyrics composed wholly or partially in female voices from Northern France. *'Biaus Douz Amis:' Songs of the Women Trouvères*, eds. Eglal Doss-Quinby, Joan Tasker Grimbert, Wendy Pfeffer and Elizabeth Aubrey (Yale University Press, forthcoming) exemplifies how expanding the corpus of women's writing will continue to transform our critical assumptions.

22 These songs have been edited by Michel Zink, *Belle: essai sur les chansons de toile, suivi d'une édition et d'une traduction* (Paris: Champion, 1978).

23 See Solterer, *Master and Minerva*, pp. 97–130.

24 See Elizabeth Alvilda Petroff, *Medieval Women's Visionary Poetry* (Oxford and New York: Oxford University Press, 1986) for an anthology of European women's religious writings.

25 See Newman, *Virile Woman*, pp. 136–67.

26 *Writings*, ed. Blumenfeld-Kosinski, p. 31.

27 In her final 'Approbatio', appended to the Latin and Middle English translations, Marguerite says that Brother John, Dom Franco of Villiers and Godfrey of Fontaines approved her work, although the latter warns that it should only be read by those strong enough to abide by its teachings; *Mirouer*, pp. 404–9.

28 Jacques de Vitry, *The Life of Marie d'Oignies*, trans. Margot King (Toronto: Peregrina, 1989). On the climates for the *béguines* at the time of Marguerite's trial, see Ellen L. Babinsky, 'Introduction,' in her edition of Marguerite Porete, *The Mirror of Simple Souls* (New York: Paulist Press, 1993), pp. 5–20.

29 Babinsky, 'Introduction', pp. 13–20.

30 *Mirouer*, p. 344, lines 94–112.

31 Newman, *Virile Woman*, pp. 136–67.

32 *Le Livre du Chevalier de la Tour Landry*, ed. Anatole de Montaiglon (Paris, 1854). The abuses of women's literacy were assumed to be the reading of 'dangerous' books, such as romances, that would incite the reader to sin or to the exchange of love letters with a man other than her husband. The Ménagier de Paris advises his young wife to imitate the queens of France by reading only letters written in her husband's handwriting; *Le Menagier de Paris*, eds. Georgine E. Brereton and Janet M. Ferrier (Oxford: Clarendon Press, 1981), p. 56.

33 Anne de France, *Les Enseignements d'Anne de France, Duchesse de Bourbonnais et d'Auvergne à sa fille Susanne de Bourbon*, ed. A. M. Chazaud (Moulins: Desrosiers, 1878).

34 As cited by Willard, *Christine de Pizan*, p. 222.

35 This term derives from a recent critical anthology on Christine (Zimmerman, ed., *The City of Scholars*).

CHAPTER TWO

To choose ink and pen: French Renaissance women's writing

Cathleen M. Bauschatz

Our picture of French Renaissance literature has been dominated by canonical male authors: Clément Marot, Maurice Scève, François Rabelais, Joachim du Bellay, Pierre de Ronsard and Michel de Montaigne. In fact anthologies such as that of Lagarde and Michard, commonly used by French students, do not include any Renaissance women writers. French women writers of the sixteenth-century have received increasing attention in the last few years, however, particularly in the Anglophone world, and reading the works of these women writers gives us quite a different picture of the period from the one we receive from their male counterparts. Through a survey of nine carefully selected women writers (among many more) of the sixteenth century in France, it is possible to come to a more balanced understanding of its literary climate. These nine writers – Jeanne Flore, Hélisenne de Crenne, Marguerite de Navarre, Pernette du Guillet, Louise Labé, Madeleine and Catherine des Roches, Marguerite de Valois and Marie de Gournay – are each important for the way in which they modify the genre (or genres) in which they write, and change its definition for subsequent authors, whether male or female.

The literary image of woman emerging from the French Middle Ages was formed through the tradition of *courtoisie* [courtliness], apparent in both male- and female-authored texts. *Amour courtois* [Courtly Love] presented by a woman writer such as Marie de France, and questioned over two centuries later by Christine de Pizan, continued to be re-examined by sixteenth-century French authors, including women. In particular, many women writers criticized the adulterous nature of *amour courtois* and pursued the *Querelle de la Rose* [Quarrel of the Rose] initiated in Christine de Pizan's response to Jean de Meung and, through him, to the strong tradition of misogynistic medieval literature. *The Querelle des femmes* [Quarrel of Women], in the sixteenth-century, will develop into a full-blown literary quarrel with male and female authors writing on each side.[1]

There are some major factors in the early sixteenth century which influenced women's literacy as well as literacy in general. Print, introduced into Europe in the late fifteenth century, brought books and reading, mainly confined to castles and monastic libraries in the Middle Ages, into upper-class and bourgeois homes. Women were active in the print trade, as wives and daughters of printers. Most importantly, print helped to spread the new ideas of Italian and northern European Humanism to women. Although women were excluded from Humanist educational reforms, they were able to receive the benefits of many of these new ideas by studying the works of Humanists in their own homes (usually in vernacular translation), either alone or in groups such as *salons* or academies.

A second factor which influenced female literacy in this period was the Protestant Reformation. Particularly in the south-west, conversions to the new religion were frequent, especially among women. In Evangelical circles, Bible reading was a common practice, as we shall see in Marguerite de Navarre's *Heptaméron*. The Protestant emphasis on reading and interpretation of the Bible by the individual believer, rather than through the mediation of a priest or monk, may have influenced women even more than men. Women were frequently those who read the Bible aloud to a group busy with sewing or other hand-work. Women had more leisure and inclination than men for devotional reading, and they were encouraged to do this by moralistic writers, both Protestant and Catholic.[2]

A third historical or cultural factor which touched women as much as or more than men in the early sixteenth century was the influence of Italy, during and after the French wars in Italy (late fifteenth to early sixteenth century). François I, widely considered the father of the French Renaissance, brought Italian arts and letters back to France, began the construction of Italian-style châteaux, and imported Italian artists such as Leonardo da Vinci and Benvenuto Cellini. The influence of the Italian Renaissance on sixteenth-century women writers was a strong one, particularly in the south of France, and especially in the Lyons region, which had frequent contact with Italy.

THE BOCCACCIAN TRADITION: DEFINING A FEMALE VOICE

The early part of the sixteenth century in France is dominated by the Italian Renaissance, and its rediscovery of 'man', as nineteenth-century scholars like Jacob Burckhardt have pointed out. Women writers were obliged to define their voice in the context of these earlier Italian male precursors. For writers of prose, the influence of Boccaccio (1313–75) is particularly apparent. Boccaccio's *De mulieribus claris* (*Concerning Famous Women*), (1355–9), was a collection of exempla, showing one hundred and four outstanding women from antiquity who could be models for contemporary women readers. Boccaccio had also incorporated the female voice into his lighter works, specifically the *Elegia di Madonna Fiammetta* (*Elegy of Lady Fiammetta*) (1343–4) and the *Decameron* (1348). In sixteenth-century France, Jeanne Flore (*Les Comptes amoureux* (*The Amorous Tales*)), Hélisenne de Crenne (*Les Angoisses douloureuses* [The Painful Anxieties]) and Marguerite de Navarre (*L'Heptaméron*) all work within the Boccaccian tradition, and take advantage of the dialogic form of the novella (frame tale), which offers male and female speakers an equal share of the story-telling. But while Boccaccio actually gave women speakers and listeners a secondary role, his three French imitators develop the female point of view more extensively, sometimes subverting the message of compliance with male desire, which they inherit from the *Decameron*.

The case of Jeanne Flore is a particularly problematic one. The *Comptes amoureux* (1537–9) are a collection of amorous tales in the tradition of Boccaccio's *Decameron* (1348). A group of women (unlike Boccaccio's mixed group) meet to exchange stories about love. In particular, these tales show the punishments which befall young married women who do not give in to the demands of potential lovers. The *Comptes amoureux* appeared in Lyons in the late 1530s, and may grow out of a contemporary controversy about the relevance of medieval courtly love to the sixteenth century, as well as about the nature of women (the *Querelle des femmes*), in intellectual Italianate circles there.

The real problem in evaluating Jeanne Flore's work is the question of her identity – who was she? Was she really a woman? Was she only one person? Recent research seems to suggest that the *Comptes amoureux* may have been a literary hoax, put together by a group of male writers, possibly including Etienne Dolet, Clément Marot and other humanists in 1530s Lyons. For the student of early modern women's literature, an analysis of the text itself should suffice to show that the work is probably not by a woman. Strong, assertive female characters are consistently ridiculed in the book. For example, Méridienne (the heroine of tale no. 2) is thrown to the dogs after refusing the commands of Venus.

Like many heroines in the *Comptes amoureux* (and in the courtly tradition which it imitates or parodies), Méridienne is a beautiful young woman married to an old man. A younger man, Pyrance, falls in love with her because of her great beauty. He dies of grief after it is clear that she will never love him. But Venus punishes Meridienne, as the goddess's statue falls on the woman's head, killing her instantly. Her body is thrown to ravenous wolves and dogs, and the other women of the town are frightened into submission, resolving never to reject a lover again. It is obvious that the 'moral' of this tale parodies that of traditional didactic literature for women, but with an exaggeration of the adulterous message of courtly love, which could hardly be viewed as 'didactic' in a conventional sense. Certainly Jeanne Flore is more audacious than Boccaccio in recommending or even requiring adulterous love, whereas Boccaccio apologized for tales which might be shocking to women, suggesting that they not read them all.

Whoever Jeanne Flore was, the *Comptes amoureux* are significant for six-teenth-century French women's literature because they raise questions which will be pursued throughout the century in books by and about women. Among these issues are the subject of women's relationship to the courtly tradition and to Italy, and the representation of images of women as speakers and listeners, readers and writers, of oral and written literature. Whether or not Jeanne Flore was female, the book creates a convincing picture of a woman writer speaking to women readers, although the message it conveys may not appear convincingly feminine or feminist.

Hélisenne de Crenne (a pseudonym for Marguerite Briet, *ca* 1515–60) was a contemporary of Jeanne Flore, but her work is very different from the *Comptes Amoureux* – so different that it provides additional evidence for the theory that Jeanne Flore may not have been a woman. Hélisenne appears in various sixteenth-century lists of educated women, and she wrote many more works than Jeanne Flore. Among these are: *Les Angoysses douloureuses qui procedent d'amours* (*The Painful Anxieties that come from Love*) (a semi-autobiographical novel – 1538) and *Les Epistres familieres et invectives* (*The Personal and Invective Letters*) (a collection of semi-fictional letters – 1539). Other lesser known works include *Le Songe de madame Helisenne* (*Madame Helisenne's Dream*) (a dream allegory – 1540), and a translation of the first four books of Virgil's *Aeneid* (*Les quatre premiers livres des Eneydes* (*The First Four Book of the Aeneid*) – 1541).

Hélisenne was born between 1510 and 1520, in Abbeville. She married (around 1530) Philippe Fournel, Seigneur de Crenne, and bore him at least one child. The marriage was not a happy one, if we are to believe that the *Angoysses douloureuses* and the *Epistres* are truly autobiographical.

By 1539 she appears to have been separated from her husband, and was living in Paris. The date of her death is not known, but she published nothing after 1560.

One factor complicating the theory that the *Angoisses* may be partly autobiographical is the fact that the book is also closely modelled on Boccaccio's *Elegia di Madonna Fiammetta* (1343–4), which had been translated into French in the early 1530s. The *Fiammetta* purports to be the unhappy autobiographical love story of a young married woman, despite the fact that it was written by a male, Boccaccio. When Hélisenne wrote her story, she took over many elements of Boccaccio's *Fiammetta*, transforming them slightly and demonstrating that her book, unlike his, really did represent the voice of a woman. Hélisenne shows more concern for the profit to be derived by women readers than did Boccaccio's *Fiammetta*, who was mostly preoccupied with the cathartic effects of telling her own story, and thus with its benefit to herself. Unlike Jeanne Flore's *Comptes amoureux*, Hélisenne de Crenne's *Angoysses douloureuses* contains the message that women should avoid extra-marital love which, she shows, will lead only to pain and suffering. This has echoes of Christine de Pizan, rather than of Jeanne Flore.

The *Angoysses* tell the story of a young girl (Hélisenne) who marries (at the age of eleven) a jealous, sadistic husband. A few years after the marriage, Hélisenne falls in love with Guénélic, a young admirer who has seen her at her window. The husband becomes aware of their love, spies on her, locks her in her room and occasionally comes in to threaten or beat her. Hélisenne meets the young man occasionally, usually at church, but their love is never consummated, unlike the situation in the *Fiammetta* or the *Comptes amoureux*. They carry on a correspondence, which is discovered and destroyed by the husband. Hélisenne tries to commit suicide (as did her model, Fiammetta) but, again like her model, does not succeed. Guénélic leaves her by the end of the novel, as his patience with her chastity has worn thin. Hélisenne is then locked up in a tower by her husband, with only two serving maids as companions.

Thus ends the first volume of the *Angoysses douloureuses*, which is the best-known section of the book. This section is frequently considered to represent the first psychological novel written in French, and for this reason it is often compared to Madame de La Fayette's *Princesse de Clèves* (1678), written over a century later. The *Angoysses douloureuses* is written in an extremely learned, Latinate style, reminiscent of the late fifteenth-century 'Grands Rhétoriqueurs'. Despite the pedantry of the book's style, it was extremely popular in the sixteenth century, and was reprinted several times during Marguerite Briet's lifetime, once (1550) with 'corrections' of the overly Latinate language by Claude Colet.

A second work of Hélisenne de Crenne which has recently received renewed attention is the *Epistres familieres et invectives* (*Personal and Invective Letters*). These letters, like the novel, seem to combine autobiographical and fictional elements. The *Epistres* were published by Denys Janot in 1539, by which time Marguerite Briet and her husband were apparently separated, and the author was living in Paris (see the fourth invective letter which describes the warm reception she has received as a writer, in Paris). The *Epistres* construct a story of sorts through letters: thirteen 'personal', and five 'invective'. Hélisenne writes letters both to and from herself in this collection, once assuming the voice of her estranged husband. As in the *Angoysses*, Hélisenne blends many literary influences here: Cicero, Ovid, Petrarch and Boccaccio as well as Christine de Pizan and other French medieval writers.

Like Jeanne Flore, Hélisenne de Crenne appears to work out of the Italianate atmosphere of the 1530s and 1540s in France. But she goes far beyond her models such as Boccaccio, to incorporate autobiographical elements into her works, which thus reflect authentic aspects of her life as a woman. More dramatically than Jeanne Flore, she presents the persona of a woman writer speaking to women readers, with a more convincing message which real women readers apparently welcomed.

Marguerite de Navarre (1492–1549) is probably the most significant woman writer of the sixteenth century in France: not only because of her prolific output of poetry, theatre, stories and letters, but also because she was the sister of François I, later married two prominent French noblemen (Charles d'Alençon and Henri d'Albret), and finally would become the grandmother of Henri de Navarre, the future Henri IV. Traditional French criticism has recognized her importance, although in the nineteenth century some scholars suggested that the *Heptaméron* (written 1540s, published 1558) may not have been her own work, attributing it rather to the male author Bonaventure des Périers, who was in her service for a time.

Today we recognize Marguerite's significance not only for her high rank and influence, and for her unusual erudition at the time, but also for her leadership role in two important contemporary cultural controversies. The first was her sympathy for the nascent Protestant Reform movement in France, more correctly called Evangelism in the 1520s and 1530s. She carried on a long spiritual correspondence with reformist Bishop of Meaulx, Guillaume Briçonnet, and became the patron of several other reform-minded French writers, such as Clément Marot and François Rabelais. In her writing we find many references to her Bible reading (especially the New Testament), the constant theme of spiritual ascent (particularly in her poetry), as well as criticism of contemporary religious mores. A second theme which is receiving renewed attention today is Marguerite's obvious interest in the *Querelle des femmes*, and her representation of the battle between the sexes, especially in the *Heptaméron*.[3] Many tales, and the story-tellers themselves, depict fundamental conflicts between the ways in which men and women see the world and their relationship to it.

Like Jeanne Flore and Hélisenne de Crenne, Marguerite de Navarre reworks Boccaccio's legacy, particularly that of the *Decameron*. Marguerite had commissioned Antoine Le Maçon to translate the book into French, and it appeared in 1545. In her 'Prologue' (apparently written around 1546), Marguerite explains that everyone at court is busy reading the book, and that a group of noble men and women had hoped to create their own collection in imitation of Boccaccio's. The *Heptaméron* (so called because it contains only 72 stories rather than 100), purports to be a collection of true stories, which the fictional story-tellers recount while they are stranded at an abbey in the Pyrenees, after a torrential rain washes out a bridge, their only way back to civilization.

This mixture of truth and fiction reminds us of Hélisenne de Crenne's reworking of Boccaccio. But Marguerite's book does not develop a persona for the woman writer, as Hélisenne's did. The narrator of the collection is generally invisible, although scholars have been able to detect events from Marguerite's life in some of the tales. Rather, the female voice is found in those of the women story-tellers or *devisantes*, who express reactions to the tales of other characters, as well as introducing and concluding their own tales.

One of the longest tales is a miniature 'novel', and shows Marguerite's influence, similar to that of Hélisenne, on the developing 'genre' of the *roman sentimental*. 'Amadour et Floride', the tenth tale of the first day, treats the theme of 'impossible love' typical of the tradition of courtly love, or *amour courtois*. But it has a more tragic ending, and highlights the differences between male and female experiences of love, more thoughtfully than either Boccaccio or Jeanne Flore. Like many tales in the *Heptaméron*, this one focuses on problems experienced by young people of differing social rank, who although deeply in love, cannot consider marrying. Amadour befriends the nobleman he thinks Floride will marry, and himself marries Aventurade, one of Floride's serving women. The two platonic lovers are separated for long periods, as Amadour goes to war in Spain. The situation goes on for several years, until Aventurade is killed in an accident. Now Amadour does not have an excuse to visit Floride, since his wife is no longer his beloved's lady-in-waiting. On his last night there, after the funeral of his wife and before returning to war, Amadour tries to rape Floride, who is now married, and whose honour he therefore considers to be safe. He believes that after his long service, he deserves to possess her. Floride is shocked, and vows never to see him again. When she learns later through her mother that Amadour is planning another visit, Floride disfigures herself by striking her face with a stone, so that Amadour will no longer love her. He tries again to rape her, however, and she is rescued by her mother. Amadour is finally (apparently) killed in battle, although we learn that his death was really a suicide. As her husband has also been killed in the same campaign, Floride withdraws to a convent, where 'all her affections henceforth were bent on the perfect love of God'.

This tale is not typical by its length and complexity, but it does illustrate several themes which are representative of the collection as a whole. The story is recounted by the *devisante* (story-teller) Parlamente, frequently believed to be the mouth-piece for Marguerite. Parlamente concludes that the tale illustrates the virtue of Floride, who resisted temptation. Parlamente's fictional husband, Hircan, (a possible representative of Henri d'Albret), responds that the story illustrates the failure of the hero, Amadour, to carry out his duty, that of possessing the lady he loves. Rape is a common phenomenon in Marguerite's stories, and is generally viewed differently by male and female *devisants*. While the women see the duty to resist rape as defining their honour, the men find that they are obliged to attempt rape, as a feature of male honour. Thus the difference between male and female moral codes is a central focus of the *Heptaméron*, and particularly of the discussions which take place after each tale.

Marguerite has taken the legacy of *Boccaccio* in a different and more serious direction than either Jeanne Flore or Hélisenne de Crenne. In addition to the accentuated criticism of the hypocrisy of priests and monks, which reveals Marguerite's evangelical leanings, her treatment of the relationship between men and women has a more feminist tinge than that of Jeanne Flore, and a more thoughtful tendency to generalize and reflect on experience than was found in Hélisenne's autobiographical lamentations. Finally, the spiritual context of Bible reading at the beginning of each day, as well as the attempts by several characters such as Floride to escape the problems of this life through prayer, and to substitute the more perfect love of God for the very imperfect love of mortals – all these factors take Marguerite and the novella genre in a new direction not anticipated by Boccaccio.

While Jeanne Flore, Hélisenne de Crenne and Marguerite de Navarre may use the *œuvre* of Boccaccio as a point of departure, the latter two writers in particular transform this legacy, creating female versions of the *Fiammetta* and the *Decameron*, and revealing the masculinist bias present in much of Boccaccio's work. These women writers fulfil the promise of the *De mulieribus claris* by presenting realistic women characters, and by addressing real women readers, offering them instruction as well as the entertainment already present in their Italian predecessor.

PETRARCHAN AND NEO-PLATONIST CONVENTIONS REWORKED: THE LOVE POETRY OF PERNETTE DU GUILLET AND LOUISE LABÉ

Two women poets of the 1540s and 1550s from Lyons, Pernette du Guillet (*Rymes*) and Louise Labé (*Œuvres*), work within the Italian Petrarchan and neo-platonist conventions of love poetry, which typically assigned to women roles as Muses, subject-matter or addressees, but which rarely gave them a voice. Unlike Petrarch and his French imitator Maurice Scève, du Guillet and Labé find a way to reverse and restate the subject–object relationship in love poetry, from a woman's point of view. But they do this in quite different ways.

As for women writers of prose in the early sixteenth century, women poets, especially in Lyons, must work out their relationship to the mostly male cultural legacy of Italy, and particularly to that of the Petrarchan love lyric. The tomb of Petrarch's Laura had been discovered near Avignon by Maurice Scève in 1533, and this discovery brought a renewed interest in Petrarchan modes for male and female poets alike. Pernette du Guillet (1520–45), however, struggles to define her voice as a poet not only in relation to Petrarch, but more specifically with respect to the work of Maurice Scève (1500–60), the author of the Petrarchan poetic sequence *Délie, object de plus haulte vertu* [Delia, Object of the Greatest Virtue] (1544), whose title we now believe to represent Pernette herself. Pernette probably met Maurice Scève in 1536 and, although there was a twenty-year age difference, they became platonic lovers and he served as her poetic mentor.

Much of Pernette's poetry is concerned with the problem of imitation, but more specifically, with that of response. How can she praise

Scève, as a woman responding to a male poet, in the way that he had praised her in a major poetic sequence? The option of anonymity or invisibility available to Marguerite in the *Heptaméron* is not a possibility for Pernette. One critic has argued convincingly that the love lyric is in fact the only genre which is completely gender-determined.[4] While the third-person narrator of epic, romance or *nouvelle* could be male or female (although we have seen subtle distinctions between the ways in which male and female writers present their characters), only in the love lyric must the speaker identify him or herself by gender. Thus the obligation to present and define her voice as a woman writer or speaker is very much present for the writer of poetry, as it is not necessarily for the prose writer. In fact, for both Pernette du Guillet and Louise Labé, this becomes the central question with which they must struggle.

Pernette du Guillet's *Rymes* [Rhymes] were published in 1545, after the author's death. Her husband, unlike the jealous and sadistic husbands presented by Hélisenne and other women writers, had actually insisted that her poems be published. In his dedicatory epistle, addressed 'Aux Dames Lyonnoizes' [To the Ladies of Lyons], publisher du Moulin explains that 'ce petit amas de rymes' ['this little pile of rhymes'] was found after the much-regretted death of their author. He describes the many accomplishments of Pernette, despite her youth: playing musical instruments such as the lute, and speaking foreign languages including Italian, Spanish, Latin and a smattering of Greek. Du Moulin also stresses the exemplary nature of Pernette's life, for women readers: 'c'est à sçavoir de vous exerciter, comme elle, à la vertu' ['that is, to practise virtue as she did'].[5] Du Moulin closes his dedicatory epistle by encouraging the women of Lyons to imitate their well-educated (female) Italian predecessors as Pernette had done, in a surprising pæan to women writers of both countries.

Pernette wrote in a variety of genres. The collection contains seventy poems, of which the majority are in her favourite genre, the short epigram, formally very similar to Scève's *dizain* (ten lines, ten syllables, and the same rhyme scheme). The order of the poems is somewhat haphazard, apparently determined by du Moulin. The major theme of the poetry is her love for Maurice Scève, but she manages, deftly and wittily, to reverse some of his Petrarchan tropes, and shows herself to be the 'woman on a pedestal' who finally opens her mouth and answers back, not always as demurely as her interlocutor might have expected.

Although Scève developed the Petrarchan themes of the pain and torment of love (as Hélisenne de Crenne had done, as well), Pernette's love is more reasonable and more spiritualized, in line with the Neo-Platonism fashionable at the time.[6] Pernette's lexicon includes words such as '*vertu*' ['virtue'], '*chasteté*' ['chastity'], '*honneur*' ['honour'] '*parfaite amitié*' ['perfect love'], '*céleste*' ['celestial'], '*devoir*' ['duty'] – which do not predominate in Scève's work. She frequently plays on his name, with puns such as '*sévère*' and '*savoir*', or, as in epigram no. 5, with direct anagrams such as '*Vice à se muer*' and '*Ce vice mueras*'.

One poem which shows how Pernette reverses the usual mythological conventions of love-poetry is *Elegie* no. 2, which retells the story of Diana and Actæon from the point of view of the woman (Diana) bathing in the fountain. She sprinkles her lover with water, and then explains that she does not want to see him devoured by dogs as in the myth, but does want to see him enslaved to her. Pernette is obviously attuned to issues of power in the conventional love lyric, and at times she skilfully manipulates these conventions to her advantage. At other times, she tries to imagine equality between herself and her lover, as in Chanson No. 9, which announces, 'Je suis la Journée, / Vous, Amy, le Jour'.[7]

Although Pernette has been the 'eternal third' in the triad of Lyons poets, after Scève and Labé, feminist scholars have shed new light on the originality and ingenuity of her seeming emphasis on conventional female virtues such as chastity and modesty. These virtues give her some independence from her male mentor, and they suggest more equality in the relationship between the two writer/lovers than he had envisaged himself.

Louise Labé (1520–66) is one of many women writers whose biography is better known than her literary work. 'La belle Cordière', ['the beautiful rope-maker'], 'la cortegiana onesta' ['the honest courtesan'], 'la femme d'amour' ['the woman of love'], 'la belle Rebelle' ['the Beautiful Rebel'], 'Dame de Franchise' ['Lady of Frankness'] – these are only a few of the phrases which have been used to describe her flamboyant and unusual lifestyle. Unlike most writers in the sixteenth century, Louise Labé was not from an aristocratic background, but from the emerging bourgeois manufacturing sector of Lyons. Both her father and husband were rope-makers (hence the epithet 'cordière'), but she sought and received fame for her gatherings frequented by the artistic and literary cognoscenti of Lyons, as well as for her writing in both prose and poetry.

Myths about Labé have outweighed fact, perhaps because so many contemporaries wrote down their various opinions about her. Not only did she collect twenty-four sonnets by other poets, in praise of herself, to publish along with her own twenty-four; but scholars have assembled many comments by contemporary and later male critics. Early feminist François de Billon described Labé, in 1555, as a woman who 'se pourra bien dire Homme' ['could call herself a man'] for her many accomplishments.[8] An anonymous song of 1557 finds Louise to exercise the profession of paid courtesan, being visited in just one night by a lawyer, public attorney, cobbler, miller and rich Florentine.[9] In 1560, Calvin describes evenings spent at the home of 'la belle Cordière' (whom he refers to as a vulgar courtesan), where women dressed as men.[10]

This flamboyant reputation, justified or not, is the first of several differences between Louise and Pernette who, as we saw above, was careful to maintain a reputation for modesty and chastity. Several other obvious differences come to mind. While Pernette had to struggle with a sense of inferiority to her poet–lover Maurice Scève, Labé is really better known than the object of her sonnet sequence, Olivier de Magny, who was also himself a poet. Any borrowing between the two is now believed to have been by de Magny, whose 'O beaus yeus bruns . . .' ['Oh beautiful brown eyes'], in two versions, post-dates Louise's sonnet no. 2 of the same name.[11] Most importantly, Pernette and Louise found diametrically opposed ways to transform the conventions of the Petrarchan love lyric, to serve their poetic voices as women writers. Pernette maintains the role of addressee, and answers back, generally as if providing the second half of a dialogue, whether the first half has been stated or not. But Louise takes on the traditional male role as speaker to a less eloquent beloved, who is praised (as women traditionally had been) for his beauty rather than for his intelligence. Labé's sonnet no. 2 adapts the typical 'blason féminin' to list the beauties of her male lover: eyes, gaze, sighs, tears, forehead, hair, arms, hands, fingers.[12] No. 10 refers to his beautiful blond hair: 'Quand je voy ton blond chef couronné' ['When I see your blond head crowned']; while no. 11 again describes the beauty of his eyes: 'O dous regars, o yeus pleins de beauté' ['O sweet look, oh eyes full of beauty'].[13]

As Petrarch had frequently done, Labé inserts many references to the importance of her own role as poet, especially in the Latinate elegies which open her volume. Elegy no. 1 finds that Apollo has finally allowed her, like Sappho, to pluck the lyre, in memory of her past suffering. Elegy no. 2 speaks of the fame she has achieved as a writer: 'Que gens d'esprit me donnent quelque gloire' ['that intelligent people have made me famous'].[14] Elegy no. 3 asks the women of Lyons not to condemn her writings (as will sonnet no. 24), but it is obvious in this elegy that her poetry was well-known ('Ces miens escrits pleins d'amoureuses noises') ['these writings of mine full of amorous ideas'].[15] The self-confidence in her role as a woman poet, displayed here, distances Labé from the more hesitant du Guillet.

Labé's prose work was better known in the sixteenth century than her poetry. In the nineteenth century, its dense rhetorical style led it to fall into disfavour. But feminist scholarship has taken a new look at both the dedicatory epistle and the *Débat de folie et d'amour* (*Debate between Folly and Love*), finding them to be well worth the effort required to digest their complexity.

The 'Epitre dédicatoire', before the *Œuvres* of 1555, uses full-blown rhetorical periods, and raises several questions central to the debate over women's education, in the sixteenth century. There are some parallels to the epistle preceding Pernette's *Rymes*, written by its editor, du Moulin (after her death). Both begin by detailing some of the author's accomplishments in her youth, including music and letters. Like du Moulin, Labé encourages women to aspire to learning, but with her own original contrast between writing and spinning, asking 'les vertueuses Dames d'eslever un peu leurs esprits pardessus leurs quenoilles et fuseaus' ['virtuous women to raise their minds a bit above their distaffs and spindles'].[16] Although Labé repeats topoi found in many women's prefaces, her own stands out for its feminist stance on women's education.

The *Débat de folie et d'amour* is Labé's major prose work. It reveals her unusual erudition, upon which many contemporaries commented. Like the poetry, particularly the *Elegies*, the *Débat* shows Louise's knowledge of Latin literature, both classical and Renaissance. The *Débat* borrows from Erasmus's *Praise of Folly*, with long declamatory speeches by various deities: Venus, Cupid, Apollo, Mercury, as well as Folly herself. The *Débat* offers a humorous explanation for the fact that Love is blind – Folly stole his eyes, and then proposed herself as his guide.

Labé's transformation of the Petrarchan love lyric is more radical than Pernette's, but her work is also more accessible than her predecessor's, which two factors may explain Labé's increased recognition at present. Although her sincerity and directness did not find many imitators at the time, her use of the sonnet was to be taken up by contemporary poets, especially those of the *Pléiade*.[17] Her sense of a shared female condition has a distinctly modern ring to it, and this sentiment will be echoed by women writers later in the sixteenth century and beyond.

WOMEN'S WORK AS LITERARY ENTERPRISE: THE *DAMES DES ROCHES*

In the second half of the sixteenth century, women writers work more in the context of their Northern European and French predecessors and contemporaries, than with the legacy of Italian humanism. The Poitiers mother and daughter, Madeleine Neveu (ca. 1520–87) and Catherine Fradonnet (1542–87), more frequently known as the Dames des Roches, are contemporaries of the late *Pléiade* poet Pierre de Ronsard, as well as of the French humanist Estienne Pasquier, whom they knew well. While Ronsard (like Petrarch) addressed women throughout his poetry, rarely offering them a chance to answer back, the Dames des Roches claim the right to speak, and more importantly, to write; disdaining distaff and spindle, they redefine 'woman's work' as the literary enterprise, and reject love and marriage in favour of the life of the mind.

Although Madeleine was born around the same time as Pernette and Louise, she lived much longer than they (40 and 20 years longer, respectively). Catherine belonged to a younger generation, however, and profited from the existence of these 'literary foremothers', and most particularly from the influence of her mother. The geographical and temporal distance between the two 'milieux' of Lyons and Poitiers explains many but not all of the differences between these two sets of women poets.

Compared to the flowering of poetry in Lyons of the 1540s and 1550s, the Dames des Roches's era, the 1570s and 1580s, represents a more serious period in French history, due largely to the contemporary wars of religion. Madeleine and Catherine both comment in their poetry on the religious troubles dividing their city, and like Christine de Pizan earlier, they have a political and social conscience which motivates them to speak out against the destruction and horror of civil war. This conscience differentiates them from their relatively apolitical predecessors, du Guillet and Labé.

Much has been written about the unusual erudition of the Dames des Roches, and about the way in which Madeleine filled for her daughter the role of mentor and guide, more traditionally reserved for males in humanist manuals of education. Like the Poitiers humanists in whose context they lived and wrote, the Dames des Roches constantly associate knowledge with virtue. Their *salon* was more like the earlier fifteenth-century Italian academies, in which serious discussions took place, although there was also a role for literary games. The Dames des

Roches' first printed work, *Les Œuvres* (1578–9)[18] represents only a fraction of their voluminous output, but it does give the reader a good sense of the writing of both women.

Madeleine was less ambitious as a writer (although she was apparently more erudite). She comments elsewhere that her youthful intellectual aspirations were cut short by the cares of two husbands, a household and three children of whom only one, Catherine, lived to adulthood. Like Pernette du Guillet and Louise Labé, Madeleine begins her section of the volume with a prose 'Epistre aux dames' ['Epistle to the Ladies'], followed by a verse 'Epistre à ma fille' ['Epistle to my Daughter'], admonishing her to strive for knowledge and virtue, which are mutually supporting endeavours. Madeleine writes mostly in the ode and sonnet genres, with many erudite classical and mythological references. Advice to women is a frequent theme: ode no. 3 suggests 'A la dame Poïtevine' / 'De choisir l'ancre et la plume' [To the Lady of Poitou / To choose ink and pen'] (pp. 97–8); and moral precepts abound, such as sonnet no. 30 'Il est certes plus beau de donner que de prendre' ['it is certainly more beautiful to give than to take'] (p. 149). Madeleine's section of the volume closes with some epitaphs, including one in which her second husband, François Eboissard (d. 1578) speaks from the grave to describe their marriage, distinguished for its 'chaste amour' ['chaste love'] (p. 157). Catherine's section of the volume is longer and more varied. She begins with a prose *Epistre* addressed to her mother, and acknowledging her as an 'exemple de vertu' ['example of virtue'] (p. 181). She claims not to care about readers' opinions, but does advise them that although she writes about love (in the 'Dialogue de Sincero et de Charité' ['Dialogue of Sincero and Charité']), this does not mean that she is in love. She also responds to the potential criticism that there are already enough poets in France, with the telling point that there are still not enough women writers.

Among the most interesting works in Catherine's section are the mixed prose and verse allegorical 'Dialogues', which, like Labé's 'Débat de folie et d'amour', try to resolve differences between faculties such as Youth and Age, Virtue and Fortune, the Hand and the Foot, Beauty and Love, etc. The 'Dialogue de Sincero et de Charité' has led to much speculation about the possible real-life model for the male lover, Sincero, with some commentators offering the name of Claude Pellejay, even suggesting that the latter may have written the speeches in his name. Sincero speaks in neo-platonic clichés, asking Charité for her 'bonnes graces' ['good graces']. Charité responds (especially in the sonnet sequence which follows the prose dialogue) that she prefers an 'amitié saincte' ['holy friendship'], and asks Sincero to be virtuous and reasonable, even suggesting that he spend more time studying!

One of the best known poems by Catherine is the sonnet 'A ma Quenoille' ['To my Distaff'], which has been compared to Ronsard's poem of the same name, and is reminiscent of Labé's dedication to the women of Lyons. She describes her dilemma as a woman, torn between domestic duties ('la quenoille', the distaff) and intellectual pursuits ('la plume', the pen). She concludes that she will try to do both: 'Ayant dedans la main, le fuzeau, et la plume' ['having in my hand both the spindle and the pen'] (Larsen, p. 293).

The Œuvres were published in 1578 by Abel l'Angelier, at the prestigious Paris house which would later print the 1595 edition of Montaigne's Essais (Essays), and most of the works of Marie de Gournay. A second expanded edition of the Œuvres was published in 1579. In 1582, l'Angelier printed the collection of blasons celebrating the flea which had landed on Catherine's bosom, one famous afternoon in 1579. The Secondes Œuvres were printed in 1583,[19] and Les Missives (a collection of letters), in 1586. Both women died of the plague on the same day in November of 1587.

The Dames des Roches are unique among sixteenth-century French women writers for having established their identity through dialogue with each other, rather than with earlier or contemporary Italian or French male authors. Despite their status as bourgeoises, they sought and found immortality through letters. Catherine in particular is remarkable for her independence, having refused marriage (to the disapproval of Pasquier) in order to devote her life to writing. The integration of traditional women's work with their intellectual life as sixteenth-century humanists makes Madeleine and Catherine des Roches stand out as precursors to the contemporary 'woman-identified' feminist intellectual.

MEMOIRS, ESSAYS, AND FEMINIST HUMANISM

Finally, two women writers of the late sixteenth century redefine the prose genres of memoir and essay, practised by their French male contemporaries. Marguerite de Valois (Mémoires), better known as 'La Reine Margot' ['Queen Margot'], responds to the French memorialist Brantôme, correcting his picture of her, and giving us her own version of contemporary events. Marie de Gournay, covenant daughter of Michel de Montaigne,[20] is best known for her posthumous edition of the Essais in 1595, but she published other works around the same time and would go on, in the early seventeenth century, to write her own collections of essays, *L'Ombre* (*The Shadow*). These essays treat subjects similar to those of the *Essais*, but from a feminine point of view. Finally, in the 1620s, she would write the first overtly feminist texts by a woman since those of Christine de Pizan, the 'Egalité des hommes et des femmes' ('Of the Equality of Men and Women'), and the 'Grief des dames' ('The Complaint of the Ladies').

The daughter of Henri II and Catherine de Médicis, Marguerite de Valois (1553–1615) was a member of the French royalty, and was qualified to be called 'Reine de France' [Queen of France] both by birth and by marriage. She could never rule in her own right, however, because the French Salic Law forbade it.[21] She was married to the Protestant Henri de Navarre in 1572, an event which hastened the Saint Bartholomew's Day Massacre in which thousands of Protestants were slaughtered, across France. The marriage did not produce children, and it was eventually annulled (1599), after Marguerite had been exiled (in 1586) to the remote fortress of Usson, in the Auvergne. There she wrote the bulk of her literary *œuvre*, much of which has been lost. The *Mémoires* (written in the late 1590s, published in 1628) describe events from her childhood, the marriage and separation from Henri de Navarre, but break off in 1582. There has been speculation that she did finish the *Mémoires*, but that the post-1582 material was either lost or censored in the early seventeenth century.

Marguerite also wrote many letters, mostly in a formal, rhetorical style, and generally to ask for favours from powerful figures at court. There are several to a lover, Jacques Harlay de Champvallon, lamenting his infidelity, and suggesting that he read more, as a consolation for the pain of love. The poetry, none of which is signed, expresses contemporary themes such as neo-platonic love, and is mostly limited to short genres like the sonnet. A humorous prose dialogue, 'La Ruelle mal assortie' ('The Ill-Assorted Bedside'), compares the pleasures of love and study, suggesting that her lover read neo-platonic authors such as Agricola, Léon Hébreu, and Ficino. Most commentators now believe that this dialogue is not authentic, although as recently as 1986, Yves Cazaux included it with Marguerite's collected prose works.

The *Mémoires* are Marguerite's best-known work. They appear to constitute the first completely autobiographical book by a woman in French, and were followed by several women's memoirs in the seventeenth century. The memoir was a genre which had been practised by males in the late Middle Ages and early Renaissance, in France, but was generally used to describe public and military events, rather than private or personal ones. Marguerite's contribution to the genre is that, in addition to chronicling public events, she also describes seemingly insignificant incidents from her childhood and adolescence, which had an impact on her personal development, rather than on the history of France. She apparently knew the essayist Michel de Montaigne (1533–92), since his 'Apologie de Raimond Sebond' ['Apology for Raymond Sebond'] (*Essais*: vol. II, no 12) is believed to have been written for and dedicated to her (*ca* 1576–9). Although Marguerite's *Mémoires* are more conventional, chronological autobiography than are Montaigne's *Essais*, the emphasis on the subjective side of human experience may have been something which she borrowed from him.

Her most productive intellectual friendship, however, was with the memorialist Pierre de Bourdeille, Abbé de Brantôme (1540–1614). Her *Mémoires* are dedicated to him, and in fact claim to respond to the overly flattering picture of her he has painted in the *Dames illustres* (*Illustrious Ladies*) (1580s). She sent him her version of many of the events he had also described, asking him in turn to correct her book, and give it shape. The fact that he did not do this attests to the power of her book to stand on its own. Like Brantôme, Marguerite does write extensively about details of public royal events, and particularly about her clothing and jewellery. But in addition to these traditionally 'feminine' topics, the *Mémoires* chronicle her developing introspective side, strong religious faith and interest in classical literature and philosophy.

Like Pernette du Guillet and Catherine des Roches, Marguerite de Valois responds to a flattering male discourse which tends to objectify her, and substitutes an authentically subjective version of herself and of events (such as the Saint Bartholomew's Day Massacre) which had previously been seen only from the outside. She is certainly not independent of men, as the Dames des Roches strove to be, but, as one of the first women to write openly about herself, she is original in claiming the importance of 'herstory', and of her version of events which had previously only been chronicled by male historians.

Marie le Jars de Gournay (1565–1645) illustrates many of the themes which we have observed with respect to earlier sixteenth-century French women writers, but in a completely original and even idiosyncratic manner. Her life and interests span the late sixteenth and early seventeenth century. Thus a discussion of her work provides at once a conclusion to this chapter, and an introduction to the next. Marie de Gournay was born to a family of lesser nobility in Paris in 1565, but the family soon moved to Gournay sur Aronde, in Picardy, when they could no longer afford the expense of urban life. To the displeasure of her mother, Gournay preferred study to all other pursuits, and spent her girlhood reading. She even claims to have taught herself Latin, by comparing Latin texts with their French translations. At the age of eighteen or nineteen (around 1584), she happened to come across a copy of the first two books of Montaigne's *Essais*, which had been published in 1580. This discovery was a revelation to her, and she resolved to meet their author, which she did in 1588. Since Gournay's father had died, Montaigne offered to grant her the title of his 'covenant daughter'. For the next four years, the friendship with Montaigne was to be the central focus of her life. He apparently visited her family in Picardy, and they corresponded after his return to the Château de Montaigne outside Bordeaux.

When Montaigne died in 1592, Marie de Gournay was devastated, but his widow asked her to help prepare a posthumous edition of the *Essais*, with additions which Montaigne had written in the margins of the 1588 edition. Marie worked assiduously on this edition, writing in addition an eighteen-page preface which was published along with the *Essais* by Abel L'Angelier, in 1595. The 'Préface' defends Montaigne from criticisms his *Essais* had received (both stylistic and thematic), but it also expresses Gournay's deep affection for Montaigne and her desire to imitate him and his work as completely as possible. Throughout the rest of her life, Gournay would continue to revise and reprint editions of the *Essais*, adding translations of their Latin quotations (in 1617), and constantly reworking the 'Préface' (in 1599, 1617, 1625 and 1635). Throughout the nineteenth century, she was best known for this editorial work, and her memory lived in the shadow of the essayist's.

In the twentieth century, however, attention turned to Gournay's other works, and particularly to her feminist writings. Gournay's first published book was, surprisingly, a romance, entitled *Le Proumenoir de Monsieur de Montaigne par sa fille d'alliance* (*Strolling with Montaigne, by his Covenant Daughter*) (1594). She had apparently recounted this story (borrowed from Claude de Taillemont's *Discours des champs faëz* (*Discourse on the enchanted countryside*) (1553) to Montaigne during his visit to Picardy in the late 1580s, and she had then written it down and sent it to him, asking for corrections. However, in a parallel to the situation of Marguerite de Valois and Brantôme outlined above, Montaigne never did this, leaving Gournay to present the novel herself, after his death. The novel recounts the story of a young woman, Alinda, who is loved and abandoned by her lover, Leontin. It contains lamentations and purports to warn young women to avoid love, much as Hélisenne de Crenne's *Angoisses doulou-reuses* had done.

In 1598, after a trip to the Low Countries, Gournay moved to Paris, and began an almost fifty-year struggle to survive as a woman of letters. During the first twenty-five years or so of the seventeenth century she established a literary *salon*, practised alchemy and wrote occasional prose and poetry, always hoping to obtain patronage. She also may have cultivated Marguerite de Valois, after the latter's return to Paris from Usson, in 1605. Topics on which she wrote included: education (1600); a pamphlet on the assassination of Henri IV in 1610; a short autobiography (1616); and several treatises on language (1618, 1619) in which she defended the language of the sixteenth-century. In the early 1620s, she wrote two feminist tracts, the 'Egalité des hommes et des femmes' (1622); and the 'Grief des dames' (1626). Finally, in 1626 she published her collected works, including essays, novel, translations and poetry ('Le Bouquet de pinde' ['A Bouquet of Poetry'], in a volume entitled *L'Ombre de la damoiselle de Gournay* [The Shadow of the Damoiselle of Gournay].

The last twenty years of Gournay's life saw her gain credit for her accomplishments. She received a pension from Cardinal Richelieu, may have been influential in founding the *Académie française* ('French Academy'), and republished her collected works (revised and expanded) in 1634 and 1641, under the title *Les Advis ou les presens de la demoiselle de Gournay* [The Demoiselle of Gournay's Presents and Offerings]. At her death in 1645 her reputation was solidly established, although she had also attracted ridicule for her unorthodox lifestyle and for her attachment to the language and values of the sixteenth century, which were now viewed as hopelessly old-fashioned.

The 'Egalité des hommes et des femmes' (1622) illustrates several of the themes which we have seen develop over the sixteenth-century. The essay is dedicated to Marie de Medicis and in this dedication Gournay exhorts the Queen that both she and her son should 'se jeter vivement sur les bons Écrits de Prudence et de Moeurs' ['studiously read good writings on prudence and behaviour'],[22] thereby illustrating her humanistic belief in the moral value of learning, as well as her feminist commitment to learning for women. The 'Egalité' begins with an original distinction between equality and superiority, for women. Gournay does not claim, like some contemporary feminists, that women are superior to men – she just asks for simple equality. She rejects the position of some men, who would confine women to the distaff alone ('la quenouille seule'), in terms reminiscent of both Louise Labé and Catherine des

Roches. Gournay goes on to stress the importance of education for women, in helping them to achieve the equality they are capable of, finding that French and English women have gone further in this respect than the women of Italy. We see here that one of the themes of early six-teenth-century women's writing, inferiority to Italy, has now been resolved in favour of France.

Gournay's career epitomizes several other tendencies which we have traced throughout the sixteenth century. One is certainly the importance of the printing industry in making contemporary books (such as Montaigne's *Essais*) quickly available to her, despite her isolation in Picardy; and in helping her own work to become well known and dis-seminated throughout France and Northern Europe. A second theme has been that of women writers' relationship to the male canon, and Gournay's was a complex and unusual one. Her adoration for *Pléiade* authors and for the essayist Montaigne seems to keep her subordinate to the male canon, but her editorial work with the *Essais* shows an ability to transform and expand the very canon which she inherited. A third theme, the creation of an authentic voice as a woman writer, was a central but very problematic issue, for Gournay. As early as the 'Préface de 1595', Gournay commented that many men refuse to listen to an opinion, once they realize that 'C'est une femme qui parle' ['It is a woman who is speaking']. But she went on later to expand this insight to form an entire short essay, the 'Grief des dames'. Here, for the first time, Gournay is able to express solidarity with other women writers, and to attack men of letters who refuse to read women's work.

Finally, the question of the relationship between autobiography and third-person discourse, which we have seen to be problematical for women writers of the sixteenth century, is played out in a new way, by Gournay. Her model, Montaigne, was one of the first to write autobio-graphical prose, and he invented the essay genre, which blends subjec-tive and objective insights. Gournay initially hoped to imitate Montaigne, without revealing herself. But towards the end of her career, she does write several short autobiographical pieces, including the poem 'Peincture de moeurs' ('A Moral Portrait') (*Bouquet de pinde*), as well as a prose defence of herself, the 'Apologie pour celle qui escrit' ('Apology for the Woman Writer'). Along with Marguerite de Valois, Gournay will serve as a model to a host of women memorialists, in the seventeenth century.

Women writers of the French sixteenth century, like their male counterparts, worked within the context of European Renaissance

Humanism. But 'humanism' seemed initially to be reserved for males, in the elitist poetics of Petrarch or in Boccaccio, Ronsard or Montaigne. Humanism had developed in Italy and later in France, with the Roman model of public civic virtue, as the goal of education and literature. This civic virtue was not well suited to the private lives of women. Women writers of the Renaissance, by adding the perspectives of the feminine and of feminism, transformed humanism into a more inclusive point of view which is fully human. It is with Marie de Gournay that this process reaches a conclusion at the beginning of the seventeenth century.

NOTES

1 See for example François de Billon, *Le Fort inexpugnable de l'honneur du sexe féminin* (*The Impregnable Fortress of the Honour of the Female Sex*) (1555).

2 See, for example, the Spanish humanist Juan Luis Vives, whose *Institution de la Femme Chrestienne* (*Education of the Christian Woman*) was translated from Latin into French in 1542.

3 The *Querelle des femmes* grows out of the *Querelle de la Rose*, initiated earlier by Christine de Pizan in her response to Jean de Meung's portion of the *Roman de la Rose*. The *Querelle des femmes* was a literary quarrel about the value of women, whether they were good or bad, superior or inferior to men, etc. Scholars disagree about whether this debate was serious, or just a literary game.

4 Jones, *Currency of Eros*, p. 7.

5 *Rymes*, ed. Graham, pp. 2–3.

6 Neo-platonism was first revived at the Florentine Academy of the fifteenth century. Marsilio Ficino wrote a commentary on Plato's *Symposium* for this academy, which became influential in sixteenth-century France. Neo-platonic love, now in a Christian context, assumed that human, physical love was only the first step toward divine love.

7 It is not possible to offer an English translation of this quotation which plays upon masculine and feminine versions of the word 'day'.

8 See Rigolot's edition of Labé's *Œuvres complètes* (1986) p. 233.

9 *Ibid.*, p. 238–9

10 *Ibid.*, p. 242.

11 *Ibid.*, pp. 227–9.

12 The 'blason féminin' was a genre of poetry in the early sixteenth century which praised women's body parts separately, rather than as part of a whole. Clément Marot was one of the best known of the 'blason' poets.

13 *Œuvres*, ed. Rigolot, p. 127.

14 *Ibid.*, p. 113.

15 *Ibid.*, p. 115.

16 *Ibid.*, p. 42.

17 The *Pléiade* was a group of seven poets in mid-sixteenth-century France.

The best known of these were Joachim du Bellay and Pierre de Ronsard, both of whom practised the sonnet form in French.

18 This is now available in an excellent critical edition by Anne Larsen. All references are to this edition.

19 The *Secondes Œuvres* have recently been edited by Anne Larsen.

20 As 'covenant daughter' [*fille d'alliance*], Gournay (whose own father had died) was entitled to protection by Montaigne. The 'covenant' relationship was a fairly common one in the sixteenth century: it was not as formal as adoption, but seems to have described a person who became an honorary member of the family.

21 The French Salic Law forbade women to rule as Queens in their own right (as was possible in England). It was feared that a Queen could marry, and thus put France under the power of a foreign King. This rule dated back to Gallic times.

22 *Fragments*, ed. Dezon-Jones, p. 112.

CHAPTER THREE

Altering the fabric of history: women's participation in the classical age

Faith E. Beasley

THE CHANGING GENDER OF LITERARY CULTURE

The seventeenth century presents an intriguing paradox. The dominant image of France's canonized classical age is the all-powerful monarch Louis XIV (ruled 1661–1715), a man who reduced the nobility to puppets and harnessed every discourse – literary, historical, philosophical – to pull his own chariot modelled on Apollo's. This would hardly seem to be a fertile milieu for female creativity. And yet seventeenth-century France witnessed a veritable explosion of women's participation in the literary and intellectual realm. During the years 1640–1715 alone, there were over 220 women who actively participated in the literary scene.[1] They shaped that scene in an unprecedented fashion, and their innovations as both producers and consumers had a profound and long-lasting influence on the French literary tradition.

To what can this seemingly sudden upsurge in women's participation in the literary field be attributed? While the sixteenth century had its literary luminaries, there was not a strong female literary tradition upon which seventeenth-century followers could draw, as would be the case for the eighteenth century. There is no single explanation for this seventeenth-century phenomenon; rather one must speak of a confluence of historical and intellectual factors that together produced the powerful female literary tradition of this period.

In terms of history, sixteenth-century France did leave a legacy of strong female actors on the political stage. Catherine and Marie de Médici's regencies remained indelibly ingrained in France's historical memory. Anne d'Autriche revived this memory when she became regent for her son, Louis XIV, upon the death of her husband, Louis XIII. Anne d'Autriche's regency (1643–61) was fraught with discord. Her foreign-born prime minister, Mazarin, was never accepted by Louis XIV's family members, who thought they should be governing in place of the usurping pair composed of Anne and Mazarin. A civil war, the Fronde, erupted, which Anne and Mazarin eventually quashed.[2] This war was to have far-reaching and lasting consequences on the young monarch's political psyche, and, as we shall see, on the literary scene.

The Fronde was a complex civil war that pitted the nobility against itself and divided the rest of France into various factions. This war is of significance for the opportunity it afforded some women to make history, to participate in and have an effect on the political realm, not in the traditional roles of spouses or mistresses, but as seventeenth-century incarnations of Amazons. Opposing the regency, the three principal *frondeuses* were the duchesse de Montpensier, the duchesse de Longueville, and the princesse de Condé, but many other women played significant roles. The duchesse de Montpensier was Louis XIV's first cousin. La Grande Mademoiselle, as she was known, was an impassioned and willing replacement for her vacillating father, Gaston d'Orléans, Louis XIV's uncle. Her principal feats include leading her troops into battle to conquer Orléans for the *frondeur* or princely party and even helping them to conquer Paris. She is etched into historical memory as the figure on top of the Bastille ordering the troops to fire upon those of the future Sun King. Anne-Geneviève de Longueville's exploits were no less spectacular and influential. She convinced her brother, Condé, to join the *frondeur* cause. When Condé and her husband were imprisoned for over a year, she assumed their positions as leaders. She organized the uprising in Normandy and even made a pact with Spanish troops to overthrow the regency. Her sister-in-law, the princesse de Condé, also took command and organized the opposition in Bordeaux. These women, along with others such as the duchesse de Chevreuse, the princesse Palatine, the duchesse de Montbazon, the marquise de Sablé, and Mmes de Fiesque, de Frontenac, de Sully, and d'Olonne thus worked to make history as would their male counterparts in the political realm on the battlefield. But the Fronde was also an untraditional arena. Many of the battles were waged on a less public field – the territory of personal intrigue and alliances. Here, too, women were often the first line of attack. They exerted crucial influence through love affairs and by forging alliances, proving decisively that the personal was very political. When the war ended in 1653, most of these women were exiled. But the legacy of their involvement in the Fronde continued to flourish, notably by having a profound effect on the literary realm. As shall become apparent, many *frondeuses* turned their energies to literature, where they waged a war whose stakes were perhaps even higher. They were certainly longer-lasting.

Louis XIV took over the reins of government in 1661, determined to alleviate all conditions that could have produced such seditious behaviour. Everyone is familiar with his absolutist political legacy according to which nobles were reduced to theatrical puppets upon a splendid stage, Versailles. Most important for our purposes was Louis's appropriation of the intellectual realm to further his political ambitions. Official history and literature reflected the Sun King's rays, and intensified their brilliance. The patriarchal figure was at the centre of theatrical productions as well as all accounts of historical events. There was seemingly little opportunity for other lights, particularly those associated with women, to shine for the remainder of the century, leading to what some term 'le grand renfermement de la femme' ['the great confinement of women'].[3]

But women's fires were never extinguished under Louis XIV. They simply took more subtle forms than that of warrior. Recent research has suggested that while many women could not write, they could read, and thus constituted a public that grew throughout the period. Education for the masses, especially for women, was very limited. But noble women as well as some bourgeois often employed tutors. For example, Madame de Lafayette, author of *La Princesse de Clèves* (*The Princess of Clèves*), among other works, was learned in Spanish, Italian, Latin and philosophy. Throughout the century, the relationship between women and knowledge was explored and debated. But the familiar arguments excluding women from intellectual pursuits had lost much of their vehemence and seduction. Women like Madeleine de Scudéry in her harangue 'Sapho à Erinne' (*Les Femmes illustres*, (*Illustrious Women*) 1642) echoed this revised reasoning on the subject. Sapho exhorts Erinne to educate herself, not only for her own good, but for the benefit of society as a whole. 'What good does it do men', she asks, 'to discuss topics with interlocutors who are not more learned than animals?'

The seventeenth-century produced a number of learned women. In 1668, Marguerite Buffet published *Nouvelles Observations sur la langue française* (*New Observations concerning the French Language*), a treatise on grammar addressed specifically to a female public, the second half of which is entitled *Eloge des illustres sçavantes* (*In Praise of Illustrious Learned Women*). The *Eloge* consists of over 100 portraits of women who merit the title 'illustre savante' ['illustrious learned women'] a title she extends to those whose knowledge is worldly as well as to intellectuals. Buffet also includes more traditional intellectuals such as Mme Dacier, known for her translations of Homer, and Marie de Gournay. Such women proved that women could equal, or even surpass, men in intellectual pursuits.

Women's intellectual and literary pursuits flourished due, in particular, to the development of a uniquely French institution, the *ruelle* or *salon*, as it has become known to posterity. The Fronde and the *salon* movement were largely responsible for fostering and inspiring the particular wave of female creativity. For centuries women had met informally for conversation and companionship, but in the seventeenth century this practice became an integral and recognized institution of French culture for both sexes. In the 1620s, Catherine de Vivonne-Savelli, the marquise de Rambouillet, opened her doors to intellectuals, writers, political personages and friends. She in fact redesigned her Paris mansion, or *hôtel particulier*, to be more conducive to these gatherings, and introduced to France the architectural concept of rooms *en enfilade*. Rambouillet's *chambre bleue* [blue room] became synonymous with distinction, poetry, good taste, and polite society. The marquise received her guests in her bedroom, and occupied the place of honour, the bed itself. She was either ill or feigned illness after having her children, perhaps to avoid future and repeated pregnancies, which were the dangerous bane of women's existence at the time. Habitués of the *chambre bleue* were seated or stood in the area around the bed, called a *ruelle*. As a result, gatherings such as Rambouillet's came to be known generically as *ruelles*. (The term *salon* dates from the nineteenth century.)

There were numerous *ruelles*, particularly during the first three-quarters of the century. Contrary to the *salons* of the eighteenth century, the seventeenth-century *ruelles* were always governed by a woman and dominated by the female participants. Interestingly, both noble women and bourgeois held *ruelles*. This institution was responsible for an unprecedented intermingling of classes. Marriages across class lines were even encouraged. The *ruelles* of the first half of the century are above all associated with the refinement of language and manners. By mid century, however, the focus shifted primarily to literary matters.

It is difficult to determine precisely what occurred within the confines of the *ruelles*. The activity was oral in nature and few records were kept. Conrart maintained a log of his friend Madeleine de Scudéry's *ruelle*, called her *samedis*, but his record was destroyed in a fire. Historians are thus forced to rely on sources such as correspondences, the literature that bears the *ruelle*'s imprint, and the descriptions by male detractors who opposed the movement, in particular DePure, Somaize, and Molière. Such accounts reveal that the primary subjects of conversation were love, marriage and literature. Increasingly marriage was viewed as slavery for women, especially in noble families where women were used to form alliances between families or even countries. In an interesting exchange of letters, two important female historical figures and writers, the *frondeuse* Montpensier and Anne d'Autriche's lady-in-waiting, Françoise Bertaut de Motteville, expressed some of their female contemporaries' thoughts on marriage. In 1660 Montpensier suggested to her friend that an ideal situation might involve marriage simply for the length of time needed to produce progeny and thus continue the human race. Separation, and thus freedom for women, could follow this hopefully brief period. In fact, the position of the widow, although reviled by society as a whole, was actually attractive to women. It is intriguing to note that many of the women writers of the period either never married or were widowed or otherwise separated from their husbands. Inspired by these discussions of marriage in the *ruelles*, women writers explored alternatives for women in their literary works.

Participants in *salon* culture examined human relationships and conduct in society, especially love, in great depth. This was a theatrical society in which everyone was aware of playing a role. The norms of *politesse* [politeness], *civilité* [civility] and other codes of conduct were severely regimented. *Salon* participants critiqued the theatrical productions of society but advanced their own equally stringent codes and expectations. One *salon* board game developed in Madeleine de Scudéry's *samedis*, the 'Carte de Tendre' – which was published in Scudéry's novel, *Clélie (Clelia)* (vol. 1, 1654) – illuminates especially well this desire to dissect society and offer other models.[4]

This map of the heart is designed to show the would-be suitor how to please his object of desire. The worthy suitor will choose a route along which he passes the towns of Sincerity, Generosity and Respect; an undesirable partner will stray and end up visiting Negligence or Forgetfulness. The destination is not passion or even consummated love, but a place called *Tendre*, where friendship and respect reign. Scudéry's 'Carte de Tendre' is the ultimate example of *salon* women's attempt to analyse the most profound and influential human emotion, love, and to redefine its territory and women's roles within that psychological space.

Just as women explored new patterns for emotional and societal life, so too did they use the collaborative nature of the *salons* to explore women's place in the intellectual world. Rambouillet's *salon* is usually associated with refinement and pleasure, although its influence on the French language cannot be negated. By mid-century, many of the *ruelles*, in particular Scudéry's *samedis*, were seen as intellectual gatherings that resembled the officially sanctioned academies, with the important difference that the *ruelles* were dominated by women whereas the academies excluded them entirely. Descartes was read and debated. The *ruelles* in general were considered the temples of taste, the places where taste, or *bon goût*, reigned supreme. Taste has many connotations, the most interesting perhaps being its association with judgment, especially of literary works. As the marquise de Lambert – a *salonnière* in her own right – states in *Réflexions nouvelles sur les femmes* (*New Thoughts about Women*), the ultimate place to acquire this 'taste' was the *ruelles*, and its purveyors were female. One of the primary activities in the *salons* was the critique of literature composed within or outside of their confines.[5] A writer needed the approbation of this worldly public, who judged according to its elusive standards of taste, *bon sens*, and *bienséance*. To be a critic one need not be well versed in scholastic models. Worldly sensibility, acquired through contact with this *salon* public, was considered sufficient and even preferable. Women dominated this form of literary criticism, even though they were virtually excluded from higher learning, because they needed only to cultivate their worldly experience and its values. This form of criticism was a collaborative venture. Participants often read works aloud and underscored what was pleasing or what did not meet worldly standards.

In addition to critiquing literature according to new criteria based on the pleasure of a text, rather than on its adherence to ancient models and capacity to instruct, the *ruelles*, especially by mid-century, were considered foyers of literary creativity and innovation. Like criticism, literary composition was often collaborative in nature. Joan DeJean has coined the term '*salon*-writing' to refer to these collective literary practices. A good example of this method is the now canonical *Maximes* of La Rochefoucauld. Correspondence of the period attests to La Rochefoucauld's constant involvement with the *salon* milieu during the elaboration of the *Maximes*, especially with the marquise de Sable's *salon*. The marquise was also responsible for her own volume of maxims. Participants added their own reflections and commented upon and revised La Rochefoucauld's. While the final version was published under La Rochefoucauld's name, it was common knowledge that the *Maximes* was the product of many voices.

Montpensier's *Divers Portraits* (*A Portrait Collection*) and her *Galerie des portraits* (*A Portrait Gallery*), collections of literary portraits, are further examples of the collaborative literary activity of the *salons*. The only signed work by Mme de Lafayette is a portrait of her friend Scudéry in these two works. In addition to portraits, toward the end of the century Scudéry published volumes of *Conversations* which had either really taken place or were modelled on *salon* interactions and later incorporated into her novels.

The collaborative nature of both *salon* criticism and literary composition which, to twentieth-century readers, appears foreign and nebulous points to the complexities of authorship in general during the seventeenth century. Many women writers did not sign their works, but not for the same reasons that inspired their nineteenth-century successors to hide behind anonymity or pseudonyms. Whether one was male or female, the act of publishing one's work was viewed as beneath the status of a noble person. As most women writers were of the nobility, it was simply beneath them to be identified as authors who wrote for money. This class consciousness, however, did not mean that women were never openly acknowledged as authors. Some women, such as Marie Catherine Desjardins, Mme de Villedieu, did sign their works. Others, such as Lafayette and Scudéry, often placed a man's name on the cover, but the veil was thin and they were known to the public as authors. Anonymity must thus be interpreted within this specific seventeenth-century context.

The women involved in the literary field and the *salons* created a powerful and creative force by mid century. But with power came opposition. Throughout the century there were disgruntled voices trying to combat women's insurgence into the cultural realm. As their influence grew so did the vehemence of the opposition. By the end of the 1650s numerous works appeared in which women's literary taste and compositions were ridiculed, notably de Pure's *La Précieuse ou le mystère des ruelles* (*The Précieuse or the mystery of the ruelles*), Somaize's *Le Dictionnaire des précieuses* (*The Dictionary of Precious Women*), and Molière's *Les Précieuses ridicules* (*The Ridiculous Précieuses*). *Précieuse* was the term eventually used derogatively to refer to women who wrote or critiqued literature within the salon milieu, and came to designate what was viewed as an exaggerated effort to impose restrictions on language to make it more polite. Molière later continued his diatribe in *Les Femmes savantes* (*The Learned Ladies*) (1672). What unites all these works and others like them is their opposition to women's influence as readers, critics and especially as writers. Many found the feminization of the literary field disturbing. Women were transgressing traditional boundaries, and their actions had a profound effect on society and literature as a whole.

Portraits, conversations and maxims, with their obvious roots in oral culture, are the most clearly collaborative *salon* literary projects, but not the most important. All three of these minor genres were incorporated into the most influential genre to derive from this milieu, the novel. The novel's principal practitioners were women, all of whom were deeply involved in the *salons* and many of whom had played a role during the Fronde. As we shall see, works such as Lafayette's *La Princesse de Clèves* reflect the milieu both in terms of style, content and conditions of composition. La Rochefoucauld and Segrais are often cited for having 'helped' Lafayette create what some consider to be France's first psychological novel, the precursor of the modern novel. While the exact process of composition will probably forever be unknown, this novel and others do reflect the *salons*' values, literary creativity and societal preoccupations.

THE POWER OF THE PEN: THE NOVEL AND HISTORY

The *salon* culture and the Fronde proved to be powerful catalysts for female literary creativity, a creativity channelled most directly into the nascent genre of the novel. The most admired genre in seventeenth-century France was theatre and playwrights such as Corneille, Racine and Molière reigned supreme. But when women turned to writing they overwhelmingly chose narrative genres, which could be more freely moulded into a vehicle for their collective and personal thoughts and designs. The novel offered fertile terrain for innovation.

The various forms of the novel attest to women's deliberate experimentation with the genre. In the early years of the century, the pastoral novel, in particular d'Urfé's *L'Astrée* (*Astrea*), was most highly regarded. In this form of the novel, aristocratic characters don the cloaks of simple shepherds and explore the many facets of love in idyllic, pastoral settings. Women were drawn to the pastoral as readers, but when it came to writing themselves they opted to develop the historical novel. Madeleine de Scudéry (1607–1701) was recognized as the master of the first type of historical novel, the heroic novel. Scudéry's principal novels, *Ibrahim ou l'illustre Bassa* (*Ibrahim, or the Illustrious Bassa*) (1641), *Artamène ou le grand Cyrus* (*Artamenes, or The Grand Cyrus*) (1649–53) and *Clélie, histoire romaine* (*Clelia, an Excellent New Romance*) (1654–60), recount the many adventures of pairs of lovers who endure wars, abductions, shipwrecks and other works of fate but in the end are united in love. As the titles of the principal works indicate, the heroic genre used ancient history as a backdrop. Despite their Greek and Roman names and their exotic settings, the characters' actions and personalities were decidedly seventeenth-century French. Scudéry's principal innovation to the genre consists of analyses of feelings and conduct, often in the form of conversations and portraits, like those practised by her contemporary *salon* public. Scudéry endowed her fiction with a carefully constructed historical context, but readers were drawn to her novels less for their ancient history than for their inscription of seventeenth-century society and its history. Readers flocked to these novels because they were *mise-en-abymes* of polite society. Critics often view them as *à clé* portrayals of mid seventeenth-century France. *Le Grand Cyrus* in particular can be analysed as a reflection of the tumultuous years of the Fronde. Published during the war, the principal characters are frequently identified as Condé and the duchesse de Longueville.

In addition to reflecting current events, Scudéry's novels incorporate contemporary concerns. One of the most interesting internal narratives in *Le Grand Cyrus*, for example, explores the issues debated in the *salons*, women and knowledge and women as writers, and the all pervasive question of marriage. In volume x, Scudéry devotes this narrative, which is almost the length of a short novel, to Sapho, whom she portrays as the consummate seventeenth-century French woman writer. Scudéry herself was known as Sapho by her contemporaries and she weaves what little was known of Sapho's life into a narrative celebrating the female mind, women's power and spiritual love founded on respect and honour. Scudéry rewrites Ovid's ending according to which Sapho commits suicide when her lover Phaon rejects her. Instead of death, Sapho chooses to retire to the country of the Sauromates, a matriarchy. She invites Phaon to join her there, but he must agree to her terms: love but no marriage, utopia according to Scudéry's 'precious' contemporaries.

Scudéry's novels remained very popular through the eighteenth century, but by the 1660s the heroic genre was considered ponderous and out-dated. Readers objected in particular to its length. It was not uncommon for the heroic novel to run to ten volumes or more. The structure encouraged such length because the main story was punctuated by numerous internal narratives that could reach hundreds of pages. The public clamoured for a new variety of historical fiction and authors responded with the *nouvelle historique*. These fictions did not contain any 'digressions' or the conversations or detailed portraits of the heroic novel, and eliminated many of the adventures and twists of fate in order to focus on love and analyses of the heart. Readers also preferred more believable stories. To this end, novelists grounded the *nouvelle* in often meticulously researched, primarily sixteenth-century French history. The resulting fictions so closely resembled history that it was difficult to distinguish fact from fiction. Novelists played upon the ambiguity of the

French term *'histoire'*, which can mean both history and story. They filled in the lines of history primarily by adding plausible motives for well-known events, often with love and women as the principal forces. As official history became more and more co-opted by Louis XIV as a vehicle of propaganda, women writers used the *nouvelle historique* to rewrite the historical record to include women, thus using the pen to revolt against a monarch who would relegate them to powerlessness and silence.

As with the heroic novel, the best writers were considered to be women, in particular Lafayette and Villedieu. Lafayette published the first official example of the *nouvelle historique* in 1662, *La Princesse de Montpensier* (*The Princess of Montpensier*). The novel reflects the changing taste of the literary public. It is short, has no digressions, focuses on love and is carefully grounded in sixteenth-century French history, to make it appear *vraisemblable*. In the case of *La Princesse de Montpensier*, while the novel's preface states that the work is entirely fictional – and thus does not relate the history of the real sixteenth-century princess – Lafayette most likely chose that particular figure to pay homage to her friend, La Grande Mademoiselle, duchesse de Montpensier. *Vraisemblance* is a more complex concept than its translation, verisimilitude, implies, and connotes plausibility as well as propriety. To be *vraisemblable* a work must not only seem to be possible, it must reflect the accepted norms of behaviour in society. Thus while the genre did not have the 'ancient' models to follow that theatre did, theorists and critics from its inception endeavoured to legitimize the genre but also to govern creativity by establishing rules. Many women writers used the genre to explore alternative notions of *vraisemblance*, rewriting history – plausibility – as well as interrogating propriety by offering alternative plots for women.

Today Madame de Lafayette (1634–93) is acknowledged as the foremost novelist, but Madame de Villedieu (1640–83) is the *nouvelle historique*'s most prolific practitioner. In her short career (1659–75) she published over fourteen novels, in addition to poetry, plays and fictional memoirs. Unlike many of her contemporaries, Villedieu signed her works and made her living by writing. She was also the historical novel's premier theorist. In her many prefaces, Villedieu explains her conception of the genre and her writing processes. She focuses primarily on the relationship between her fictions and history. She offers her novels – such as *Les Annales galantes* [The Galant Annals] and *Les Désordres de l'amour* (*The Disorders of Love*) – as alternative but equally valid versions of history, stating for example that she is unveiling the 'ressorts secrets' ['inner workings'] of general history, the underlying motives neglected by 'L'Historien judicieux', the judicious historian or novelist, or the official, public historian. Women are often at the centre of this *histoire particulière*, or particular history, as it was called.[6] Villedieu's novels, like those of many of her female contemporaries, advance that their loves and secret intrigues actually determined the well-known events of history. Novelists such as Villedieu and Lafayette thus inscribed into literature the philosophy embodied by the Fronde: 'private' history, with women at the forefront, has a profound effect on the official historical record.

Such a position on the venerable genre of history naturally provoked controversy. Pierre Bayle accused Villedieu of deforming truth: 'on n'ose croire ce qui au fond est croyable' ['one doesn't dare believe what really is true']. Other critics such as Boileau in his *Dialogue des Heros de roman* (*Dialogue of the Heroes of Novels*) attacked the novel, especially Scudéry's, for portraying male historical figures, even monarchs, as hapless and ineffectual victims of love. In 1678, Mme de Lafayette's *La Princesse de Clèves* incited one of the century's greatest literary debates. In what is now considered to be France's first modern novel, Lafayette tells the fictional story of a princesse de Clèves at the very real court of Henri II. As required by the genre, Lafayette grounds her fiction in a meticulously researched history in order to make it appear *vraisemblable*. But her fictional princess's actions were denounced by some as an affront to plausibility and propriety. The princess falls in love with the duc de Nemours, but rather than succumb to her adulterous passion, Mme de Clèves tells her husband that she wishes to withdraw from public life. M de Clèves guesses the reason and dies of jealousy. Free at last, the princesse de Clèves refuses to marry Nemours, even though society would have condoned it. She does so not simply out of respect for her dead husband but because she is sure the playboy Nemours will not remain faithful to her once they are married. 'Mais les hommes conservent-ils de la passion dans ces engagements éternels?' ['But how long does men's passion last when the bond is eternal?'] she pessimisticly queries. Rather than risk rejection, the princess decides to live alone and dies young. Many readers and critics denounced the princess's avowal to her husband and her rejection of Nemours and passion as *invraisemblable*, thus not only as implausible but also as a violation of the rules of propriety. Significantly, the princess's principal critic, Valincour, could find only one precedent for such behaviour, Scudéry's Sapho. No historical background, especially one as feminocentric as the history Lafayette constructs for *La Princesse de Clèves*, could make this fiction *vraisemblable*.

Lafayette's *La Princesse de Clèves* illustrates to an exceptional degree the ways in which women novelists used the nascent narrative genres to explore issues as diverse as the construction of the historical record, the role of women in history, the relationship of women to knowledge, passion, love, marriage and women's place in society. The *nouvelle historique* and fictional memoirs became increasingly popular during the last third of the century. Lafayette and Villedieu had many successors, namely Catherine Bédacier (Mme Durant), Catherine Bernard, Anne Ferrand, Charlotte-Rose de Caumont de La Force, Anne de la Roche-Guilhem, Marie-Jeanne l'Héritier de Villandon and the comtesse de Murat. Remarkably between 1687 and 1699, at least one third of all novels published in France were by women. By the end of the century, women writers had succeeded in significantly altering the literary field, just as many of them had changed the historical arena as *salonnières* and as *frondeuses*.

A NEW LITERARY LANDSCAPE

Like the present chapter, most literary histories highlight the names of Scudéry, Sévigné and Lafayette in their descriptions of seventeenth-century France, but the rest of this female literary community has until recently been consigned to oblivion. Historians and critics have begun to shed light on this black hole and are altering our perceptions of France's classical period. In addition to the novel, many other genres bear a female imprint. In a break with the confining code of *vraisemblance*, some women developed a genre often associated with a female oral tradition, a genre in which one's imagination could go wild, the literary fairy tale. Today Charles Perrault's name is inseparable from the French fairy tale. But Marie-Catherine d'Aulnoy (1650–1705), Catherine Bernard (1662–1712), and L'Héritier de Villandon (1664–1734) all published prose tales before Perrault did in 1697. The majority of fairy tales in the seventeenth century were composed by women. Indeed, d'Aulnoy's works outsold Perrault's throughout the eighteenth century. These fairy tales should not be conflated with the simplified and revised versions propagated by nineteenth-century editors in collections destined for children. Authors like Caumont de La Force and Henriette-Julie de Murat composed their tales for an adult, *salon* public. Many tales, such as d'Aulnoy's fascinating *La Chatte blanche* (*The White Cat*), were the length of novels. Like the novel, the genre was intricately connected to the *salon* milieu. Many were first told orally in the *salons*, and they all reflect the concerns and values of this particular public. The story-tellers examine social issues, such as marriage, and the status of women. They pushed social commentary to the limits of acceptability using the thick veil of extraordinary fictions. In *La Chatte blanche*, for example, d'Aulnoy rewrites the expected happy ending by having her female cat, once she regains her human form, magnanimously give the king and his sons kingdoms while maintaining three for herself, instead of quietly marrying her prince and becoming his possession.

Fiction was not the only vehicle for female literary expression in classical France. Particularly from the mid-century on, many women turned to a genre traditionally reserved for male government officials, memoirs. Women radically altered the genre and used it to challenge the historical record that excluded them. Most of these efforts were not published until after Louis XIV's death in 1715, indicative of their subversive qualities, but many circulated in manuscript. In contrast to previous examples of the genre, women's memoirs have a more interiorized perspective, are occasionally introspective, and focus on aspects of life considered unimportant for the historical record – women's activities in the 'private' and public realm. The first person voice, which was being developed at the time, is very present in these texts. Many seventeenth-century female memorialists say that they are following in the tradition of Marguerite de Valois, whose *Mémoires*, illustrating this more personalized form, was published in 1628.

The most direct continuator of Marguerite de Valois is her granddaughter, Montpensier (1627–93), Louis XIV's first cousin. Montpensier's *Mémoires*, which she composed from 1653–86, recounts her exploits during the Fronde as well as her intriguing life as a member of the royal family and one of the wealthiest women in France. Compared to the memoirs composed by her male contemporaries, Montpensier's four-volume opus is clearly feminocentric. She revises history by unveiling the intrigues and more 'private' occurrences behind well-known events, underscoring that women are frequently at the centre of such happenings. Similarly, another figure active during the Fronde, the duchesse de Nemours, composed her memoirs to inscribe women's actions during the civil war. Traditionally, women's memoirs have not been considered as rival histories because they were categorized as private musings that their authors never destined for public consumption, much less publication. But research into the period and a re-examination of women's texts has inspired a redefinition of the categories 'private' and 'public' as well as notions of authorship. Montpensier and other female memorialists clearly inscribe a public into their works and advance them as additions to the collective memory.

Like her friend Montpensier, Motteville (1621–89) wrote *Mémoires pour servir à l'histoire d'Anne d'Autriche* (*Memoirs for the History of Anne of Austria*) to present an alternative vision of history, one which foregrounds women's central roles. After the queen's death in 1666, she devoted the rest of her life to composing the *Mémoires* from notes she had scrupulously taken since 1643. In the preface to the *Mémoires*, she distinguishes her work, which she characterizes a history, from other accounts, explaining that her privileged relationship to Anne (as her lady-in-waiting), afforded her access to knowledge no-one else could obtain. Like other female memorialists as well as novelists of the period, Motteville blurs the distinctions between the private, which these women would refer to as 'the particular' and the public, or political sphere. Motteville's *Mémoires* clearly demonstrates how the particular realm, associated with personalities, intrigues, and secret motivations, not only affects but determines the public events of the official historical record.

In addition to rewriting political history, many female memorialists used memoirs to comment on the social fabric of their time from a consciously female perspective. Mme de la Guette, for example, describes how her life was affected by fortune as well as by her husband and son. Appearing in 1681, her text, along with those of Hortense and Marie Mancini (1646–99 and 1639–1715), are the only female memoirs not published posthumously, although de la Guette's were published in Holland, the capital of clandestine publishing. De la Guette's memoirs read like many of the novels of her contemporaries, underscoring the extent to which real life in seventeenth-century France was often implausible, fact could resemble fiction and fiction fact. For instance, she adopts male garb when it could prove useful, as when she ran off to join her husband against the expressed wishes of her father. Like Montpensier, de la Guette was actively involved in the Fronde, on the royal side, in contrast to her husband's and son's allegiance to the Frondeur party. Her memoirs recount the courage of a woman who could oppose male authority – her father's as well as her husband's – and take an active role in politics. Her text is also intriguing because she deliberately blends her historical account with fiction. While the historical events she recounts are verifiable, the 'I' who relates them is a construction. De la Guette portrays herself as a noble woman, for example, although she was a provincial who had no claims to nobility. De la Guette uses the pen to rewrite her own reality while maintaining the essence of truth at the core of her text.

Hortense and Marie Mancini's *Mémoires* also seem the stuff of fiction, but, while their lives may appear implausible, they are true. Hortense and Marie were the colourful nieces of the Cardinal Mazarin, Anne d'Autriche's prime minister. With the exception of Marguerite de Valois, they were the first in 1675–7 to publish their life stories, which they used not to add to the historical record, as did Motteville and Montpensier, but to justify their often scandalous existence. Both were known for their peregrinations across Europe, and primarily for escaping the dominating hold of their husbands. Hortense's memoirs can also be viewed as a legal document with which she attempts to obtain financial independence from her husband. Hortense tried for years to obtain a legal separation from the man chosen by her uncle as his successor and as her partner for life, Armande de la Meilleraye. Her account of this struggle bears witness to women's lack of control over their own marriages and thus lives. Meilleraye even had complete authority over Hortense's dowry. Hortense depicts her escape to Italy to join Marie, and her eventual move to London, where she continued her legal battles to obtain a separation and the financial means with which to live, to no avail. After her death, her memoirs were in some sense justified. The insane man she describes proved to be unbalanced as he obtained his wife's body in England and proceeded to travel with it all over France for an entire year, forcing his wife to accompany him in death because she had refused to do so in life.

Marie composed her memoirs in part to validate her sister's, but also to contest a series of false, fictional memoirs attributed to her. Like her sister, Marie was a strong, free spirit determined to live according to her own rules and desires. The fact that her life inspired so many fictional accounts attests to the extraordinary nature of these desires, but also to the ways in which real life could and did nourish fictions. In fact, Hortense's life is often seen as the inspiration for one of the first pseudo-memoirs in France, Villedieu's *Mémoires de la vie de Henriette Sylvie de Molière* (*The Memoires of the Life and Rare Adventures of Henrietta Sylvia Molière*). In this fascinating text, Villedieu's heroine is more successful than her real-life counterparts at conquering the many obstacles fate places in her path. Like Hortense and Marie, Henriette Sylvie de Molière travels all over France, often disguised as a man, and flaunts the conventions governing female conduct. Villedieu uses her fiction as a kind of literary wish fulfilment for her female contemporaries. She also pays homage to the many strong-willed women, such as Hortense and Marie, who acted on the stage of classical France.

By inscribing women's participation in the public and particular spheres, memorialists and novelists endow women with the kind of immortality advocated by Scudéry in *Les Femmes illustres*. Sapho/Scudéry urges Erinne, her young protégé, to make her indelible mark on the world by using the pen and her mind, stressing that only writing can ensure immortality. Scudéry's friend Lafayette had this in mind when she wrote the life of her friend, Henriette d'Angleterre, who was the wife of Louis XIV's brother, Philippe d'Orléans. Lafayette composed her *Histoire de Madame Henriette d'Angleterre* (*The Secret History of Henrietta, Princess of England*) intermittently from 1665–9. Around 1673 she added a minute-by-minute, poignant description of the princess's premature death in 1670. Approximately ten years later she completed the work with a detailed preface in which she explains the work's genesis and compositional history. The *Histoire* was not published until 1720, but Lafayette's careful framing of the manuscript and inscription of a public are proof that she envisioned this text for publication and as an addition to History. Lafayette also wrote *Mémoires de la Cour de France pour les années 1688–9* (*Memoirs of the Court of France*), further underscoring her passion for historical writing. In the preface to her work on Henriette, she recounts her friendship with the princess, and the princess's suggestion that Lafayette be her scribe because of her reputation as an accomplished author. The princess furnished her with material which she wove into an historically accurate 'particular' history of court life under Louis XIV. (In contrast, Lafayette's *Mémoires de la Cour de France* is devoid of intrigues and focuses on politics.) Lafayette highlights the princess's active role in important political affairs, such as her help in securing a treaty with England, as well as Henriette's intrigues with their novelistic overtones. She endows Henriette with literary immortality and concurrently legitimizes the fictions, such as *La Princesse de Clèves*, which she draws out of real history. If Henriette's story, which appears novelistic because of the intrigues, is actually true history, then readers may also perceive Lafayette's historically grounded fictions as plausible (hi)stories, even when the female protagonists go beyond society's expectations. And if such fictions could be passed off as real, their impact would be greatly enhanced because they could not be dismissed as mere fantasy. Memoirs, history and fiction thus all conspire under women's pens to offer alternative and often exceptional plots for women.

Some women developed the epistolary genre for many of the same reasons as the memorialists. The most famous, and now canonical, of the seventeenth-century *épistolaires*, male or female, is the marquise de

Sévigné (1626–96). Sévigné's enormous corpus, spanning forty-eight years, is autobiographical and historical. She gives a spirited and detailed account of life as a member of the lesser nobility (the title of marquise was accorded her merely as a courtesy), an occasional visitor at Louis XIV's court, a very active member of Parisian society, and especially from 1671, when her daughter left Paris for Provence, as a devoted mother. It is the highly developed maternal quality in the later letters that has helped Sévigné to achieve canonical status, for she can be elevated as a model of 'correct' female comportment. But Sévigné's letters do much more than paint a portrait of maternal love. They are historical documents that depict an entire age, penned by a woman who chose to remain a widow when her husband died in 1652, thus living a life of relative autonomy. Sévigné herself drew the parallel between widowhood and freedom when she wrote that 'le nom de veuve emporte avec lui celui de liberté' ['the word widow connotes freedom'].[7] This liberty allowed her to move freely in society, and write about it without constraint. Far from being private reflections destined only for her correspondents' eyes, Sévigné's letters are the consummate example of *salon*-writing. In seventeenth-century *salons*, correspondents often shared letters, critiqued them, and even composed them collectively with friends. Sévigné was famous for her letters, which were often written in the company of friends or shared in the *salons* frequented by Sévigné as well as those of her correspondents. Her letters were copied as premier examples of the genre and were even offered to Louis XIV. Sévigné used the letters to construct a public and personal identity, and celebrated her position as author as the key to her social status and identity.

One female letter writer, or *épistolaire*, would have preferred that her personal correspondence remain outside the public domain. In 1668, Villedieu's editor, Claude Barbin, published her love letters to M de Villedieu without the author's consent. The short, but very passionate *Lettres et billets galants* (*Gallant Letters and Notes*) resembles the anonymous *Lettres portugaises* (*The Portuguese Letters*), also published by Barbin, which appeared in French in 1669. *Les Lettres portugaises* is viewed either as the real-life lamentations of a Portuguese nun abandoned by her French lover or hailed as a masterful fiction penned by Guillergues. Both volumes reflect the public's penchant for works that straddle the boundaries of fact and fiction. In addition, like Scudéry's epistolary fiction, *Lettres amoureuses de divers auteurs de ce temps* (*The Love Letters of Various Authors of the Time Period*) (1641), and Villedieu's *Henriette Sylvie de Molière*, an epistolary novel, these works are the first French examples of the narrative form that would become so popular in the eighteenth century.

In addition to fiction, memoirs and epistolary works, seventeenth-century women writers contributed to a number of other genres, often with great success, although such public recognition was eventually extinguished. Villedieu, for example, is remembered almost exclusively for her works of fiction. Before she turned her attention completely to novels, however, she was celebrated by her contemporaries as a poet as well as a playwright who wrote both tragedy and comedy. Of particular importance are her tragedy, *Manlius* (1662) and her comedy, *Le Favory* (1665), which was performed by Molière's troupe for Louis XIV. Villedieu's foray into the esteemed genre of theatre led her to be recognized and taken seriously by the principal intellectuals of the day. She was even asked her opinion of Boileau's *Satires*, and entered a debate of prominent intellectuals over their merits.

Other women writers also excelled in what were considered at the time to be the more serious, official genres, as opposed to fiction. Françoise Pascal was another recognized playwright. There were numerous poets such as Jeanne de la Motte Guyon (1648–1717) who composed sacred poems and canticles, Mme Deshoulières (1638–94) and her daughter, and Catherine Bernard. Both Deshoulières even received the prestigious prize for poetry from the French Academy, joining Scudéry, who in 1671 had received the Academy's prize for eloquence. Mlle Deshoulières, Scudéry and other female contemporaries such as Catherine Bernard were inducted into the learned Académie des Ricovrati de Padoue, which, unlike the French Academy, accepted women among its ranks.

Like poetry and theatre, the essay was exercised primarily by male writers and as such was highly valued by the literary establishment. It was thus a less welcoming venue for female expression than the novel. Nevertheless some women succeeded in making their mark with it, notably Marie de Gournay at the beginning of the century and as we have seen, Marguerite de Buffet with her *Nouvelles Observations sur la langue française*. Anne Thérèse de Lambert (1647–1733) took up the pen to explore many of the same subjects that had attracted Marie de Gournay, namely the role assigned to women by society and education for women. Although not published until the early eighteenth century, Lambert's *Réflexions nouvelles sur les femmes, Conseils importants à une amie* [*Important Advice to a Woman Friend*], and *Avis d'une mère à sa fille* (*Advice from a Mother to her*

Daughter), among her other works, all reflect the preoccupations of seventeenth-century women. But whereas Scudéry and Buffet had celebrated women's intellectual parity with men and painted an optimistic, if not at times idealistic portrait of women's capacity to go beyond the boundaries prescribed by society, Lambert's tone is decidedly more pessimistic as well as perhaps more realistic. In her *Réflexions sur les femmes*, she looks back at the *salons* and intellectual milieu of the mid-seventeenth century as an almost utopian moment of female influence that has since been critiqued and ultimately suppressed. While Lambert's pessimism is perhaps exaggerated – after all, there were more women writers at the end of the century than at any previous period in France's history – she nonetheless captures the climate as the seventeenth century drew to a close. Women had reached unprecedented heights in the cultural realm, but their success and influence had sparked a reaction against them. At the close of the century authors such as Fénelon in his *De l'éducation des filles* (*The Education of Girls*) (1687), (composed under the influence of Mme de Maintenon, Louis XIV's second wife), picked up on Molière's satires of *salons* and intellectual women and advocated a more domestic role than those occupied by many of the century's prominent women. The backlash against women writers and women's participation in and influence on culture attests to their influence on the sphere as a whole. They were recognized not just as separate voices but as a powerful force that changed the very fabric of literary culture.

If one were to return to the Great Century and ask these women writers what they think of the preceding history and the premise of the present volume, they would most likely be surprised. Why is there a separate history devoted entirely to women? They would have considered themselves, and their contemporaries in fact viewed them, as a cultural force on all of society, not as a separate sphere of creativity. The full significance of women's participation in and their influence on the literary world will only be appreciated when authors such as la Rochefoucauld, Perrault and Boileau are studied in conjunction with Sablé, d'Aulnoy and Scudéry. Only then will we have a clear picture of how the whole literary and intellectual culture functioned and a truer sense of what 'the splendid century' really was.

NOTES

1 In *Tender Geographies*, Joan DeJean provides a useful appendix of women active in the seventeenth-century literary scene.
2 '*Fronde*' can be translated as 'slingshot'. In seventeenth-century France the

word was used to refer to illegal or disorderly activities in general. Contemporaries referred to the civil unrest of 1648–53 as the 'Fronde'. See Orest Ranum, *The Fronde: A French Revolution* (New York: Norton, 1993), p. 5.

3 'Grand renfermement' is a term coined by Albistur and Armogathe, *Histoire du féminisme français*, vol. I, pp. 196–200.

4 See DeJean, *Tender Geographies*, pp. 55–7 and 87–90.

5 See Beasley, 'The Voices of the Shadows', in Goldsmith and Goodman (eds.), *Going Public*.

6 See Beasley, *Revising Memory*, pp. 29–41.

7 Letter 781, in *Lettres*, ed. Emile Gérard-Gailly (Paris: Gallimard, Bibliothèque de la Pléiade, 1972–8), 3 vols., vol. II, p. 999.

CHAPTER FOUR

The eighteenth century: women writing, women learning

Jean Bloch

Men's writing has traditionally dominated the literary history of the French eighteenth century. Men have, entirely justifiably, been hailed for their achievements as precursors of the Enlightenment, as *philosophes* and *Encylopédistes*, as experimental novelists and successful dramatists. Literary women of the period have tended to achieve fame and notoriety more for their influential salons or political opinions than for their writing. Only recently have eighteenth-century women begun to emerge from the shadows as novelists, pedagogues and pamphleteers of note.

The particular problem which beset women's writing in eighteenth-century France was the importance accorded then to scientific, philosophical and political writing. How could inadequately educated women compete with Montesquieu (educated by the Oratorians and the law faculties of Bordeaux and Paris), Voltaire (by the Jesuits at Louis-le-Grand) or Buffon (who had followed legal, medical and botanical studies)? The problem was compounded by the dubious status of the female author, or *femme-auteur*. We know that intelligent and even erudite women failed to put their ideas into writing or, if they wrote, failed to have their work published. In his *Traité des Sensations* (*Treatise on the Sensations*) (1754) the famous philosopher, Condillac, paid homage to a Mlle Ferrand. He credited Ferrand not only with invaluable help in the preparation of his work but with having illuminated every aspect of the treatise. Although one must be wary of the customary exaggeration of a dedication, the wording of Condillac's recognition of Ferrand rings true. Acknowledging his intellectual debt to her, he claims that her modesty and generosity prevented her from producing her own work. His words reveal the unenviable position of the intellectual woman of the mid-eighteenth century, whose self-effacement prompted her to facilitate her friend's creative thinking rather than produce her own work. Responding to the criticism that he had taken the basic idea for his *Traité des Sensations* from Diderot's *Lettre sur les sourds et muets*, Condillac claimed that it was Ferrand who had given him the idea for his treatise many years previously. He thus appropriated her originality as the vindication of his own right to be considered original in the disputed territory of competing males.

Yet, some eighteenth-century Frenchwomen did commit their ideas to paper and published in spheres beyond the acceptable areas of works of the imagination, correspondence and memoirs. Often, however, their works were published anonymously (at least in the first instance) and sometimes by friends or relatives without the author's consent.[1] Marie Huber took part in theological disputation, Angélique Marguerite Le Boursier du Coudray published a manual of midwifery, Anne Louise Élie de Beaumont collaborated in the work of her lawyer husband, signing her name to a few publications, Marie Anne de Roumier Robert wrote 'philosophical' novels underpinned by the Cartesian adherence to democratic reason, Sophie de Grouchy, marquise de Condorcet, translated Adam Smith's *Theory of Moral Sentiments* to which she appended her own eight *Lettres sur la sympathie* [Letters on Sympathy].

The outstanding example of what a privileged intellectual woman might, if she were determined and wealthy enough, achieve is offered by Émilie du Châtelet (1706–49). Taking lessons in advanced mathematics from distinguished tutors and with a good working knowledge of English and Latin, she undertook the translation into French of Mandeville's *The Fable of the Bees* and Newton's *Principia mathematica*. Her own position is set out in her *Institutions de physique* [Introduction to Physics] of 1740, in her *Dissertation sur la nature et la propagation du feu* [A Dissertation on the Nature and Propagation of Fire and heat] (which was entered alongside an essay by Voltaire for the 1738 competition of the Académie des Sciences, for which both received honourable mention) and in her works of Biblical exegesis, 'Examen de la Genèse' ('An Examination of the Book of Genesis') and 'Examen des livres du Nouveau Testament' ['An Examination of the Books of the New Testament'] (which were never published). She also worked on an uncompleted *Grammaire raisonnée* [An Analytical Grammar] and wrote a *Discours sur le bonheur* [Discourse on Happiness], published posthumously in 1779. True, she was Voltaire's companion for a number of years and could benefit from his stimulating intellect, but her style and method of analysis are totally distinct from his; some would in fact argue that she was his superior in both mathematics and philosophy. Despite her achievements, however, she did not overcome the problems of being a woman philosopher, or *femme-philosophe*. She kept her writing of the *Institutions*, the *Dissertation sur le feu* and her translation of the

Principia a secret. Erica Harth comments: 'No matter how philosophical her text, it seems that it was impossible for her to transcend her gender.'[2]

The acceptable areas for women's writing were correspondence, memoirs and fiction. Correspondence has for long been accepted as unquestionably part of the French literary tradition. In the eighteenth century it occupied a position centre-stage, both as private correspondence destined for later publication and as one of the most popular and successful fictional genres of the period, the epistolary novel. Women were commonly associated with letter-writing and in some cases credited with producing masterpieces of the art. The model before eighteenth-century eyes was that of Mme de Sévigné (1626–96) whose letters began to appear in print from the year of her death.

Her successors in eighteenth-century France have enjoyed less universal success, but the correspondence of Marie de Vichy, marquise du Deffand (1697–1780), has for long been accepted as an example of epistolary art.[3] Her fifteen-year-long correspondence with Horace Walpole, with whom she had fallen in love, is often claimed to be her best on grounds of its gaiety, wit, literary judgments and sincere comments on life, but the heights of her wit are probably reached in her letters to Voltaire. She is praised for her simple, clear and balanced sentences and her apt and sober vocabulary. Her memoirs constitute a valuable portrait of the society of her time.

Very different are the letters of du Deffand's protégée and rival, Julie de Lespinasse (1732–76), who was known for her spontaneity and the fervour of her romantic attachments. Lespinasse's letters to the comte de Guibert hold a median position between private correspondence and the fictional soliloquy of the famous seventeenth-century *Lettres portugaises*; Lespinasse's letters can be read as literary masterpiece and emotional outburst at one and the same time.

The writing of memoirs was already traditional in France by the eighteenth century. In this period, the social status of the memorialists widened, so that as well as the contributions of top-ranking nobles and politicians, we find a tax-farmer's son, Charles-Jean François Hénault, leaving his memoirs for posterity and the Girondist Marie-Jeanne Phlipon, Mme Roland (1754–93) feverishly composing an *Appel à l'impartiale postérité* (*An Appeal to Impartial Posterity*) nowadays published as *Mémoires*, from her prison cell as she awaited execution. Not only do the latter contain accounts of recent political events, but her *mémoires particuliers*, inspired by Rousseau's *Confessions*, portray her bourgeois upbringing in the artistic circles of Paris.

Manon Phlipon had married a man twenty years her senior with whom she collaborated on a number of technical and scholarly works and for whom, once he had been appointed Minister of the Interior in March 1792, she composed many important political documents. It is claimed that she saw these writings as a demonstration of her conjugal devotion and rejected all idea of publishing under her own name.[4] Even a more personal work, her account of their travels in Switzerland, was published by friends without her consent. Very different, and much more centred on herself are the *Mémoires* written in her prison cell as she awaited the guillotine, though even here, it is claimed, her intention was the rehabilitation of her husband's reputation.

The comparison of her *mémoires particuliers* with Rousseau's *Confessions* is explicit. She frequently evoked Rousseau as her literary model and wrote in a letter of October 1793 about her memoirs: 'Ce sera mes *confessions*, car je n'y veux rien céler . . .' ['These are to be my *Confessions*, in which I wish to hide nothing']. As Rousseau had sought to vindicate himself in the face of what he felt was calumny, so she attempted to justify herself against the adverse criticism she had attracted for her political activities. She presents both the historic events and political personalities with which she was familiar and traces a disarmingly frank portrait of her background, childhood and early adult life.

The area of women's writing which grows most significantly in the course of the century is that of pedagogy, partly to enable women to argue their case for access to knowledge, but also to prescribe new methods of teaching young children. Women's writings on education are important not only because they allow us to see women's deprivations and aspirations, their limitations, conservatism or radicalism, but also because they reveal the strategies women employ to make their case and the sense of identity to which their reflections on their own and others' education sometimes lead.

Anne-Thérèse de Marguenat de Courcelles, marquise de Lambert, wrote much more widely than in the simple area of pedagogy, but she is nowadays best known for her *Avis d'une mère à sa fille* (*Advice of a Mother to her Daughter*), her *Avis d'une mère à son fils* (*Advice of a Mother to her Son*), and her *Réflexions nouvelles sur les femmes* (*New Reflexions on the Fair Sex*). Although the *Avis* were published between 1726 and 1728, there is every reason to believe that they were written in the 1690s. The celebrated *salonnière* thus forms a link with the thinking of the late seventeenth century, yet at the same time leads into the Enlightenment with her influential salon, which rose to fame by 1710 and which nurtured the young Marivaux and Montesquieu.[5]

In the latter part of the seventeenth century pedagogical treatises were normally written by clerics. By choosing the briefer form of the *Avis* Lambert could opt for a different emphasis from the Christian educators of her time. Writing as a member of polite society, she is explicitly interested in the 'world' and its proprieties, not in a specifically Christian education and life. Although she conventionally accords the deity the highest place in the universal order, she reduces the role of religion in comparison to Fénelon, whose advice in his *Éducation des filles* (*The Education of Young Gentlewomen*) guides her thinking on her daughter's education. Although a prominent cleric (he became archbishop of Cambrai in 1695), Fénelon himself had begun to focus more than his predecessors on education for life on earth and Lambert boldly follows his lead. In the *Lettre à mon fils* she spends only two paragraphs on religion, implicitly suggesting that this is not her goal. Though, in line with convention, she allots more space to religion when addressing her daughter, overall she places so little emphasis on its role that her world view could easily be transposed into totally secular terms.

Effectively, the marquise substitutes a moral education, which cultivates the heart more than the mind, for the usual spiritual and moral education offered by Christianity. She is eager to cultivate sentiments in her daughter which will develop the character, conduct the mind, govern the will and guarantee the solidity and endurance of human virtues. She places the highest value on *honneur* (moral dignity) and by this she does not mean simply keeping up appearances. Accepting, however, that a woman should not take public opinion too lightly, for society will judge her, she finds it more important to live up to standards one has set oneself. As a young man on the point of entering society, she wishes her son to pursue *gloire* (an honourable reputation), which in his case will include military virtue. By cultivating the feelings, the son is to aspire to be an *honnête homme*, which in the marquise's sense indicates the truly honourable man who fulfils his duties and obligations in line with his social rank. Although close in the standards they require of both men and women, her suggestions retain a certain social conformism in their gendered differentiation of *honneur* and *gloire*.

Alone in representing the parental view of education at the turn of the century, Lambert's willingness to accept the outside world constantly feared and censored by Christian educators marks her out from her contemporaries. Though not strictly a conduct book, her *Avis* have close affinities with that tradition and were quickly assimilated into it. Despite their implicit radicalism, they represent acceptable exhortations to the young and as such were set to become classics of their kind in both England and France. Lambert was to hold her own beside the names of illustrious male pedagogues such as Fénelon, Rollin, Locke and Crousaz. Lord Chesterfield was still praising her *Lettre à mon fils* in 1775.

By the mid-eighteenth century we find a cluster of women writing on education and the number is sustained as the Revolution approaches. Some of these were upper-class governesses, the best known of whom is Mme de Genlis (1746–1830), governess to the children of the duc de Chartres, who both wrote on education and produced educational stories and plays for children.[6] Also well known for her publications and a similarly prolific writer was the somewhat earlier Marie Leprince de Beaumont (1711–80).

Leprince de Beaumont spent a number of years as a governess in England where she composed her famous *Magasins*, variously translated as *The Young Misses Magazine, The Misses Magazine*, etc. She always wrote in French and had her works published in France, though some of the first editions were produced in London. Most of her educational writings convey their lessons in the form of conversations between pupils and tutor or governess, varying the didactic content with Biblical, moral and imaginative stories, some of which are fairy tales, the best known being her version of *Beauty and the Beast*.

Her *Lettres diverses, et critiques* [Diverse Letters and Criticism] (Nancy 1750) contain an *Avis aux Parens & aux Maîtres* [Advice to Parents and Teachers], which she was subsequently to refer to as her *Traité d'éducation* [Treatise on Education]. Many of her underlying pedagogical convictions are similar to those that would be put forward by Rousseau in 1762 in his *Émile*. Leprince de Beaumont shares with Rousseau the belief that it is the father's most important duty to educate his children, that the teacher should have a sense of vocation and be a friend to the pupil, that the child's regime should be frugal, hard even, and he or she kept constantly occupied with varied instructional games and entertainments. She is even, like Rousseau, wary of La Fontaine's *Fables*, in her case on the grounds that children should be taught only what is true.

Though she would seem to be in the vanguard of modern pedagogical ideas largely inspired by Locke, there are major differences between Leprince de Beaumont and the radical modernity of a Rousseau, which ally her as much with the tradition of the Christian educators as with the proponents of modern methods. For her the child belongs to God and should be made aware of the importance of baptism and the need to reject mortal sin. Using a strong scriptural apparatus, Leprince de

Beaumont strives to convince children of the 'proofs' which reveal the divine nature of the Scriptures. Her successive levels of *Magasins* provide tales which constantly endorse the values of the Christian faith.[7] Yet, her prime aim is the achievement of earthly happiness, which for her cannot be attained without virtue. In line with her male contemporaries she also stresses the importance of reason. Rejecting memorizing as insufficient she exposes her teaching material to the pupil's rational scrutiny from the earliest possible age. For boys and girls alike she aims at developing a rigorous mind; her practical experience of female pupils showed her that this is entirely achievable. Though she differentiates between the content of the instruction to be offered to girls and boys, she demonstrates faith in girls' ability and the rapidity with which they acquire knowledge.

In the course of reflecting on her own education, as well as her experience of female pupils, Leprince de Beaumont acquires a firmer sense of self and of women's potential. Her later pedagogical writings suggest that most upper-class women would be capable, by their own efforts, of acquiring sufficient Latin to instruct their young sons, a surprising statement in a period when it was common to deride any woman who acquired a smattering of Latin.

Madeleine de Puisieux barely wrote about education in the sense of intellectual instruction, but she produced a slim volume titled *Conseils à une amie* [Advice to a Womanfriend] (1749), which takes a form reminiscent of Lambert's advice to her son and daughter on their entry into society. She differs from Lambert, however, insofar as she is more concerned with how to operate satisfactorily in society than with establishing the rules of conduct which should be observed by honourable, upper-class men and women. Since, in addition to a number of works of the imagination, she also published two volumes of *Caractères* (*Characters; or, reflections on the manners of the age*) in 1750 and 1751 and *Réflexions et avis sur les défauts et les ridicules à la mode* [Reflections and Advice on the Ridiculous Manners of the Age] (1761), which are intended to follow on from the *Conseils*, we can see her as primarily an observer of human types and social behaviour, who specifically applies her observations to the conduct of young women. Madeleine de Puisieux is nowadays credited with the authorship of a feminist text *La Femme n'est pas inférieure à l'homme* [Woman is not inferior to man] (1750) and the identical text of *Le Triomphe des dames* [The Ladies' Triumph] (1751), the authorship of which was for long attributed to her husband Philippe Florent de Puisieux. [8]

Right from the start Puisieux makes clear her unwillingness to be patronized by a man and reveals her conviction that she is more talented than others (particularly other women). The *Conseils à une amie* do not, however, speak with her voice; they are presented as advice offered by a woman of sharp mind and extensive knowledge of society to an intelligent girl before she leaves her convent, with its lives of saints, Bible stories, moral essays and sermons, for the very different reading and values of the world outside. The tone of the *Conseils* is set by recommending caution with such wordly reading as Crébillon, Prévost or Marivaux before marriage, while suggesting that afterwards, if a woman's mind is deranged by reading fiction, then this will be her husband's problem! This somewhat cavalier attitude recurs throughout the work, though moderation, cultivated taste and the benefits of a virtuous life come through as the dominant message. A number of statements highlight the dangers to women represented by other women who, envious of each others' successes (particularly with men), are constantly concerned to damage their rivals' reputations. Despite this feeling of lack of female solidarity, the most striking parts of the work highlight the injustices and advantages of men, who are held responsible for women's lack of generosity. The dilemmas experienced by women, especially in the area of sexual liaisons, are stressed. Women are presented as enslaved by the requirement of *bienséances*, even if it is only the appearance of propriety and not the practice of it; men escape unscathed, though it is usually they who have enticed women in unwise directions.

This realistic appraisal of the conditions of life for an upper-class woman leads to an emphasis on the need for self-reliance. This does not, however, lead to support for intellectual study, which is placed low on the list of priorities for a young woman, with the added injunction that knowledge should be discreetly veiled. The 1761 *Réflexions et avis sur les défauts et les ridicules à la mode* highlights the way in which all avenues, bar notoriety, are closed to women and the extent to which men flee those women they might feel obliged to respect. The author criticises female exclusion from membership of the academies. She suggests that her young 'pupil' (now approaching marriage) has pointlessly wasted her best years on an education which leads nowhere.

The most telling section of the *Conseils* is developed around the subject of marriage and is presented as the female adviser's (i.e., the supposed narrator's) own experience. The disillusionment of an arranged marriage and the husband's subsequent philandering is recounted with greater emotion than the rest of the text and culminates in the recommendation of a voluntary retreat to residence in a convent, which alone guarantees autonomy for a woman. Life is a juggling-act for women despite the supposed equality of the marriage partners, but Puisieux blames women themselves for having allowed men to gain the upper hand.

The tone of the later *Réflexions* is different. Instead of the satirical mocking of the *Conseils*, which lends ambiguity to her statements, the voice of the later work is serious and despondent. There is no flippant ending of the kind which closes the *Conseils*; here the voice of a saddened woman rings true. Despite the differing tone of her works, however, Puisieux's view remains essentially the same. The world is a hard one for women and those who try to make a name for themselves rarely receive compliments either from their own sex or from men. The greatest injustice, however, is to be found in the inequalities which separate the male and female spheres. In such a world it is pointless for a woman to seek advancement via her pen. Puisieux's whole approach is very different from that of the conventional Leprince de Beaumont. Yet Leprince de Beaumont grows in personal assurance as a writer and opens up new possibilities for women, whereas Puisieux starts with a flamboyant rejection of male patronage, but never satisfactorily finds solidarity with other women, most of whom she denigrates. Her disappointment fluctuates between the consciousness of injustice and the conviction of her own disregarded merit.

The closing down of the Jesuit *collèges* in 1762 focused attention on the need to reform education, in particular that offered by the school system. Women could play little part in this, but on the other hand they could participate in the contemporary debates sparked by Rousseau's groundbreaking treatise *Émile*. Much has been written on women's enthusiasm for Rousseau's emphasis on child care, for his pleas for the kindly handling of young children and a healthier lifestyle. Reactions from women to his ideas on girls' education (presented through the portrait of the imaginary Sophie) were, however, mixed. An early example is Mlle d'Espinassy's *Essai sur l'éducation des demoiselles* [Essay on the Education of Young Ladies] of 1764. Displaying conventional modesty with regard to her status as a writer, the author consciously chooses anonymity, whilst at the same time allowing her sense of patriotism and public service to push her towards publication (*Avis de l'auteur*). Beneath the polite formulation and conventionally humble female authorial stance, the reader senses that d'Espinassy feels she has something worth saying and has been stimulated to react to that part of *Émile* which specifically targets women.

To position herself in relation to Rousseau she seizes on one specific point, that women 'govern' men. She cleverly contrasts this with his apparently contradictory underestimation of women's capabilities and his belief that they should always defer to their husband's judgment. Rejecting his general principle that woman should be educated in relation to man, she transforms his claim that women 'govern' men into the idea that a *properly educated woman* (my emphasis) can become an acceptable guide for her husband. At the same time, however, she indicates that Rousseau's detailed recommendations for Sophie's education are not dissimilar to her own. She is, therefore, criticizing the general framework he posits, while diplomatically supporting at least some of his specific suggestions. This leaves her entirely free to offer her own proposals for the education of girls, which she explicitly presents as designed to make them worthy of their husbands' admiration and respect. She returns to Rousseau's insistence on women's power over men only at the end of her essay when her educational programme is complete.

In the development of her essay d'Espinassy undermines the radical potential of her rejection of Rousseau's theory of female nature by following a conformist and conventional line. She suggests that the end is to produce sensible, agreeable women who will guarantee the stability of society. Given a good education they will gradually achieve respect; by becoming virtuous they will in the course of time produce a virtuous society. Her essay thus provides us with two rather different discourses. If we look at the stance she consciously takes in relation to Rousseau she seems far-sighted, radical even, cleverly taking advantage of his emphasis on female moral and psychological domination of the male to suggest the legitimate pursuit of an education designed to promote intellectual and moral capacities in the female. When we look at her actual suggestions, however, we see the limits of her reform. Women are to be given access to knowledge to the point at which they acquire a satisfactory veneer, designed to give them a dignified respectability in public and they are to be educated in accordance with religious and moral principles that will make them aspire to virtue and willingly fulfil what she sees as their natural obligations to educate their children.[9] Though she has spotted the Achilles heel of the education of Sophie she has not taken on board the implications of covert power for the female over the male. Believing she has countered the apparent disadvantages by opening up intellectual studies for women and giving them equal importance with the moral and psychological advantages suggested by Rousseau, she has merely espoused a modest reformist line, which will in no way encourage women to become creative innovators, front-line researchers or distinguished public figures.

Later pedagogical writers display similar advances and reticences in a variety of areas. Louise Tardieu d'Esclavelles de la Live d'Épinay (1726–83), for example, was an author from Rousseau's own circle. Her successful *Conversations d'Émilie* (*The Conversations of Emily*) (published in Leipzig in 1774)[10] both counter his ideas on the education of women and share certain basic pedagogical assumptions with him. Written in dialogue form between a mother and her daughter this work clearly has affinities with the conversations of Mme Leprince de Beaumont's class with their governess or, indeed, the real-life pedagogical programme of the pupils of Port-Royal, who had for long enjoyed instruction in the form of conversations. Here, an informal discussion between a young child and her mother serves to concretize widespread contemporary suggestions for a better education to be delivered by the mother to her offspring; it also serves to demonstrate the changes brought about by the incursion of new theories of knowledge via the work of Locke and Condillac backed by Rousseau's pedagogical methods. In the *Conversations* the mother clearly holds the key to already established knowledge, but she attempts to convey this to the daughter by means of child-centred experiential learning springing from the concrete observation of a physical object or experiment.

There are major differences, however, between the d'Épinay text and *Émile*. Whereas Rousseau defers all moral and social topics for the male until adolescence, the *Conversations d'Émilie*, dealing with a pupil up to the age of ten, are concerned with contemporary upper-class morality and preparation for life in adult society. D'Épinay encourages Émilie to understand the operations of social morality, to explore subjects such as marriage, female reputation, attitudes towards servants and the poor. Whereas Rousseau restricts the young Émile to what he claims is a purely sensitive, juvenile form of reasoning linked to experience of the physical world, Émilie also learns about the conflicts of reason and feeling and the importance of social conventions.[11]

The significance of the *Conversations* for an analysis of women's writing is, however, less its intertextuality with *Émile* than the pedagogical exercise it proposes and the close relationship it posits between mother and daughter in the learning process. The text does not depart radically from what is assumed suitable for the education of girls, but is innovative in its teaching method, assuming the presence of an enlightened and even knowledgeable woman, who is capable of manipulating conversation through a series of interlinked stages, which appear logical yet sponta-neous at one and the same time. The subject matter extends to high levels of reflection on what constitutes the human mind and how it oper-ates or how the physical and human spheres interconnect. The *Conversations d'Émilie* thus offer a fascinating example of the application of new pedagogical methods (intended for boys) to the education of girls.[12]

That the subject of women's education became the focus of public debate in the latter years of the *ancien régime* shows up in the choice of competition essay subjects by provincial academies. In 1777 the Académie de Besançon set the hominocentric question: 'Comment l'éducation des femmes pourroit contribuer à rendre les hommes meilleurs' [In what way might the education of women contribute to the moral improvement of men?], while in 1783 the Académie de Châlons-sur-Marne wondered: 'Quels sont les moyens de perfectionner l'éduca-tion des jeunes demoiselles?' [In what ways might the education of young ladies be improved?].

Manon Phlipon responded to Besançon.[13] Twenty-three at the time and an avowed enthusiast for Rousseau, Phlipon decided simply to back the suggestion that a better education for women will improve male beha-viour. Her essay emphasises the importance of feeling as the directive force behind human action, seeing it as the adjunct to knowledge and the faculty which 'judges' human conduct. Allowing feeling to guide her own pen, her prose takes on an effusive sentimentality as she argues the value of the emotions and particularly the human propensity for compassion and looks for ways in which this can be preserved and developed.

Phlipon assumes that it is woman's natural role to assist the improve-ment of the male. She credits woman with a natural gentleness and sen-sibility, which serves as compensation for her physical weakness and leads to the subjugation of male hearts. Accepting that women are meant to be more decorative than decisive and active, she believes they are incapable of abstract thought and high-level intellectual activity. This reasoning results in the stereotypical, Rousseauistic response that men are made to govern empires while women govern men's hearts.

Accepting the dual function of goodness (*bonté*) towards oneself and towards others as the basis of society, Phlipon sees sexual attraction as the foundation of, first the united couple, then the family (with the birth of children cementing the bonding process), then society. In this woman provides the essential element which unleashes the emotions and, through her own immediate experience of physical suffering, kindles the propensity for compassion in the male heart. Her preliminary conclusion is that it is important to cultivate women's sensibility.

The second part of her essay seeks to cultivate female sensibility through suitable education. She is not opposed to women having access to knowledge, but she subordinates knowledge to feeling. Realizing that a political programme is necessary to escape the frivolity and artifice of the modern world she calls for just laws, equable punishments and rewards and an equal distribution of wealth. It is only in these conditions that she believes society will be able to rediscover human goodness and virtue. Despite the Rousseauistic flavour of many of her statements, her distance from him over women's access to knowledge is made clear. For Phlipon, Rousseau's attitude to female knowledge presents an obstacle to the growth of feeling. If men are to be influenced for the good and children raised satisfactorily, women will need both to think and act well. Yet, despite the fact that she holds on to access to knowledge for women relatively more enthusiastically than does Rousseau, Phlipon's final position endorses the moral domain as women's proper sphere of influence. The future Mme Roland seems to have fallen prey to the lure of sensibility as the most important and beneficial gift controlled by women.

The comtesse de Miremont also thought that she could bring about a moral revolution by means of women's education.[14] Her *Traité de l'éducation des femmes, et cours complet d'instruction* [A Treatise on the Education of Women and a Complete Course of Study] of 1779–89 argues that better education will produce more virtuous women and that this will, in turn, have an effect on men, thereby bringing about a general moral reform of society. Her position is essentially a reformist one, but what she does is different from Phlipon. She presents a one-volume educational treatise and a complete course of studies devised for women, but presented as also suitable for boys and many gentlemen (i.e., not scholars). This runs into six volumes and offers a *précis* of each discipline. Here is someone who takes intellectual studies for women seriously.

Genlis's successful pedagogical novel in epistolary form, *Adèle et Théodore, ou Lettres sur l'éducation* (*Adelaide and Theodore: or Letters on Education*), appeared in 1782. She had already published several volumes of moralistic plays for children in her *Théâtre à l'usage des enfans & des jeunes personnes* (*Theatre of Education*) (1779–80) and was to bring out her collected stories for children under the title *Les Veillées du château* (*Tales of the Castle*) in 1784. With its practical proposals for educational aids and teaching methods, *Adèle et Théodore* represents the post-Rousseauan ideal that either or both parents should be willing to devote themselves completely to the education of their children. It also mimics the contrived, model dialogues of Rousseau and d'Épinay (whose *Conversations d'Émilie* are to be used for Adèle between the ages of seven and eight) and produces moralistic tableaux promoting the values of late eighteenth-century sensibility. Although this fictitious correspondence focuses on the education of a representative of each sex and an exchange of ideas between a number of male and female correspondents, it is Genlis's own voice which is projected through the principal character of the baronne d'Almane and which dominates the discourse.[15] The author is very aware of the different lives men and women must ultimately lead and her text provides an important discussion of the education of girls. Genlis recognizes the limitations imposed on women by society and the consequences these hold for their education, but she proposes quite an ambitious programme of study for them all the same. She articulates the tensions and inconsistencies that mark women's lives, thus making an important step towards a greater female awareness, which could eventually lead to a desire for emancipation. Yet, in the final analysis, she presents her *baronne* as the dominant voice of morality and common sense of her novel, an exemplary model of motherly devotion, who fails to undermine her gloomy assessment and recommendation of compromise by any trace of irony.

This espousal of a moderate, even conformist position is a problem which recurs constantly in eighteenth-century women's writings on education. Though a number express an awareness of the tensions and inconsistencies facing women, they settle for compliance to custom, while attempting through their suggestions for curriculum changes to extend women's minds and activities as far as possible within the confines of the socially acceptable.

Mlle Le Masson le Golft (1749–1826) is slightly different. Her *Lettres relatives à l'éducation* [Letters concerning Education] (1788) are conventional enough in their presentation, that of a series of apparently authentic letters addressed to a high-born mother predictably seeking advice on her daughter's education, but their content marks a difference. The author is careful to back her letters with documents, which testify to her own credentials as an authority on education. The public value of the published version of these letters is vouched for by Le Masson le Golft's membership of the Académie royale des Belles-Lettres d'Arras as well as the Cercle des Philadelphes of the Cap Français in Haiti. Le Masson le Golft was a resident of Le Havre and had had the opportunity of meeting Haitians. She includes an extract from a letter from the Cercle des Philadelphes, praising one of her letters on education, and part of a letter from the Arras Academy referring to her other publications, *La Balance de la Nature* [Nature's Scales] (Paris 1784), her *Tableau du genre humain* [Survey of the Human Race], her *La Rumination, attribuée inconsidérément aux mouches communes* [On the ill-considered attribution of rumination to the housefly], as well as two of her letters on education, which are said to demonstrate the astonishing extent of her knowledge. We are, therefore, not simply in the presence of a woman writer but of a woman scientist and academician.

At moments these letters voice the limitations placed on a woman's knowledge and apparently accept that this will be so. Women's exclusion from politics and the public sphere is not debated; religion and philosophy, on the other hand, are dealt with at length. Overall, Le Masson le Golft takes a firm stand on the side of Christianity and expresses her hostility to deism, impiety and atheism. She puts philosophy and science to the service of religion, arguing that it is at the point where philosophy and religion coincide that one finds certainty. It might be tempting to think that she includes religion to avoid controversy, and that her focal interests are philosophy and science, but her comments on the existence of a creator and her acceptance of revelation and the Christian faith is reaffirmed too extensively to be simply a gesture of conformism. Her letters demonstrate the desire to reconcile the discoveries of modern science with divine purpose.

Le Masson le Golft is above all anxious to equip upper-class women with an up-to-date knowledge of science that explains the operations of the physical world and which can be applied to the lives they lead. She does not suggest that women should study mathematics or that they should venture into the theoretical domain, merely that they should have a good understanding of experimental physics. She believes, unlike others, that there are adequate elementary textbooks explaining science, which are accessible to women and that, with the aid of tutors and public lecture courses, women can acquire considerable knowledge. In this way, she challenges women to help themselves and to take advantage of the possibilities offered by Enlightenment science.

Women's writings on education thus show us the extent to which, hedged about with conventions and restrictions, women tend to remain conservative in at least one major area of their thinking at the same time as they are opening up new avenues to their fellows, suggesting that women can learn Latin, understand physics and attain a high level of rational analysis. By the eve of the Revolution women become more political and we find them writing petitions, pamphlets and articles, arguing their case for improved conditions and often specifically for a better education. They commonly argue the latter on the grounds that women, like men, possess the powers of reason. The *Pétition des femmes du Tiers-Etat au Roi* [A Petition to the King by Women of the Third Estate] (1 January 1789), claims that women deserve 'une éducation saine et raisonnable' ['a sound, rational education']. A clearer and more developed example is that of Mme L— to the *Journal des Dames* (24 April 1791) *Première lettre d'une femme sur l'éducation de son sexe* [A First Letter from a Woman on the Education of her Sex], in which Mme L— puts forward a strong, straightforward challenge to men, based on the argument that women possess intelligence and reason, and links this to the contemporary recognition of rights. Her point is that those who argue that women must necessarily receive a different education from that of men need to demonstrate that male and female intelligence is actually different. Though men frequently criticize the idea that a woman should be *savante* [learned] and push this in the direction of pedantry, she claims that their real fear is that women might appear rational, since this constitutes a threat to men's newly obtained rights. Indeed, the Jacobins were to close down the newly founded women's clubs and stifle the call for women's rights. The playwright and pamphleteer, Olympe de Gouges (1748–93), author of the *Les Droits de la femme* (*The Rights of Woman*) (September 1791) – which systematically applied the 1789 *Déclaration de l'homme et du citoyen* [Declaration of the Rights of Man and the Citizen] to women – was sent to the guillotine in 1793 for her open opposition to the Jacobins. Women were encouraged to accept that true patriotism resides in republican motherhood. They readily produced patriotic hymns, odes, songs, republican catechisms and plays. In a 1793 proposal for the daily schooling of lower-class girls the Citoyenne Hardou wrote:

Il y aura des époques dans la journée où on enseignera à lire et à écrire et l'arithmétique; les jeunes élèves en qui on découvrira de l'aptitude à d'autres connaissances, seront instruites de l'histoire de notre Révolution; des idées qu'elles doivent se former des droits et des devoirs des hommes réunis en société; on ne négligera rien pour leur laisser les impressions les plus vraies de ce qui peut contribuer à les rendre bonnes mères et filles reconnaissantes de la patrie qui les protège.[16]

There will be periods in each day for the study of reading, writing and arithmetic; young girls who show a capacity for further learning will be instructed in the history of our Revolution and the ideas they should have on the rights and duties of man in society. Every effort will be made to foster a true awareness of what constitutes a good mother and a grateful daughter of the fatherland.

There is, therefore, a contrast between the early Revolution, where we see women becoming aware that the area of individual rights might be extended to them, and the support offered by women themselves from 1793 for the ideal of republican motherhood. This is mirrored by changes in legislation, which in the early years of the Revolution move in the direction of greater equality between the sexes, only to meet with resistance under the Jacobins and subsequent reversal by the Code Napoléon. Most women endorsed, at least for a time, the calls for republican motherhood and the growing bourgeois emphasis on the desirability of hearth and home.

NOTES

1 Manon Phlipon (Mme Roland), for example, was furious when friends published her travel journal, *Voyage en Suisse* (Tour through Switzerland), without her permission.
2 *Cartesian Women*, p. 199.
3 In Hervé de Broc's *Le Style épistolaire* (Paris: Plon, 1901), she was accorded a place alongside Cicero, Pliny the Younger, Saint-François de Sales, Balzac, Voiture, Mme de Sévigné, Mme de Maintenon and Voltaire. Also of interest are the letters of one of du Deffand's relatives, Diane de Vichy, who, consciously recalling Mme de Sévigné, charmingly recounted in letters to her daughter the winter of 1767–8, which she spent in Provence (see bibliography).
4 Mary Trouille reiterates these points in her 1994 article. Bosc's 1795 edition of the memoirs emphasises Roland's view, *Appel à l'impartiale postérité* (Paris: Louvet), see 'Avertissement de l'auteur'.
5 Pierre Carlet de Chamblain de Marivaux (1688–1763), playwright, novelist and 'journalist'/essayist, is mainly remembered for his successful comedies. As well as Mme de Lambert's *salon* he also attended that of Mme de Tencin and portrayed both women in his novel *La Vie de Marianne* (*The Life of Marianne*) (1731–42). Charles de Secondat, baron de Montesquieu (1689–1755) is known for his political philosophy, but also as the author of the highly successful *Lettres persanes* (*The Persian Letters*) (1721), which made him a fashionable figure in the Paris *salons* of the 1720s.
6 Interestingly, Genlis's professional title was the masculine *gouverneur* to the Orléans children, not the feminine *gouvernante* with its inferior connotations of (mere) child care.
7 In the nineteenth century some of her tales were published under the title *Le Trésor des familles Chrétiennes* [A Treasury for Christian Families].
8 See the arguments of Laborde *Diderot and Madame de Puisieux*, pp. 58–63.
9 Between 1766 and 1771 she produced a seven-volume *Nouvel abrégé de l'histoire de France à l'usage des jeunes gens* (Paris: Saillant), which was intended for both sexes.

10 The expanded second edition of the *Conversations d'Émilie* was awarded the Prix Monthyon by the Académie française in 1783 beating Genlis's *Adèle et Théodore*.

11 Rousseau had, of course, suggested that the female should be socialized from an early age, which would suggest introducing morality and social conventions earlier than for the male.

12 Contrasting with d'Espinassy's engagement with Rousseau and d'Épinay's modern approach to girls' education, there is also resounding female endorsement of Rousseau's plans for Sophie at this time (see, for example, Mme de Montbart's *Sophie, ou l'éducation* (Berlin: n.p., 1777)).

13 The essay was first published in M. P. Faugère's edition of the *Mémoires* (Paris, 1864), vol. II, pp. 333–57.

14 That this was a common view at the time and not restricted to women is illustrated by Riballier's *De l'Éducation physique et morale des femmes* [The Physical and Moral Education of Women], Brussels and Paris, 1779. He argues that a better education for women will lead to the reform of society, then takes the argument into a more political direction, arguing that this will lead to the regeneration of the nation.

15 She recommends her own *Veillées du château* and her *Théâtre à l'usage des enfans & des jeunes personnes* as if these had been written by the *baronne*.

16 Reprinted in Elke and Hans-Christian Harten *Femmes, Culture et Révolution*, pp. 516–19.

CHAPTER FIVE

Eighteenth-century women novelists: genre and gender

Martin Hall

It would be possible to write a history of the eighteenth-century French novel which referred only to works by women. The result would be a rather strange route-map, with some of the dominant features of the landscape blotted out (no Marivaux, Prévost, Diderot, Rousseau, Laclos), but it would cover most sub-genres of the novel and give a reasonably accurate indication of the evolution of the genre over the century. As eighteenth-century readers and critics knew, women were not occasional and marginal novelists. They were part of the mainstream.

Women were successful as novelists partly for negative reasons: the problems of apprenticeship and work opportunities made a career in music, painting or as a playwright a difficult one for a woman.* By comparison, the novel allowed a more ready outlet for their creativity. This is not to suggest that the genre offered dilettantes an easy opportunity to publish. Many eighteenth-century women novelists lived by their pen, often out of necessity, had to negotiate with publishers and agents, promote their works, and, in a general way, develop their name and reputation – for many, writing novels was a profession.

The success of women novelists was in part the result of a double depreciation, of the *genre*, and of women. The critical establishment of the period was male, and conservative. It viewed the novel as a *parvenu* genre. This conservatism also manifested itself in the disparagement of women as writers, and, more generally, in a misogynist suspicion of women's growing prominence in the social sphere. In conservative eyes, modern society was already suffering the consequences of this trend, and women's success in writing novels was further evidence that their concerns were becoming important. Love was the dominant theme of the novel and excessive interest in this subject was both a sure sign of female preponderance and of cultural decline.

Critical reaction was never entirely hostile, and with the growing popularity of the novel, condemnation turns to approval. Overt misogyny correspondingly turns to condescension: the prominence of women in modern society is accepted, and the success of the novel tolerated. This attitude still preserves the essential equation which identifies gender inferiority with genre inferiority. It insinuates that women's shallow minds find pleasure in a superficial form of literary entertainment purveyed by second-rate female writers who cannot aspire to true literary success in the more prestigious genres. The third phase follows on from recognition of the novel's popular success. The critical establishment shifts its stance again, and applauds this success. It is important to note that approval is accompanied by devalorization of the contribution of women to the development of the novel. Women are still deemed capable of a significant contribution, but one which is limited by their intellectual and biological inferiority: they are granted the 'feminine' virtues, finesse, sensitivity, spontaneity, but 'male' virtues, strength, imagination, creative capacity, are deemed necessary to create truly 'great' novels. The late eighteenth century sees the beginning of the process dubbed 'le sacre de l'écrivain' [the writer consecrated] by Paul Bénichou: the writer as priest, seer, prophet is beginning to emerge, but the priesthood which comes into being is one which excludes women.[1]

Eighteenth century criticism, in its depreciation of women as novelists and in its valorization of their efforts, anticipates and explains their later fall from public esteem: only as long as the genre is considered a backwater, can it be left to female cultivation. Once it becomes the lead-genre of eighteenth-century literature, it is colonized by men. In recognition of talents supposedly special to them, women are still granted a place, but only in a sort of literary ghetto.

The decades either side of 1700 are usually considered a period of change and experiment in the novel, foreshadowing the achievements of later novelists such as Prévost and Marivaux. However, this threshold, or 'entre deux siècles' can also be defined by the literary careers of a remarkable group of women novelists. For contemporary readers, the 1690s were marked by the 'nouvelles historiques' of Catherine Bernard (1662–1712), by Marie-Catherine d'Aulnoy's (1650–1705) best-selling *Hypolite comte de Duglas* (*Hypolitus Earl of Douglas*) (1690), Anne de La Roche Guilhen's *Histoire des favorites* (*The History of Female Favourites*) (1697), by the fairy-tale collections of Charlotte-Rose de La Force (1697) and d'Aulnoy (1697–8). Most of these writers remained active into the early years of the eighteenth century.

Historical fiction and fairy-tale remained popular in the first half of the eighteenth century, and seem to have been particularly favoured by women writers. The fairy tale's relative freedom from literary prescriptions and constraints was no doubt an important attraction. This freedom was expressed in a playful and ironizing form of writing, essential to the exploration of thematic material – dream and the erotic – which could not find ready expression in other forms of literature. Women writers who made distinctive contributions to the genre include Louise Lévesque (1703?–45) and Catherine de Lintot (dates uncertain). The most flamboyant author of fairy tales is Mlle de Lubert, in whose tales some of the characteristic motifs of the fairy tale (e.g., metamorphosis, magic, monsters, violence) are amplified and distended to the point of surrealism. However, one fairy-tale deserves particular mention. The only piece of women's prose-fiction which is known to a readership vastly greater than the specialists of the eighteenth century is *La Belle et la Bête (Beauty and the Beast)*.[2] Its success cannot be adequately explained in this chapter, but in the perspective of women's writing of the eighteenth century, it is plausible to suggest that it offered one of the most powerful expressions of women's fears and hopes about marriage.

Like the fairy-tale, the historical novel of the first half of the eighteenth century has its origins in the seventeenth century. It survives into the mid-eighteenth century largely in the work of women novelists. Compared to the fairy-tale it may seem a rather conservative form of fiction whose typical plot gravitates around a high born heroine's painful sacrifice of love to 'devoir', or more specifically, parental 'diktat'. Often, she embraces her fate as evidence of her virtue. Female virtue, in other words, consists in obedience to and consolidation of the established order.

The relative conservatism of the sub-genre no doubt constituted part of its appeal and success. The historical novel offered a way of representing women's lives which both glamorized them and emphasized their dismal constants. The beautiful princess forced to marry a man she cannot love might seem a remote and unreal figure, but was this predicament so very remote from so many girls' apprehensions about marriage, and so many wives' distaste for it? Moreover, it is clear from examining some of the more successful historical novels by women writers that the genre allowed more adventurous representations of women's lives than has been suggested, and might indeed be used to quite subversive effect. The most representative writer in this context is Marguerite de Lussan, the main plot of whose *Anecdotes de la Cour de Philippe-Auguste* [Tales from the Court of Philip-Augustus] (1733–6) contrasts two heroines, one of whom dies from her refusal to disobey her parents, the other of whom triumphantly resists.

Three women novelists of the first half of the century warrant particular mention. The first of them, Madeleine-Angélique de Gomez (1684–1770) is an outstanding example of the professional woman writer in this period. One of many obliged by marital circumstances to write for a living, she published poetry, a tragedy, and a wide variety of novels including historical novels and an imitation of the seventeenth-century 'grand roman'. Her most distinctive works are collections of tales, *Les Journées amusantes* (*La Belle Assemblée, or the Adventures of Six Days*) (1722–31) and *Les Cent Nouvelles Nouvelles* (*One Hundred New Novellas*) (1732–9). The first uses the form of framed narratives, in which the social and conversational context of the tales is given particular importance. The second is a compendium of tales taken from all manner of sources, a hotchpotch indeed, but distinctive in the fact that the most compelling tales insistently return to the feminocentric topic of women caught between love and social constraints.

Two other novelists, Alexandrine de Tencin and Françoise de Graffigny, are distinctive for having produced fiction which breaks with or subverts received forms, and each illustrates, in a different way, the manner in which distinctively female voices emerge in eighteenth-century fiction. Alexandrine de Tencin (1682–1749) wrote four novels, of which three appeared during her lifetime, and one was left incomplete. Two novels are particularly interesting. *Le Siège de Calais* (*The Siege of Calais*) (1739) is loosely based on the events leading up to the surrender of Calais during the Hundred Years War. It illustrates how novelists, and especially women novelists, used the antiquated conventions of 'galant' historical fiction to new and surprising ends. The novel begins with a bizarre and implausible episode in a country house, in which a man takes sexual advantage of a woman who believes him to be her husband. Once the heroine discovers the truth, she behaves with understandable coldness to the man, even after her unpleasant husband's death, and despite her attraction toward the man, and his attempts to earn her forgiveness. She only relents when, in a strange gesture of repentance, he takes the place of one of the sacrificial burghers of Calais. This is rewriting history with a vengeance: one of the most famous episodes of medieval history is 'hijacked' to become the resolution of private quarrels. It also becomes the scene of very public male abasement, the noble hero forced to expiate his initial imposture by adopting the doubly disgraceful disguise of burgher and of captive. Throughout the course of the novel a series of oppositions are played against one another: dress and undress, the private darkness of the marital chamber and the bright light of public ceremony, male opportunism and submission, female passivity and decision.

A similar play of gender inversions and echoes constitutes a distinctive feature of Tencin's first and best known novel, the *Mémoires du comte de Comminge* (*Memoirs of the Count of Comminge*) (1735), a cocktail of gloomy dungeons, cloisters and castles, where love is associated with pain and death, and with violent and tyrannical fathers and husbands. Hero and heroine are cousins, fall in love, but are frustrated by Comminge's father, who imprisons his son and blackmails the heroine into marriage to another man as the price of her lover's freedom. Once released, the hero disguises himself, and seeks her out, but his impetuous revelation of his identity leads to her being disastrously compromised. The hero wounds the husband and flees. Believing his beloved dead, he enters La Trappe.[3] Some three years later, called to witness the death of a fellow monk, he discovers that the latter is in fact his beloved. Imprisoned and given for dead by her husband, she has been freed by his death. Disguised as a man, she has sought out her lover, and entered the monastery to be near him. She dies, and he retires to a hermitage to mourn her.

The final scene has an almost 'grand guignol' quality, as the dying heroine, stretched out on a bed of ashes, explains to the assembled Trappists how she has insinuated herself into their community in order to be near her lover. Her dying confession, whilst it is couched in the language of religious repentance, comes over as an affirmation of profane love, but also of female superiority. After all, the hero has made a disaster of simply disguising himself as a painter, whereas she has managed three years as a Trappist monk. Throughout the novel, her voice has scarcely been heard. When she does finally speak, when she reveals the full extent of her 'fol amour', it is in the midst of a community of men dedicated to silence. Very few women wrote male-voiced memoirs-novels, and Tencin's is remarkable for the manner in which it ends with the scandalous voice of a woman resounding in and taking over a male space. This 'scandalousness' in the exploitation of discourse which was in the cultural tradition of the period thought of as male (history, memoirs) is perhaps the most distinctive feature of one of the most playful novelists of the century.

Françoise de Graffigny (1695–1758) is remembered for the *Lettres d'une péruvienne* (*Letters Written by a Peruvian Princess*) (1747), one of the most popular novels of the century, largely for reasons which now make it seem whimsical and dated: its 'Inca' exoticism. The *Lettres* is the story of Zilia, an Inca princess, destined for marriage to Aza, the heir to the Inca throne. Both are captured by the conquering Spanish, but whilst he remains in Spanish captivity, she is seized by French sailors, who take her to France.

The novel consists for the most part of letters written to her absent lover by a forlorn woman, a figure heavy with connotations in French epistolary fiction: passive, constrained or captive, waiting, unfulfilled in the absence of the man. Such is Zilia in the opening letters, but the novel is essentially the story of her emancipation from dependency, and of her intellectual awakening as she discovers European civilization. In the early letters her interest in knowledge and learning is associated with her love for Aza. She has studied 'pour te plaire . . . mériter ton estime, ta confiance, ton respect . . .' ['to please you . . . to earn your esteem, your trust, your respect'] (lettre II). As the novel progresses, the heroine embarks upon a quest for knowledge in which reference to Aza recedes as a stimulus before 'l'excellence du plaisir' ['the sheer delight'] which she discovers in reading (lettre XX). This new pleasure is accompanied by growing awareness that her project relies on material security. These problems are resolved by the acquisition which her French protector arranges of a small country house and estate (with her captured wealth), so that she may have her independence, 'une vie indépendante' (lettre XXXII). This episode is fundamental to the novel's feminism: a woman can only emancipate herself, and pursue her intellectual interests if she has the time and space – and money. No other eighteenth-century French novel makes this point so explicitly.

Free from material dependency, Zilia must confront the more insidious dependency which binds her to Aza and her protector Deterville. Aza typifies the figure of the absent male, cause not only of the heroine's grief and yearning, but of her compensatory emotional investment. Zilia comes to realize Aza is not the superman she had constructed, but a fairly ordinary man. Her relationship to Deterville is more interesting. In lettre XII, Zilia seeks to express her gratitude for his kindness. Language is a problem: he speaks French, she speaks Inca. She learns his language, he does not learn hers, and it is in his language that she must try to thank him. The result is misunderstanding: the terms she uses are taken from his expressions of love and are inappropriate for her expressions of gratitude. As the relationship develops, it is *his* use of language which becomes the critical problem, as he forces her to listen to expressions of love which she does not want to hear. The issue of language, highlighted in the first instance by Zilia's inadequate command of French becomes the means of exposing the selfishness of male desire. Beyond this, the novel has a much more radical thrust: it questions the very possibility of true communication in the heterosexual relationship, where the language of communication is imposed by one sex on the other.

The climax of the novel comes in lettre XXXVIII, entitled 'La résolution où elle est de vivre libre' ['Zilia's resolve to be free']. Aza renounces her, but this reinforces Zilia's commitment to him: she will never marry, out of fidelity to the pact which bound them. The man's breach of their contract is answered by the woman's assertion of its continuing validity. The resolution of her relations with Deterville is more difficult. She cannot love him, but persuades him to accept a relationship of friendship. The novel proposes a solution to the problem of heterosexual relationships which is quite common in the eighteenth century: true intimacy and real equality between the sexes can only exist once sexuality is renounced or exhausted. Zilia finally 'converts' Deterville, who responds, if not in Inca language, in terms which are clearly derived from Zilia's emotional and intellectual 'language'.

In the second half of the century, there were more novels, more novelists, more readers, and a more ambitious conception of what the novel might express, and of the subjects which it might address. Subject matter expanded: domestic issues which had previously been deemed trivial and boring became fashionable, so that issues concerning household management, children and parenthood became legitimate topics in the novel. The capacity to be moved, to feel intensely, is associated with an enthusiasm for the good. The expression of this new 'sensibilité' became more exalted and hyperbolic. The demand that feelings (and love in particular) be granted greater freedom of expression and fulfilment becomes more insistent. The period is also marked by the dominance of the epistolary novel which seems to have held a particular attraction for women novelists. In explanation, it has been argued that this form constituted a natural progression from private correspondence, in which many women would have wide experience, and that the essentially private nature of letter-writing offered a particularly appropriate means for expressing concerns, domestic and affective, in which they would be particularly interested. The important influences which feed into the work of most novelists in the second half of the century are those of Richardson and Rousseau, and the latter's La Nouvelle Héloïse (1761) is rightly seen as a work of primary importance in the evolution of the novel in the last four decades of the century.[4]

Before discussing these later developments, mention must be made of the work of two contemporaries of Rousseau, who begin their careers and write their most distinctive novels around the middle of the century, and who remain relatively untouched by the developments prompted by his novel. Marie Jeanne Riccoboni (1713–92) and Jeanne Marie Leprince de Beaumont (1711–80) are two of the most distinctive voices in the eighteenth-century French novel, and perhaps the two women novelists who most obviously articulate individual and specifically feminist points of view in their novels. They are also notable as women who made their career by the pen. Both escaped from unhappy marriages, and subsequently lived without a male partner.

Riccoboni's status as a major novelist was widely recognized during her lifetime, and although her reputation later declined, her novels never fell entirely from view. Most of her novels are epistolary in form and the dominant voice is usually a woman's. They are primarily concerned with amatory relationships and with the analysis of the differences between male and female emotions. Her most successful novels are her early ones. The first, *Lettres de Mistriss Fanni Butlerd* [Letters of Mistriss Fanni Butlerd] (1757), is composed of 116 letters, mostly fairly brief, written by the eponymous heroine to her lover, Alfred. We have none of his letters, although it is clear from hers that he does reply. The novel charts their love-affair, a matter of greater intensity and graver consequences for her than for him. She loves him, she gives herself to him, and he abandons her for an advantageous marriage. Fanni's letters cover a wide range of feelings, but what comes over very clearly is the greater honesty and emotional commitment of the heroine compared to her lover. She invests in a relationship which, ultimately, is one-sided, and in which he takes more than he gives. The last letters, as Fanni's feelings turn to anger and contempt, are marked by a bleakness of tone redeemed by her lucidity and dignity as she severs contact. The novel achieves a tragic dimension in her realization that her love has been wasted on a phantom: 'Vous n'êtes pas celui que j'aimais, non, vous ne l'êtes point; vous ne l'avez jamais été' [You are not the man I loved, no, you are not; you have never been the man I loved'] (letter CXIV).

Male selfishness and insensitivity are recurrent motifs in Riccoboni's novels, and Alfred is only the first of a number of men whose behaviour towards women ranges from insensitivity to perfidy. The central figure of *L'Histoire de M le marquis de Cressy* (*The History of the Marquis de Cressy*) (1758), betrays a young woman to whom he is morally and emotionally committed, in order to marry a wealthy widow. He then seduces her young *protégée*, and is responsible for his wife's subsequent suicide. Widows are wary of committing themselves to a second marriage, since their first one has been so awful (*Lettres d'Adélaïde de Dammartin, comtesse de Sancerre*, (*Letters from the Countess de Sancerre*) (1767). Men are opportunists who will seduce a young woman who means nothing to them (*Lettres de milady Juliette Catesby*, (*Letters from Juliet, Lady Catesby*) (1759).

Riccoboni's presentation of gender relations is more sophisticated than these examples suggest. Male generosity and nobility are depicted, and if men are presented as unjust or insensitive in their behaviour towards women, it is not simply because they are men, but because of the society of the period. Men are presented less as gender-determined villains than as morally weak opportunists, who exploit material, legal and social advantages to the detriment of women. Men can acquire money more readily than women. The legal system favours them hugely in this respect. An unmarried woman who enjoyed a relatively protected environment before her marriage will find herself defenceless once she is married. Socio-moral factors also play an important part. A young woman who has an affair with a man runs enormous risks – that he will expose her socially, and thereby ruin her reputation, whilst running no comparable risk himself; that she will become pregnant, an unmarried mother and social pariah. A husband's adultery will be considered a peccadillo, a wife's grounds for sequestration. Riccoboni is a social realist in that her plots are founded on these facts, and her position as one of the most important women novelists of the eighteenth century rests on this realism as much as on her psychological insight.

Leprince de Beaumont was an important writer on education, as was shown in the previous chapter, and her novels were written with a similar didactic purpose, driven by a conservative Christian ideology. The founding principle of a woman's destiny must be the fulfilment of her duty as a woman, subordinate to man. Women are not placed in this world to enjoy themselves, but to become wives and mothers. As wives, they must defer to their husbands, and accept male authority. Even when her husband transgresses Christian principles (typically through sexual infidelity) she must continue to cherish him, and seek through meekness and exemplary behaviour to win him to virtue. Such behaviour will require the sacrifice of her own appetites, and devotion to others.

This programme is elaborated in Leprince's three epistolary novels, *Lettres de Madame du Montier* [Letters of Madame du Montier] (1756), *Lettres d'Emérance à Lucie* (*Letters of Emerance to Lucy*) (1765), *Mémoires de*

Madame la baronne de Batteville (*The Virtuous Widow, or Memoirs of the Baroness de Batteville*) (1766). In the first of these novels, the core exchange of letters is that between a mother and her daughter. The basic structure is simple: the young bride, married to an older man, writes to her mother for advice, and the mother answers. It soon becomes apparent that the daughter needs little advice in her progress to virtue. An older friend's advice to her young *protégée* similarly forms the basis of the *Lettres d'Emérance à Lucie*, and the same pattern emerges, whereby a young bride gradually accedes to the same wisdom and competence in the management of her life as her elder. In the *Mémoires de Madame la baronne de Batteville*, the exchange is more equal (Mme de Batteville is writing to a friend rather than mentor), but the overall effect is similar: the reader is invited to admire a Christian heroine, and subscribe to a conception of feminine fulfilment in endurance, sacrifice and submission.

However, the extremism of Leprince's views leads to a curious reversal of perspective. Her conception of female duty and fulfilment creates heroines who 'opt out' of the worldly cycle of desire and satisfaction, and as a result acquire considerable autonomy. This is most evident in the figure of the widow, still relatively young, who refuses a second marriage which, in the eyes of the world, would fulfil her. Her refusal is ostensibly motivated by altruism, but has the effect of ensuring that she does not return to the subordination which marriage requires of the woman. Leprince works within a Christian feminist tradition, which, paradoxically, secures female autonomy through apparent sacrifice. Women give up the world, profane love and carnal commitment, and they are rewarded with freedom, freedom essentially from a world of heterosexual engagements. In this perspective, Leprince's heroines constitute some of the most distinctive heroines of refusal in feminocentric fiction of the eighteenth century.

The love-interest was, of course, central to most novels in the eighteenth century, and one of the distinctive developments after Rousseau is the manner in which the conception and evaluation of love change. Simplifying Rousseau's complex dialectic of love and virtue, novelists produce tales in which virtuous lovers skirt perilously close to adultery. Françoise Albine Benoist (1724–1809) was a prolific writer, whose novels can be seen as exploitations of the fashion for exalting love and virtue, often in rather ambiguous ways. The title of one of her novels, *Célianne ou les amants séduits par leur vertus* [Célianne, or The Lovers Seduced by their Virtues] (1766), is almost a summary of this association. In novels such as *L'Aveugle par amour* [Blinded by Love] by Fanny de Beauharnais

(1781), the same exaltation of passion and sensibility found in Benoist becomes almost formulaic.

The identification of love with virtuousness is accompanied by a tendency to underline the status of lovers as victims of social oppression, and to justify their right to happiness. In feminocentric fiction, this sometimes leads to startling explorations of marital situations. A particularly powerful evocation of a young girl's revulsion at marrying an older man is found in *Caroline de Litchfield* (1786) by Isabelle de Montolieu (1751–1832), which, it has been argued, can be read as a variation on the theme of *La Belle et la Bête*.[5] Towards the end of the century, we find the same trends in the work of a younger generation of novelists such as Adélaïde de Souza (1761–1836) and Sophie Cottin (1770–1807), whose early novels, respectively *Adèle de Sénange* (1794, but written before 1789) and *Claire d'Albe (Dangerous Friendship)* (1799), both develop the situation of the young girl married to an older man, and illustrate distinctive aspects of late eighteenth-century sensibility. *Adèle de Sénange* is an interesting variation on the theme: the sweetness of the couple and of the young man who loves Adèle, and whom the old man befriends, leads to an innocent *ménage-à-trois*, which is happily resolved when the old man dies, having done his best to ensure that the young people will marry and be happy. The novel is a fantasy in which the old, possessing generation does the decent thing and dies, leaving the younger generation to be happy. *Claire d'Albe* is altogether more sombre: its eponymous heroine, married in adolescence to an older, but kindly man, falls in love with a young man, a 'romantic', impulsive figure. Although both are presented as deeply sincere and virtuous, they commit adultery (the scene is more ambiguous than this term suggests: he uses force but she may be read as acquiescent and responsive). She dies repentant and he becomes a wanderer, never to be seen again. What is both typical and distinctive about these novels, however different they are, is the way in which the complexities of the relationship between love and virtue have been simplified in such a way as to justify the impulse to love as a virtuous one.

Whilst the love-interest generally remains central, other issues and themes also make distinctive appearances. Félicité de Genlis (1746–1830) resembles Leprince de Beaumont in her conservative Christianity, didacticism and pedagogic aims. Her *Adèle et Théodore (Adelaide and Theodore)* (1782), discussed in the previous chapter, was an outstanding success in the field of educational fiction. Genlis lived on well into the nineteenth century, and wrote many novels in quite different styles – ranging from novels which shade into the Gothic to works which are clearly attempts to revive the 'nouvelle historique' of the late seventeenth century. The guiding thread in her work is her hostility to the Enlightenment and the Revolution, and to what she sees as the misguided and morally dangerous enthusiasm of a writer like Sophie Cottin. In *Les vœux téméraires* (*Rash Vows*) (1798), for instance, she presents a heroine who is undone by her excessive valorization of 'sensibilité'.

The *Lettres du marquis de Roselle* (*The History of the Marquis de Roselle*) (1764) by Anne Elie de Beaumont (1730–83) is a good example of the way in which domestic and rural life are valorized. The eponymous hero is rescued from the clutches of a scheming *fille d'opéra*, and happily married to a sweet and gentle girl of an old provincial noble family, to live out a life of domestic contentment. The novel is distinctive in its evocation of family life, and the pleasures of a simple country existence. Its celebration of the rural idyll also promotes a conservative and nobilitarian vision of society, in which the secure values and social stability of the country are promoted over the dissatisfactions of town-life.

The epistolary novel was not the only one in which women novelists wrote, and the late eighteenth century sees two instances of women resorting to quasi-autobiography in the *Histoire de Madame de Montbrillant* (*Memoirs and Correspondence of Mme d'Épinay*) (1757–70, but only published in mutilated form in 1818) by Louise d'Épinay (1726–83) and the *Mémoire de madame de Valmont* [Madame de Valmont, a Memoir] (1788), by Olympe de Gouges (1748–93). In each case, the initial impetus to write was polemical and apologetic. D'Épinay was writing to forestall what she anticipated would be Rousseau's misrepresentation of her in his *Confessions*, and Gouges was seeking to obtain recognition and redress from her natural father. They constitute important documents because they testify to the fact that women were ready to discuss details of their private lives which previously would have been more heavily disguised. Interestingly enough, d'Épinay and Gouges, in writing these self-revelatory pieces, renew a form of female 'auto-fiction' which is occluded throughout the greater part of the eighteenth century, but which has ancestors in the *Mémoires de Mme la comtesse de M**** (*Memoires of the Countess of Dunois*), and yet earlier seventeenth-century memoirs.[6]

Of all the women novelists of eighteenth-century France, Isabelle de Charrière (1740–1805) is arguably the greatest. She was born into the Dutch nobility, learnt French at an early age, and felt an attraction towards the language and its culture matched by her distaste for her native environment. The need to escape seems to have prompted her to marry M de Charrière, a Swiss gentleman. Marriage proved a disappointment, and she sought fulfilment in writing. Her early novels, which were based upon her experience of marriage and of Swiss provincial life, appeared in 1784 (*Lettres neufchâteloises* [Letters from Neuchâtel] and *Lettres de Mistriss Henley*) and 1785 (*Lettres écrites de Lausanne* (*Letters from Lausanne*), whose second part, *Caliste*, published in 1787, is her best known work). These explore the pettiness and constrictedness of everyday provincial life. They also offer an indictment of the eighteenth-century marriage-system.

Lettres de Mistriss Henley is a short work, clearly autobiographical in inspiration. Set in England, and comprising six letters written by the eponymous heroine to a woman friend, it relates her marriage to an older man, a widower with a young daughter from his previous, happy marriage. She marries him, not out of necessity, nor from love, but because he is so obviously a worthy man. The couple settle to country life on his estate, Hollowpark. Their marriage is a series of tragi-comic disasters, as she attempts to adapt herself to her new circumstances, and to introduce improvements. All her efforts are failures, benignly accommodated by her laconic and tolerant husband. His exasperating kindness, and the naïvety of her reliance on spontaneity and goodwill make a terrible combination. Nothing really happens – a painting is repositioned, a servant is allocated new duties, furniture is shifted – but in each case, unhappiness, or loss of confidence and intimacy is the result.

In the last letter's final paragraph, the implications of this simple tale become apparent: in this stable, benign little world, a woman is heading for breakdown, madness, even perhaps death. She will, for the sake of the child she bears, not seek to end her own life. She will 'carry on', and ends with this prediction to her friend: 'Dans un an, dans deux ans, vous apprendrez, je l'espère, que je suis raisonnable & heureuse, ou que je ne suis plus' ['In a year or two, you will learn, I hope, that I am reasonable and happy, or that I am no longer']. Reasonable like her husband? Happy like her husband? It seems impossible. She is not a victim, tyrannized by some ogre-like husband, nor does she suffer obvious deprivation, but she is suffocating in 'reasonable' Hollowpark. The 'reason' and 'happiness' proposed are those of her husband, male notions to which a wife must conform. The conclusion holds out little hope that she will be able to survive.

The *Lettres écrites de Lausanne* are a diptych, two tales of women caught in a social and economic trap. The first part consists of the letters of a mother to her cousin, relating her anxieties about her daughter's future. The latter's marriage prospects are poor, since she is of genteel birth, without fortune, and trapped within a narrow social circle. Cécile is seen through her mother's loving but honest gaze. Far from being some ideal novel-heroine, she is simply a high-spirited, attractive, good-natured, lovable person. A young man, a good 'catch', is attracted to her, but too indecisive to propose to her. That is the sum of the tale which remains incomplete. Its poignancy lies in this incompleteness, which is less a sign of the author's incapacity to conclude than the representation of a seemingly hopeless situation.

The second part of the diptych is usually referred to as *Caliste* owing to its eponymous heroine. Caliste is her stage name. She is given no other, just as she has neither family nor recognized social position. Put on the stage by her mother in preparation for a life as a 'fille entretenue', she becomes the mistress of an older man. He sees to her education, makes of her an accomplished courtesan, and dies satisfied and penniless, 'bequeathing' her to his uncle. Caliste's story is told in retrospective narrative by the man who fell in love with her. He has been too weak to flout paternal and social norms by marrying her. She, in turn, could only yearn for a marriage, which she knew the man's weak conformism made impossible. She finds security in marriage to another man, whilst he makes a socially acceptable marriage. Her health undermined by the after-effects of miscarriage, and by her continuing love, Caliste dies, leaving the narrator a broken man, haunted by regrets.[7]

Cécile's and Caliste's stories are complementary. In the first, an amiable girl finds herself in an ordinary enough situation for someone of her time, class and gender: even a mediocre happiness is elusive and dependent on the inclination and actions of a prospective husband. The exceptionally talented and beautiful Caliste is condemned to a different but equally depressing passivity in social marginality, where even her strength of character and passionate commitment cannot overcome the irresolution of the man she loves. Both women live in societies in which their qualities weigh little against the conformism of society, and the power of the 'marriage-machine'.

Charrière has been compared to Jane Austen in her wit, lucidity and economy, but she eschews the romance-plot which allows Austen to reward her heroines with a happy ending. However, Charrière transcends the pessimism which these tales suggest. The delineation of mother–daughter love in the *Lettres écrites de Lausanne* possesses genuine poignancy, whilst the almost nightmarish quality given to the bland everyday in the *Lettres de Mistriss Henley* is without parallel in eighteenth-century fiction. In addition, Charrière's technical mastery, evident in her construction of characters through their writing about another person (the mother on her daughter, the ex-lover on Caliste) is as sophisticated as anything in eighteenth-century prose-fiction. Her genius lies in understatement and suggestion, qualities all the more distinctive because so rare in the late eighteenth-century novel.[8]

Charrière's later career as a writer extended through the Revolution, and much of her later prose-fiction engages with the issues and events of the last decade of the eighteenth century. More decisively than any other novelist, Charrière sets her novels in the contemporary context of upheaval, political debate and exile, and seeks to understand the origins and possible consequences of the Revolution. From a relatively safe position in Switzerland, but in regular contact with 'émigrés', sympathetic to many of the ideas which led to the events of 1789, but deeply distressed by what she saw as the excesses of the Jacobins, Charrière attempted in her *Lettres trouvées dans des porte-feuilles d'émigrés* [Letters found in the Document-Cases of Emigrés] (1793) to understand the events which were unfolding, the different political positions adopted in what she presents as a civil war. In addition, she offers a perceptive view of the social causes which precipitated the Revolution, and suggests the benign social changes which it might bring about, changes which might actually release women from the old social constraints.

Charrière sits between two extremes as a writer about the Revolution. Not the extremes of left and right, but of writers who respond as political activists, and those – the majority – whose novels do not engage at all with the political issues of the Revolution. Few writers were as directly involved in politics as Olympe de Gouges, whose feminist radicalism and proclaimed hostility to the Jacobins led her to the scaffold. The greater part of her political writing after 1789 consisted of pamphlets and plays. Her only important piece of prose-fiction is *Le Prince philosophe, conte oriental* (1792), a politico-philosophical 'conte' which puts forward a strongly feminist message. Her case illustrates a general point, that the novel was not a genre to which writers seeking to make an immediate political impact would resort. At the opposite end of the political spectrum, we find confirmation of this point in another writer mentioned earlier, Félicité de Genlis, whose royalist sympathies took her into exile in 1791. Like Gouges, she wrote works which engage directly with political events, and she also continued to write novels, but the two sorts of writing remain largely distinct.

Gouges and Genlis were activists as well as writers, and in this they were exceptional. Most novelists carried on writing novels after 1789 which are as devoid of political reference as those written before this date. This is not to say that the Revolution and its consequences do not figure in the novels of the time. The massive disruption of lives which revolution and emigration provoked could be assimilated into the well-worn routines of the adventure-novel, and it would hardly be an exaggeration to say that their disruptive effects replaced the pirates, wars and earthquakes of earlier novels. Moreover, the Revolution, by providing such an effective means of casting hero and heroine out into a world of uncertainty and danger, often served as a means of representing them as innocent and virtuous victims of a malign fate.

Joan Hinde Stewart, discussing critics' use of the term 'feminist' to describe Riccoboni's novels, argues that it is legitimate to do so 'if what we mean by feminism entails a forceful statement of prevailing gender inequities and a demand that they be addressed'.[9] The *statement* holds true for most of the novelists discussed in this chapter. They write works which refer us to the condition of women, to the legal and economic dependence they suffer, to the different standards of sexual morality which apply to men and women, to the consequences for women's hopes and aspirations.

Whether there is a *demand* that injustice be *addressed* is a more complex issue. If it is a demand that injustice be remedied, it implies a demand for change, which in turn supposes the possibility of change, but what sort of change? Almost all women's novels are set in an upper-class context, and this constitutes a limitation, for this world is presented as unchanging, and women's lives as seemingly unchangeable.[10] Above all, what is constant is that the dependence of women arises from the institution of marriage. Women's lives are determined not by the choices open to them, but by the accommodations they contrive with this institution.

Indeed, the sceptic might ask whether it makes sense to talk of feminocentric fiction in the eighteenth century. Is this notion not better expressed by 'marriage-centred fiction'? It is certainly true that almost all eighteenth-century novels (whether written by women or men) which take a woman as their principal figure will organize her tale in relation to marriage. The balance may be different: one novel will conclude with marriage, another will focus on the married woman, another will throw the centre of gravity towards widowhood. In whichever case, marriage constitutes the point of reference which orders the tale. Feminocentric fiction of the eighteenth century is almost inevitably 'marriage-centred' fiction, and hence, it could be argued, 'man-centred' fiction.

This is not to imply that women novelists spent their time writing tales of 'waiting for Mr Right'. The weak young lover and the oppressive father/husband probably constitute the defining representations of the male in feminocentric fiction of the eighteenth century. It does mean that it is more apposite to refer to escape from the system rather than change of the system as the principal remedy proposed by women novelists. Alternative representations of women exist to the marriage-defined woman. Mothers and maternal love are occasionally foregrounded, but the principal alternative figure is the widow. She is the most powerful representation of feminine freedom, because she has the experience and opportunity to choose whether to remain within the system, or to step outside it. Re-marrying widows are common enough, satisfying the powerful expectation of the happy ending, but it is the refusers who constitute the most distinctive group of heroines (to which can be added rare cases such as Graffigny's Zilia of unmarried women who refuse marriage). Various motives may induce women to refuse a second marriage, but what is perhaps more important is that their refusal constitutes a refusal of the heterosexual economy, and its servitudes. Autonomy, where it is envisaged as a possibility, is not advanced as a possibility resulting from some improbable change in society, but as a consequence of opting out of this economy.

NOTES

* Some women did write successful plays in eighteenth-century France. Space precludes discussion of them here, but further information is to be found in Beach, *French Women Playwrights before the Twentieth Century*.
1 *Le Sacre de l'écrivain 1750–1830* (Paris: José Corti, 1973).
2 *La Belle et la Bête* has been attributed to Suzanne-Gabrielle de Villeneuve, and first appeared as an intercalated tale in *La Jeune Amériquaine et les contes marins* (1740). It was later cut down and re-worked by Jeanne Marie Leprince de Beaumont, and appeared in volume 1 of her *Magasin des enfants* (1756). In its basic outline, this fairy-tale is the story of a young girl coerced into marriage with someone she finds repulsive. Both the Villeneuve and the Leprince versions offer some sort of optimistic resolution to the heroine's predicament, a predicament which, in the eighteenth century, can hardly be described as unusual.
3 The monastic community of La Trappe was famous in the late seventeenth and early eighteenth century for the austerity of its rule. The monks were pledged to silence.
4 The English novelist Samuel Richardson enjoyed considerable success in France, especially with his *Clarissa Harlowe* (1748). His novels were translated into French soon after their appearance, and established the vogue for epistolary novels. Rousseau's *La Nouvelle Héloïse*, his only novel, was an even

greater success and further consolidated the prestige of the novel as a serious genre.

5 Stewart, *Gynographs*, pp. 136–51.

6 Henriette de Castelnau, comtesse de Murat, *Mémoires de Madame la comtesse de M****, Paris, 1697. On this and other women's memoirs of the seventeenth century, see René Démoris, *Le Roman à la première personne à l'âge classique* (Paris: Colin, 1975).

7 There are many similarities to Constant's *Adolphe* (1815). Charrière and Constant were close friends.

8 Béatrice Didier makes some very interesting suggestions about Charrière's style in relation to women's writing. See Béatrice Didier, *L'Ecriture-femme*, pp. 107–10.

9 *Gynographs*, p. 76.

10 Charrière alone was alert to the possibility of escape into work. In the *Lettres de Lausanne*, Cécile imagines running off to work and live with her mother, for whom this notion is mere adolescent fantasy. Charrière leaves unspoken the issue of how feasible such escape is.

CHAPTER SIX

The nineteenth century: shaping women

Rosemary Lloyd

While the eighteenth century allowed a considerable degree of intellectual freedom to women in the upper echelons of society, the Revolution of 1789 and its aftermath mushroomed forth a series of depictions of the Republic, symbolized by woman as devouring virago, driving young men into the destruction of conflict and war.[1] Intimately connected with such iconography, the removal of women's suffrage, in 1793, remains a potent symbol of just what *fraternité* can mean. The puritanism of Napoleon's public ethics used the changing iconography of the times in an attempt to restrict women to roles connected with children, the Church and the kitchen. The Napoleonic code of 1805 formalized the dichotomy between masculine public space and female private space, assigning to women the legal and metaphorical role of minors in the new society, controlling the way they dressed and the kinds of work they could do. Typical of this restriction of women's freedom was the suppression of the 1792 divorce law in 1816: divorce would not be made legal again until 1884. Adultery was punishable by imprisonment, with the female offender technically liable to remain incarcerated for as long as the husband wanted. As the century progressed and as women came to be seen as possessing a powerful role as consumers in an increasingly industrialized state, their intellectual and physical freedoms went through various revolutions reflected in a wide range of genres. The misogyny that stamps the 1880s and 1890s, a hatred of women that is also a hatred of self and that is linked to the anti-Semitism so much in evidence in the Dreyfus affair,[2] coincides with the time when powerful critics such as Brunetière, Faguet and Gourmont were beginning to delimit the academic canon. As a result, many women writers have been thrust into minor roles or fallen into the oblivion of out of print books. Nevertheless, the century remains one in which women produced an extraordinary array of texts.

Throughout the century, women's roles and influence can to some extent be indicated by reference to those who were most in evidence. French Romanticism owed much of its initial impetus to the voracious reading and incisive intellect of Germaine de Staël. The first collection of Romantic poetry to be published in France was, contrary to what school manuals might tell us, not that of Lamartine, but Marceline Desbordes-Valmore's *Elégies et Romances* [Elegies and Romances] (1818). Women contributed to the tradition of the confessional novel, with Louise Colet's *Lui* and Marie d'Agoult's *Nélida,* to mention only those two. Marie d'Agoult, writing under the pseudonym of Daniel Stern, played a central role in the 1840s and 1850s as art critic and social historian. George Sand's vision of an ideal society produced a long series of novels that counteract the bleaker realism of Balzac and Champfleury. The imaginations of generations of French people were indelibly stamped by their childhood reading of Mme de Ségur's children's books, published in Hachette's series, *La Bibliothèque rose.* Juliette Adam, as a result of her role as editor of the *Nouvelle Revue,* exerted considerable political and literary influence in the Third Republic, while Judith Gautier, through her support of Wagner's music and her highly romanticized novels set in India and China, opened up a larger world to a France that had turned inward after the defeat of the Franco-Prussian war. In addition to these prominent and successful women writers, there are also a large number of women who wrote clandestinely, hiding behind pseudonyms, publishing anonymously, or ghost-writing for men. Marie d'Agoult frequently served as ghost-writer for Liszt. Others, like Augusta Holmès, the greatly talented musician, who wrote the libretti for her own operas, fell into obscurity after death, when personal charisma could no longer outweigh the calumnies of envy and the outrage of prudery. Women were writing biographies, as well as imaginative educational material, such as Mme J. Macé's *L'Arithmétique de grand-papa* [Grandpa's Arithmetic Book] and her *Soirées de ma tante Rosy* [Evenings with my Aunt Rosy]. Félicie de Choiseul-Meuse is just one of those who produced erotica, while others devoted themselves to spiritual writings and feminist polemics.

As this brief list suggests, it is always useful, in considering the women writers of this period, to set them in a broader cultural context, and especially to see them responding to other artistic movements of the time. While a few of them, such as the diarist and letter-writer, Eugénie de Guérin, lived lives isolated from the cultural existence of their age, most of them, like their male counterparts, drew sustenance from the social possibilities of such large cities as Paris or Lyons, or maintained an active correspondence with friends to keep in touch with the cultural life of the cities. Several, like George Sand, Flora Tristan and Suzanne Voilquin, traveled widely, and wrote voluminously about their travels. Germaine de Staël and Juliette Adam, to mention but two, were at least potentially powerful political figures, whose thinking and influence shaped the future of France. The image of the women writers we inherit from Balzac's novels or Daumier's cartoons, though witty, is inevitably mis-leading. What this chapter will attempt is an exploration of an, admit-tedly limited, but representative sample of these women, with the aim of revealing their complexity, their gifts and their legacies less as women than as writers.

Women's ability to speak publicly and gain a wide audience was closely dependent on education, and it was really with the installation of the Third Republic (1870–1940) and its belief in the liberating power of the ability to read that women gradually regained some of the influence they had exerted in the preceding century. This is not to imply that edu-cation was not on the political agenda during the intervening years. Earlier educational reforms opened more opportunities to boys from poorer families, but they were less able to assist girls. Guizot's law of 1833 obliged every commune to maintain a public school, but it did not mandate that such education be either free or compulsory, and no sep-arate provision was made for girls. In 1850 Falloux's law re-enacted that of Guizot, going beyond it in that the new law forced communes of more than 800 inhabitants to provide separate schools for girls. But it is only when education was made obligatory, free and secular with Ferry's law of 1882 that illiteracy levels in women began to fall substantially. For all that, even educated women were to remain at a considerable disadvan-tage for many years.

The social changes that mark the nineteenth century and that led to the increasing dominance of the bourgeoisie and the growing literacy and leverage of the working classes also inevitably affected the position of women. Moreover, the increasing power of the press, the prolifera-tion of newspapers and periodicals once advertising had been intro-duced in the 1830s, and the surge in the numbers of printed books and pamphlets gave women a much broader audience and a much wider array of venues through which their views could be made known. One of the areas in which they were most prolific, because they were not restricted by so many laws, was that of journalism.[3] Feminist periodicals such as the *Athénee des Dames* (1808), edited by Sophie de Renneville, chal-lenged phallocratic images of society and provided women with a forum for alternative visions. Later in the century, the more working-class *Tribune des femmes* (1832–4), under the leadership of Suzanne Voilquin, the *Journal des femmes* (1832) and the *Gazette des femmes* (1836–8) all gave opportunities to women who might otherwise have found no outlet for their convictions and talents. The second half of the century saw a rapid growth in the number of periodicals in general, and of feminist publications in particular, notably the *Droit des femmes* which ran from 1869 to 1891, and *La Citoyenne* of 1881 which espoused the cause of women's suffrage. Among female journalists fighting for the poor and oppressed is the prolific writer Séverine, whose legal name was Caroline Rémy (1855–1929). For many years she worked alongside the radical thinker and writer Jules Vallès. When Vallès died, she took over direction of the paper he had founded and on which both had worked, *Le Cri du peuple*. Her novel, *Line*, a study of a little girl's gradual awareness of the meaning of her position as female, is somewhat sentimental and conventional, although its psychological insights and its quick-fire journalistic style are undeniably appealing.

While journalism thus offered many women the possibility of finding a voice, for others travelogues were a more acceptable vehicle for self-expression. Whether they accompanied husbands or traveled alone, visited other European countries or explored further afield, whether they perceived the foreigners whose lands they visited as barbarians or realized that to the foreigners they themselves were, in Flora Tristan's expression, the pariahs, they seem to have responded to a growing hunger for the exotic and for adventure among their own compatriots of either sex. While such writing has until very recently been rejected as popular and non-literary, its discovery by scholars exploring the interrelationship of gender and colonialism suggests that in many cases it offers more than such a derogatory classification might suggest. Indeed, as Bénédicte Monicat argues so forcefully, 'le récit de voyage est peut-être l'espace du discours où le 'féminin' s'inscrit de la manière la plus complexe dans le genre littéraire.' ['within literary genres, the traveler's tale is perhaps the space in which 'feminine' discourse inscribes itself in its most complex form'].[4] Travel writings, most importantly, allow for an exploration of the self against the background of an exploration of the other in ways that prefigure the psychological explorations of the twentieth century. They were, in addition, highly readable. The dangers encountered by Mme de Saint-Amant in her voyage to California (*Voyage en Californie*, 1851), or by Mme Langlot-Dufresnoye as she and her husband sought diamonds along the Amazon (*Quinze ans au Brésil,*

[Fifteen Years in Brazil], 1861) are recounted with a sense of the dramatic and a conviction of the narrative value of what was being told that many novelists would envy. Yet, as feminist critics have noted, such writers found themselves in a double-bind: where it was essential to the male-adventurer to present himself, with however much false modesty, as exceptional in his bravery and endurance, women struggled to avoid the tag of adventurer because of the sexual slurs they would incur. Nevertheless, by conforming to certain norms and presenting themselves as victimized and threatened by the exotic world they had discovered, they were able to suggest images of female power and strength in the face of such dangers and suffering. Among the many women who wrote such works were Cristina Belgiojoso, who related her travels to Asia Minor and Syria, that 'curieuse infatigable' ['indefatigably curious woman'],[5] Olympe Audouard (1830–90), whose travels took her to the Middle East, Russia and North America, Suzanne Voilquin, whose autobiography includes a section on her travels in Egypt as part of a utopian colony, and Carla Serena, who recounted her travels to Persia (1881).

Whether seen in relation to their compatriots or in contrast to those whose countries they explored, what unites many of these women writers is the emphasis placed on the image of the self, the discovery of the individual's own nature and needs, and the ways in which the individual can alter society to fulfil that nature and those needs. But they are frequently united, too, by a subtext that reveals how difficult it was for women to see themselves as men's equals in an age consistently given to decrying their talents, debasing their contributions, and delimiting their sphere. Nevertheless, throughout the century women reacted vociferously to shifts in laws and mores that affected their status.

The repressive nature of the Napoleonic code, for instance, was attacked with force and passion by the working-class feminist, Claire Démar (1800–33) in her *Appel d'une femme au peuple sur l'affranchissement de la femme* [A Woman's Appeal to the Nation] of 1833, while women inspired by the utopian Saint-Simonian movement used the journal, *La Tribune des femmes*, to voice their convictions and their growing anger with the discrepancy between the movement's stated support for women and its domination by men. Suzanne Voilquin (1801–77), who joined the self-styled utopian Enfantin's expedition to Egypt, gives expression to the hypocrisy and double standards revealed by Saint-Simonian men in her racy autobiography, *Souvenirs d'une fille du peuple* [Memoirs of a Daughter of the People] (1866). Her sharpest criticism, all the more powerful for its understatement, occurs when she recounts how, as members of

Enfantin's Saint-Simonians, Suzanne and her husband were encouraged to confess past errors to Enfantin himself. In her husband's presence, she reveals an earlier rape she had suffered:

Ces messieurs, à travers mes paroles entrecoupées, purent à peine comprendre la chute, mais non ce qui l'expliquait, et, j'ose le dire, l'excusait complètement. Voilquin se jeta en pleurant dans les bras du Père [Enfantin], mais, dans ces premiers moments, aucun des deux ne me tendit la main! . . . Cette inique répartition de la justice mâle m'arrêta mes larmes. (p. 115)

Those gentlemen could barely understand, through my broken words, the fact of my fall and were quite unable to comprehend what explained it and I make bold to say completely excused it. Voilquin threw himself in tears into the arms of the Father [Enfantin], but, in these first moments, neither of the two held out his hand to me! . . . That unjust division of male justice brought an end to my tears.

Elsewhere she refers to this sudden flash of insight into patriarchy as 'cette minute d'*expansion* ou plutot d'*explosion*' ['that moment of *expansion* or rather of *explosion*'] (p. 107). Typical of feminist writers in the 1830s and 1840s who shared that sense of explosive outrage is Flora Tristan (1803–44) whose *Pérégrinations d'une paria* (*Peregrinations of a Pariah*) (1838) and *Promenades dans Londres* (*Flora Tristan's London Journal*) (1840) chart the appalling conditions of women in Peru and England respectively and draw on these arguments to make an urgent plea for the importance of female emancipation. Her vast theoretical work, *L'Union ouvrière* (*The Workers' Union*) (1843), examines the ways in which she believed the working class needed to organize itself to gain equality with the bourgeoisie and the rich.

If the decades leading up to 1848 saw a gradual rise in support for women's emancipation, the failure of the Revolution of 1848, and the loss of many utopian hopes, ushered in a particularly difficult time for women. While the Saint-Simonians and such Fourierists as Pierre Leroux had at least paid lip service to the right of women to enjoy equal opportunities in the work place, the Second Empire (1852–70) was marked more by the openly anti-feminist thinking of such phallocrats as Proudhon, who limited women to two spheres, that of the housewife and that of the courtesan, and Michelet, who presented women, more insidiously, as inherently suffering and feeble. Nevertheless, women continued to argue their cause with force and conviction. Jenny d'Héricourt published *La Femme affranchie* [The Enfranchised Woman] in 1860, and Léodile Champseix (1824–1900), writing under the pseudonym André Léo, attacked Proudhonism in *Les Femmes et les mœurs* [Women and

Customs] of 1869, while the first woman to successfully complete an
education and be granted the baccalauréat in France, Julie-Victoire
Daubié (1824–74), wrote prolifically on questions concerning working
women. Daubié's 1862 study, *Du Progrès dans l'enseignement primaire* [On
Progress in Primary Teaching], argued for equal treatment of both girl
students and women teachers, while in 1871 she published ten brochures
collectively entitled *L'Emancipation de la femme* [Female Emancipation],
advocating female suffrage. Daubié believed that the right to vote should
be earned on grounds, not of gender, but of merit. She also wrote for
the feminist journal *Le Droit des femmes*, and its later avatar, *L'Avenir des
femmes*. Her major work, however, is the two volume study *La Femme
pauvre au XIXᵉ siècle* [Poor Women in the Nineteenth Century], published
between 1866 and 1869. This intensively researched survey of the situation of women who work for a living is written with amazing passion and
constitutes not merely a powerful feminist argument, but also a rich
source of information for social historians. Focusing on working women,
she seeks above all economic emancipation, which she sees as the key not
merely to personal happiness but to the well-being of the entire nation.

The way in which Daubié's powerful contribution to the feminist
debate was for so long ignored bears eloquent witness to the frequently
noted fact that for arguments in favour of feminism to attract attention,
they had to be proffered by men. Among those feminists writing at the
end of the century, Louise Michel (1830–1905), stands out for her ardent
republican views and her impassioned espousal of political causes.
Closely associated with the Commune, a revolutionary regime that controlled Paris from 18 March to 28 May 1871, she was a founder member
of the *Association pour le droit des femmes,* and after the repression of the
Commune turned, like many of her contemporaries, to anarchism. Her
memoirs and novels all bear poignant witness to her feminist convictions. These final decades of the century were marked equally by
growing misogyny and by a series of conferences and congresses devoted
to furthering women's status and promoting women's rights.

Many of the women whose writing dominates the nineteenth century
were proficient in a range of different genres. To some extent this is
symptomatic of the age: Hugo above all epitomizes this desire to excel
in all forms, while both Balzac and Baudelaire longed to write successful plays, and Mallarmé devoted many hours to journalism. Such
flexibility was certainly one of the characteristics of Anne Louise
Germaine Necker (1766–1817). A highly intelligent, deeply passionate
woman, she married the Swedish ambassador to Paris, Baron Staël-

Holstein, in 1785, and published under the name of Mme de Staël although the marriage lasted only a few years. She grew up in the political and intellectual environment that surrounded her parents, the brilliant financier Jacques Necker and his highly cerebral wife, Suzanne. Under the influence of this environment she developed a deep conviction of liberalism and a profound understanding of the mechanisms of modern society. Her character, Delphine, as described by her lover in the following passage, reflects many of Mme de Staël's own beliefs:

Vous aimez la liberté par un sentiment généreux, romanesque même pour ainsi dire, puisqu'il se rapporte à des institutions politiques. Votre imagination a décoré ces institutions de tous les souvenirs historiques qui peuvent exciter l'enthousiasme. Vous aimez la liberté, comme la poësie, comme la religion, comme tout ce qui peut ennoblir et exalter l'humanité: et les idées que l'on croit devoir être étrangères aux femmes, se concilient parfaitement avec votre aimable nature, et semblent, quand vous les développez, intimement unies à la fierté et à la délicatesse de votre âme. (*Delphine,* p. 543)

You love liberty through a generous emotion, one might even say a highly romantic emotion, because it is linked to political institutions. Your imagination has decorated those institutions with all the historical memories that can arouse enthusiasm. You love freedom as you love poetry, religion, everything that can ennoble and exalt humanity: and ideas that are generally held to be alien to women find a perfect harmony with your kindly nature, and seem when you develop them to be intimately connected to the pride and delicacy of your soul.

Mme de Staël's views, and her ability to express them, made her a formidable opponent to Napoleon, who on several occasions responded by banishing her from his capital. Thrice exiled from Paris, she settled in Coppet, Switzerland, where her salon gathered many of the influential and original thinkers of the time. In 1810 Napoleon pursued her even in Switzerland and she traveled to England through Moscow, St Petersburg and Stockholm.

Madame de Staël is one of the founding figures both of modern historiography and of modern liberal political thought, one of the first to envisage a united Europe and to understand the value of credit in the contemporary world. That would be enough to establish any man's reputation, but Mme de Staël also made considerable contributions to the history of literary criticism and to the field of comparative studies. Her theoretical writing played a central role in introducing the ideas of German and English Romanticism to the French reading public, and she also suggested important links between literature and the society in which it is produced, in *De la littérature considérée dans ses rapports avec les institutions sociales* [*On Literature Considered in its Relationship to Social Institutions*]. In addition, she is the author of two psychologically penetrating novels, whose central characters explore the predicament of sensitive and intelligent women in post-Revolutionary France.

Delphine, which Mme de Staël published in 1802, is in many ways the practical test of theories she had expressed from a very early age. An essay on fiction appeared in 1795, while her exploration of the emotions, *De l'influence des passions* (*On the Influence of the Passions*), dates from 1796, and her *De la littérature*, published in 1800, gathers together political and literary preoccupations in ways that prepare the ground for her first extended novel. She was also able to draw on experience gained in writing her short novel, *Zulma*, and three tales, published under the collective title of *Morceaux détachés* [Unconnected Pieces] in 1795. An epistolary novel, *Delphine* draws on a long eighteenth-century tradition of such works, not only in France and Germany, with Rousseau's *La Nouvelle Héloïse* and Goethe's *Die Leiden des jungen Werthers* [The Sufferings of Young Werther], but also in England, with Fanny Burney's *Evelina* and Richardson's *Clarissa*. While the form was to fall out of favour in nineteenth-century France, it does offer a writer as gifted as Mme de Staël numerous possibilities to experiment with narrative voice and time. Moreover, it allowed her to create a heroine whose sensitivity, enthusiasm, unshakeable loyalty to friends and resolute belief in the value of freedom make her not only very likeable but also very convincing. Based in part on the character of Mme de Staël herself, Delphine is at once extremely vulnerable and yet possessed of an inner strength that society cannot corrupt.

There is in Mme de Staël a strong desire to inform, instruct and teach. Her preface to *Delphine* insists on her belief that the circumstances of our existence are too fleeting to teach us as much about lasting truths as 'fictions fondées sur ces vérités' ['fictions anchored in these truths'] (p. 82). In this she reveals herself very close in spirit to the great educational reformers of the Revolution. But she is also very much a product of her time in the importance placed throughout the novel on the value of liberty and the emphasis on the individual. As this suggests, *Delphine* is of course above all a forerunner of French Romanticism, and its central character sets the patterns for many subsequent heroines, especially, perhaps, those of Stendhal. 'La bonté, la généreuse bonté' ['goodness, generous goodness'] (p. 217) is, as she herself claims, 'le culte de ma vie' ['the cult of my life'], one to which she will sacrifice the deepest love.

Psychological insights, often expressed in the form of aphorisms, abound in this generous novel: 'J'ai souvent remarqué que c'est par ses défauts que l'on gouverne ceux dont on est aimé' ['I have often noticed that it is by their weaknesses that one rules those who love us'] (p. 94). Fascinated in her theoretical writing by the function of the imagination, a theme that was to become increasingly important over the next fifty years or so, she continues her thinking on this aspect of the mind in the novel: 'Les peines d'imagination' ['The suffering of the imagination'], one of Delphine's correspondents affirms, 'dépendent presqu'entière-ment des circonstances qui nous les retracent; elles s'effacent d'elles-mêmes, lorsque l'on ne voit ni n'entend rien qui en réveille le souvenir, mais leur puissance devient terrible et profonde quand l'esprit est forcé de combattre à chaque instant contre des impressions nouvelles' ['depend almost exclusively on the circumstances that depict them for us; they fade away of their own accord, when we neither see nor hear anything that awakens the memory of them, but their power becomes terrible and deep when the mind is forced at every instant to fight against new impressions'] (p. 119).

For all the richness and suggestion of Mme de Staël's *Delphine*, an ade-quate reading of it demands that a modern reader set aside contempo-rary conceptions of the novel form. Even Balzac's baggier monsters seem masterpieces of concision and careful construction in comparison with a work in which the primary aim is far less narration than psycho-logical and philosophical speculation. The second half of the novel is above all concerned with manipulating private emotions and exploring the intermittences of the human heart with a minuteness and intricacy that ultimately suggests not so much any possibility of lived experience, however transmuted, as a laboratory experiment in which emotions are isolated and observed *in vitro*. Given the social opprobrium associated with divorce, illustrated clearly in the novel, the tragic trap is irrevocably sprung from the moment Léonce, despite his love for Delphine, marries Mathilde: the rest of the novel can only record the distress of the two lovers, without offering even the glimmer of ultimate hope. While this situation precludes any narrative interest, it does allow Mme de Staël to focus exclusively on the present moment and to concentrate on what will remain throughout her life her central philosophical preoccupations: the pursuit of happiness, the power of the passions, and the conflicting demands of society and of the generous heart.

Similar preoccupations are explored both in her second novel, *Corinne*, and in a more theoretical mode in her study, *De l'Allemagne* (*On Germany*), which privileges feeling over form, imagination over reason, and north-ern mysticism over southern paganism. This analysis, which occupies a central position in the development of French Romanticism, revealed to French readers the greater writers of the German tradition, and was to have a profound influence on French thinking. Its persuasiveness was such that, in 1810, when it had just been published, Napoleon ordered the pulping of *De L'Allemagne*. She republished it in 1813, and revised it several times.

Adélaïde de Souza (1761–1836), who was exiled as a result of the 1789 Revolution, published her first novel, *Adèle de Sénange*, in London in 1794. *Emilie et Alphonse* which appeared five years later continues the theme of unhappy marriages inflicted on young men and women by a rapacious and insensitive older generation. Written in the form of letters, this novel reveals a fine degree of stylistic variety, with Emilie's letters marked by the sensitivity and effusions of late eighteenth-century emotionalism, her mother's revealing a far more severe practicality marred by snobbery, and those of the would-be seducer the Chevalier de Fresque being crisply calculating. While Alphonse is seen from the outside, as a suffering Byronic hero, for most of the novel, he relates his story to Emilie, who retells it through letters, a clumsy narrative device that nevertheless adds to the gothic nature of the novel. The conclusion is wonderfully melodramatic, typical of the kinds of novels read with such fervour by Jane Austen's heroine Catherine Morland in *Northanger Abbey*. Souza's novels place few intellectual demands on their readers, but they do reflect the disarray of an aristocracy in which the expectations of privilege are no longer underpinned by any sense of self-sacrifice to name or country, and in which the growing force of Romanticism has released in both men and women an overpowering egocentrism.

In 1823 and 1825 there appeared two short novels, *Ourika* and *Edouard*, written by Claire de Duras (1778–1828). Each explores, with considerable psychological finesse, the situation of an individual whose suffering arises from something beyond his or her control. Ourika is a black woman, who has been brought up in an upper-class family in France, and suddenly becomes aware that her colour will forever bar her from the happiness of the kind of marriage a white woman of her station could achieve. Edouard is a talented young man who falls in love with a young woman who belongs to a higher social class: his passionate love, expressed in astonishingly physical terms, leads to their mutual destruction. Both stories have considerable charm in the way in which they are presented, and each is remarkable for its insight into suffering individuals, yet they may well strike modern readers as somewhat thin, with their single focus on the central character or pair and their lack of secondary themes, characters and intrigues. Each finds a slightly contrived way of reporting a first-person narrative through a second narrator, but each nevertheless manages to offer singularly profound psychological observations.

Like so many women of this period, Delphine de Girardin (1804–55) explored many literary genres, becoming well known in her lifetime for her journalistic writing. Her husband Emile owned the highly influential daily, *La Presse*, in which Delphine frequently published chronicles entitled *Lettres parisiennes* [Parisian Letters], using the pseudonym of vicomte de Launay. In addition to short stories, a collection of which she published under the title *La Canne de M. Balzac* [M Balzac's Walking Stick], she produced two volumes of elegiac poetry, *Essais poétiques* [Poetical Essays] and *Nouveaux Essais poétiques* [New Poetical Essays]. Inspired by Ossian, Chateaubriand and Russian legends, these poems are typical of early French Romanticism, both thematically, in their depictions of natural beauty and their spiritual longing, and technically, in their frequent use of standard alexandrines and rhyming couplets, and in their privileging of expansive rhetoric over any kind of energetic inspiration. Delphine de Girardin is also remembered for her plays, especially, perhaps, *Lady Tartuffe*, a lively if somewhat conventional and certainly contrived comedy that hinges on a young woman being (briefly) condemned for caressing a young man. Her innocence is accepted when she explains that she caressed him to save him from the attacks of the family guard dog.

While the early years of the century thus saw women experimenting in various prose genres, it was also marked by the rise of several women whose main vehicle was poetry. The finest woman poet of the nineteenth century is arguably Marceline Desbordes-Valmore (1785–1859). Her writing was admired by literary figures throughout the nineteenth century, but she suffered through the imposition of the misogynistic canon in the first seventy years or so of the twentieth century. Over the last two decades she has been rediscovered and her works have begun to receive the attention they deserve. For most of her life she supported herself and her family by acting and by her writing, living on the borderline of poverty and revealing considerable understanding and sympathy for the oppressed. In addition to *Elégies et Romances* of 1818, a collection now acknowledged as inaugurating the Romantic period of French literature, her best collections are *Les Pleurs* (1833), *Pauvres Fleurs* [Poor Flowers] (1839) and *Bouquets et Prières* [Bouquets and Prayers] (1843). While she shares some of the themes explored by Romantic poets

– the love of nature, the value of individual experience, and the suffering of the unhappy lover – she avoids many of the clichés, thematic and linguistic, that dogged many Romantic poets, and also introduces themes that draw strongly on her experience as a woman and mother. She writes intensely of maternal love, but she also explores with remarkable openness and power the emotions of a woman abandoned by the man she loves. Again it is symptomatic of the prevailing mores that while nineteenth-century male poets abandoned by a lover almost universally place the blame on the woman, Marceline Desbordes-Valmore's female voice is far more likely to believe herself guilty of a fault she feels she must unwittingly have committed. Her poetry has a spontaneity and a freedom that few of her male contemporaries managed to achieve, and while Baudelaire may dismiss this ability as mere insouciance, it gives her a particularly important position in the growing experimentation with poetic form that develops through the course of the century. In addition to poetry, she also wrote short stories, and produced one of the century's few studies of a woman artist in her novel *L'Atelier d'un peintre* [A Painter's Studio] (1833). Although this work ultimately fails to rise above the humdrum because of its author's apparent desire to remain within the confines of the 'artist novel', while still making her female protagonist place love above artistic ambition, it nevertheless reveals the enormous difficulties set in the path of women who sought careers outside the family.

A poet roughly contemporaneous with Marceline Desbordes-Valmore, and greatly enthused by the Romantic movement, Aimable Tastu (1795–1885) exploits a wide variety of poetic forms and explores many varied themes in her beautifully produced collection, *Poésies* (1826). Poems in praise of industry, love, and the beauties of nature vie with those exploring politics or offering transpositions of works of art in this diverse collection, which attracted the praise of Sainte-Beuve. Like Marceline Desbordes-Valmore, she lamented her lack of formal training, and on several occasions makes the art of poetry the central subject of her poems.

Among the women poets active in the first half of the century, the precociously intelligent Elisa Mercœur (1808–35) who published her first volume of poetry at the age of sixteen, offers a stark contrast to the spontaneity of Desbordes-Valmore and Tastu, with poetry that tends to preciosity and a somewhat awkward display of erudition. Her collected works, *Œuvres complètes*, published posthumously in 1843, includes a tragedy and essays as well as her poetry. Louise Colet also published several volumes of poetry, and received prizes from the Académie française for four of her poems. Her first collection appeared in 1836 with the title *Les Fleurs du midi* [The Flowers of the South], and suggests a fund of talent that could have been harnessed had she not given way to the love of abstract and rather shallow philosophizing that characterizes her 1846 volume, *Les Chants des vaincus* [The Songs of the Vanquished]. Louise Ackermann (1813–90) illustrates with particular clarity the difficulties often placed in the way of women with poetic gifts. Her autobiography, *Ma Vie* [My Life], which reveals the intoxicating joy she found as a child in reading, and her pleasure at writing poetry from a very early age, also insists that she never mentioned her poetry to her husband, fearing that to do so would be to lose his esteem (*Œuvres complètes*, xv–xvi). She began publishing her poetry only after his death, producing her *Poésies philoso-phiques* [Philosophical Poems] in 1871. Her writing reveals the value placed on formal considerations and the Hellenistic inspiration that marks the Parnassian poets. She was, however, deeply influenced by Darwinian theories and saw science as one of the great sources of poetic inspiration, writing one poem, for instance, to the comet of 1861.

As if in an attempt to give herself, and her poems, greater authority, several of Louise Ackermann's poems are dedicated to a woman who refused to be cowed by current scorn at women writers. Marie de Flavigny, comtesse d'Agoult (1805–76), is yet another writer whose prolific output covers many genres and offers a revealing series of reflections of contemporary social and political life. Her *Essai sur la liberté* [Essay on Freedom] (1847) and *Esquisses morales* [Moral Sketches] (1849) both argue for the emancipation and education of women. Her novella, *Valentia*, which hovers uneasily between male-view eroticism and feminist plea, was first published in *La Presse* in 1847. It demonstrates the difficulty d'Agoult, and not only she, experienced in pitching her writing for a broader reading public. Many women, either using their own names or writing under a pseudonym (sometimes masculine, as was the case of Marie d'Agoult herself when she wrote art criticism for *La Presse* under the name Daniel Stern, sometimes aristocratic or fanciful), made use of the vogue for serialized novels, which had first been introduced into the French daily newspapers in the 1830s, to enter into a publishing world which was often hostile to them. Writing for this form demanded rapid adventures, little psychological development, and an accessible style. *Valentia* draws on countless Romantic clichés, continues the attack on current concepts of marriage launched by George Sand, and carries vague echoes of the contemporary fascination with lesbianism revealed by such writers as Gautier, Baudelaire and Balzac. Disentangling the complex threads of this tale, the reader is nonetheless struck by d'Agoult's evident determination to impose on those readers for whom such ideas were anathema a sense of pity for young women commodified by marriage, a vision of the differences between male and female friendships and concepts of loyalty, and a linking of political revolt and women's rebellion against the demands of patriarchy. Writing to support herself, d'Agoult could not afford to deny her audience's demands for titillation and melodrama, but she clearly also has her own agenda.

That agenda is more forcefully expressed in her confessional novel, *Nélida*, the title of which offers an anagram of part of her pen name, Daniel Stern. While in male-authored confessional novels, the heroine conveniently dies in order to force the hero into a clearer knowledge of his own flaws, this work allows the heroine to survive and instead kills off the erring male. The protagonist's discovery of her own freedom and her determined seizing of independence when she realizes the weaknesses of her lover makes this confessional novel quite different from the standard form of the sub-genre. Rich in episode and frequently entering into close psychological explorations not only of the central characters, as is the case with male-authored confessional novels, but of minor figures as well, *Nélida* also includes evocations of natural beauty and moments of sharply observed social behaviour. What it lacks in comparison with, say, *Adolphe*, is the ironic self-perception that marks the older narrator's presentation of his younger self. Yet such irony is a form of manipulation of the reader that d'Agoult avoids by her more open and naked pleas for the reader's goodwill.

A variation on the confessional novel is provided by Louise Colet (1810–76) who also explored a wide variety of genres, including poetry, children's literature, novels and polemical writing. Volatile and vindictive, she wrote a punchy and barely fictionalized account of her relationship with the poet Musset in a novel entitled *Lui*, which also contains an interpolated account of Musset's relationship with George Sand. Framing Musset's narrative in this way allows her to draw on the conventions of the confessional novel, but it also gives her the ability both to curtail his story, and to control our reading of it. While it offers some lively dialogue, this first-person novel is curiously lacking in irony or self-judgment: the frame narrator's physical and intellectual narcissism and her tendency to emotional blackmail, as well as the vindictive portrait of Flaubert that the novel includes, are in the end too heavy a freight for this rather flimsy vessel to carry.

The dominant female novelist of this period is, of course, George Sand (1804–76), who was born Aurore Dupin and whose love affairs and unconventional life style have frequently attracted more attention than her writing. As prodigiously energetic and as politically engaged as Mme de Staël, George Sand played an active role in the revolutionary movements leading up to 1848, wrote a twenty-volume autobiography, experimented with plays for both the conventional and the marionette theatres, and produced scores of novels, travelogues and polemical tracts. Her earlier novels, especially *Indiana*, *Lélia* and *Valentine*, examine the predicament of women locked into unhappy marriages, and deplore the abuse of female potential in a patriarchal society. Intensely Romantic in their intertwining of natural surroundings and inner feelings, and in their privileging of the self over concepts of state or class, they also tend towards the gothic in their sharp dichotomies of good and evil, love and hate, devotion and exploitation. Her liaison with the musician Chopin informed her love of music and inspired two long novels, *Consuelo* and its continuation *La Comtesse de Rudolstadt*, in which musical sensitivity combines with humanitarian and socialist yearnings to create works of considerable intensity and complexity.

George Sand's ability to find ways of discussing the political within a novelistic framework has few equals in the nineteenth century, and continued to inspire those of her works written after the collapse of the Second Republic and the attendant loss of socialist faith that she suffered. While they are sometimes summarily dismissed as 'pastoral' novels, her works produced in the immediate aftermath of the 1848 revolution and the collapse of utopian hopes are far richer than this derogatory tag implies. *La Petite Fadette*, for instance, offers a many-sided study of the development of the individual, through its three central characters, the boy twins and Fadette, who gradually agrees to abandon her tomboyish and independent ways to force her immediate society to adapt its images and expectations of invidual responsibility and behaviour. The novel's psychological insights into the effect on children of losing their mother, into female adolescence, and into the complex relationship of twins to each other and to their families make this both a pioneering study and one of considerable depth.

More complex and certainly more ambitious is the novel *Les Maîtres Sonneurs* (*The Master Pipers*), which George Sand wrote in a burst of energy between 31 December 1852 and 26 February 1853. Here she seizes on the possibilities of what Gide was to call that lawless genre, the novel, to capture the songs, traditions and ways of life that the industrial revolution was threatening to destroy forever. These form the decor of a novel whose main themes are intimately connected to George Sand's thinking about the nature of revolution and the apparent impossibility of bringing about social change except through violence, that in turn created its own victims. *Les Maîtres Sonneurs* is also an exploration of the nature of the gifted individual, in this case a young musician, who, while scarcely capable of speech until he finds a way to express himself through playing first the flute and then the bagpipes, eventually succeeds in giving form to the most complex and intense passions. In true Romantic fashion, his gift is revealed to be ultimately destructive, in a society that greedily attempts to monopolize even art and music, and in which genius is always intrinsically suspect. Of equal interest is her exploration of maternal love, and her insistence on the fact that learning to love a child may demand acts of abnegation and will, rather than being a natural instinct common to all women. Most radical is the novel's linguistic experimentation, in the way George Sand allows her first-person narrator to express himself in a diction that draws strongly on the syntax and lexicon of the local peasants. A novel of exploration in which the characters discover music, love, nature, language and above all their own selves, and which includes analyses of childhood and old age, erotic love and friendship, violence and self-control, *Les Maîtres Sonneurs* is also a political novel which allows George Sand to offer a solution to the dilemma posed by 1848. Here the two regions in central France, the Bourbonnais, with its independence, rootlessness, violence and creativity, and the Berri, with its placidity, timidity, good sense and love of comfort, come together to create a potentially perfect blend through the marriages of the central characters.[6]

George Sand also drew on, exploited, and refined a typically 'women's' genre, that of the autobiography. Her *Histoire de ma vie* (*The Story of my Life*) blends historical exploration, psychological analysis, and social fresco to create a multi-volumed, many facetted image of French society in the nineteenth century. This autobiography is particularly fine in its presentation of childhood and its insistence on the child's awareness of adult preoccupations from an early stage. Her child's eye view of Napoleon's Spanish campaign, and later of the retreat from Russia, is both deeply convincing and highly moving in its exploration of the ways in which the child's mind builds monuments of extraordinary coherence from the disparate fragments of information it receives. Equally fascinating for the light it sheds on French Romanticism is the child's response to place and to nature.

Autobiography, in fact, and by this I mean the exploration of the individual's personal formation rather than memoirs, which analyse the social world in which the writer found herself, increasingly became the domain of women writers during this period, and attracted writers from the poorest classes as well as the leisured and wealthy.[7] It provided several women with the possibility of exploring the conflicting forces and tensions at work on them, in a society in which women's abilities were so consistently rejected. Athénaïs Michelet, for example – the daughter of an American mother and a French father – presents herself in *Mémoires d'une enfant* [A Little Girl's Memoirs] (1866) as longing, from early childhood, to reconcile her mother's puritanism and the warmth of Provence, in which she grows up. She is equally eager to win her mother's affection despite the resultant loss of individuality and to keep her father's admiration for her mind despite his derogatory remarks about her appearance. The sense of revolt this triggers is abruptly broken when she overhears a discussion between two village girls, suggesting that the mother's deep happiness with her two older children was destroyed by the arrival of Athénaïs herself. Her response is one of immediate apology: 'J'aurais volontiers demandé pardon de ma naissance. Mon assurance en fut diminuée. Je fus et je restais timide' ['I would willingly have asked for forgiveness for having been born. My self-assurance was diminished by this realization. I became shy and remained so'] (p. 62). That same sense of apology for existing also dominates her reaction to her father, with whom she nevertheless claims affinities of character and intelligence: 'Toute parole de lui était article de foi' ['Everything he said became an article of faith for me']. The emotions her father awakens in her are presented as being extremely intense: hardly surprising, then, that at the age of puberty her body rebels against all this mental submission and she suffers long months of fever, only brought to an end, at least in the autobiographical presentation, by the deaths of her brother and father. This is one of the most disturbing of childhood recollections of revolt and submission, and its structures, language and suggestions are rich in reverberations.

As autobiography flourished in the nineteenth century, partly under the influence of such eighteenth-century autobiographers as Rousseau and partly under the emphasis placed by the Romantic movement on the value of the individual and particularly on the importance of childhood, so also did writing for children. In part the surge in works written for children, and particularly the shift away from moralistic and didactic works to books that aimed at encouraging greater literacy through entertainment, was due to the foresight and energies of the publisher

Hetzel, who commissioned stories from such leading writers as George Sand and Alexandre Dumas for his periodical, *Le Nouveau Magasin des enfants*. But it also arose from the signing in 1855 of a contract between Mme de Ségur (1799–1874) and Hachette, whose collection of children's literature, *La Bibliothèque rose*, played a central role in the imaginations and memories of generations of French people. While it has become *de rigueur* to deplore Mme de Ségur's sadism, and while it is undeniable that her work reveals undercurrents of death and suffering, it is no doubt more accurate to focus on the liveliness of her children. Their fascination with the external world and all it entails offers a salty realism and an uncomplicated sense of humour that very few of her contemporaries were able to produce and that had immense appeal for her child and adult readers. Her depiction of Sophie, the character for which she is probably best known, reveals the complex elements of cruelty and pity, selfishness and altruism of childhood, and refuses the conventional gender demarcations of the time. Ségur's vast production presents a complex and vivid portrayal of French society during the Second Empire, and wittily reveals the changing perception of childhood during the course of a political age frequently seen as portentously serious.

If the desire and ability to explore several literary genres is thus characteristic of many of the women of the early years of the nineteenth century, it only rarely lead to lasting success in the theatre. Nevertheless women did succeed in getting their plays performed and published, especially if they had male supporters already associated with the theatre. Virginie Ancelot (1792–1875), whose husband was a now all-but-forgotten playwright, is typical in that she wrote not only novels and plays, but also memoirs, especially of the Paris salon over which she presided for forty years, from the 20s to the 60s. She wrote more than twenty plays, including *Marie et les trois époques* [Marie and the three ages] (1836), *Clémence* (1839), and *Les Honneurs et les mœurs* [Honours and Morals], first performed in 1840. This talented woman was also an artist, illustrating her own collected dramatic works, *Théâtre complet* (1848). More importantly, no doubt, she also made some of her female characters painters, giving them more active and intelligent roles than that provided by many of her male contemporaries.

While breaking into the theatre posed women particularly problems throughout a century which in any case produced few lasting dramatic works, they were able to flourish as writers of wonderfully evocative, intelligent and above all readable letters. Although this is not a genre that has always been placed among the classics of literature, good arguments have been made for reconsidering such classifications, and the wider reading public has long shown considerable enthusiasm for the often vivid illumination (and, no doubt, manipulation) of everyday life in the past that such writing offers. Hortense Allart (1801–79), also known for her largely autobiographical novel, *Les Enchantements de Prudence* [The Enchantments of Prudence] of 1872, and her apologia in favour of free love, *La Femme et la démocratie de notre temps* [Women and the Democracy of Our Times] (1836), was the author of a long, rich and witty series of letters to the critic Sainte-Beuve. After marrying in her 40s, a decision she amusingly examines by casting herself in the role of Britain's Queen Elizabeth deciding among her many lovers, she discovered that marriage was not her vocation and returned to the calmer pleasures of liberated spinsterhood. The passages in which she responds to Sainte-Beuve's protests against such a decision are striking for their lack of self-pity, their frankness and their rejection of the commonplaces of contemporary propriety. Dismissing marriage as a 'devil's error' she adds: 'Je suis charmée d'avoir su bien ce que c'est que le sort de la femme, j'en parlais et je n'étais pas mariée! C'est à présent que je le sais.' ['I am delighted to have really learnt what a woman's fate is, for I talked about it before and was not married! Now, I do know.'].[8] Pressed by Sainte-Beuve she adds:

J'ai cru que ce que la loi du mariage avait d'oppressif et mauvais n'était rien avec l'amour et les promesses d'un homme, mais le plus généreux, s'il est violent et jaloux, s'appuie de la loi dans son transport et dit à la femme: Je veux. . . . Vous autres hommes, vous ne saurez jamais ce que c'est. Il y a là oppression de la force et en définitive du bras. Aussi honneur à Marie, à Lélia, à toutes celles qui n'ont pu supporter le joug! J'aime assez le mari, je déteste le mariage. Ajax n'a rien compris, c'est le sort d'Ajax (p. 83).[9]

I believed what was oppressive in the marriage laws had nothing to do with a man's love and his promises, but the most generous of men, if he is violent and jealous, leans on the law in his rage and says to the woman 'I want'. . . . You men, you will never know what it is like. There is in all this the oppression of strength and, in the final analysis, all the oppression of the hand. So, all honour to Marie, to Lélia, to all those who were unable to support the yoke. I'm pretty fond of the husband, but I detest marriage. Ajax understood nothing, but that is Ajax's fate.

Few women, it must be confessed, were able to reveal with such apparently calm acceptance that their husbands had physically abused them.

The shift away from Romanticism, towards realism and its off-shoot naturalism, that marks much male-authored prose writing is less evident in women's writing. Those publishing in the second half of the century tend either to robustly imaginative tales, or to unbridled romantic adventure, or to a form of decadence that seems less cynical but also less consciously assumed than in the case of many male writers.

One of the most prolific of novelists working in the latter part of the century published over 70 novels under the pseudonym Henry Gréville, and certainly preferred imaginative entertainment to realism. Alice-Marie-Céleste Durand (1842–1902) was a highly talented pianist, for whom the composer Félicien David predicted a spectacular performing career. Durand, however, chose to devote herself to writing. Widely travelled, she spent fifteen years in Russia, and drew on her experiences for many of the novels, plays and journalistic articles she wrote. She contributed to the *Revue des deux mondes, Le Journal des débats, Figaro, Le Temps* and *Le Siècle*, all of which were highly esteemed periodicals. In addition, she wrote entertaining, witty and very popular romances, with central female characters more reminiscent of the plucky heroines of contemporary England or the spunky girls that appeared in so many American stories. *Dosia*, for instance, which spawned a sequel, *La Fille de Dosia* [Dosia's Daughter], was crowned by the French academy and went into 150 editions. Set in Russia, partly, no doubt, to provide a spice of exoticism, and partly to grant the heroine a freedom French bourgeois fathers might not like to allow their own daughters, this novel is an amusing study of a young tomboy gradually acquiring womanhood, while not entirely sacrificing the independence of mind and the spontaneity of behaviour that make her so charming. While there is a sense in which womanhood is defined in terms of what must be left behind, Dosia succeeds in reining in the excesses that make her ridiculous while retaining the unpredictability that renders her so seductive. There is a remarkable and surely significant gap between the image of young women that such women writers produced, and that found in most male-authored works: *Dosia* undeniably adds to our image of nineteenth-century models of female behaviour, and enhances our awareness of the imaginary universe accessible to many women of the time.

Equally unattracted by the bleaker side of realism, Judith Gautier (1845–1917), exploits several different genres for their potential to offer imaginative escape. The daughter of the dancer Ernesta Grisi and of the writer Théophile Gautier, she was an autobiographer, playwright, poet, critic and novelist. She was passionately interested in the music of Richard Wagner, who was passionately interested in her: *Parsifal*, which she translated into French, is said to have been inspired by her, and she was godmother to Wagner's son Siegfried. A great lover of the exotic in general and the Far East in particular, Judith Gautier learnt Chinese as a young woman, and wrote several novels set in China. Her novels (for example, *Le Dragon impérial* [The Imperial Dragon] (1869), *La Conquête du paradis* [The Conquest of Paradise] (1890) and *Mémoires d'un éléphant blanc* [Memoirs of a White Elephant] of 1893) frequently have exotic settings, such as China, India or Japan, and while her depiction of these countries has little to do with any geographical, political or social reality, it does offer a wonderfully imaginative creation of a world in which landscape, architecture, and human relationships body forth intense passions and especially sexual love. Some critics, even recently, have rejected them for their lack of realism but reading her novels gives us an unexpectedly sharp insight into the imaginations of women whose outer lives seem hidebound and dull, and suggests something of the exuberant dreamworld open to the housewives of the Second Empire and the Third Republic.

A poet and playwright as well as a novelist, she was an assiduous visitor to Leconte de Lisle's salon, and after his death dedicated to his memory a series of poems, *Les Rites divins*. He in turn admired and respected her writing, and his sonnet, 'L'Orient', appeared as the liminary poem to her novel *Iskender* when it was published in 1894. She and Pierre Loti collaborated in 1903–4 to write the play *La Fille du ciel* [Heaven's Daughter], which they created for Sarah Bernhardt, but which she declined. When their play was first performed in an English translation in New York, at the Century Theatre, on 12 October 1912, it was greeted with 'endless applause' and 'to escape the enthusiasm of the crowd M Pierre Loti had to leave the theatre by a back door'.[10]

Nevertheless, much of this production has been neglected in favour of her autobiography, *Le Collier des jours* [The Necklace of Days], which includes an evocative study of a rebellious childhood torn between the two very different cultures represented by her father and her mother. The triangular patterning of much of the autobiography, as Judith seeks to model herself, first on the world of ballet represented less by her mother than by her mother's cousin, the famous ballerina Carlotta Grisi, and then on the world of writing embodied by her father, gains much of its strength from frequent outbursts of revolt against either possibility. There is, of course, in all this the sense of the child's or indeed the adult's desperate attempt to assert her own individuality in the wake of famous parents. The later volumes of these memoirs provide a highly readable image of the intellectual and cultural life of the Third Republic.

Like Judith Gautier, Juliette Adam (1836–1936) is probably better known for her autobiographical writings than for her fiction. According to her highly romanticized autobiography, Juliette Adam experienced a tumultuous and highly politicized childhood, married disastrously at the age of sixteen, and in 1868, after her first husband's death, married the left-wing freethinker, Edmond Adam. In the 1860s her salons attracted such figures as Marie d'Agoult, Louis Blanc and Léon Gambetta. The Third Republic brought writers, actors, artists and musicians. Most importantly, Juliette Adam was the energetic and influential editor of the republican periodical, *La Nouvelle Revue*, which published essays by Bourget and Valéry, and, in serial form, novels by, among others, France, Vallès and Pierre Loti, the last of whom Juliette Adam always claimed to have launched from nothing. Although she did write feminist polemics, such as her attack on Proudhon's misogynistic views on women and marriage (*Idées antiproudhoniennes sur l'amour, la femme et le mariage* [Anti-Proudhonesque Ideas on Love, Women and Marriage]), most of her energies as a writer went into novels. *Païenne* [The Pagan Woman], for example, is an epistolary novel celebrating the joy of sensual pleasures and especially of erotic love. While it may strike modern readers as both arch and relentlessly cerebral, and its central female figure exhibits a cloying tendency to manipulate sexual stereotypes while demanding that she herself be judged on non-essentialist terms, it is nevertheless striking for its non-judgmental vision of sexual mores.

Juliette Adam is, however, more likely to be read as a memorialist, above all because of her close connection with leading figures in the republican movement. Her account of her early years, however romanticized, is fascinating for its politicization of childhood, and charming in its evocation of the little girl's passionate interest in learning. The later volumes of her autobiography evoke the struggles, preoccupations, and gossip of a particularly rich period in France's political history, that which saw the evolution of the Third Republic, the destructive tendencies of the Dreyfus affair, and the coming of war.

The misogyny which had become such a commonplace in the final decades of the century is to be found in the writings of several women. Taught to despise themselves and their gender by fathers who would have preferred sons, they often seem to have espoused phallocratic convictions, even while their works reveal the bitter unhappiness and repressed anger of such a position. Typical of these women is Rachilde. Born Marguerite Eymery (1860–1953), she dressed as a man, described herself as an *homme de lettres*, and her first novel, *Monsieur Vénus* (1889), explores the question of cross-dressing and gender roles in ways that were seen at the time as scandalous. Many of her works deal with eroticism, and particularly with what one might consider perverse sexual drives. *L'Animale* [The She-Animal], for instance, explores the sexual development of a young girl who finds her greatest pleasure in prowling the roofs of Paris by night, in the company of her tomcat, Lion, who is filled with such fury on seeing her make love to a man that he kills her. The novel is well constructed, beginning *in medias res* with Laure gazing out of the window at night while her lover sleeps, increasingly convinced that her life is closing in around her. This leads to a psychological exploration of her childhood, before turning to her solution of exploring the roofs. The metaphorical possibilities of these rooftop prowls are also well realized, with Laure constantly running the risk of plunging into abysses of despair, as she gazes at stars that are counterfeited by the fake and costume jewelry her working class admirer offers her. Rachilde certainly writes with power and muscle, uncompromising in her ferocious descriptions of human weakness, and forceful in her evocation of sexual longings. This power, together with her stylistic flexibility, is also revealed in her Breton novel, *La Tour d'amour* [The Tower of Love], written to some extent in dialect. The muscular evocation of the sea and the harshness of life on a lighthouse provides an intense background for the study of necrophilia that adds to the image of Rachilde's misogynistic self-loathing.

The final decades of the century saw several women who played a significant role in public and political life. Sibylle de Mirabeau (1849–1932), who published under the name Gyp, was a leading figure of the nationalist right. Through her satirical portrayals of political figures and central issues, her cartoons and her many novels, she left an undeniable imprint on the thinking of many of her contemporaries. A bigotted woman, she was determinedly independent as a thinker, whose right wing politics did not lead her to endorse the monarchist cause, despite efforts to encourage her to do so, and whose individualism nevertheless did not result in her espousing the beliefs of those feminists struggling to help other women express their own individualism. Fiercely anti-Semitic, she avoided the ponderousness of other writers who attacked the social and financial position of Jews in France, exploiting her undoubted ability to produce rapid-fire, witty dialogue and to create farcical situations which make her novels at once repulsive and highly comic. Of her many novels and countless journalistic articles, very few are likely to gain any permanent status, but she does symbolize the growing possibilities women enjoyed at the end of the century to move into domains that had previously been carefully guarded against them, and her writing will continue to be read for the acid light it sheds on the mentality of a large cross-section of French society during the Third Republic.

While Gyp was a product of the aristocracy of the post-Napoleonic age, Maria Deraismes (1828–94) bears all the hallmarks of the enlightened bourgeois opposition, anticlerical, Voltairian and republican. Her writing is largely polemical, highly rhetorical in nature, and dedicated to the aim of emancipating women as part of a much larger social reform. She determinedly placed the question of female suffrage at the centre of her political debate, editing and contributing to a range of feminist periodicals, the most important, perhaps, being *Le Droit des femmes* and *Le Républicain*. Energetic, indefatigably curious and open-minded, she was one of the most important feminist thinkers of the 1870s and 1880s. Her greatest contribution was probably the unshakable belief in the complete equality of men and women, linked to her conviction that the cause of women was also that of all oppressed people. Arguing that women should be judged by what they were, and not by what they had been made into, she insisted that freedom for women would be achieved through education and work. In many ways, her writing points forward with remarkable insight to the existentialist beliefs of Simone de Beauvoir: 'La femme est une personne, partant de là une force, une liberté. Or, on n'anéantit pas une force, une liberté. Comprimée d'un côté, elle rejaillit de l'autre: lui interdit-on la droite voie, elle prend le chemin de traverse; elle pouvait être favorable, elle devient pernicieuse'.[11] ['A woman is a person, and therefore a force, an aspect of liberty. Now, you cannot annihilate liberty. Crushed on one side, she will burst free on the other side; if you forbid her to take the path straight ahead, she will take a side-track; she could have been favourable, but now she becomes pernicious.']

While such writers chose polemics to argue their case, others turned to more conventional forms. Several women poets writing in the second half of the century achieved fame during their life times. Louisa Siéfert (1845–77) published her first volume of poetry, *Les Rayons perdus* [The Lost Rays] (1868) to great acclaim. Reminiscent in some ways of the writing of Marceline Desbordes-Valmore, her poems often focus on children, a subject her contemporaries may have found acceptable for a woman, and are likely to strike modern readers as sentimental in their unquestioning representation of childhood innocence and naïve in their acceptance of the stated values of patriarchy. Marie Dauguet (1860–1942), published her first volume of poetry, *La Naissance d'un poète* [Birth of a Poet], in 1897, and went on to produce two more collections, *A travers le voile* [Through the Veil] (1902) and *Par l'amour* [For the Sake of Love] (1904). Well-received by the critics, her poetry is largely inspired by nature and by love, and, while technically sophisticated, it recalls the late Romantic period far more than that of symbolism.

At least one woman poet achieved a lasting position as a poet among the proliferating schools of the end of the century. Marie Krysinska (1864–1908) claimed, with a fair degree of plausibility, that she had invented *vers libres*, a claim refuted by several of her male contemporaries, who argued that, far from revealing any invention, she simply showed her foreigner's inability to understand and command French prosody. Nevertheless, she published three volumes of poetry, *Rythmes pittoresques* [Picturesque Rhythms] (1890), *Joies errantes* [Wandering Joys] (1894) and *Intermèdes* [Intervals] (1904). Her writing has a determined modernism, ironic in its presentation of human relationships and unsentimental in its depiction of landscapes. Her laconic cynicism, together with the imaginative vision of poems that deal with nature, deserves to be better known.

What strikes the reader of women writers across this century is the sense of energy that they collectively convey. Whether writing educational tracts, feminist propaganda, the traditional genres of novel, theatre and poetry, or erotica, letters, diaries or autobiography, they succeeded, often against enormous odds, in side-stepping the restrictive forces of poor educational backgrounds, blinkered social mores and repressive publishing laws. Many of them managed to fulfil their duties as wives and mothers; some, like George Sand and the comtesse de Ségur, supported a large number of dependents, and nevertheless produced works of great variety. While many of them inevitably reveal a willingness to accept male society's condemnation of creative women and deploy a series of tactics aimed at winning readerly benevolence by calumniating their own sex, others show remarkable fortitude in rejecting such traps and temptations. Less divisible into schools and movements than their male counterparts, more varied in their interests and less predictable in their techniques, the women writers of the nineteenth century offer adventurous readers a wonderful range of abilities and themes, views and convictions. Above all, perhaps, it is only when their voice is fully reinstated into the period that we will begin to understand many of those ongoing conversations that give the nineteenth century its particular dynamism.

NOTES

1 See Gutwirth, *Twilight of the Goddesses.*
2 The Dreyfus affair refers to a political and social crisis surrounding the arrest and imprisonment of a French officer wrongly accused of transmitting military secrets to the Germans. See Patrick Hutton *et al.*, *Historical Dictionary of the Third Republic 1870–1940* (New York: Greenwood Press, 1986).
3 See Sullerot, *La presse féminine.*
4 Bénédicte Monicat, 'Discours féminins sur les harems', in *Correspondances: Studies in Literature, history, and the arts in nineteenth-century France*, ed. Keith Busby (Amsterdam: Rodopi, 1992), p. 139.
5 Audouard, *Les Mystères du sérail et des harems turcs*, p. 12.
6 See also the introduction to *The Master Pipers*, trans. R. Lloyd (Oxford University Press, 1994).
7 See, for instance, A. Bardin, *Angélina, une fille des champs* [Angelina, a daughter of the fields] (Paris: Bonne, 1956), J. Bouvier, *Mes mémoires*, A. Esquiros, 'Souvenirs d'enfance', BN cat, no. Ye676 (1849?)
8 *Lettres inédites à Sainte-Beuve*, p. 82. Further references appear in parenthesis in the text.
9 Marie is Marie d'Agoult; Lélia is George Sand's heroine in the novel of the same name.
10 Quoted in Richardson, *Judith Gautier*, p.182.
11 Deraismes, *Ce que veulent les femmes*, p. 83.

CHAPTER SEVEN

1900–1969: writing the void

Alex Hughes

For women in France, the first seven decades of the twentieth century were characterized by a combination of stasis and change, of tradition and transformation. If the late 1960s and the early to mid-1970s represented a revolutionary epoch, after and as a result of which the rights and lives of French women and the contours of the *condition féminine* would never be the same again, the preceding years of the century were significantly less marked by radical, gender-related socio-cultural change.

In the preface to her *Promenade femmilière: recherches sur l'écriture féminine* (1981), Irma Garcia argues that to disassociate women's writing from (women's) history is to disregard the particularly marked imbrication of female creativity and its socio-historical context. The discussion that follows here takes its cue from Garcia's sense of the way in which women's writing and its historical environment are connected. The particular focus of this chapter is a series of selected fictional texts published by Colette, Simone de Beauvoir, Violette Leduc, Christiane Rochefort and Monique Wittig. The intention is to examine the varied accounts of gendered evolution and experience offered in these texts, and to assess the extent to which modern French women's writing is marked by the socio-historical situation in which women in France found themselves at various points in the twentieth century. It is no more possible, in a single chapter, to cover this period in its entirety than it is to address the work of all of the women authors whose literary careers coincided with these years of the twentieth century. Consequently, this analysis will foreground two specific periods in modern French history: (i) the decade following World War I, and (ii) the years 1944–69. If discussion focuses on post-war history, and on the influence it exerted on French women's writing, this is because the aftermath of conflict brings with it social change, and, generally speaking, social evolution and shifts in gender ideology tend to go hand in hand.

The earliest years of the twentieth century have been classified as the *Belle Epoque* of French feminism.[1] This reflects the fact that by the time World War I broke out, French feminist activism pre- and post-1900 had helped to bring about legal changes relating to education, divorce and women's control of their financial affairs. It had given birth to a wide range of feminist congresses and newspapers (thirty-five publications came into being between 1875 and 1914), and seemed to be winning the campaign for female suffrage. Given the gains French feminists achieved prior to 1914, French society – and its legislature – might have opted, after the armistice of 1918, to sanction further gender-related reform. In fact, no such reform came about. Two factors help us to understand why, in post-1918, interwar France, women were not accorded a greater degree of civil liberty.

For one thing, the French women's movement – reformist rather than radical – had achieved relatively little by the eve of the Great War, and was also deeply divided (by tensions between bourgeois/suffragist and socialist feminists). These facts suggest that the *mouvement des femmes* in France stood only a limited chance of generating significant gender-related social change in the interwar period. Secondly, the Great War has been, somewhat mythically, viewed as the scene/source of a reconfiguration of social and sexual relations which enhanced French women's freedom; a freedom emblematized in the image of the *garçonne*, or sexually independent woman, which entered the French popular consciousness after the end of the First World War. Contemporary historians have argued, however, that because the '14–'18 conflict helped to consolidate traditional gender models and gave rise to a rearguard action against female emancipation brought about by perceived wartime changes in women's situation and the anxieties they provoked, it cannot be considered to have facilitated a lasting shift in gender orthodoxy.

The notion that, in France, the Great War failed to further the cause of women's independence is confirmed by various historical facts. First, while World War I ran its course, women in France certainly gained access to new sectors of the labour market, and assumed new financial and legal responsibilities. Once the war ended, however, and the Frenchmen who survived it came home, women workers were dismissed *en masse* from those traditionally male forms of employment to which they had been temporarily admitted, and, by 1926, represented a smaller proportion of the workforce than they had before 1914. Secondly, World War I halted the momentum of the pre-war women's suffrage campaign, and enabled the French Senate to delay and then finally, in 1922, to reject a bill sanctioning the women's vote which the more liberal *Chambre des députés* had passsed in 1919. Thirdly, the contribution made by war deaths to France's existing demographic problems encouraged the French government to legislate in 1920 and 1923 against contraception, abortion and the dissemination of information pertaining to anti-conceptional practices, thereby preventing France's *citoyennes* from easily controlling their fertility. Taken together, these facts suggest two things: (i) that in the 1920s, French women were faced with the threat of a forced 'redomestication' which militated against the relative liberty and higher public profile they had enjoyed during the hostilities, and (ii) that the socio-political ethos of post-1918 France favoured an anti-feminist reactionism. This was born in part out of the limited shifts in women's socio-sexual status, employment patterns and rights that the war engendered. Its manifestations included what has been termed a 'régression des droits féminins' ['a reversal of women's rights'], and an 'éloge de la ménagère promue reine' ['revalorization of the housewife'].[2] A symptom of the anti-feminist backlash of the 1920s was the publication of newspaper articles and literary works lampooning the rise of the 'New Woman' and/or cautioning against sex-role transgression. Although the dissemination of ideas promoting conservative notions of gender normativity failed to discourage many French women either from continuing to work outside the home or from taking illegal steps to avoid compulsory motherhood, it did contribute to the emergence, in interwar France, of an ideological climate in which, it has been argued, a 'critique virulente de la femme emancipée et du féminisme' ['virulent critique of the emancipated woman and of feminism'] was able to flourish.[3]

If, for all that it is popularly associated with the figure of the emancipated, crop-haired, childless *garçonne*,[4] the era (*les années folles*) following the armistice of 1918 witnessed an upsurge of socio-sexual conservatism in France, what then was its effect upon French women's writing? Repressive phenomena such as the 'Back to the Home' campaign, along with the upset in gender-role expectations caused by the experience of war, encouraged a number of women authors – such as Jeanne Galzy, Marthe Bibesco and Marcelle Tinayre – to produce works of fiction in which the relationship between gender, identity and power was interrogated and an alternative vision of gender relations was articulated. This sense of the 'resistant' dimension of 1920s–30s women's writing is confirmed by the contestatory stance *vis-à-vis* patriarchal gender norms apparent in specific texts written in the post-1918 period by Colette

(1873–1954). The fictions in question – *Chéri* (1920) and *La Fin de Chéri* (*The Last of Chéri*) (1926) – cast doubt on the acceptability of a gender orthodoxy according to which sexed positions must remain inflexible and hierarchical, and women must play a subordinate role. In the light of this, we need to establish why it is that Colette, whose literary career predated the outbreak of World War I, should have produced post-1918 works of fiction in which gender conventions are contested.

Colette's textual creations cannot be unproblematically classified as the products of a political–feminist consciousness because her writing style consistently favours the individualistic and the personal, and avoids any overt polemical stance. Additionally, her work does not offer the reader the kind of baroque treatment of gender/sexual variance evidenced by the decadent fictions of her predecessor Rachilde. Nonetheless, from its inception, her literary *œuvre was* marked by a desire to reflect on and rethink questions of gender enactment, sexual morality and desire. In view of this, it should come as no surprise that the Colettian fictions under scrutiny here offer a tacit *critique* of restrictive gender norms. They were, after all, written when their author was in her middle age, was an established journalist and novelist and, according to the autobiographical *La Naissance du jour* (1928), was reaching that phase of a woman's life when, as Diana Holmes puts it, '(hetero)sexual love ceases to occupy any significant place in female identity'.[5]

How does Colette's critique manifest itself? An investigation of the accounts of sexed behaviour contained in *Chéri* and *La Fin de Chéri*, a duo of fictional texts featuring the same textual *personae*, might offer a response to this question. Both works subject masculinity and femininity to scrutiny. Equally they signal the extent to which modes of gender conduct are inflected by or imbricated with socio-historical phenomena and the age and maturity of the gendered subject. A close reading of these texts illuminates Colette's reluctance to present an individual's adherence to gender norms as a 'natural', permanent or entirely non-harmful activity.

In *Chéri*, written in 1920 but focused on events taking place between 1906 and 1913, a key theme is the *compelling* nature of gender (and social) convention. The 'message' inherent in volume one of Colette's history of Chéri is that, while it is not impossible to live outside the gender/sexual rules of the social order, the strength of these rules will frequently oblige those individuals who opt to ignore them to recognize the impermanent, 'illegal' nature of their transgressions and, in the end, to give them up.[6] The sections of *Chéri* in which manifestations of gender

– and generational – non-conformism are charted are those that tell of the love affair between Chéri and Léa. Chéri is the product of a fatherless upbringing (pp. 28–9) which appears *not* to have taken him through that Œdipal psycho-sexual phase after which, Freud argues, a definitive masculine/paternal identification and an entry into the world of sexed being are made by the infantile male subject.[7] It is his 'blâmable éducation' ['deplorable education/upbringing'], we sense, and specifically its lack of a solid gender formation, as well as Léa's 'unsuitable' age which enable Chéri to embark upon his liaison with his elderly courtesan-mistress. This liaison enables its participants to 'perform', and perhaps even to exchange, masculine/feminine roles in ways that are less than typical *and* to enjoy a 'mother–son' erotic bond. As is indicated by the segment of Colette's text devoted to the time Chéri and Léa spend in Normandy in 1906 (pp. 39–49), this relationship affords much pleasure to its participants, even if it admits some degree of conflict. As other parts of the novel reveal, however, it cannot and does not last.

While she is far from explicit on the subject, Colette offers clues as to the fundamental cause of the collapse of the Chéri–Léa bond. Various aspects of the lovers' relationship, including the unusual gender performances it encourages, transgress a set of socio-sexual norms which, despite the text's bohemian character, penetrate the universe depicted in *Chéri*. Colette's novel intimates that modes of gender conduct should be 'proper' and immutable, and that love should only be enjoyed between 'appropriate' partners. The rite of marriage – the epitome of socio-sexual correctness – represents a key emblem of these norms. By revealing that it is as a result of Chéri's marriage to Edmée that the Chéri–Léa affair is ultimately destroyed, Colette implies that if the lovers' liaison founders, this is because it has somehow 'sinned' against that order of social/gender conformism which the marital contract symbolizes, and has been punished for so doing. Colette's textual 'lesson' is reinforced in those parts of her novel which address the aftermath of Chéri's wedding. Once this symbolic ritual has occurred, Chéri comes gradually to recognize that he must at least try to move into male adulthood. This process forces him to substitute his given name, the more masculine 'Fred', for his favoured androgynous sobriquet, and to engage, with Edmée, in the marital 'duel de femelle à mâle' ['male–female duel'] (p. 103). After her lover's marriage has taken place and she has also witnessed the spectacle of another ancient courtesan, *la vieille Lili*, cavorting with a very young 'fiancé', Léa eventually assumes the gender status which has always awaited her, accepting that she must henceforth live the life of a 'vieille femme' who has had her allotted portion of lovers. Chéri and Léa do not give in overnight to the rules of gender/social convention. Towards the end of Colette's tale, the lovers make a last attempt to revive the sexual idyll they once enjoyed. Their efforts are, however, doomed – and doomed by the insidious effect upon Chéri of his integration by marriage into the world of socio-sexual normality. No longer seduced by, or even tolerant of, Léa's age – whose marks become increasingly evident as Colette's narrative progresses – and oppressed by the 'enfance retrouvée' and the pluralistic set of gendered behaviours he has previously enjoyed in her company (pp. 177–8), Chéri opts in the concluding part of the novel to return to the adult, gender-conventional realm from which he has briefly (re)escaped. Thus, as the first *volet* of Colette's brace of texts reaches its close, the conventional patterns of gender-role behaviour which conservative opinion in the France of the early 1920s was determined to (re)endorse are established as triumphant.

Set predominantly in 1919, the action of *La Fin de Chéri* (1926) takes place at the very beginning of the *années folles*. Having selected as her focus a period marked in France not only by the aftershock of World War I but also by a resurgence of that gender orthodoxy whose influence haunts *Chéri*, Colette turns back, in *Chéri*'s post-war sequel, to the issue of sex-role *non*-conformism. The characters who most patently exemplify this phenomenon are Edmée and Chéri. Their individual gender-trajectories are, however, very different.

All the principal women characters depicted in *La Fin de Chéri* are portrayed as escaping their traditional roles of wife and mother and in so doing they undermine what Yannick Resch has referred to as 'le mythe de l'éternel féminin' ['the myth of the Eternal Feminine'] (p. 20). In order to emphasize their sex-role transgressions, Colette adopts a variety of strategies. The gender non-conformism of Charlotte Peloux is, for instance, signalled in an almost caricatural fashion by Colette's narrator, who dwells on the incursions into masculine cross-dressing practised in the materialist post-1918 era by this commercially minded ex-courtesan-turned-speculator (pp. 35, 43, 75). Edmée, on the other hand, escapes the comic treatment to which Colette subjects Charlotte, and it is she who is shown to depart most significantly from the traditional *mère–ménagère* paradigm. Although the epitome of convention in *Chéri*, in *La Fin de Chéri*, as Resch observes, she turns herself into a kind of 'New Woman', refusing any longer to play the submissive wife, or to remain a 'jeune femme effrayée qui subissait, muette, les remarques sardoniques de son mari' ['scared young woman willing silently to tolerate her husband's sardonic remarks'] (p. 12). Having embraced the kind of professional freedom World War I made accessible to many French women, Edmée's experience of hospital management encourages her to ensure, in the post-war era, that subordination will not henceforth be her lot. While she never quite becomes one of those 'jeunes filles du monde qui, pour avoir bénévolement conduit des camions pendant la guerre, n'aimaient plus que le cigare, l'automobile et la camaraderie de garages' ['fashionable young women who, having driven lorries as volunteers during the hostilities, were interested only in smoking cigars, driving fast cars and enjoying the camaraderie of the workshop'] (p. 137), she profits from the expansion in her horizons which professional independence/success affords her. In so doing, she is able to reject future ways of gendered being – specifically motherhood – which will put at risk her new-found autonomy (pp. 152–3). By the end of Colette's novel, confronted with the spectacle of her husband's descent into mental and emotional confusion, Edmée manifests a distance – and a 'male' self-satisfaction ['complaisance masculine'] (p. 171) – which speak volumes about the gender-metamorphosis this previously docile personage has undergone.

If Edmée's (female) trajectory, as recounted in *La Fin de Chéri*, suggests that escape from gender convention is an enabling phenomenon, the fate of Chéri reveals that when masculine gender norms prove to be both overarchingly influential *and* impossible to adhere to, disaster will inevitably ensue. Colette's sequel to *Chéri* depicts 'the return of soldiers from World War I and the industrious escapism of the early 1920s in terms of the drama of masculine subject formation'.[8] As this drama unfolds, the reader becomes aware both that, while Chéri *did*, apparently, during the hostilities, accede temporarily to the masculine/adult realm, he is neither capable nor desirous of doing so in the post-1918 epoch that provides the setting for *La Fin de Chéri*; and that his failure to take up his 'proper' place in the inter-war masculine–social domain is a key factor in his suicide-inducing collapse.

In the era depicted in Colette's sequel, an individual's masculinity is emblematized in – and assessable in terms of – his financial, commercial and sexual prowess. Indifferent not only to women (pp. 54–5) but also, importantly, to money (p. 49),[9] the Chéri of 1919 cannot embrace a normative gender mould which, in spite of the exemplary 'maleness' conferred by his wartime status as a soldier, remains alien to him. His sole desire is to return to Léa and to achieve – by reviving in her company an erotico-affective bond that will permit him to regress into a semi-fœtal state – a blissful, genderless 'immobile' mode of existence

which will heal the torments inflicted upon him by the frenetically materialist post-1918 era, by its gender expectations, and by a (male) adulthood he finds intolerable (pp. 140–1). When this desire is thwarted
because Léa comes to value an 'abdication de la féminité' as well as to
enjoy a 'dignité sans sexe' [asexual dignity] (p. 87) which precludes
further physical relationships, Chéri slides towards breakdown.
Eventually he commits suicide in a rented room which, decorated with
photographs of Léa, reproduces that primal womb-space in which a
nascent individual knows neither gendered being nor the passing of
time.

In *Chéri* and *La Fin de Chéri*, both of which were written during, and,
it seems, at least partially in reaction against, a war-inflected historical
period which is considered to have been profoundly conservative in its
view of gender relations, Colette succeeds not only in problematizing
that period's notions of gender propriety but also in signalling the perils
that gender conformism potentially brings in its wake. Neither of these
narrative fictions constitutes a vehicle for the kind of self-consciously
polemical feminist writing evident, for example, in Marcelle Tinayre's
L'Ennemie intime [The Intimate Enemy] (1931): a novel which is set around
1930, and whose contents reveal that the inter-war period, even if it
brought independence to a minority of determined and hardened
women, was one in which women in France, wealthy women included,
generally remained in thrall to the patriarchal order and its codes of
sexed conduct. Nonetheless, because Colette implies that escape from
gender norms may be a positive experience and that the overpowerful
effects of such norms can put the vulnerable at risk, it is clearly the case
that *Chéri* and *La Fin de Chéri* can be read as countermanding the gender
orthodoxies/discourses of the historical moment during which they
came into being. In addition, the 'subversive' dimension of these
Colettian creations serves to point up not only the contestatory echoes
which a repressive gender ideology can generate within the literary
domain but also the sexual–political challenges which historically
marked women's fictions regularly proffer.

In 1938, married women in France ceased to be legal minors. In 1944
French women belatedly acquired the vote, partly as a reward for their
activities in the Resistance. In 1946, the Constitution recognized their
equality with men in most domains. By the late 1940s, then, French
women were finally granted some of the essential civil liberties to which
they had been not been given access after the end of World War I. Many
believed that other changes in women's status would, in the years and

decades following the Liberation, issue naturally from their civic enfran-
chisement. It became apparent, however, that legal and political emancipation did not necessarily put an end to deep-rooted prejudice and
sexual oppression.

In *Women's Rights and Women's Lives in France 1944–1968*, Clare Duchen
reveals that, while there were quite significant differences between the
1950s and 1960s, as far as French women's socio-sexual situation was
concerned, for many of the women who lived through them, both post-
war decades represented a time when nothing happened, and an era in
which the pattern of most women's lifestyles rarely departed from a
'"traditional" model' (p. 3). The socio-sexual victories which French
women eventually won in this era and some of the persistently 'traditional' aspects of their lives in the 'void' period (1944–67) point up the
ways in which the gender specificities of French women's historical situation, as it evolved in the years that separated the end of World War II
and the revolution initiated by May 1968, are reflected in a series of
female-authored fictions published between 1954 and 1964.

Radical neo-feminism of the kind that flourished in the 1970s, in the
wake of the May events, was not yet born in the France of the 1950s and
1960s. However, the existence of progressive groups such as *Jeunes
Femmes*, the *Mouvement Français pour le Planning Familial* and the *Mouvement
Démocratique Féminin*, along with the reflections on the 'woman question'
contained in the writings of individuals such as Colette Audry, Françoise
Giroud, Andrée Michel, Evelyne Sullerot and Simone de Beauvoir,
attest to the fact that in the immediate post-war era, and especially by
the early-to-mid 1960s, gender politics was by no means moribund in
mid-century France, even if there was no coherent 'ground-swell of
[feminist] opposition.'[10] The activities and analyses of these groups and
individuals are viewed by Duchen as 'precursors for a later, more radical
brand of feminism.'[11] Moderate as it may have been, the (re)nascent
feminism of '50s and '60s France helped to generate the freedoms to
which French women finally acceded in the mid-to-late 1960s. They
were brought into being by hard-fought laws which, passed in 1965 and
1967, allowed married women finally to have full control over their own
financial assets and gave women access if not to abortion then at least to
legal contraceptive methods. Neither of these laws, in the form they
finally took, was entirely satisfactory. The 1965 Marriage Reform law left
intact the husband's status as head of the family, so that the traditional
power balance of the marital contract was largely preserved and the
1967 *Loi Neuwirth* legislated only to allow contraception via prescription.

Nevertheless, the socio-legal changes they ushered in went some way towards enhancing French women's sense of autonomy, in what remained a deeply male dominated socio-cultural climate.

If the period 1944–67 was crowned in France by a series of partial feminist gains, as far as women's existences were concerned it was nonetheless one during which, certainly in the early post-war era, a traditional, domestic/maternal format remained very much in place. That this is so is indicated by data relating to women's situation *vis-à-vis* motherhood and family life and employment. In the late 1940s and 1950s normative notions about what marriage and motherhood should entail were deeply entrenched in French society.[12] Even though, in theory, the Fourth Republic (1946–58) was committed to promoting women's equality and rights as workers, married women were generally expected to stay at home, devoting themselves to husband, housework and family. Furthermore, a whole spectrum of family organizations, Catholic associations, conservative political groups and women's publications combined to convey the ideological message that they should do so. Things changed, to a degree, in the 1960s. Working mothers (by the 60s, married women were increasingly rejoining or remaining in the labour market) were accepted as a social reality. However, in the latter part of this period, the pressure on women to bear children was still present,[13] even if the pro-natalist family lobby was in quite significant decline in the post-'baby boom' France of the mid-60s. While numerous publications – including Jacques Derogy's *Des enfants malgré nous* [Our Unwanted Children] (1955) and Marie-Andrée Weill-Hallé's *La Grand'peur d'aimer* [The Fear of Love] (1960) – highlighted the perils of unwanted pregnancy and stressed the need for immediate re-legalization of birth control, compulsory motherhood remained until 1967 something that many French women found impossible to elude – a fact which, as Derogy's book reveals, brought suffering to great numbers of them. It is the case that during the period 1944–67, evolving conceptions of, and discourses on, French women's maternal role went hand-in-hand with debates around the home-versus-career thematic. It is difficult, however, to build up a complete picture of French women's employment patterns in mid-century France. Duchen notes that, in the decades following the Liberation, women did not have the same right to work as their male counterparts, women workers were kept at the bottom of the wage hierarchy, professions deemed to be 'feminine' were devalued, and women were denied access to the political and economic elites that they were increasing well-qualified to join.[14]

Women in France were certainly not yet fully emancipated by 1967, but had made legal and civic progress, particularly in the immediate period preceding the outbreak of the May 1968 revolution. This process was undoubtedly helped on its way by the renewal of reformist feminism. Women of the post-war period did not, however, have access to that empowering space of highly public, politicized 'sisterhood', or feminist community, which was a feature of the radical neo-feminist upsurge – described as 'cette révolution identitaire collective'[15] – of the 1970s. The abiding 'second-class citizenship' that was still part of French women's mid-century social lot was mirrored by their marginal position within the *institution littéraire*. It is certainly not the case that no French women authors were writing and publishing during these years. Between the mid-to-late 1940s and the late 1960s, many well-known women writers were either embarking upon their literary trajectories, or were pursuing careers already flourishing before World War II. These included Françoise Sagan (b. 1935), whose *Bonjour Tristesse* (1954) and *Un certain sourire* (*A Certain Smile*) (1956) initiated a corpus of work that has been too readily dismissed as 'upmarket' popular romance; the Belgian-born Marguerite Yourcenar (1903–87), whose best-known post-war fictions, *Mémoires d'Hadrien* (*Memoirs of Hadrian*) (1951) and *L'Œuvre au noir* (*The Abyss*) (1968), juxtapose an Ancient World setting with more modern thematic concerns; Marguerite Duras (1914–96), whose *Un barrage contre le pacifique* (*The Sea Wall*) (1950), *Moderato Cantabile* (1958) and *Le Ravissement de Lol V. Stein* (*The Ravishing of Lol V. Stein*) (1964) manifest a nascent preoccupation with the related issues of narrative style and sexual desire that was to become the hallmark of Durassian writing after 1968; and Nathalie Sarraute (b. 1900), who, like Duras, was associated with the avant-garde experimentalism of the French New Novelists. However, in the 1950s at least, even when they managed to overcome the material difficulties and cultural prejudices that impeded women from writing works of literature and getting them accepted for publication, French women authors regularly found that their creative productions were excluded from, or categorized as 'lightweight' in, the literary histories and cultural annals of the day.

Some of the French women writers of the post-war era eschewed an overtly woman-focused stance. Yourcenar, for instance, claimed not to 'write as a woman', and adopted what have been taken to constitute 'male' writing strategies (including an exploitation of categories of thought and value-systems conventionally conceived of as masculine).[16] The protagonists of Yourcenar's fictions, with the exception of those of

the prose poems contained in the prewar *Feux* (*Fires*) (1936), tend not to
be predominantly female, and the accounts of sexuality offered in post-
war novels such as *Les Mémoires d'Hadrien* and *L'Œuvre au noir* focus on *male*
homoeroticism. This phenomenon has encouraged critics to categorize
Yourcenar as, at best, someone who sought to resist a limiting assimilation into the ghetto of 'female writing' and, at worst, as an author bent
on selling out to a patriarchal model and to a pursuit of power made possible by a sustained, textual engagement with male-identification or
transgenderism.[17] Many mid-century French women writers did
however opt in their novels to treat the feminine condition in order to
record, critique or rethink its parameters and limitations. Examples
include Simone de Beauvoir (1908–86), Violette Leduc (1907–72),
Christiane Rochefort (1917–98) and Monique Wittig (b. 1935) – four
women writers whose intentions and styles are different, but whose pre-
'68 fictional work can be classified as 'feminist', insofar as it seeks to challenge the gender norms and assumptions of patriarchal culture. The
works that will receive particular consideration are: Beauvoir's *Les
Mandarins* (*The Mandarins*) (1954); Leduc's *Ravages* (1955); Rochefort's *Les
Stances à Sophie* (*Stanzas to Sophie*) (1963) and Wittig's *L'Opoponax* (*The
Opoponax*) (1964). These narratives have much in common: all are fictional but are autobiographically inflected, and all of them (in contrast
to the female-authored, poetic, experimental texts which proliferated
in the post-'68 period) are grounded in social reality. All, moreover,
unlike the historical fictions of Yourcenar or Duras's surreal *Le
Ravissement de Lol V. Stein*, focus squarely on women and/in the (mid-
century) social. Discussion of the texts selected for analysis here will
centre on their treatment of three key themes: the 'problem' of female
subjectivity, and the formative effect upon it of gender relations and
determinants; feminine sexuality; the absence/impossibility/potential
of female intersubjectivity (that is, of relations and relationships between
women).

By 1950, mainly as a result of the publication of *Le Deuxième Sexe* (*The
Second Sex*) (1949), Simone de Beauvoir was one of the 'stars' of Paris's
literary and intellectual firmament. Her fourth novel, *Les Mandarins*
(1954),[18] is a document which bears witness to the historical and cultural
specifics of the epoch during which it was written and set. A chronicle
of intellectual and political life in France during the late 1940s and early
1950s, it offers a meditation on what it was like to be a woman at a time
when feminine identity was still defined more or less exclusively through
and against a masculine standard. Additionally, however tacitly, *Les*

Mandarins denounces the depredations inflicted on women's subjectivity and autonomy in a male-centred social order. That this is the case should come as no surprise, given that Beauvoir's novel post-dates by only five years her groundbreaking analysis, in *Le Deuxième Sexe*, of the 'Otherness'/subordination inherent in the feminine condition, as it is constructed by and under patriarchy.

Beauvoir's fictional treatment, in *Les Mandarins*, of the gender situation in which French women found themselves in the 1940s and 1950s is, of necessity, both partial and class/milieu-specific. It proceeds primarily via the depiction of two (bourgeois) female protagonists: Anne Dubreuilh, whose voice and view dominate the novel, and her friend Paule. This latter, secondary figure constitutes a 'complete example of *The Second Sex*'s analysis of the *amoureuse* . . . who tries to make her own being vicariously through the loved one.'[19] She incarnates, further (see I: pp. 9–38, pp. 470–1), albeit caricaturally and imperfectly, the kind of ideologically inflected femininity valued in a cultural climate that exhorted women to seek their true fulfilment in the private life of the home.[20] In creating Paule, and in playing off against Anne's self-reliance her crazed, concubinic dependence on her ever more indifferent lover, Beauvoir condemns not only the 'feminine' weaknesses Paule displays but also, implicitly, the socio-sexual norms of the early post-war world in which she was writing; norms which, over-privileging the ideal of the *femme au foyer*, can be taken to represent a root cause both of Paule's folly and of her eventual descent into breakdown.

It might appear, on first reading, that it is solely through her account of Paule's desperate attempts to preserve her status as the object of Henri's love and as the tutelary deity of his domestic universe (cf. I: pp. 130–2) that Beauvoir formulates her critique of the disempowering social construct that was femininity in 1940s/50s France. However, Anne, too, is used by the creator of *Les Mandarins* in order to highlight the negative aspects of a historically situated womanhood. She is a practising psychoanalyst, with a thriving career, but for all her independence and her awareness of the dangers, for a woman, of the belief that love is everything (II: p. 246), Anne's world comes to be contoured by her relationships with two very different men. These are her husband, Robert, an intellectual, aptly described by Fallaize as playing an asexual 'Pygmalion role in her life, assigning moral and political meaning to the world about her through their conversations and his writing',[21] and her American lover, the writer Lewis Brogan, in whose company she (re)discovers a powerful enjoyment of sexuality repressed in her marriage.

Caught between these masculine figures and between the existential and
sexual options they represent, Anne is revealed by Beauvoir, as the tale
of her 'two lives' develops, as a woman who in fact also fails to live
entirely 'for-herself' within an androcentric universe (cf. II: pp. 354–5),
even if the passion she brings to her affair with Lewis, and the choices
she makes concerning it, show her to be a far more 'authentic' individual than Paule.[22]

In the narration of *Les Mandarins*, then, by dint of plotting segments
of the life-trajectories of not one but two, apparently oppositional
women protagonists, Beauvoir does two things. First, she maps out a
sexed 'space' which is historically, culturally and socially specific and
which is portrayed as governed by a status quo whereby male subjects
are able to over-dominate, and manipulate the direction taken by, the
lives of their female counterparts, even if they do not seek to do so.
Beauvoir's evocations of this 'space' imply, in line with her analysis in *Le
Deuxième Sexe*, that if women find it difficult to enjoy an uncomplicated
relationship with their sexuality and with the motherhood that is their
'lot' or to find solace in female–female bonds that seem habitually to be
poisoned by various forms of rivalry (evident in the troubled dynamic
between Anne and her daughter Nadine), this is a function of the fragile,
ambiguous subject-status allotted them in a 'man's world'. Second, in
weaving her tale of intellectual and political life in 1940s/50s France,
Beauvoir subtly works up an indictment targeted as much at the gender
hierarchies of the post-war society invoked in her narrative fiction as at
those amongst its women characters who are complicit with 'traditional',
disabling feminine modes of behaviour. Beauvoir was not, at the time of
writing *Les Mandarins*, the committed feminist she became in the 1970s.
Her novel does not address gender issues in the kind of consciously
'political' fashion we might expect to find in the work of more contemporary women writers. However, *Les Mandarins* is for all that a 'feminist'
production, insofar as its account of female gendered being quietly
invites the reader to speculate as to the causes and sources of the nature
of the feminine condition.

A year after Beauvoir published *Les Mandarins*, Violette Leduc's
Ravages appeared.[23] Its genesis had been lengthy and difficult – Leduc's
publisher, Gallimard, had insisted on the excision of an opening section
devoted to an account of adolescent lesbian love in a boarding school –
and had helped to propel its author into the mental collapse that blighted
her life for years afterwards. *Ravages* is less overtly historically contextu-
alized than *Les Mandarins*, containing no dates or temporal pointers.

However, it may be taken nonetheless to offer a testament to the gender situation in which French women found themselves during a particular epoch (specifically, once again, the 1940s/50s era during which Leduc's novel came into being). The testament in question is not a positive one. *Ravages* deals, in predominantly realist mode, with the urban/suburban lives of a group of lower middle-class Parisian individuals, chief amongst whom is a young woman named Thérèse. In telling the tale of Thérèse's sexual and emotional adventures – or, rather, in allowing her narrator-protagonist to recount it herself – Leduc reproduces a social milieu that is very far from the elitist intellectual enclave inhabited by Beauvoir's Mandarins. Leduc's story of Thérèse's disastrous marriage to Marc, and of the degradations that result from her (impermanent) desire to embrace the feminine/maternal gender role, is not only historically and socially anchored, but is also distinguished by various 'political' features that pinpoint the contestatory potential of women's writing referred to in the first part of this chapter. First, by dwelling on the grotesque and inadequate nature of the 'home life' Thérèse and Marc share after they marry, Leduc's fiction offers a bleak parody of the *femme au foyer* ideal prevalent in discourses on/of the feminine produced during the period in which it was written and published. Second (cf. pp. 49–54, p. 160), *Ravages* calls into question the notion, widespread in the France of the 1940s and 1950s, that motherhood was a woman's natural – indeed heroic – destiny and that raising children was the summit of a woman's achievement.[24] Third, its account of Thérèse's near-fatal dealings with the elderly woman who eventually procures her backstreet abortion silently makes the kind of point addressed openly in studies such as Derogy's *Des Enfants malgré nous*. At stake in Leduc's treatment of her heroine's trajectory are all sorts of things which issue from the personal obsessions of her own, highly individual literary universe, and the 'case' she evokes is a special one. However, her account of Thérèse's exploits does appear to signal that, in *Ravages* at least, Leduc writes of the feminine condition in a more forcefully and instinctively feminist mode than Beauvoir, even if she herself did not openly acknowledge that she was doing so.[25] That this is the case is intimated by her treatment of woman-to-woman relationships. As we saw earlier, these bonds are not depicted as successful or enabling in Beauvoir's *Les Mandarins* – a textual phenomenon indicative, perhaps, of the absence, in 1950s France, of a culture of sexual–political 'sisterhood'. In *Ravages*, however, which focuses amongst other things on Thérèse's pre-marital lesbian affair with an older woman, Cécile, and, in its closing pages, on her renewed relationship with the mother from whom marriage has estranged her, feminine inter-subjectivity *is* permitted to represent something that can be (relatively) positive and nurturing, albeit also potentially stifling (cf. pp. 49–50, p. 85, p. 89, p.110).

Les Stances à Sophie (1963) and *L'Opoponax* (1964) were written during a period when women's rights were being discussed in France more pub-licly and more extensively than hitherto, and when women were on the point of attaining new civic and sexual freedoms. This is reflected in their overtly feminist tenor which is evident in the way in which they not only openly signal conventional gender roles and practices to be exter-nally imposed, deforming constraints, but also in the way they frame lesbian love as a space of resistance, out of which an alternative kind of female subjectivity – and language – may potentially emerge.

Christiane Rochefort's *Stances* takes as its focus the world of the French bourgeoisie of the late 1950s and early 1960s.[26] Its setting, in other words, is a realm in which marriage and motherhood still dominated as key ref-erence points in women's lives. Rochefort invokes the moment and the class environment within which her tale is situated by referring both to the inequalities intrinsic in married life in mid-century France (cf. p. 30, p. 118, p. 195, pp. 210–11) and to the normative notions of wifely being ingrained in 1950s/60s French bourgeois culture. In so doing, she creates a fiction that at once denounces a set of historically specific socio-cultural phenomena and vehicles a degree of gender-role satire absent in both *Les Mandarins* and *Ravages*. Her novel charts the (pre-marital, marital and post-marital) doings of Céline Rodes. Céline is the source of the perky, ironically analytical *voice* of Rochefort's narrative; however, in her role as the *protagonist* of the *Les Stances à Sophie*, she also features as Mme Philippe Aignan; an 'exemplary' pre-'68 bourgeois wife. As she chronicles, in *Bildungsroman* mode, Céline's liberty-sapping encounters with the gender mores, sexual 'rules' and social structures of her time and, especially, of her husband's milieu, Rochefort contrives to mount an attack on a historically grounded sex/class value-system which she patently deplores and which her central protagonist eventually rejects in favour of her pre-marital, 'liberal' mode of existence. Rochefort does this, firstly, by inserting her reader into an oppressive, androcentrically organized universe which, as an older and wiser Céline acknowledges at the start of her narrative (pp. 7–8), represents an alien territory wherein women are given no maps or designs for living, and their status as auton-omous subjects is easily eroded – by, amongst other things, the Myth of Absolute Love. Secondly, she signals that within this realm certain entities or phenomena exist that run counter to, and are potentially subversive of, the dutiful, passive, decorative feminine identity-mould into which Céline and her fellow *bourgeoises* are expected uncritically to slot. The first of these is female–female desire. Céline and her friend/lover Julia refuse to designate themselves with the 'political' label of lesbian (pp. 138–40). However, their short-lived erotico-affective idyll, brought to an end by Julia's premature death, does nonetheless function as a form of anti-patriarchal resistance, working as an antidote to the power play which *Les Stances à Sophie* reveals to be part and parcel of the heterosexual love dynamic, as it operated in the bourgeois milieu in the period. The second focus of 'feminist' rebellion evoked in *Stances* is language. In the mouths of men, language is shown by Rochefort's novel to constitute an instrument of oppression. Céline's husband Philippe, when not endeavouring to curb his wife's proclivity for 'inappropriate' expletives, uses particular kinds of terminology and linguistic tricks in order to compel Céline, as she herself informs him (pp. 188–9), to recognize and remedy the gender/social 'defects' he deplores in her. When used by women, however – on their own terms, amongst themselves, and, above all, rigorously – language can represent a jumping-off point for an analysis of patriarchal structures that brings not only understanding but also liberation in its wake. This latter phenomenon is signalled in those sections of Rochefort's novel which address Céline's efforts to give new, demystifying meanings, in the *Dictionnaire Sémantique Néo-Bourgeois* she is determined to produce, to the types of ideologically inflected word or cliché – 'Amour', 'Obsession' – which the likes of Philippe exploit in order to keep their female partners in their allotted 'place' (p. 184, p. 188).

Language – and its relation to sexual ideology – also represents a central focus of *L'Opoponax*.[27] Language, together with the socio-cultural discourses it sustains, is shown in Wittig's text to constitute a key element within the process whereby evolving human beings are 'interpellated' into the gendered/sexual 'obedience' required by the broader ideology of modern Western society.[28] However, language – patriarchally marked language included, provided that it is 're-appropriated', resistantly – is revealed in *L'Opoponax* as a tool which enables the not-quite-fully-socialized subject to articulate the forbidden feelings and desires that the social order seeks to repress. In order to convey the role played within gender/sexual socialization by language and discourse, Wittig retraces the post-war infancy and early adolescence of Catherine Legrand, a fictional protagonist whose perspective, the reader gradually realizes, filters the events recorded in the present-tense narrative of *L'Opoponax*.[29] Catherine's story – if we can so designate Wittig's disconcerting, stream-of-consciousness *récit* – exposes the language/discourse-types we are introduced to during our formative years as forces which help to compel the youthful human subject out of the ungendered, unindividuated, sexually polymorphous state that is childhood (encapsulated in the neutral '*on*' that is the dominant narrative pronoun of *L'Opoponax*) and into the gendered individualism/conformism patriarchal society expects from us ('Sur le mur de l'école il y a écrit d'un côté de la grande porte école de filles et de l'autre école de garçons' ['On the school wall "girls's school" and "boy's school" are written on either side of the main entrance'] (p. 126)). But Wittig's tale also signals that the language/discourses of the male-centred, man-made world – evoked insistently in *L'Opoponax*, via references to such variant language-forms as schoolyard taunts ('qui c'est qui veut voir ma quéquette' ['who wants to see my willy'] (p.7)); classroom dictation exercises ('Liliane lave le linge' ['Liliane is doing the laundry'] (p. 16)); and the texts of high culture ('Des tresses de perles attachées à ses tempes descendaient jusqu'aux coins de sa bouche, rose, comme une grenade entr'ouverte' ['Her beaded tresses fell from her temples down to the corners of her mouth, pink, like an opened pomegranate'] (p. 147)) – can be made to signify something other than that which patriarchal ideology means them to signify, provided that their user is sufficiently determined to make them do so.

Wittig hints that language can and should be 'remade' differently – and from inside – early on in her story, when she evokes the 'unseemly' spectacle of the child Reine Dieu's messy school exercise book (p. 36). However, it is via her account of Catherine Legrand's adolescent dealings with the linguistic/discursive realm that Wittig foregrounds the message that the female subject – particularly the female *desiring* subject – needs to take back and remould patriarchal language from within, in order to use it to 'find a voice'. As Catherine grows up, she grows into a state of desire – lesbian desire – whose object is her classmate Valerie Borge. This is a desire which has no 'place' in the social (even/especially in the microcosm of the social that is the girls' convent school Catherine and Valerie attend), and for which there are no 'man-made' signifiers. In the face of this linguistic lacuna, Catherine invents a being – *l'opoponax* – which is a bizarre word-entity of her own making, and which she employs to symbolize a desire she cannot 'speak'. Concomitantly, she 'borrows' the language of key texts from French male literary history (especially Baudelaire's 'L'Invitation au voyage' and Scève's *Délie*) in order to articulate her love, along with the new, 'aberrant' subjectivity it bestows upon her. By dint of expanding, via a process of 'lesbianization', the significatory potential of this language, Catherine transforms *and* transgresses the boundaries of a poetic tradition wherein, historically, the female desiring voice has been occluded. In revealing her as so doing, Wittig's narrative – which in no way demonizes the male texts she and her protagonist reappropriate – eschews a didactic, politically strident approach. It does, however, quite patently invite the reader to rethink and critique the complex dynamic which, in Western culture, binds language and discourse to sexual and gendered subjectivity and its formation. And it is by virtue of its combination of sexual–political reticence and forcefulness, rather than via the exploitation of an overtly historically anchored narrative setting, that *L'Opoponax* – arguably the most politically charged of the fictions under scrutiny here – signals itself to be a text of its (transitional) time.

This chapter began by invoking Irma Garcia's belief in the interpenetration of women's writing and women's history. In each and every one of the texts discussed in the foregoing pages, this phenomenon is palpable. Some of the works in question – those of Colette (especially *La Fin de Chéri*), Beauvoir and Rochefort – clearly illuminate the history of gender relations, as they evolved within the context of early-to-mid twentieth-century France. Within this first group of narratives, stamped as they are with readily identifiable historical markers, temporally specific aspects of French women's situation feature as part of the narrative content/plot. On the other hand, in the writings of Leduc and, especially, of Wittig, it is primarily narrative *tone* and what might be termed narrative *politics* that appear to be historically inflected, i.e., to bear witness to the (gender specifics of the) moment during which the texts vehicling them were produced. These differences aside, all of the fictions examined in this chapter help us better to understand what was happening to women, and to gender relations and norms, during a modern era which, regardless of the changes it witnessed, never brought full emancipation to France's Second Sex.

NOTES

1 Montreynaud, *Le XXᵉ siècle des femmes*, p. 84.
2 See Thébaud, 'La Grande Guerre' in Duby and Perrot (eds.), *Histoire des femmes*, vol. 5, p. 67 and p. 69.
3 *Ibid.*, p. 69.
4 For an account of the nature of the image of the *garçonne*/emancipated

woman – created by Victor Margueritte in a 1922 novel of the same name – and its influence on French women of certain classes and on French fashion, see Montreynaud, *Le XXe siècle des femmes*, pp. 148–9.

5 Holmes, *Colette*, p. 127.

6 All page references in the text refer to the 1920 Fayard edition of *Chéri* and to the 1983 Flammarion edition of *La Fin de Chéri*, which is prefaced with an illuminating essay by Yannick Resch.

7 For an account of psycho-sexual evolution in the male subject, and the role of Œdipus within it, see Sigmund Freud, *On Sexuality* (Harmondsworth: Pelican Freud Library, 1977), vol. VII, pp. 315–22.

8 Holmes, *French Women's Writing*, p. 136.

9 In Freud's taxonomy of psychic symbolism, money represents a symbol of the phallus.

10 Duchen, *Women's Rights and Women's Lives*, p. 4

11 *Ibid.*, p. 170.

12 *Ibid.*, pp. 96–127.

13 See *ibid.*, p. 114 for post-war birth-rate figures; these reached a peak in 1964.

14 See *ibid.*, pp. 128–64, especially p. 131, for employment figures.

15 By Marcelle Marini, 'La Place de femmes dans la production culturelle: l'exemple de la France', in Duby and Perrot (eds.), *Histoire des femmes*, vol. V, pp. 275–96, p. 281.

16 See Robinson, *Scandal in the Ink*, pp. 228–32.

17 For details of these debates, see Robinson, *Scandal in the Ink*, together with Eric Bentley, 'We Are in History', in Stambolian and Marks (eds.), *Homosexualities and French Literature*, pp. 131–2.

18 Page references in the text refer to the two-volume Folio edition of *Les Mandarins* (Paris: Gallimard, 1954).

19 Fallaize, *The Novels of Simone de Beauvoir*, p. 109.

20 See Duchen, *Women's Rights and Women's Lives*, p. 65.

21 Fallaize, *Novels of Simone de Beauvoir*, p. 105.

22 There is no space here to develop the Existentialist reading of *Les Mandarins* that Beauvoir's novel invites. However, it is worth noting that, in Existentialist terms, it is possible to view Anne's love, unlike Paule's, as the kind of freely chosen *projet* which, according to Sartre, brings transcendence and freedom in its wake.

23 All page references in the text relate to the *édition blanche* of *Ravages* (Paris: Gallimard, 1955).

24 See Duchen, *Women's Rights and Women's Lives*, p. 102.

25 For an account of Leduc's relationship to feminism, see my *Violette Leduc*, chap. 4; see chap. 2 for a reading of *Ravages*.

26 Page references in the text refer to the Livre de Poche edition of Rochefort's novel (Paris: Grasset, 1963).

27 All page references refer to the 1964 Editions de Minuit edition of *L'Opoponax*.

28 For an illuminating analysis of this process, see Jennifer Birkett, 'Sophie

Ménade: the Writings of Monique Wittig', in Hughes and Ince (eds.), *French Erotic Fiction*, pp. 93–119.

29 As in *Ravages*, there are no dates in *L'Opoponax*. A reference to bomb craters (p. 69), along with the generally 'modern' nature of toys and clothing referred to in Wittig's novel, suggests however that her narrative setting post-dates World War II.

CHAPTER EIGHT

From order to adventure: women's fiction since 1970

Leslie Hill

Impossible de *définir* une pratique féminine de l'écriture, d'une impossibilité qui se maintiendra car on ne pourra jamais *théoriser* cette pratique, l'enfermer, la coder, ce qui ne signifie pas qu'elle n'existe pas. Mais elle excédera toujours le discours que régit le système phallocentrique; elle a et aura lieu ailleurs que dans les territoires subordonnés à la domination philosophique–théorique.

A female practice of writing can't be *defined*, and this impossibility will not go away. No-one will ever be able to *theorize* this practice, enclose it or codify it, which doesn't mean it doesn't exist. But it will always exceed the discourse of the phallocentric system; it takes place, and will continue to take place, elsewhere than in those territories subject to philosophical–theoretical control.

Hélène Cixous, 'Le Rire de la Méduse'

The early 1970s in France were witness to a complex series of deep-seated historical changes. In the political and social sphere, the events of May 1968, together with de Gaulle's resignation from the presidency which followed a year later, marked the end of what was felt by many in France, despite the substantial economic changes that came in its wake, to be an often backward-looking era of paternalistic and autocratic rule, and which had found its most telling embodiment in the self-mythologizing persona of General de Gaulle himself. Little wonder then, during the years that followed, that one of the first reactions to de Gaulle's fall from power was for historians, film-makers, and novelists alike to embark on the task of retrieving – and rewriting – the history of the previous thirty years.

One of the most immediate and striking consequences of this renewed interest in the recent past was that, largely for the first time, the many unflattering and sometimes shocking secrets that lay buried beneath the Gaullist myth of unified national – and nationalist – resistance during the Occupation were brought to light. The questions at issue were of course more than simply archival ones and interest in them more than academic. Indeed, the myth of France's unified war-time resistance to the Occupation was largely in fact what lent the institutions of the Fifth Republic, embodied in de Gaulle's own persona, their apparent legitimacy as an expression of French national identity. However, in point of fact, as many were aware, that legitimacy was at best belated, founded more on the retrospective logic of the popular plebiscite than on the principle of democratic self-determination. In May 1958, de Gaulle had returned to power thanks only to an unconstitutional coup, supported by the colonialist military, with the sole purpose of filling with the prestige of his own charismatic and mythic persona the interval or void at the centre of power that, however necessary it was to the exercise of democracy as such, had tended under the Fourth Republic to express itself only in the form of the notorious parliamentary instability of successive administrations. During the 1960s, de Gaulle occupied that gap with exemplary, self-mythologizing zeal. But during the early 1970s, once he had gone from power, it was as though there was once more a void at the heart of the political process, one that none of the numerous contending government or opposition parties had much chance of filling on its own, given the disarray and disunity that had been the legacy of the events of May not only for those on the left but for those on the conservative right as well.

The political consequences of the end of Gaullism were many and far-reaching; indeed, directly or indirectly, it not only led to the break-up of the conservative right and the refounding of the French Socialist Party in 1972 and, with it, in time, the construction of a new presidential majority around the figure of François Mitterrand, but also brought about the remorseless decline of the once dominant Communist Party, and the re-emergence of the racist extreme right. The implications in the intellectual, ideological and cultural sphere were no less remarkable; for what the 1970s ushered in, alongside a reorganization of the political arena, was a new and critical phase of reassessment and re-examination affecting France's historical and cultural self-identity. Indeed, while the 1970s saw little of the government instability that was routine twenty years before, what they did witness, however, on the part of many French men and women, was an increasing awareness of the discrepancy between public image and private experience, between political discourse and lived reality. Already this gap between representation and represented had been the underlying motive behind the rebellious events of May 1968; and as May had implied, the problem was not necessarily one that could be resolved by a new regime, for what was at issue, even more than France's own particular self-image at the time, was the principle of representation itself, in both the cultural and political sense, and in years to come it was this that was increasingly to be thrown into question by many of France's most influential intellectuals. Indeed, what is most significant of all about the years that followed May '68 is perhaps the extent to which in France numerous different groups and individuals – from women and homosexuals to peasants, prisoners, former immigrants and psychiatric patients – began actively to contest the right of the French State to speak for them, in their place and on their behalf.

The effects of these many historical and cultural shifts were arguably most marked in those areas where public authority and private experience, control by the State and the singularity of the body impinged on each other, overlapped, and came into conflict. Just as May 1968 had opened up the possibility of a new kind of politics, in which the personal was always already political, and the political itself irreducible to received notions of parliamentary representation, so new areas of social reality came to be the object of significant renegotiation. Of particular importance in this regard were questions of sexuality and the family, and much important legislation was enacted in this area by the French government in the 1970s, with the result that significant changes took place, affecting not only the law on abortion and the rules governing the availability of contraception, but also the legal framework for relations between the sexes within the family. For many intellectuals, however, these reforms were still somewhat piecemeal; and there was considerable tension between, for instance, the demands of feminists and the capacity of traditional forms of political representation to satisfy those demands. Indeed, in the aftermath of May '68, one of the most important developments in the political and cultural sphere, alongside the birth of numerous other so-called single-issue social campaigns, was the emergence of an autonomous women's movement operating with distinctive, very loose modes of organization outside of all established political parties.

The effects of these various developments spilled far beyond the political sphere in the narrow sense, with the result that the 1970s not only saw many social and political changes, but also witnessed a considerable upsurge of interest in avant-garde artistic experimentation as such. The result was a new, progressive climate in the cultural sphere, that served to put writing – and the writing of fiction – high on the agenda of cultural intervention. The phenomenon affected literary activity in many different ways, but the impact on writing by women was particularly impressive. For it was from that moment on, in France, that writing by women in general – and not just the works of a token canon of women authors such as Colette, Elsa Triolet or Simone de Beauvoir – began to be taken more seriously than ever before. Important issues were at stake. For the challenge facing women writers at the time, and in far more explicit and collective fashion than ever before, was the question of how far it was possible for women to create a different, distinctive, yet also pluralistic voice of their own. The compelling need on the part of women, so to speak, was to learn how to reinvent the legacy of the past in order to address the future. Instead of endorsing an established order of representation, the goal women writers began increasingly to give themselves, in breaking with the old order, was that of finding a language, both a form and an idiom, for an entirely new adventure, that of writing, and of writing otherwise.

Most prominent of all among the many theoretical or polemical claims put forward in the early 1970s was the assertion, associated primarily with the work of Hélène Cixous (b. 1937), that women's writing – *écriture féminine* – because it was more multiplicitous, and less subject to sublimation than that of men, was fundamentally transgressive of all social and sexual hierarchies. Women's writing, wrote Cixous, was less concerned with identity and property or propriety than that of men; it was more open to otherness, ambiguity and change, and thus more welcoming to the potentiality of the future. As Cixous explains, in a celebrated passage from *La Jeune Née* (*The Newly Born Woman*) (1975):

Je dirai: aujourd'hui l'écriture est aux femmes. Ce n'est pas une provocation, cela signifie que: la femme admet qu'il y ait de l'autre. Elle n'a pas effacé, dans son devenir-femme, la bisexualité latente chez la fille comme chez le garçon. Féminité et bisexualité vont ensemble . . . A l'homme, il est bien plus difficile de se laisser traverser par de l'autre. L'écriture, c'est en moi le passage, entrée, sortie, séjour, de l'autre que je suis et ne suis pas, que je ne sais pas être, mais que je sens passer, qui me fait vivre – qui me déchire, m'inquiète, m'altère, qui? – une, un, des?, plusieurs, de l'inconnu qui me donne justement l'envie de connaître à partir de laquelle s'élance toute vie. (p. 158)

Let me say: today, writing belongs to women. This shouldn't be taken as a provocative statement, it means that woman accepts that there is otherness. Women, in their becoming-woman, have not erased the bisexuality that is as latent in girls as it is in boys. Being female and being bisexual go together . . . For men, it is far more difficult to allow otherness to pass through you. Writing, for me, is the passing through, the going in, the coming out, the inhabiting of that other which I both am and am not, which I don't know I am, but which I can feel passing through me, and which makes me feel alive – which tears me apart, worries me, changes me from what I am, and who am I? Am I female, male, or several people at once? It's the unknown that is precisely what gives me the desire to know and which is the basis of life itself.

From the outset, though, it was clear that this was a view not without major theoretical difficulties, many of which derived from an unresolved antagonism between description and prescription, and a confusion as to whether what was being claimed here reflected the socio-economic circumstances under which women lived, or whether it was the result of some unchangeable, biological condition. Did *écriture féminine* identify how women already wrote or how they were meant to write? If the latter, by what authority? Did the theory have universal validity, or was it bounded by cultural relativity? Did it apply to all women – and men – without exception, or did it just invoke a general tendency? If one of the hallmarks of *écriture féminine* was its multiplicity, and its refusal of all forms of strict gender identity, how far was it logical to think of *écriture féminine* as being feminine (or female) at all? To an extent, powerful though they were, these objections missed the point. Properly speaking, *écriture féminine* did not aspire to the status of a systematic or global theory at all; it was intended primarily as an intervention into an avant-garde cultural debate in which explicit discussion of sexual difference was conspicuous by its very absence.[1] Its function was rather that of an injunction, or promise. As such, its importance cannot be overestimated; indeed, throughout the 1970s, the idea of *écriture féminine* continued to serve as an important platform for all kinds of experimental literary work written by women, irrespective of how far these were consistent – or, more often, inconsistent – with the position first articulated by Cixous.

Nevertheless, it is the early fictional texts of Cixous herself that provide perhaps the best example of the kind of avant-garde opening to otherness that the call for *écriture féminine* sought to embody. Indeed, in a novel such as *LA* (1976), with its untranslatable title neatly suspended between feminine article (as in *la femme*, say) and spatial deictic (as in *là*, there), between generality and singularity, it is not hard to see how Cixous's commitment to fluidity and excess gave rise to a poetic approach to textuality in which Joycean wordplay took priority over the linearity of plot, and unconscious fantasy over objective narration, even as the text itself drew on traditional Western and non-Western myths (notably the Tibetan *Book of the Dead*) both as a means of giving its protean fluidity some minimal narrative coherence and as a way of circumscribing the arena into which it sought to intervene, convinced as

Cixous was that the whole challenge of writing today was to engage with myth rather than reason, *pathos* rather than *logos*, for the simple reason that assumptions about sexual difference, like cultural myths themselves, were ultimately fantasmatic in provenance. Effusive, lyrical, prolix and constantly reinventing themselves as theoretical and autobiographical confessions, Cixous's novels are a radical and affirmative response to the hopes and anxieties of the future. But at the same time, to the extent that they endeavour to dispense with much of the traditional scaffolding of narrative, they can often seem strangely flaccid and verbose. Though at times excessively – and provocatively – indulgent towards themselves, these are texts that are also exceptionally demanding of their readers; and it is perhaps not surprising that, faced with the choice of plunging totally and unreservedly into the sensual materiality – the matrix – of Cixous's writing, or, less patiently, simply moving on elsewhere, many a reader has more than once preferred the second of these courses of action.

But if one is disappointed, as some readers undoubtedly are, by the apparent gulf between Cixous's ambitions and the seeming limpness of her writing, to what other texts might it be possible to go? In a famous footnote to her article, 'Le Rire de la Méduse' ('The Laugh of the Medusa'), which first appeared in the special Simone de Beauvoir issue of the magazine *L'Arc*, Cixous lamented the relative dearth of writing by women in twentieth-century French literature (unlike its Anglo-American counterpart).[2] Eventually, she put only three names forward for inclusion within the pantheon of modern, truly *féminin* writers: Colette, Jean Genet and Marguerite Duras. This last name was not a haphazard choice, and in the years that followed it was indeed Duras (1914–96) who came to be promoted most actively, by author and critics alike, as France's foremost experimental woman – feminist? – novelist.[3] Admittedly, during the mid-1970s, there seemed to many readers to be a fairly easy equivalence between the vision of contestatory, bisexual femininity put forward by Cixous and Duras's interest in cultural exclusion, female desire and madness, and a number of Duras's texts and films written in the wake of May 1968, alongside much of the discussion with Xavière Gauthier published in *Les Parleuses* [*Woman to Woman*] (1974), certainly appear to endorse many of the key emphases of the *écriture féminine* position. In the novel (and film) *Détruire dit-elle* ('*Destroy*', *She Said*) (1969), for instance, set in a kind of alternative hotel or sanatorium, Duras explores the dramatic impact on Elisabeth, a depressed, conventional middle-class housewife, grieving over a painful miscarriage and an unhappy love affair, of her encounter with a much younger woman called Alissa, an encounter that has the effect of suspending the boundaries between the pair and undermining the (neurotic) identity to which Elisabeth had formerly been clinging. 'Nous nous ressemblons tellement' ['We are so alike'], Alissa tells her, adding, in more provocative vein: 'Je vous aime et je vous désire' (p. 101) ['I love, and desire you']; and indeed it is as though this invocation of undifferentiated, same-sex desire between the pair is sufficient to work an affective and socio-political revolution in the text, one that leaves no stable identity in its wake and fuses together, male and female alike, the hieratic community of nomadic individuals living in the hotel.

By 1977, however, Duras had begun in interviews to declare *écriture féminine* a mistake, on the grounds that literature as such resisted all compartmentalization and was deeply inimical to any moral or political agenda, including a feminist one. This shift of opinion on Duras's part was perhaps in some measure an idiosyncratic one. It does however give an indication of the extent to which, by the late 1970s, feminism in the literary field in France had begun to forfeit the quasi-unanimity among avant-garde women writers it had enjoyed half a decade earlier, and, by a writer such as Duras (who since her days as a Communist Party activist in the late 1940s had always been quick to dissociate herself from any kind of ideological consensus) was now being perceived as laying down conformist dogma. There were other signs, too, that women writers in France were increasingly reluctant to find themselves labelled – ghettoized – as feminists. In this respect, Duras's decision to reject *écriture féminine* was symptomatic of a more general unease; and while Duras, like other women, maintained her political support for the demands of feminists for equal rights and equal representation, she became increasingly wary of the transformation of feminism into a list of desirable moral objectives which it was the duty of a writer to disseminate through her work.

Such an instrumental view of literature was, for Duras, disturbingly reminiscent of the *littérature engagée* of the post-war years, and it was one she vehemently refused, not because it was politically progressive, but because it implied a subordination of literature to non-literary values which, however desirable they might be in their own terms, served only to limit the writer's freedom to challenge established meanings. As far as Duras was concerned, taking her lead from Georges Bataille and Maurice Blanchot, literature was contestatory or it was nothing; and it is this that explains Duras's literary (and political) fascination with all those dissident voices and experiences – whether belonging to madness, exclusion, sexual violence, Judaism or the Shoah – that remained beyond the pale of traditional literary or political representation and defied the attempt to enclose them within legal norms or narrative conventions. It was here, at that fragile limit where reason, authority, meaning and narrative suddenly take leave of themselves and plunge into disorder and violence, that literature, for Duras, has its empire. 'Écrire', she insisted in *La Vie matérielle* [*Practicalities*], 'ce n'est pas raconter des histoires. C'est le contraire de raconter des histoires. C'est raconter tout à la fois. C'est raconter une histoire et l'absence de cette histoire. C'est raconter une histoire qui en passe par son absence' (pp. 31–2) ['Writing isn't just telling stories. It's exactly the opposite. It's telling everything at once. It's the telling of a story, and the absence of the story. It's telling a story through its absence.']

Throughout the 1970s and 1980s, Duras in her work sought, then, to dispense with traditional forms of narrative in order to respond to experiences or events that refused to give rise to stories. The strategy was, of course, only one among many. Other women writers, for instance, rather than rushing to abandon conventional narrative structures, were more concerned to exploit the transformative potential of story-telling as such. If telling stories was a way of shaping the world, it was argued, then perhaps the most efficient way of changing the world was to transform the stories that structured the world; indeed, if readers could be encouraged to stop being the passive consumers of dominant narrative forms, they might therefore become the active producers of their own emancipated narratives. In the mid- and late 1970s, the approach had many attractions. It enabled women novelists, in an undogmatic way, to reconcile literary activity with broad political commitment. But in addition, contrary to the strictures of an increasingly isolated literary avant-garde, it encouraged writers to experiment with narrative form while still endeavouring to appeal to a mass readership; for indeed, if the tactic were to work at all, both requirements needed to be satisfied, and perhaps the most successful texts of the second half of the decade were those that managed most cogently to ally a high degree of narrative self-consciousness with an equally high degree of literary accessibility.

The novels of Marie Cardinal (b. 1929) are a case in point. In her first major work, the best-selling novel *Les Mots pour le dire* (*The Words to Say It*) (1975), Cardinal presents her reader with the story of a first-person woman narrator – whom many readers assumed, at least half-mistakenly, to be an autobiographical portrait of the author – who finds herself beleaguered by a whole range of distressing physical symptoms mainly affecting the regularity and heaviness of her menstrual periods. In the novel, the narrator refers to this insistent but indeterminate ailment as 'la CHOSE', or 'THING', thus implying, as the text goes on to explain, that her symptoms are not purely physiological ones, but are the product of a painful inability on her part, the result of a dysfunctional family and a repressive Catholic upbringing, to name her own body with an appropriate, and confident sense of belonging. To this extent, they were not pathological in an individual sense, but simply the price paid by the protagonist to a male-dominated culture in which the words simply do not exist with which to address her experience, sexual, psychological and cultural, as a young woman growing up in French Algeria, and subsequently France itself, through the middle years of the twentieth century.

For Cardinal's narrator, reconstructing her past in the very act of recounting it to her largely unspeaking (male) psychoanalyst, bodily symptoms come to be understood as already constituting a – repressed – form of language, and indeed much of the interest of the novel lies in the slow process by which the protagonist learns to translate the silently eloquent language of her own body into clearly articulated words and narrative structures of her own. As she does this, the narrator comes to realize that the real story of her life is significantly at odds with the – alien – story told her by her family, and crucially by her own mother, and which she was expected to live out, passively, by the prudish and male-dominated culture into which she was born. The novel pays homage to the therapeutic potential of psychoanalysis as a way of liberating individuals like Cardinal's narrator from the unspoken traumas of the past; but more important still, perhaps, is the tribute paid by the novel to the transformative and curative resources of story-telling. For it is by (re-)constituting and (re-)articulating her story in words that Cardinal's narrator succeeds, by the end of the text, in appropriating for herself the means of reproduction of her life. And this is at least one reason why, for Cardinal, her protagonist's emancipation from the past was not just a private matter; it had political implications, too, as the novel acknowledges by concluding with an emblematic invocation of the events of May 1968, and thus not only with the narrator's rebirth but with the renascence of an entire community of women.

The story told by Cardinal's narrator in *Les Mots pour le dire* was necessarily more on-going process than finished product, and it was no doubt to emphasize this point that, eight years later, Cardinal followed up the book with another novel, a companion volume, so to speak, entitled *Le Passé empiété* and dealing with much the same material as the earlier book, albeit from the perspective of an older woman, now a professional weaver, who, like her predecessor, is confronted with a major crisis and a turning point in her life. Again, Cardinal's title provides the reader with an embryonic reading of the text; for as the narrator points out, the phrase is taken from sewing, and refers to a stitch which constantly returns back upon itself before moving forward. As with weaving fabrics, so with writing texts, and indeed much of the narrative in *Le Passé empiété* is taken up with the narrative's movement through time, as it tracks backwards into the past in order to find a way forward towards the future. In that process, the narrator finds herself not just spinning anew the story of her own life, but also (re-)writing, in the first person, in a startling instance of textual cross-dressing, the forgotten, suppressed, at any rate unspoken story of her own father's life up to the moment of the narrator's own conception and birth. This story-within-a-story is not however the only material from which Cardinal's novel is woven, for it is supplemented, on the distaff side, by a lengthy reworking of the story of Clytemnestra, which functions as a parallel narrative thread reworking, in mythological vein, the story of the narrator's repressed – oppressed – mother. Telling these stories for the novel's protagonist is not just to set them down and pass them on to her own children; it is also to re-embody them, and, by doing so, transform them into stories that have become changed and re-invented from within, not only for the benefit of the narrator, whose stories they are, but more importantly, for that of the reader, whose stories they aim to elicit, reshape, and reform.

(Re-)telling stories in the novels of Cardinal, even when the stories (as they often do) tell of misfortune and hardship, is in itself a dynamic, transformative process. Much the same is true of the first-person narratives of Annie Ernaux (b. 1940), *Les Armoires vides* (*Cleaned Out*) (1974), *Ce qu'ils disent ou rien* [The Things They say, or Else] (1977), and *La Femme gelée* (*A Frozen Woman*) (1981). Again, for reasons of personal history and background, the emphasis falls on the narrator's experience of exclusion from the canonic story lines of modern culture and on her inability to recognize herself in the roles that contemporary society and literature attribute to her. The student narrator of *Les Armoires vides*, for instance, the independently minded Denise Lesur, who spends the bulk of that novel suffering from the physical and mental after-effects of a backstreet abortion, is keenly aware that of the texts she is given to read at university not one properly addresses her present experience as a woman, even more so a woman who has just undergone an illegal abortion: 'Travailler un auteur du programme peut-être, Victor Hugo ou Péguy', she muses at one point. 'Quel écœurement. Il n'y a rien pour moi là-dedans sur ma situation, pas un passage pour décrire ce que je sens maintenant, m'aider à passer mes sales moments' ['Perhaps I should just get started on one of the authors on the course, like Victor Hugo or Péguy. It all makes me sick. There's nothing in all of that about what's happening to me now, not a single passage to describe what I'm feeling at this moment, to help me get through the worst'].

Denise's words sum up the predicament faced by all Ernaux's narrators. Denied access to their own stories because of the narrow parameters of the culture of which they are allegedly a part, they end up, as a result, each repeating, in spite of themselves, the stereotyped life-story that society imposes upon them. And it is this that causes Denise the prematurely emancipated student to find herself in the parlous state of isolation and lost hope dramatized in *Les Armoires vides*.

Set alongside the novels of Cardinal, these early texts of Annie Ernaux read like so many studies in abject personal failure. The dynamism that sustains Cardinal's characters in their endeavour to overcome adversity and discover freedom finds an almost exact inverted reflection in Ernaux's stories of emancipated individuals falling foul of the oppressive stereotypes governing male and female behaviour in the society of the 1950s and 1960s. But to say no more than this is to forget a crucial aspect of both Ernaux's writing and that of Cardinal. For what is fundamental for both writers, and inseparable from the very practice of writing itself, is the realization, which confounds these tales of dashed hopes and unfulfilled aspirations, that there is an irreducible, ironic discrepancy between the defeats experienced by the protagonists in the novels and the language used – and used *by* the protagonists themselves in their capacity as first-person narrators – to narrate their troubles. Writing, for Ernaux, though it may chronicle private disaster, is transformative and life-affirming for at least two reasons. First, it creates narrative where formerly there was only the oppressive silence of exclusion. Secondly, and more importantly, it allows the author, and the narrator–protagonists who are her sisters, to disown the standardized, conventional discourse of mainstream school and society and to forge for herself an idiom that, in its geographical and social singularity, in its unmistakable rhythms and movement, functions as an affirmative act of self-emancipation and self-invention. By fashioning a literary language of her own making, interwoven with the colloquialisms and regional expressions that are the mark of her own singular life's story, Ernaux's narrator is able to transform defeat into victory, exclusion into speech, and isolation into hope. This is what the last lines of *Les Armoires vides* tell the reader, by adapting the words of a song by Boris Vian, made popular in the 1960s by Serge Reggiani: 'Je ne voudrais pas crever. La concierge est toujours en bas, le dimanche, à la Cité' (p. 182) ['I don't wanna die. The concierge is always there, on Sundays, in the Residence']. Words themselves supply the possibility of hope, solidarity with others, the future; and it is, so to speak, the very language of Ernaux's novels that defies the silence from which her characters stand to suffer so much.

In their narratives, both Cardinal and Ernaux engage in constant dialogue with the real world in which their stories are enmeshed, and it is easy to read their texts for that reason as contributing to some kind of feminist project, however loosely defined. By the early 1980s, however, for many women writers, the reference to feminism had become less necessary, and in the eyes of some writers and film-makers even somewhat inhibiting. Indeed, with the exception of Hélène Cixous, whose own later work, notably for the theatre, had itself turned to more detailed scrutiny of the material circumstances of historical change, the theoretical debate about sexual difference in the literary field in France found itself more or less stalled, even though issues of sexual difference continued to exert a significant impact elsewhere, as for instance in the philosophical work of women such as Luce Irigaray, Sarah Kofman, or Michèle Le Dœuff, not to mention the influential writings of Jacques Derrida. For numerous reasons, after the election of Mitterrand to the presidency in 1981, the 1980s became a period of increasing retrenchment. Nevertheless, throughout the decade, a growing number of women writers began publishing their work. But if they did so, increasingly, in the absence of explicit reference to any large-scale feminist project of the sort envisaged in the early 1970s, this did not mean they were any the less willing to confront the challenges of inventing new writing forms and, in much of their work, obliquely but consistently, began to push back once again the boundaries of what women were allowed to write.

Typical of the new climate that resulted was the award of the prix Goncourt to the seventy-year-old Duras for her autobiographical text, *L'Amant* (*The Lover*). What the prize rewarded of course was not autobiographical certainty, but a more contestatory mixture of veracity and divagation, and a heady brew of sexuality, politics, exoticism, confession and verbal improvisation. Admittedly, the price of consecration by the literary establishment was not negligible, for it meant that overnight Duras was transformed into a mythic entity, a kind of archetypal *diva*. The disadvantages of this were plain to see, but what the lionization of Duras did also show, in the mid-1980s, perhaps for the first time, was the extent to which it was possible in France to be taken seriously simultaneously as a writer and as a woman writer. Duras during those years was an author whose sex and gender were central to all that she wrote; for all that, her status was that of a writer *tout court*, not a woman writer. To that extent, Duras's refusal to be relegated to the compartmentalized world of women's writing had paid off. The move was an important one; and it was indicative of a new and increasing self-confidence on the part of women writers in general in France. In turn, this made it possible for women writers to adopt a greater degree of frankness or permissiveness in the years that followed, and in 1988, for instance, the novelist Alina Reyes (b. 1956) enjoyed some considerable notoriety for the explicitness of her erotic novel *Le Boucher* (*The Butcher*), a steamy account of the daily doings of a butcher, penetrating and piercing flesh with his blade, as a result of which Reyes not only found herself widely translated, but adopted too by Philippe Sollers for inclusion in the series associated with the literary periodical *L'Infini*, which published two of her subsequent novels, giving the reader to understand that what her fiction lacked in originality or subtlety it made up for in timeliness and marketability.

Of the new direction being explored by other women writers throughout the 1980s and 1990s perhaps a more interesting example is that provided by the novels of Marie Redonnet (b. 1948). The name is a pseudonym, originally taken from the author's mother.[4] On Redonnet's part, the gesture is a clear expression of her preference for the matrilinear principle, representing circularity and return, and her rejection of the patrilinear logic characteristic of all end-dominated, progressive conceptions of history (and narrative). At the same time, the key realization informing all Redonnet's work is a sense of the unredeemed negativity and inevitability of history. The antagonism between these two competing principles – supplying the reader with images of recurrence and decay, fatality and hope – is what gives Redonnet's narratives their strange mixture of grimness and light-heartedness. Examining the depredations of the past, as she does in almost all her novels, Redonnet is more essentially concerned with the question of the future, and with the need to inquire, obliquely, into the possibilities of the future and, in particular, into the possibilities for women in the future.

This dilemma is what is perhaps most visibly at issue in her best-known work, the three-novel sequence, *Splendid Hôtel* (1986), *Forever Valley* (1986), and *Rose Mélie Rose* (1987). In the first two of these short texts, the reader is given a pair of falsely cheerful, even whimsical first-person narratives, recounted by women, which ultimately turn out to be far more sinister than at first appears; these are stories, so to speak, that belie their own titles, and deal not with glamorous futures, but with the effects of lost heritages and remorseless physical, social and psychological decline. But as with the novels of Annie Ernaux, in both texts it is as though writing itself were not only the inevitable witness of decadence and dissipation, but also the best and only antidote to the phenomenon of dissolution. Alongside its two bleaker predecessors, the third part in this triptych, *Rose Mélie Rose*, functions as a story of redemption and rebirth. Indeed, from the outset, this possibility of rebirth is signalled not only by the circular structure of the title of the book, but by the strange and fantastical coincidence, with which the narrative begins, conflating the death of Rose, a souvenir-shop owner, and the first menstrual period of Mélie, the foundling first discovered by Rose under a waterfall. Death and regeneration coincide, then, and dispatch Mélie on a journey that takes up the rest of the novel. That journey, too, is circular, and the novel ends with Mélie giving birth to a child named Rose whom, in a ritualistic re-enactment of the past, she promptly abandons in the grotto by the original waterfall. Against a general background of loss and abandonment, then, a circular, matrilinear movement, coupling ending with renewal, and fresh life with the inevitability of death, seems to hold out the prospect of a transfigured future, without it ever being clear, however, whether Redonnet's characters will ever be successful in the attempt to elude the crushing weight of their own past or able to release the present from the sombre and corrupt political legacy that bedevils the movement for social reform, as described for instance in the political fable, *Nevermore* (1994).

Throughout Redonnet's work, the inherent tension between fatalism and eschatology leads the author to abandon literary realism in preference for a self-consciously archaic mode of story-telling in which the use of fantasy is tinged irremediably with anxiety and despair. In its very distance from realism, as a result, Redonnet's writing hovers uncertainly between the utopia it promises and the dystopia it reveals. Much the same ambiguity is also a key characteristic of the novels of Marie NDiaye (b. 1967). There, too, a woman writer finds herself refashioning inherited narrative forms in order to inscribe within them other desires and hopes, without it ever being evident whether these will successfully be realized or satisfied. In *Quant au riche avenir* [As for the Affluent Future] (1985), for instance, the author's first novel, published when she was only eighteen, NDiaye explores with thrilling virtuosity the hypotactic structure of French syntax, using it as a way of dramatizing the complex mental and verbal constructions erected, in a series of endless conjectures, by her young (male) protagonist, 'le jeune Z', to negotiate his increasingly remote relationship with the outside world and to protect himself from impending emotional disaster. This is language not as revelation but concealment, words used as a kind of rampart, designed seemingly to ward off distress, but only in full, anxious knowledge of the fact that whatever words are meant to protect against has insidiously and unavoidably already taken root within them, as the author was to demonstrate even more incisively in *Comédie classique* [A Classic Comedy] (1987), a text that, despite being over one hundred pages long, consisted of a single sentence!

Elsewhere in NDiaye's fiction, as in the texts of Marie Redonnet, the concerns that recur are those of inheritance and continuity, the past and the future. In *En famille* (*Among Family*) (1990), NDiaye's longest and most ambitious work, though perhaps not her most successful, the plot, which stands midway between *The Castle* and a desolate version of *Sleeping Beauty* or *Cinderella*, revolves around the outsider status of the heroine, a young woman of whom the reader is told only that her name is not Fanny, who embarks on a foolish quest for her aunt Léda, who was absent from her christening, in the belief that with Léda lies the secret that will lead to the re-establishment of family harmony. But by the end of the novel, the family is not restored to integrity or unity, indeed rather the reverse, and Fanny is left in suspense between the evidence of her complaint that family life is not what it was, and the fact that her own actions to reconstruct the family do more to cause further bitterness than to repair the past. A similar lesson is at the heart of *La Sorcière* [The Witch] (1996). Here, in an entertainingly satirical romp, the narrator, an unsuccessful, married witch, loses husband, children and parents as a result of her inherited gifts. The past, then, is more poisoned chalice than munificent tradition, and there seems little escape for the protagonist from the disasters that dog her actions, well intentioned though they seem, to pass on her gift to her two daughters, reconcile her parents, and maintain a happy marriage. Throughout, NDiaye's concern is with the status of the outsider, and in her work there seems no possibility of reconciling what on the part of the outsider features as undiminished nostalgia for integration, and what confronts the outsider in the guise of her or his insurmountable exclusion.

Interestingly, the dilemma explored in NDiaye's books is one that, though it affects women, and does so at times severely, is hardly specific to them. On the contrary, it is as though the persistent concern with the inability – or refusal – of women to inherit the world as it is offered to them has given way in NDiaye's work to a more broadly based, less gender-specific exploration of the condition of the outsider as such. This theme of historical or cultural marginalization is one that recurs in the work of many other contemporary French women novelists, and finds particularly powerful expression in the critically acclaimed work of Sylvie Germain (b. 1954). In her first novel, the prize-winning *Le Livre des nuits* (*The Book of Nights*) (1985), Germain uses the resources of a kind of magical realism to construct a haunting half-legendary, half-historical narrative, dealing with the fate of the Péniel family, or more exactly of Victor-Flandrin Péniel and his four successive wives, each of whom produces a set of twins before dying shortly afterwards. What the story explores, from this obliquely transfigurative perspective, is the long, brutal – and brutish – history of war and destruction in France from the Franco-Prussian War till the Occupation. History here is not an object of national or nationalist celebration, but a series of faceless acts of slaughter that exact from those who are most remote from its so-called glorious achievements the harshest and most daunting sacrifices. Indeed, in all Germain's novels, it is the excluded, anonymous, marginal individual who suffers most the pain and torment that history imposes on the humble. And if her protagonists acquire in the process a gentle innocence that is little short of saintliness, it is because for Germain exclusion from history seems to be the only possible ground for insight into the intensity that lies beyond it. Such at any rate, it would seem, is the lesson of *Immensités* [Vast Perspectives] (1993), the story of Prokop Poupa, a former Prague literature teacher dismissed from his university post after the events of August 1968, and who, in a private and original response to this defeat by history, discovers the spiritual vastness still to be found, paradoxically, in his exiguous flat, in the traces of damp left like so many florid inscriptions on the walls and ceiling of the WC.

As these examples suggest, many of Germain's protagonists, though far from all of them, are men, and it is clear that, in the endeavour to grapple with the impasses of history, the author herself is as much concerned with the male as with the female line. However this should not be taken to represent an abandonment of the explicit commitment to feminism that was such an important article of faith for Germain's predecessors in the 1970s. The reality is perhaps more nearly the reverse.

Indeed, increasingly, in the 1990s, women novelists in France began once more to write, paradoxically, with what one might call a newly discovered innocence: an innocence that is not the result of congenital feminine naïvety, but rather the fruit of an adventure that has led women writers in France to explore many different possible narrative strategies, only for them then to return, fortified and transformed, once more to their starting point. But starting over, so to speak, in this way, they of course find themselves, as in the beginning, once again entrusted with the challenge of discovering and inventing a literary idiom capable of speaking the diversity and complexity of what it is, in France, on the cusp of the third millennium, to be a woman, writing.

NOTES

1 One symptom of the relative neglect of questions of sexual difference by the textual avant-garde of the early 1970s, common both to the *nouveau roman* and to the writers associated with *Tel Quel*, was the belief in the subversive potential of male-authored eroticism and pornography (in the work, say, of Sade, Bataille, Robbe-Grillet, Guyotat and others), without there being a corresponding interest in so-called transgressive writing by women. Indeed, Julia Kristeva, perhaps the foremost theorist of the avant-garde literary text in the years after 1968, waited till 1987 to publish her sustained critical account of a woman writer. This was Marguerite Duras, whose work Kristeva analyses, in rather tepid fashion, in her *Soleil noir: dépression et mélancolie* (*Black Sun: Depression and Melancholia*), pp. 227–65.

2 See Hélène Cixous, 'Le Rire de la Méduse', *L'Arc*, 61 (1975), 39–54 (at 42).

3 Duras's relations with feminism were in fact far more complicated, as I attempt to show in my *Marguerite Duras: Apocalyptic Desires*.

4 See Fallaize, *French Women's Writing*, p. 160.

CHAPTER NINE

Changing the script: women writers and the rise of autobiography

Michael Sheringham

The early 1980s saw the publication of four important works of auto-biography by women writers. *Enfance* by Nathalie Sarraute (1983), and *L'Amant* (1984) by Marguerite Duras, came from the pens of established novelists at the peak of their careers. *La Place* (1983) by Annie Ernaux, and *L'Amour, la fantasia*, by Assia Djebar (1985) were by younger writers for whom the switch to autobiography would represent a decisive point in their evolution. Published within a brief space of time, these texts marked a crucial moment in the development of both autobiography and women's writing in France. From this point on autobiography has been at the centre of a number of important currents in French litera-ture and culture, and the contribution of women writers to this domain has been considerable.[1] This moment is, then, a vantage point from which to look back at women's autobiography in the earlier part of the twentieth century, and forwards to more recent developments in auto-biographical writing, where Ernaux and Djebar, along with other women writers, have continued to be prominent.

Sarraute (1900–99) and Duras had both been linked with the *nouveau roman* movement. Their motive in turning to autobiography was not the conventional one of seeking to record a life for posterity, nor did it involve abandoning or breaking stylistically with their earlier creative work. Whilst they would soon be emulated by male colleagues (notably Alain Robbe-Grillet, who published *Le Miroir qui revient*, the first volume of a trilogy of autobiographical texts, in 1985), these women writers were the first to exploit the possibilities afforded by a radical reassessment of the nature of autobiography, and its promotion from the sub-literary side-lines to the centre of serious critical attention, that had occurred in the previous decade. The key date is 1975, which saw the appearance of three texts which, in different ways, contributed massively to the repositioning of autobiography. *Roland Barthes par Roland Barthes* was the work of a writer who had been at the forefront of the movement in French thought which – initially under the banner of structuralism, and propelled by new developments in linguistics, anthropology, psychoanalysis and history – had mounted an onslaught on the conventional humanist view of identity, and, in the literary context, on the commonplace idea of the author as self-evident originator of meaning. In this context, autobiography, often assumed to be a genre where an individual confidently ascribes secure meanings to the events of his or her life, could be seen as a bastion of outmoded ideas. What then was Barthes doing writing an autobiography? Both in the way it was written and in some of its prominent themes, Barthes's text showed that if it marked a 'retour du sujet', a desire to bring subjectivity back into the frame of discussion, this was by no means to be construed as a return to the old humanist psychological subject. Presenting his autobiography as a series of fragments in alphabetical order, and oscillating constantly between first- and third-person pronouns, Barthes evaded the imposition of chronological order, associated with causality and determinism, and constantly questioned his enterprise, treating himself as if he were a fictional character, while at the same time sticking to the verifiable facts of his life.

Published in the same year, Philippe Lejeune's *Le Pacte autobiographique* was to have a major impact on both literary critics and would-be autobiographers. By offering close readings of major works in the French autobiographical tradition, notably Rousseau, Stendhal, Gide, Leiris and Sartre, Lejeune not only demonstrated the remarkable inventiveness they had demonstrated in writing about their lives, but quashed any idea that a single set of assumptions about human lives underlay the genre called autobiography. Defining it in terms of a pact or contract with the reader, Lejeune's approach to autobiography underlined the creative flexibility it allowed, and emphasized that, far from being reducible to a single motive, autobiographical texts could be harnessed to a range of different projects. The third important work published in 1975, Georges Perec's *W ou le souvenir d'enfance*, exemplified this perfectly. Here, chapters from an autobiographical narrative which sifts and scans a meagre stock of childhood memories, enshrined in talismanic traces such as torn photographs and scraps of paper, alternate with chapters from a fictional story written when Perec was an adolescent. Progressively it emerges that both narratives point to a horror neither kind of text can name – the annihilation of the author's mother at Auschwitz. Perec's work is concerned not only with the individual past but with historical memory and testimony, and it showed how versatile a mode autobiography could be, and how potentially stimulating its combination of public and private, fact and fiction, literariness and referentiality.

The new-found prestige of autobiography in the late 1970s involved more than the development of a heritage. It marked one of those points in intellectual history when the potential of autobiography to map and probe important aspects of human reality matched new currents in the way the constitution of the individual subject was viewed.

Autobiography now had much to offer subjects and communities of subjects in search of ways of articulating a new sense of identity. In the front line of these were women writers, and writers from the ethnic margins.[2] Where women's writing in France is concerned, the immediate context for the resurgence of autobiography was another forum where the return of subjectivity was perceptible. This was *écriture féminine*, associated particularly, as shown in the previous chapter, with Hélène Cixous. 1975 saw the publication of 'Le Rire de la Méduse' ('The Laugh of the Medusa') and *La Jeune Née* (*The Newly Born Woman*), key texts in which Cixous calls for the exploration of feminine subjectivity in writing. Based on the postulate that language itself bears the marks of gender division, *écriture féminine* involves ways of writing aimed specifically at giving direct expression to feminine experience. But the emphasis on otherness and difference, whilst focusing attention on body and senses, tends to lead away from individuation, and thus in fact away from autobiography. There is no room for Lejeune's pact with the reader, guaranteeing the common identity of narrator, author and protagonist, in a mode of writing which, if it is closely tied to the individual psyche, has no commitment to external reference. If, in its concern for the essence of femininity, *écriture féminine* deals with lived experience, the focus tends to be on the immediacy of the body's 'vécu', or lived experience, and on the processes through which femininity can be articulated and celebrated, rather than on historically rooted experience. To some degree, the emergence of the autobiographical writing of Duras, Sarraute, Ernaux and Djebar can be linked to a resistance to *écriture féminine*, whilst on the other hand a *rapprochement* between *écriture féminine* and autobiography will occur, notably in the work of Cixous, at the end of the 1980s.[3]

Where women writers are concerned, therefore, the turning point with regard to autobiography occurs in the 1980s, and is epitomized, in different ways, by the four texts mentioned at the outset. If we look at these autobiographies globally, and ask why they are important and successful, we can situate the change that takes place at this point in relation to four aspects or tendencies:

(*i*) The prominence given to the relationship with significant others, especially parents
(*ii*) Empowerment through writing
(*iii*) The search for new autobiographical forms
(*iv*) The grounding of individual experience in historical and material reality.

The first two features are perennial in women's autobiography, but are given a new twist in the 1980s by the third, largely through the elaboration of new autobiographical devices by Sarraute and Duras. The fourth aspect, subsuming and developing the others, belongs squarely to the 1980s, and finds particularly striking expression in the texts by Ernaux and Djebar, as well as in the autobiographical work of Marguerite Yourcenar and Hélène Cixous. The first three aspects can be considered together.

Since the 1970s, the rise of a dual interest in women's writing and autobiography studies has led critics to revisit the literary past with a view to identifying canonical features in female-authored autobiographical texts. In the French context this has led to the investigation of common ground in such writings as George Sand's *Histoire de ma vie* (*The Story of my Life*), the memoirs of Madame Roland and Daniel Stern (Marie d'Agoult), and twentieth-century works by Colette, Clara Malraux, Simone de Beauvoir, Violette Leduc and Marguerite Duras. A central point in the general consensus that has emerged is that the issue of gender and the fact of femininity are particularly prominent in female autobiography, and are linked to a number of constraints, real or imagined, to which these writers consistently refer. For example, in delineating the structure of their lives as they perceive them, women autobiographers characteristically place much greater emphasis than their male counterparts on familial networks as well as on different types of dependency that are held to constrain the range and nature of their existences. The immensely detailed account of her father's life with which George Sand opens her autobiography is often cited in support of the view that the most pervasive feature of female autobiography is the tendency to define the self in relation to significant others rather than in terms of self-creation. This may be associated with the fact that, by contrast with male autobiographers, women do not tend to perceive themselves as representative of their epoch, nor as possessing essential and sovereign selves enjoying a privileged existence in the eyes of God. If women perceive themselves as representing anything it is the fate of womanhood, a common lot rather than an individuating destiny, and this tends to militate against the identification of an inviolable core of individuality. As one critic puts it: 'the subject of women's autobiography is a self both occulted and overexposed by the fact of her femininity as a social reality'.[4] Inevitably, therefore, canonical women's autobiographies tend to have a similar pattern, involving the struggle with social and cultural constructions of femininity in the context of complex familial relationships, and against the background of the biological realities of the female condition. Where bodily experience (puberty, sexuality, pregnancy) is invoked it is often in ambivalent or negative terms. The mother–daughter relationship receives prolonged attention, as the site of ambivalent emotions of identification and repulsion, while the father–daughter relationship is often linked to the question of liberation from the constraints of femininity.

For the majority of female French autobiographers who are writers, a central feature of the traditional pattern is the achievement of freedom through writing itself. It has been observed that 'writing as a vocation and as a locus of identity is paradigmatic'.[5] In what has been called the 'valorized trajectory' in female autobiography, it is the pen that enables the subject to transcend the feminine condition. Because writing is perceived as a masculine preserve, the role of writer is not represented as the gift of genes or genius, but as a status won through a gradual and dramatic process of experiment and authorization. This emphasis on rebirth as an autonomous being through literary and intellectual achievement means that many female autobiographies tend to bracket bodily experience as an obstacle to be surmounted and thus to remove the mark of gender from the autobiographical text. In doing so they achieve assimilation into a genre which, in its canonical forms, 'fails to interrogate gender as a meaningful category'. Thus, for Nancy Miller, it is the autobiographical fictions of Colette, featuring 'a textual "I" [that] is not bound by genre',[6] that offer readers a true grip on gendered subjectivity. One of the achievements of recent autobiographies by French women writers is in fact to find solutions to this problem, through ways of making autobiography and gender coalesce. First, however, we should consider a view that both complements and questions Miller's. For Bella Brodski and Celeste Schenk, one of the strengths of female autobiography, cutting across traditional and modernist manifestations of autobiographical practice, is its strongly relational character. Lacking a secure, externally sanctioned, basis of selfhood, women autobiographers give more space to the role of the Other in the constitution of identity, and in doing so come closer to reflecting contemporary versions of the subject than male autobiographers whose narratives consecrate the imaginary self. Like Miller, Brodski and Schenk are sceptical about the capacity of traditional autobiographical narrative to deal with gendered subjectivity as opposed to sexuality. But in their account of both a traditional text and an experimental text they emphasize the ways in which women autobiographers, by foregrounding the relational nature of identity, have challenged established representations of women.[7]

Whilst the importance of Colette in the field of twentieth-century French women's writing, and the crucial place of autobiographical elements in her work, are not in doubt, it would be perverse to give excessive prominence to a writer who always strongly resisted the referential commitments of autobiography. Colette preferred autobiographical fictions, or memoirs, or a strategy that later became known as *autofiction*, where the writer figures in the text under his or her real identity but in a narrative containing manifestly fictional elements, making it impossible for the reader to gauge the degrees of truth or fiction. In *La Maison de Claudine* (*My Mother's House*) (1922), which she declared to be her most 'truthful' work, the title, literally 'Claudine's House', displays the name of a fictional alter ego, heroine of a series of earlier partly autobiographical novels, rather than Colette's own *nom de plume*. Moreover, even if they involve an engagement with memory, and a renegotiation of the relationship with her mother (continued in *Sido*, 1936), the chapters of *La Maison de Claudine*, each having the characteristics of a short story, lack narrative continuity, and this not only militates against any overall synthesis of past experience but also against the kind of relationship with a reader that is a mark of autobiography.

In many respects Simone de Beauvoir's *Mémoires d'une jeune fille rangée* (*Memoirs of a Dutiful Daughter*) (1958) bears all the marks of canonical women's autobiography. The account of liberation and independence achieved through education, academic distinction and incorporation into the ranks of intellectuals and writers is closely tied both to the question of the social status of women and to relationships with significant others, notably mother and father, lovers and mentors, a close friend, Zaza, who fails in the same struggle, and finally Jean-Paul Sartre who sanctions Beauvoir's mature identity by treating her as an equal and by becoming her partner. One of the great distinctions of this work is the sustained, closely focused attention Beauvoir brings to her childhood and adolescence, through an account that is strongly linear. Whilst thematically and intellectually the question of gender is in the forefront of *Mémoires d'une jeune fille rangée*, this has little impact on the text's formal or stylistic identity. In this respect it conforms to the general pattern of women's auto-biographies up till then, staying within the bounds of autobiographical convention rather than breaking new ground. The subsequent volumes of her autobiographical trilogy – *La Force de l'âge* (*The Prime of Life*) (1960), *La Force des choses* (*Force of Circumstance*) (1963) – are closer to memoirs, focus-ing on Beauvoir's participation in the intellectual life of her time, record-ing personal matters, such as her affair with an American writer, through extensive quotation of diaries and other materials. The compelling inter-est of Beauvoir as an autobiographer lies less in the inherent literary qual-ities of these works than in the way later books such as *Une Mort très douce* (*A Very Easy Death*) (1964), *Tout compte fait* (*All Said and Done*) (1972), and *La Céremonie des adieux* (*Adieux: A Farewell to Sartre*) (1981) continue and develop an increasingly dominant autobiographical project.

It is instructive to compare Beauvoir as autobiographer with Violette Leduc, a writer who was her fanatical admirer and protégée. In the important prefatory essay she wrote for *La Bâtarde* (1964), a first volume of autobiography which brought Leduc fame and fortune after the failure of her earlier autobiographical novels, Beauvoir claims that, in her relations with others, Leduc 'n'avait fait qu'assumer son destin. Elle lui invente un sens imprévu quand elle s'oriente vers la littérature' ['had done no more than accept her destiny. She invents an unexpected meaning for it when she turns to literature'].[8] But if the prominence of personal relationships and the discovery of writing are canonical, Leduc's autobiographical practice differs radically from Beauvoir's and has increasingly placed her at the forefront of female French autobiog-raphers. This can be linked to the fact that, where for Beauvoir writing is a vocation that is seen to emerge and acquire meaning by virtue of a chain of experiences and influences on which the autobiographer reports, for Leduc writing is, as Beauvoir herself puts it, the outcome of a process of choice and self-invention. And, as Beauvoir further implies, this process is not only attested to in *La Bâtarde* but enacted in its pages. In *La Bâtarde* autobiography becomes a performative mode, in other words a transitive process, a transaction with feedback, where the way writing is carried out transforms the writer, the text and the reader, as well as the relations between these poles. In this respect *La Bâtarde* bears one of the hallmarks of authentically innovatory autobiographical texts: a recognition that the self in the text is in significant respects inseparable from the text itself, and therefore enshrined as much in the style, voice, or practice of the autobiographer, made manifest by the adoption of a particular device or devices. The device – a personal stamp or trademark

– provides the text with its individual signature. In Leduc's case the devices that together make up her signature, and thus the textual identity she forges for herself in the text, include the sentence-by-sentence texture or atmosphere of her prose, the roles she allocates to her readers and the way she foregrounds her body and physical appearance. Consistently at stake in Leduc's autobiography is the desire to renegotiate her relationship to her own past. Writing is crucial because it is as a writer that Leduc can claim to have appropriated her own past identity, becoming active agent rather than passive victim: her original illegitimacy (she is 'une bâtarde') will have been superseded by a new legitimacy vested in the persona of the writer. She therefore turns writing into a performance, and conscripts her readers as witnesses to this process. In doing so she makes a spectacle of herself, and thus makes the transaction being staged in the writer–reader process a mirror for other processes. First, a mirror for the acute bodily awareness that gives her a profound insight into the ways the female body is ideologically controlled and produced. Second, a mirror for the dynamic at work in her relationships with others which perpetuates the chronic imbalances and insecurities of her childhood. The devices deployed in *La Bâtarde* and in Leduc's subsequent works of autobiography, *La Folie en tête* (*Mad in Pursuit*) (1970), and the posthumous *La Chasse à l'amour* [Hunting for Love] (1973), contrive to show that autobiography – as a mode of writing, literary in the stylistic strategies and registers it can accommodate, but crucially referential in its orientation to the real world and real time – can engender change and create new identities.

Leduc was arguably the first French woman writer to exploit the inherent potential of autobiography in this way and, particularly in the light of more recent developments, the importance of her work, previously overshadowed by Beauvoir, is increasingly recognized. At all events, when we turn to the major autobiographical texts produced twenty years after *La Bâtarde* by two of Leduc's approximate contemporaries, the affinities are more with her work than with that of Beauvoir. In both cases perennial features of women's autobiography – significant others and the trajectory that leads to the discovery of identity through writing – are refashioned by the adoption of devices that make autobiography an act and a performance.

In Nathalie Sarraute's *Enfance* (*Childhood*) (1983) the salient devices that give the text its signature are fragmentation and the splitting of the narrating voice into two channels. The latter device involves a dialogue between a first narrator and an alter ego who responds to its partner in a variety of ways, ranging from censure to collaborative encouragement. This keeps the main focus initially on the narrating present, and on the process of remembering (and negotiating with memory), rather than on the narrated past. Instead of a continuous sequence, we are presented with a succession of plunges back into the folds of memory and this engenders a text made up of some seventy fragments, each a few pages long. The book recounts a childhood scarred by a broken marriage. Each fragment is based on a particular moment, often involving a phrase uttered by an adult in one of the child's provisional households. Sarraute seeks to demonstrate the way words encapsulate extremely powerful forces at work in the intersubjective space of human relationships.

In most of the fragments of *Enfance* two voices delve into the emotional currents exposed by the decision to pursue the ramifications of a particular piece of linguistic behaviour, frequently a prohibition, as when the child is told not to plunge her scissors into a sofa, or a warning, as when she is told to chew her food properly. The first voice usually identifies with the child, and with submission to the emotional currents rekindled by the remembered phrase. The second voice is often more detached and critical, pointing to flaws and inconsistencies in what the first voice claims to remember, and drawing attention to the pitfalls of hindsight, false memory, self-delusion and literary embellishment. But, through its transformations, the dialogue device tends to authenticate rather than discredit the autobiographical act, construing it as an open-ended, interrogative process rather than a matter of laying down the law. As in the case of Leduc, the autobiographer's devices enact a process, in this case an active pursuit of elusive truth on the borderline between language and the inarticulate, and between the past and the present. If in Sarraute's case the autobiographical process is not generated by a pressing need to negotiate a new sense of identity, it is nevertheless geared to negotiating a new relationship with the past, and to establishing continuity between childhood and adult identities. There is an obvious similarity between the way the child progressively gains control over the powerful forces at work in her family relationships by finding ways of ordering and distancing her experience, and the way the two narrating voices collaborate in probing the truth about the girl's past feelings and their (often only implicit) repercussions in the adult.

Like *Enfance*, Marguerite Duras's *L'Amant* (*The Lover*) (1984) is a fragmentary text where a central device serves to emphasize the conjectural aspect of the autobiographical process, and to probe the nature of autobiographical memory. Here the device is that of an imaginary

photograph that could have been taken at a particularly crucial junc-
ture in the autobiographer's life. The fact that the photo does not exist
raises questions about the event it would have recorded, but in fact is
used to draw attention to the problematic status of all memories of past
events. For even if the photograph had been taken (and there is considerable evidence to suggest that a real photograph, similar to the one
imagined in *L'Amant* in all respects save the context in which it was
taken, forms the basis of the author's reflections) it would still have been
necessary to decipher it, to explore its meaning by attempting to
imagine its link to a given context, and by interpreting the elements it
makes visible. Duras in fact proceeds as if the photo – which would have
depicted her, aged fifteen, on a ferry crossing the Mekong in French
Indo-China on the occasion when she met a rich young Chinese man
who was to become her lover – actually existed. In other words she
interrogates the imaginary image as she would a real one, venturing
hypotheses as to what it reveals. In doing so Duras endorses Roland
Barthes's extemely influential theories about the photographic image
outlined in his *La Chambre claire* (1980). Here Barthes insists on the par-
adoxical status of the photograph, which both constitutes the material
trace of a past event that *must have* happened (and to which, if it depicts
us, we are linked as by an umbilical cord), and, at the same time, pro-
claims the absolute pastness, the death, of the moment it commemorates, and thus allows unlimited scope for the play of conjecture.
Absent or present, real or imaginary, the photograph of oneself in the
past generates a potentially endless process of self-scrutiny driven by the
way we see ourselves and the way we think others see us. The photograph in *L'Amant* points to a self that is partially of the order of the
image, and hence, as Barthes again suggests in his autobiography, of the
order of the imaginary (conceived in psychoanalytical terms as a
process of objectification which incorporates the way we think we are
seen and the way we would like to be seen). The fifteen-year-old Duras
is dressed in glamorous but bargain-basement clothes, notably a man's
hat and a skimpy dress, that make the image susceptible of multiple
decodings. It enfolds (and reveals to the elderly narrating self) the girl's
precocious sexuality, her self-awareness as an object of desire, and her
aspiration to see desire as the antidote to her family. It reveals (and
therefore serves as a line back to) the girl's dismal family circumstances,
evoking her sad, crazy mother, partly responsible for decking her out in
these unsuitable clothes, her feuding brothers and the deprived poor-
white colonialist milieu she was brought up in. The photo also gives

access, through the expression in the girl's eyes, to the avenues of writing and desire (and therefore the close links between these two things) that will provide the girl's escape route from the family to which, as the photo also predicts, she will nevertheless remain wedded.

L'Amant gives prominence to those staples of women's autobiography, the mother-figure, family relationships, and writing as a source of identity. But, as in *Enfance*, this canonical material, along with other themes relating to gender, the body, intertextuality, and history, is marshalled in new ways and exposed to new kinds of investigation. The invention of a device which gives the autobiographical text its unique character accompanies the invention of new kinds of autobiographical strategy. *L'Amant* points to features – the prominence given to the photographic image, and to the notion of the trace, the interaction of individual and collective memory – that are central to the way French women writers have been instrumental in reshaping the agenda of autobiography.

By the early 1980s there were many signs that the rehabilitation of autobiography was by no means a narrowly literary matter but a symptom of a much wider phenomenon cutting across and linking a diversity of fields, including literary theory and practice, sociology, ethnography and history, and sponsoring a widespread blurring of distinctions between established genres. The crisis of identity engendered by structuralism and poststructuralism spawned new ways of thinking, inspired by interdisciplinary practices where the talk was not of the 'death of the author' but of a plural subject dispersed across various zones (sexual, juridical, political, ethnic, historical, etc.), and finding agency and identity, if not unity and continuity, through participation in a variety of processes and transactions. Autobiography, by virtue of its inherently hybrid status, on the border between fiction and reference, offered itself as the ideal vehicle for a subject conceived as process, and for a process conceived in terms of the production of (always provisional) identities through an engagement with heterogeneous elements. In this context, class, gender, and ethnicity emerged among the most significant elements in the production of individual and cultural identities to which autobiography could contribute. In Annie Ernaux's *La Place* (*Positions*), for example, autobiographical enquiry takes over from fiction and combines with other discourses and strategies, including those of biography, sociology and ethnography, to explore class, gender and family. In Assia Djebar's *L'Amour, la fantasia* (*Fantasia: An Algerian Calvacade*), gender, ethnicity and colonialism are explored through an autobiographical project fusing personal testimony and historical evidence.

Over the last twenty years the work of Annie Ernaux has evolved from autobiographical fiction to a fusion of autobiography and biography rooted partly in sociological or ethnographic enquiry, and then to another form of autobiographical writing, affiliated to the diary, where attention falls on the subject's interactions with her present everyday environment. *Les Armoires vides* (*Cleaned Out*) (1974), her first book, is in many ways a standard autobiographical novel about a young woman from a working-class background who has transcended the limits of her milieu by academic success, but is then riven by feelings of class guilt and betrayal. Having pursued the vein of autobiographical fiction in two other novels, Ernaux adopted a different mode in *La Place* (*Positions*), carefully retracing her father's life. The change was partly dictated by the feeling that literary embellishment constituted a betrayal not only of her father but also of her own past self. If understanding her father was to serve as a means of understanding herself it was important to record the reality of his world as objectively as possible, substituting an *écriture plate* [flat style] for literary artistry, and assembling the 'signes objectifs d'une éxistence que j'ai aussi partagée' (p. 24) ['the objective signs of an existence I have also shared']. Objectivity is here conceived as a route to the exact 'placing' of subjective experience, and thus to an understanding of the strata of one's identity. And the 'objective signs' on which Ernaux focuses in *La Place*, as in a subsequent work on her mother, *Une Femme* (*A Woman's Story*) (1986), are to be found in the kinds of material which would be the quarry of the social historian, the sociologist, the socio-linguist or the practitioner of *ethnologie rurale*: photographs, family rituals, public and private space, linguistic behaviour, gestures, attitudes. Yet Ernaux, as narrating 'Je', does not simply enumerate or describe. Like its successors, *La Place* is a highly self-reflexive work in which the author constantly probes her own methods and motives, echoing the consistently self-questioning nature of genuine autobiographical enquiry. One of Ernaux's concerns is memory, and particularly the interconnections between individual memory and social or class memory, preserved in memory traces. Ernaux found that unearthing buried memories was harder than inventing fictional ones: the memory triggers were not Proustian associations but the sight of ordinary people in everyday situations:

C'est dans la manière dont les gens s'assoient et s'ennuient dans les salles d'attente, interpellent leurs enfants, font au revoir sur les quais de gare que j'ai cherché la figure de mon père. J'ai retrouvé dans des êtres anonymes rencontrés n'importe où, porteurs à leur insu des signes de force ou d'humiliation, la réalité oubliée de sa condition. (*La Place*, p. 100)

It's in the way people sit and get bored in waiting rooms, chivy their children, say their goodbyes on station platforms that I sought the image of my father. It was in anonymous people I met here and there, unwitting bearers of the marks of force or humiliation, that I found the forgotten reality of this condition.

Ernaux reconstitutes the 'réalité oubliée' [forgotten reality] of her father's condition, and a crucial dimension of her own identity, via glimpses of strangers, ordinary people like him, shouting at the kids, or yawning in waiting rooms.

Journal du dehors (*Exteriors*) (1993) is a series of fragmentary texts mostly centred on incidents observed in public spaces – the metro, the RER, supermarkets and other small shops, or *commerces*. Certain themes recur: class privilege and culture, the theatricality of everyday life, social injustice. But more important than this ideological content is the attempt to register what has been observed as neutrally as possible, holding on to the way minor events seem to reveal things that help the writer understand herself and her participation in a wider social order. The epigraph from Rousseau 'Notre *vrai* moi n'est pas tout entier en nous' ['Our *true* self is not entirely within us'] points to a dimension of the subject – an aspect of individual truth – that is not inner but outer, *transpersonnel*, to use a word Ernaux has adopted to talk about her work. At one point she coins another word to describe her method: *ethnotexte*: 'Aucune description, aucun récit non plus. Juste des instants, des rencontres. De l'ethnotexte' (p. 65) ['No description, or narrative. Just moments, encounters. Ethnotext']. A consistent aim in *Journal du dehors* is the interaction between individual identity and its possible reflections in the surrounding world. In one fragment Ernaux recalls recognizing her mother's phrases and gestures in a woman in the supermarket, and this reaffirms her sense that her own past existence is deposited like archaeological evidence in the passenger she sees in the corridors of the RER or the housewife on the escalators in the Auchan shopping mall:

C'est donc au-dehors . . . qu'est déposée mon existence passée. Dans des individus anonymes qui ne soupçonnent pas qu'ils détiennent une part de mon histoire, dans des visages, des corps, que je ne revois jamais. Sans doute suis-je moi-même, dans la foule des rues et des magasins, porteuse de la vie des autres. (p. 106)

It's therefore outside . . . that my past life is deposited. In anonymous individuals who are quite unaware that they possess a little of my history, in faces, bodies, which I never see again. No doubt I am myself, in the crowded streets or shops, a carrier of the lives of others.

In *La Honte* [Shame] which centres on an incident from Ernaux's adolescence when her father attacked her mother in a murderous rage,

Ernaux explicitly seeks to become 'ethnologue de moi-même' (p. 38) [ethnologist of myself]. Rather than simply attempting to reanimate and transcribe her recollections of this event and its repercussions, she treats her memories as 'documents' and attempts to locate them in the context of 'traces matérielles' ['material traces'] of that year, traces through which she seeks to reconstruct the social world of her family and her childhood. She pays a visit to the Archives de Rouen and reads through the back numbers of the *Paris–Normandie* newspapers delivered to her parents, including the issue for the day of the 'incident'. But this exercise proves frustrating because the socio-political events of summer 1952 recorded in the newspaper, while indicating 'signes collectifs' ['collective signs'], have no direct connection with her life. Ernaux learns from this that it is her own archive that must be consulted and where necessary reconstituted. If, on the one hand, 'il n'y a pas de vraie mémoire de soi' (p. 37) ['there is no real memory of the self'], in the sense that we remember with the mental equipment, attitudes and verbal ability of the person we are in the present, it is equally true that impersonal information about the past cannot fill in what is missing. In this dilemma, Ernaux seeks to become her own archivist and ethnologist, patiently sifting the traces of her existence in 1952 to reconstruct the mental and social horizons of her twelve year-old self, beginning with 'les règles du monde de mes douze ans' (p. 69) ['the rules of the world I inhabited at twelve'] – the borders of the territory felt to be 'chez nous', and the 'usages collectifs' enshrined in daily gestures and rituals, and particularly in words and phrases. Applied in the area of personal experience, archival and ethnological enquiry make it possible for Ernaux to approach a uniquely painful dimension of her memory.

Ernaux's visit to the Rouen Archives, the decision to establish her own archive through classification and inventory, and then to open this archive, through interrogation and speculation, are profoundly symptomatic. The notion of the archive, associated with documents, traces and inventories, is central to autobiographical practices since the 1980s, and specifically to the major contribution women writers make at this point. Before looking at this in more general terms let us consider another woman who goes into the archive, Assia Djebar (b. 1936).

Djebar's *L'Amour, la fantasia* (1985) is an immensely ambitious autobiographical text where 'traces matérielles', and questions of historical, social and ethnic memory, are constantly to the fore. Djebar splices together a number of different archives, exploring parallels and oppositions between them: fragments (never a linear narrative) of her own experience, primarily as an adolescent; fragments of the history of her family and ancestors; published eye-witness accounts of various phases of the French conquest of Algeria in the nineteenth century; a sound-bank of voices from the Algerian revolution of the 1950s and 60s; quotations from writers connected with Algeria. By intercutting between these areas, necessarily fusing autobiography with fiction, Djebar transforms an individual stock of memories into an archive, in other words a quasi-objective, semi-public body of experience with which she does not immediately identify. And this enables her to explore the paradoxes of a divided identity – both French and Algerian – as one who uses the language of the conqueror to explore the complexities of belonging and not belonging. Although the word 'roman' appears after the title, this is not an autobiographical novel in the conventional sense but, as is made manifest in a variety of ways, an autobiographical project whose complex narrative and structural devices are more akin to those of experimental fiction than to conventional autobiography.

Yet there is another reason why Djebar is hesitant about using the word autobiography. As an Algerian woman, to choose to write in French is potentially to deny the very origins she is seeking to rediscover. But to the extent that Djebar, thanks to her school-teacher father's decision to give her a French education, has herself been appropriated by Frenchness, she is now able to identify as much with the conquerors as the conquered. One of the most striking features of *L'Amour, la fantasia* is the alternation in the first section of chapters focusing on the Algerian child's initiation into the French language and chapters recounting the French campaign to conquer Algeria in the 1830s. Rather than basing her retelling on the work of historians, Djebar chooses to go into the archive, and to reconstitute the voices of men who witnessed the campaign at first hand. Djebar's mode, the devices through which she fuses autobiography and fiction, enables her to find points of insertion into the archive. Her 'mémoire nomade' ['nomadic memory'] enables her to switch memory banks, to wander and intervene in a network of texts and discourses that make up the palimpsest in which she can decipher and assemble traces of her identities. In the first sections, mingling her voice with those of the chroniclers of conquest, she identifies with her defeated ancestors, but also with the European witnesses: 'ces capitaines oubliés [dont les] lettres parlent, dans le fond, d'une Algérie-femme impossible à apprivoiser . . . je suis étrangement hantée par l'émoi même des tueurs, par leur trouble obsessionnel' (p. 69) ['these forgotten captains [whose] letters speak, ultimately, of a female Algeria that cannot be tamed . . . I am strangely haunted by the emotions of the killers, by their obsessive ambivalence']. Letting herself be haunted by the French voices, appropriating their archive, orchestrating and splicing different versions, rewriting the conquest with their accounts but in her perspective, Djebar creates a new archive, and thus a new future. By opening up a host of possible kinds of identification and solidarity, writing in the 'langue adverse' ['opposing langauge'] turns out to permit the creation of a new voice. Writing in a foreign tongue (like Augustine, the father of autobiography, who was an Algerian who wrote in Latin) Djebar seeks to forge a new kind of autobiography, always aware of the pitfalls and delusions that accompany her efforts: 'L'autobiographie pratiquée dans la langue adverse se tisse comme une fiction, du moins tant que l'oubli des morts charriés par l'écriture n'opère pas son anesthésie. Croyant "me parcourir", je ne fais que choisir un autre voile. Voulant, à chaque pas, parvenir à la transparence, je m'engloutis davantage dans l'anonymat des aïeules!' (p. 243) ['autobiography in the opposing language weaves something that resembles a fiction, at least as long as the forgetting of the dead brought about by writing does not exert its anaesthetizing effects. Believing that "I survey myself", I simply choose another veil. Wanting, with each step, to achieve transparency, I am submerged even more in the anonymity of my female ancestry']. In Djebar autobiographical writing by no means gives access to secure identity or personal apotheosis. In giving voice to others it engenders separation and exile, as much as fusion and community. But in doing so, autobiography explores and clarifies the space between self and others, the public and the private, the individual and history.

In both Djebar and Ernaux autobiographical writing involves negotiating with public and private archives. The theme of the archive and a concern with the status of the document and the trace, is an important thread in contemporary French thought[9] and it is not surprising that this finds clear echoes in the rise of autobiography, given a common concern for the borders of individual and collective experience, self and history. It is symptomatic of this convergence of interests that the work of two other important women writers, Marguerite Yourcenar and Hélène Cixous, increasingly gravitated towards the archival in the 1970s and 1980s.

In Yourcenar's autobiographical trilogy *Le Labyrinthe du monde* [The World's Labyrinth] the explicit focus is rarely on the author herself, but on her ancestors – her maternal family in *Souvenirs pieux* (*Dear Departed*) (1974), her father's line in *Archives du Nord* (*How Many Years*) (1977), and later phases in the life of her father and other relatives in the unfinished and posthumous *Quoi? L'Eternité* [What? Eternity] (1988). If this reflects indifference to conventional autobiography it also indicates where Yourcenar's true interests lie. While she is by no means unconcerned with individual experience, what fascinate Yourcenar are the processes of time and history, 'les fils de la toile d'araignée où nous sommes tous pris' ['the threads in the cobweb that enmeshes us all'].[10] As the title of the second volume suggests, Yourcenar explores her family archives, basing her narrative on numerous documents, photographs, letters and mementoes (including the 'souvenirs pieux' issued after the deaths of various family members, referred to in the title of the first volume). But, by means of a number of stylistic devices, she contrives to keep her own shadowy existence in the picture, hinting at signs of her own proclivities and illuminating her life history from unfamiliar angles: 'Les incidents de cette vie . . . m'intéressent surtout en tant que voies d'accès par lesquelles certaines expériences l'ont atteinte' (p. 369) ['The incidents of this life . . . interest me primarily as entry points via which certain experiences made a mark on it']. Rather than being interested in family history for its own sake, Yourcenar seeks to catch reflections of her own existence in the 'jeux de miroir entre les personnes et les moments du temps' ['mirror-play between individuals and moments in time'].[11] As a result, although her essentially metaphysical world-view, and her tendency to see existence from the standpoint of eternity, distance her from contemporary preoccupations, Yourcenar's autobiographical mode, with its emphasis on material traces, documents, and archives, carries many echoes of the developments we have been outlining. Working on the borderlines of biography, history, autobiography and fiction, Yourcenar consistently questions her own methods and achievements, pointing to her reliance on gap-filling and speculation, but insisting on the finite and mysterious character of the concrete data with which she works, aware also that 'la mémoire n'est pas une collection de documents déposés en bon ordre au fond d'on ne sait quel nous-même; elle vit et change; elle rapproche les bouts de bois mort pour en faire de nouveau de la flamme' [memory is not a collection of documents deposited in an orderly fashion in the depths of I know not what self; it lives and changes; it brings together bits of dead wood to rekindle a flame'].[12]

As was noted earlier, the *écriture féminine* of Hélène Cixous, elaborated at a theoretical level in the 1970s and thereafter in Cixous's numerous works in various genres, kept its distances from autobiography. But there are clear signs in Cixous's writings of the 1990s that the radical reassessment of autobiographical practice occurring in the previous decade had an impact on the way she conceives her ongoing project as a creative writer. For example *Hélène Cixous: photos de racines (Rootprints: Memory and Life Writing)* (1994), co-written with Mireille Calle-Gruber, contains numerous references to autobiography and ends with a section, 'Albums et légendes', where photographs from the family album form the basis for a narrative of Cixous's childhood and family history. If Cixous continues to affirm that 'il ne peut pas y avoir d'écriture autobiographique' ['there can be no autobiographical writing'] in the traditional sense,[13] she shows a clear awareness that autobiography can no longer be defined in this narrow way, and that a number of strands in her writing have distinct affiliations with contemporary autobiographical strategies where autobiography is no longer considered to be a generic straitjacket but a multi-faceted and essentially hybrid set of practices having in common a basis in the referential (whilst not excluding the fictive). For example, she recognizes that her desire to capture the pulse and rhythms of 'la vie même' ['life itself'] through a poetic writing attuned to the fluidity of affective experience aligns her not only with certain practitioners of the diary but also with an autobiographer like Stendhal whose *Vie de Henry Brulard*, full of telegraphic annotations and self-questionings, is quoted extensively by Cixous. Not only is Cixous's writing, in texts such as *Jours de l'an (First Days of the Year)* (1990), geared to tracking down a 'Je' secreted in the act of writing itself, but increasingly the family archive has figured in her work, most notably in *Or: les lettres de mon père* [Gold: My Father's Letters] (1997) where the discovery of some of her father's letters gives rise to extensive commentary and self-interrogation.

The evolution of Cixous's work bears out the central theme of this chapter. If the decade between 1975 and 1985 represented a watershed in the development of autobiographical practice, placing it at the forefront of contemporary literary and cultural preoccupations, the contribution of French women writers has been decisive. Whilst women autobiographers, from Madame Roland to Simone de Beauvoir, have sometimes featured prominently in the development of the genre, it is at the point when autobiography comes into its own as a literary practice enjoying crucial connections to other disciplines and concerns – gender, ethnicity, psychoanalysis, ethnography, history, sociology – that major female-authored texts open new horizons. A flourishing autobiographical culture is a conspicuous feature in the contemporary French literary and intellectual scene, and the ongoing work of Ernaux and

Djebar, along with many new participants, is likely to ensure that women writers remain at the front of the field.

NOTES

1 See M. Sheringham, 'Autobiography' in A. Hughes and K. Reader (eds.), *Encyclopaedia of Contemporary French Culture* (London: Routledge, 1998).
2 On this see Ashley, *et al.*, *Autobiography and Postmodernism*.
3 For a general overview see 'L'Autobiographie des femmes' in Lecarme and Lecarme-Tabone, *L'Autobiographie*, pp. 95–124.
4 Nancy K. Miller, 'Writing Fictions: Women's Autobiography in France' in Brodski and Schenck (eds.), *Life/Lines*, p. 51.
5 *Ibid.*, p. 53.
6 *Ibid.*, p. 61.
7 See 'Introduction' in *Life/Lines*, pp. 1–15.
8 Gallimard 1964, Folio edition, 1980, p. 14.
9 See P. Ricoeur, 'Archive, Document, Trace', in *Temps et récit*, III (Paris: Seuil, 1985), pp. 171–83; Arlette Farge, *Le Goût de l'archive* (Paris: Seuil, 1989); and Jacques Derrida, *Mal d'archive* (Paris: Galilée, 1993).
10 *Archives du Nord*, p. 214.
11 *Quoi? L'Eternité*, p. 182.
12 *Souvenirs pieux*, p. 274.
13 *Photos de racines*, p. 95.

CHAPTER TEN

Women poets of the twentieth century

Michael Bishop

To speak of French women poets of the twentieth century is still, paradoxically at the beginning of the twenty-first century, something of a novelty. Very little of their abundant and ever-increasing production is quoted in anthologies or histories of literature or poetry often otherwise outstanding in their coverage. There are only two mentions in the twentieth century section of Marcel Arland's *Anthologie de la poésie française*, three in Michel Décaudin's *Anthologie de la poésie française du xxᵉ siècle*, none in Alan Boase's *Poetry of France 1900–1965*, one in the Lagarde et Michard *xxᵉ siècle*, none in Robert Leggewie's *Anthologie de la littérature française* (vol. II), and one in Anthony Hartley's *Penguin Book of French Verse*. Even many anthologies of contemporary poetry do no better – two women are retained in Henri Deluy's *Poésie en France: 1983–8* (1989), one in Jacques Roubaud's *128 poèmes composés en langue française* (1996), and three in Emmanuel Hocquard's *Tout le monde se ressemble* (1995). Recent critical studies or histories, fine as they are in many respects, barely touch upon poetry by women.[1] Fortunately, Jeanine Moulin's remarkable *Huit siècles de poésie féminine* (1963) continues to give readers a healthy perspective on a creative wealth masked by factors of either partiality or indifference, naïve underrating or simple carelessness, factors inevitably reflecting socio-economic and political parameters as well as the dominant psychological structures of our modernity. Other contemporary anthologies have followed very recently, as well as critical assessments of the work of these writers.[2]

Many fine poetic texts by many women publishing over the past hundred years cannot be dealt with here. Had space permitted, it would have been both instructive and pleasurable to examine the other powerful poetic voices that our discussion cannot embrace. The analysis that follows, then, involves a compacted choice of poets, especially with respect to the proliferating production of the past twenty years. It nevertheless demonstrates the emotional intensity, the conceptual vigour and the modal dynamism at work in the poetry of the women of the twentieth century.

Anna de Noailles (1876–1933) enjoyed the friendship of Colette and Proust, and was admired by Cocteau whose last work, *La comtesse de Noailles: Oui et Non* [La Comtesse de Noailles: Yes and No], reveals a woman simultaneously loved and despised. Regarded by Apollinaire as a true poet, Anna de Noailles ran foul of Gide and other contemporary intellectuals, and her literary reputation never recovered from what has recently been termed '[sa] première malédiction [qui] ne fut pas l'oubli mais la gloire' ['the first curse upon her [which] was not oblivion but fame'].[3] Her poetry – from *Cœur innombrable* [The Countless Heart] (1901) to *Les Forces éternelles* [Eternal Forces] (1920) and *L'Honneur de souffrir* [The Honour of Suffering] (1927) – reveals a person more viscerally simple and more psychologically private than her public persona might have led one to believe. If the 'heroic' appealed to her enthusiasm, it was no doubt because she deemed it a 'life-affirming' quality (*L'Offrande*, [The Offering], p. 41) in a universe haunted by death and viewed with a lucidity only occasionally tinged with mysticism or a sense of cosmic complexity. It is in the context of this delicate interlacement of the strictly mortal and the metaphorically 'divine' and 'mysterious' so central to a poem such as 'Les Rêves' ('Dreams') (p. 26) that other persistent elements of Anna de Noailles's poetics may be understood. Her sense, for instance, of the 'honour of suffering', whilst justifiable, is matched by the intuition that, as she puts it in 'Ceux qui, hors du rêve et des transes . . .' ['Those who out of dream and trance . . .'] (p. 71), 'la souffrance / Est l'unique et sombre péché' ['suffering / Is the sole and dark sin'], that her own vaguely and paradoxically masochistic manner of later years can only sensibly be modified by an affirmation of life's endlessly emergent lightness. Anna de Noailles knows that the growing obsession with death that marks her work is in contradiction with the wisdom of the logic of pleasure, happiness and love, however difficult such a logic proves to be in the living: 'je ne veux pas d'autre force' ['I want no other force'], she writes in 'C'est vrai, je me suis beaucoup plainte' ['It is true, I have much lamented'] (p. 38), 'Que ma fatigue et son ardeur' ['Than my tiredness and its burning']. Passion, desire, self-affirmation despite all, she knows to be the only energies upon which she can thrive. Her first words to Rilke – 'M Rilke, qu'est-ce que l'amour pour vous, que pensez-vous de la mort?' ['Mr. Rilke, what is love to you, what are your thoughts upon death?'] (p. 11) – should not be thought of as romantically, or even gratuitously dramatic; they are, rather, the sure sign of someone centred upon what concerns us all, the fundamental meaning of love and the ontological status of what we call mortal 'life'. The very modernity of Anna de Noailles's thought is rooted in this sense of the urgency of our ephemeralness. A reverie of desire always, at least implicitly, takes her beyond the traumas of deaths and illnesses to a recognition of the beauties of both 'la loi suprême de l'instinct' ['the supreme law of instinct'], as she calls it in the prose poem 'Gratitude' (p. 46), and 'le goût de l'infini' ['the taste for the infinite'] whose idealness may not be readily realizable – as 'Vivre n'est pas un bien' ['Life is not a Possession'] (p. 49) tells us – but whose dream is never forgotten in the experience of love.

The crucial existential function of love is at the heart of Anna de Noailles's work. And writing remains, throughout, a vivid inscription of this function. 'J'écris' ['I write'], she unambiguously asserts, 'pour que le jour où je ne serai plus / On sache comme l'air et le plaisir m'ont plu, / Et que mon livre porte à la foule future / Comme j'aimais la vie et l'heureuse Nature' (p. 50) ['so when I am no longer / People may know how my delight was air and pleasure / And so my book may bear forth to the crowding future / How I loved life and the bliss of Nature']. Many poems bear witness to the truth of this assertion. Love, as the poem 'Éros' (p. 51) makes clear, offers no having, no possession; rather, for Anna de Noailles, it is pure experience, pure being. It is, however, clothed in certainty despite being caught in existential becoming, for it penetrates everywhere and everything; and it is, in fact, the underlying meaning for her that, despite difference, erases difference – as other poems such as 'Si je n'aimais que toi en toi' ['If I loved but you within you'] (p. 68) both wittily and reflectively affirm. Where the troubling obscurities of doubt, anguish and seeming solitude threaten, then, love reminds us of a clarity and simplicity that is still available, buoys us up in an intensity, an innocence (of self and other) that can make death almost irrelevant. All of this is conveyed in a form that is broadly classical in its prosody, although it is loosened somewhat at times by a freer stanzaic arrangement, by the insertion of prose texts alongside verse structures and by the use, above all, of cascading anaphoric rhythms. As Yves Bonnefoy argued for Marceline Desbordes-Valmore, form, in Anna de Noailles's poetry, as in her life, is not what it is or was all about.

Renée Vivien (1877–1909), who was born in London and christened Pauline Tarn, escaped to Paris in 1898 where she plunged into what was to be a short but intense and often socially conspicuous *fin de siècle* bohemian life. The pains, the pleasures and the utopian dreams of her lesbian life are often finely portrayed in an *œuvre* that extends beyond her poetry to translations – *Sapho* (1903) and *Sapho et huit poétesses grecques* [Sapho and Eight Greek Poetesses] (1904), for example – the lesbian fairy tales of *La Dame à la Louve* [The Lady of the She-Wolf], and novels such as *Une femme m'apparut* [A Woman Came to Me] and the only very recently appearing *Anne Boleyn*, whose earlier publication was disrupted by Renée Vivien's premature death.

The eroticism and implicit or explicit feminist drive of Renée Vivien's poetics may be read against a backcloth of post-Baudelairian and 'decadent' symbolist modes and fascinations. 'Roses du soir' ['Evening Roses'], for example, from *Évolutions* (1903), whilst comparable to Marceline Desbordes-Valmore's 'Les Roses de Saadi' ['The Roses of Saadi'], ventures beyond the latter in its hauntingly languorous sensuality and subtle unspokenness. Other poems such as 'Douceur de mes chants, allons vers Mytilène . . .' ('Sweetness of my songs, let us go towards Mytilene') or 'Les Solitaires' ('The Solitary Ones'), also from *Évolutions* (Moulin, p. 201), confirm the predilection for formal artifice combined with expressive boldness, quasi-mystical solemnity combined with gothic obsession. Yet, if it is not wrong to suggest that, in Renée Vivien's dream of establishing an artistic lesbian enclave on Lesbos during her stay there in 1904 with Natalie Barney, one finds a 'feminist and lesbian counterpart of the male ivory tower'[4], it is important to remember the truly lived suffering of this exceptional woman, the degree to which any idealness is firmly grounded in visceral, unesoteric experience. 'Le Pilori' ('The Pillory') from the 1906 *À l'heure des mains jointes* [The Hour of Clasped Hands] makes such distinctions clear. 'Pendant longtemps', the poem begins, 'je fus clouée au pilori, / Et des femmes, voyant que je souffrais, ont ri. // Puis des hommes ont pris dans leurs mains une boue / Qui vint éclabousser mes tempes et ma joue' (Moulin, p. 205) ['Long was I nailed to the Pillory, / And women, seeing my suffering, laughed. // Then men took up in their hands a mud / That splashed about my temples and my cheeks']. Anger, hatred and a feeling of definitive exclusion follow; the 'hell' of Monique Wittig's *Virgile, non* (*Across the Acheron*) is amply prefigured here. There is nothing hermetic about this poem, nothing effetely conceived. And if an ironically titled poem such as 'L'Amour borgne' ('One-eyed Love') (Moulin, pp. 206–7) from the same collection can tempt us into believing that the other is loved '[d'un] œil sinistre / Où luit la colère du rhum' ['with a sinister eye / Wherein gleams the wrath of rum'] and that this deteriorates further into a masochistic, self-condemning desire 'que de tes dents tu crèves / Mon œil où se brouillent les rêves, / Comme un ara, d'un coup de bec' ['that with your own teeth you may put out / My eye where dreams fog over, / Like a macaw, with one gouging peck'], if there is some understandable (self)-deflation, then, there is far more that reveals an *œuvre*, a mind and a heart, of great resilience, great compassion or 'active passion' *à la* Wittig. As Luc Decaunes argues, 'chez Renée Vivien, ce qui est beauté inoubliable, c'est le halètement secret du texte, un texte tout formé d'appels, de caresses, de gémissements, physiquement nommés' ['with Renée Vivien, what is unforgettably beautiful is the secret breathing of the text, a text entirely shaped by her ways of calling out to us, by caresses, moanings, physically named'].[5] But, as with Anna de Noailles, form is but the homologue for another desired perfection.

The poetics of Marie Noël (1883–1967), a Catholic poet and prosist, whose first collection, *Les Chanson et les heures* [Songs and Hours] appeared in 1920, is a complex one of youthful astonishment and celebration, of bold confession and questioning, of ageing submission and continuing quest. Her poems are often titled and conceived of as 'song', 'dialogue', *fantaisie*, even, but other notions clearly govern Marie Noël's imagination: 'prayer', 'vision', 'canticle' and so on. There is also the conformist, but surprisingly lively *Le Rosaire des joies* [Rosary of Joys], her second volume, which appeared in 1930.

Many of the poems of *Les Chansons et les heures* display a gentleness and charm of mind, as well as a great vigour and intensity of spirit, displaced upon the folk song modes that, precisely, permit a wider range of expression and exploration than Marie Noël, as a pure lyric poet, might otherwise have been inclined to allow herself. She is in effect an avowedly good listener to both the voices of those around her – their words, songs and emotions – and the voice that wells up within her, as she tells us from the outset, in 'Les Chansons que je fais . . .' ('The Songs I Make . . .').[6] These are often the voices of innocent desire, nascent or brimming love – of the simple things of the earth, of life's energy, of God, and, more often than not, of the desired other. Zeal is uncluttered, natural, uncloistered; sentiments are expressed with grace and relative ease; loss and necessity are addressed with buoyancy and independence. A poem such as the fine 'Connais-moi . . .' ('Know Me . . .') (1908) runs through a vast gamut of lucid and audacious self-appraisal and physical-cum-spiritual yearning. The psychology of Marie Noël's work is in fact complex and two traumatizing spiritual and emotional crises – one she describes in her *Notes intimes* [Personal Notes] (1959) as 'L'Enfer des trois jours. Souvenir de février 1913' ('The Three-Day Hell. Memory of February 1913'), the other being termed 'L'Enfer de sept semaines et de plusieurs années, 1920–22' ('The Seven-Weeks-and-Several-Years Hell, 1920–22')[7] – make it more enigmatic and give it even greater complexity. Later texts such as 'Impropères et chant du linceul' ('Improperia and Shroud Song') and 'Sortie' ('Exit') or 'Quand un soir sur nous . . .' ('When One Night Upon Us . . .'), from *Chants et psaumes d'automne* [Autumn Songs and Psalms] (1947) and the *Chants d'arrière-saison* [Late Season Songs] (1961) respectively (Moulin, pp. 240–4), convey well the darker, apocalyptic stirrings of a poetical imagination whose will for love is unable to transcend the nightmarish ravages of obsessions with death and the 'evil' of violence and war. Even the early 'Prière du poète' ('Poet's Prayer'), from *Les Chansons et les heures* (pp. 114–16), recognizes the tensions and contradictions that already begin to inhabit her mind. This is a poem that begs for their resolution and that expresses just how incapable she is, and always will be, of pretence, just how desperately clear she must be in the difficult articulation of what she is. Love, she concludes, is what will give her the strength needed to write, the power to inspire in others that same love of life that, despite all, Anna de Noailles's work sought to confirm.

The influence of oriental, especially Buddhist thought, as well as of the platonist and stoicist traditions, is marked in the poetry and other writings of Catherine Pozzi (1882–1934). Her formal studies in Paris and, briefly, in Oxford, inclined her towards the sciences, however, particularly biology – on which she published articles in *Le Figaro*. Her metaphysical and philosophical readings and personal reflections tend, however, to shift her away from pure scientific relativism. Although also an accomplished musician, it was perhaps her somewhat tempestuous eight-year-long liaison with the poet, Paul Valéry, from 1920 (a period during which she also began to suffer violently from tuberculosis), that brought Catherine Pozzi to develop what has been termed '[cette] voix singulière, inimitable, qui se fait entendre dans [s]es six poèmes canoniques':[8] 'Ave', 'Vale', 'Scopolamine', 'Nova', 'Maya', 'Nyx'. The poetic *œuvre* of Catherine Pozzi is very slight, quantitatively, and she herself had a sense of the special genius the above six poems convey, reworking and rethinking them scrupulously as has been shown by her only recently edited *Journal*. Indeed, she specifically asked that these six poems be gathered together after her death. Of these poems, only the exquisite 'Ave' appeared in print in Pozzi's lifetime. The morphine and opium-based medication used to offset Catherine Pozzi's suffering may or may not account for certain visionary tendencies in these poems, but her work bears witness to great poetic concentration and delicacy, celestial and wild, as she writes in 'Vale' (p. 26).

More manifestly *voyante* and surreal in her mode, and given to generating a poetry of greater mythical depth where the intimate is always
suffused with the cosmic, the legendary and the occult, is the poet Claire
Goll (1891–1977). In a poem from *L'Ignifère* [Igniferous] (1969), 'Le Feu du
regard' ['Gaze of Fire'], for example, Claire Goll spontaneously exploits
various repetitive and associative modes, parataxis and ellipsis. The gaze
at the centre of this poem's preoccupations is both visceral and psychic.
It 'deforms' and destabilizes, not according to some Cubist aesthetics of
reharmonization but seemingly quite beyond any aesthetics of order. A
lightness and unearthly transmutation of being is generated and André
Breton's notion of 'convulsive beauty' is pushed to its most 'corrosive'
limits. Ambivalence characterizes the inner and outer forces with which
she at once struggles and finds fascination. We are far from the flowers
that fired the poetry of Renée Vivien, further still from those of
Marceline Desbordes-Valmore. Claire Goll's gaze here, and elsewhere
in her poetry – from the *Poèmes de la jalousie* [Poems of Jealousy] (1926) to
the *Chansons indiennes* [Indian Songs] (1952) or *Le Cœur tatoué* [Tatooed
Heart] (1958) and beyond – alights upon 'signs' that are beyond the perceptible limits of space and time. She constantly dips into the pandora-
like 'boîte cristalline du crâne' ['crystal box of the skull'] (p. 20) to
recount what she calls the teeming mosaics of dream (p. 27), structures
which are at once half-emprisoning and half-liberating like all symbolist
or surrealist obsessions. Fear and madness seem to hover about her work
and, relatively dismissive of the options afforded by the quotidian, it is
to the hothouse of inner rhythms and visions that she returns.
'Reconstruis ton palais', she tells herself in 'Roi de trèfle' ('King of
Clubs') from *L'Ignifère*, 'avec la musique des images' (p. 39) ['Build over
your palace with the music of images'].

Georgiana Colvile has subtly demonstrated the particular logic
behind dealing with Alice Rahon and Valentine Penrose, both
poet–painters, in the same context.[9] Valentine Penrose is no doubt the
better known of the two poets, partly through her marriage to the
English surrealist, Roland Penrose, but also because of the generous
texts Paul Éluard has devoted to her writing. While her husband could
speak of the 'originality of her talent',[10] Éluard, in his preface to her *Dons
des féminines* [Gifts of the Feminine Ones] (1937), did not hesitate to write
of 'the wise marvel of her language . . . the simple objectivity of her
[accompanying] collages, [that] give me trust in myself and in the virtues
of the truth that is given'.[11] Elsewhere, in his preface to Valentine
Penrose's *Herbes à la lune* [Moon Grasses] (1935), Éluard describes her

language as 'poetically limpid, a fleet language, escaping reflection. An unreasoned, an indispensable language' (p. 13). As in much surrealist poetry, being is redefined as other, shifting, metaphorical, metamorphosing. Exchanges and affinities enter the realm of the marvellous and yield new knowledge.

Alice Rahon (1904–87), who is perhaps best known for her painting, has also written some remarkable poetry, including *À même la terre* [Within the Earth] (1936), *Sablier couché* [Prostrate Hour-glass] (1938) and *Noir animal* [Animal Black] (1941). In the summer of 1936 (after the dissolution of her passionate involvement with Picasso), she travelled to India with Valentine Penrose who, as Georgiana Colvile has argued, 'had just chosen solitude and independence over marriage'. The intertextual factors at play between *Sablier couché* and *Noir animal* and Valentine Penrose's *Poèmes* (1937) and *Sorts de la lueur* [Glimmering Fates] (1937), have been well demonstrated by Colvile who concludes that 'for both artists poetry and painting remained an eternal Baudelairian "chambre double" of correspondences, synaesthesia and occultation of memories, a never-ending "invitation au voyage" to a land whose language is one of feminine analogy and where woman's body weaves a ceaseless poem'. Alice Rahon vigorously and innovatively exploits the modes of surrealism in ways which might be said to be exemplified by her last known poem, 'Le Pays de Paalen' ('Paalen Country').[12] The poem is followed by a dedication to her long-divorced husband who had recently committed suicide. The memorial text is written in a characteristic nominal style in which all verbs disappear and, through their absence, bestow upon the poem a gestalt-like, pictorial aura in which the medium becomes, at least in part, the message, and ground and figure fuse. The repetition throughout the poem of the word *pays*, as totemic as the Pacific coast Paalen visited and Alice Rahon loved, focuses attention at once upon places known and the place of more absolute being that Surrealists never ceased to dream into their creations.

André Malraux has written perceptively and movingly of Louise de Vilmorin (1902–1969), author of *Fiançailles pour rire* [Engagement for a Laugh] (1939), *Le Sable du sablier* [Hour-Glass Sand] (1945) and *L'Alphabet des aveux* [Alphabet of Confession] (1955), whom, at the time of her death, he deemed to be 'notre dernier poète *de la voix*' ['our last poet *of voice*'].[13] Louise de Vilmorin's poetry is, Malraux suggests, less textually 'engraved' than much post-Mallarméan work. 'Quelqu'un parle' ['Someone is speaking'], he asserts. Poulenc and Béart, alert to this, have set much of her poetry to music. Malraux also talks of Louise de

Vilmorin's disregard for 'les problèmes capitaux de notre poésie [contemporaine] – entre tous, l'image et sa puissance créatrice' ['the capital problems of our contemporary poetry – above all, the image and its creative power'], and considers that she elects a position of 'marginality'. That marginality is, of course, one of *other* centrality, or what Malraux, who sees it as a 'key' to her genius, calls 'une fantaisie impulsive et féerique' ['an impulsive, impish fancifulness']. As with Anna de Noailles, something of Louise de Vilmorin's social 'legend' has brought about a certain 'disfigurement' of the poetic *œuvre*. Malraux is right to say, for example, that her unusual gift for verbal acrobatics – 'Je méditerai – Tu m'éditeras' ['I shall meditate – You will edit me, mate'] she begins a poem to Gaston Gallimard – has often misled readers in their appreciation of all that is hauntingly grave and magically atemporal in a work where enchantment blends with a thematics of subdued but desperate desire.

Formally speaking, Louise de Vilmorin's work adheres to versified rhythm, but it is not uncommon to find shifts within stanzas (as in 'Fleurs' ['Flowers'], 'L'Hirondelle' ['The Swallow'] or 'Les deux Voix' ['The Two Voices']) and, as in 'Amour' ['Love'], there are even utterly unpredictable rhythms that somehow never develop into a consistent use of free verse. She wittily (and later, bravely, given her own illness) defined her poetry as 'coughing'. Malraux recounts a fine exchange with her along these lines, and, already in 1939, she gives us the poem 'J'ai la toux dans mon jeu' ['I cough in my play'] (pp. 24–5). There is, however, nothing grating or harping in Louise de Vilmorin's voice. A wit, an irony and what she terms '[une] parole [qui] est oiseau' ['a bird-like speech'] (p. 36) – free, capable of singing many tunes and in many registers – give her writing an unexpectedness and a buoyancy which are never submissive and always sensitive to the self's part, or a certain chosenness, in the existential theatre she depicts.

Joyce Mansour, who was born in England and brought up in Cairo, offers a reading experience unlike any other. She had no recognizable literary ambition and yet her work inspired illustrations by painters such as Matta, Bellmer, Alechinsky, Camacho and Lam. Hubert Nyssen, writing in 1991 at the time he was gathering together the *œuvre complète* of Joyce Mansour (1928–86), tells us that

il faut se pencher, se risquer même pour goûter au vertige et peut-être à l'outrage, pour être emporté par le déboulis des mots, le flot des images, le flux et le reflux des imprécations, pour partager la révolte du sexe, l'insurrection des chairs, le broyage des corps, la désobéissance des sens, les déchirures de l'œil, la fronde du verbe, la terreur des astres, la damnation de la mort, pour soudain s'immerger dans l'angoisse de telles *histoires nocives* ou pénétrer dans l'abyssal silence des questions éteintes.[14]

One must incline oneself, take risks even to taste the vertigo and perhaps the contemptuousness, to be swept away by the tumble of words, the flood of images, the ebb and flow of curses, to share in the sexual revolt, the insurrection of flesh, the pounding of bodies, the sensual disobedience, the renderings of the eye, the uprising of language, the cosmic terror, the damnation of death, to suddenly plunge into the anguish of such *noxious tales* or enter the abyssal silence of extinct questions.

Her first collection, *Cris* [Screams] (1953), contains seventy-four texts, all untitled, separated/joined by asterisks. Every poem is astonishing and strange, sometimes troubling. This is poetry as 'scream', as *déchirure*, as *pandemonium*, as 'black holes' – as the various titles of Joyce Mansour's work suggest. It is poetry as a painful, exhilarating, violent, liberating activity, half-visionary, half-blind, (self-)exorcizing and plunging being into a radical otherness not provoked, moreover – as is usual in surrealist strategy – but rather unexpectedly 'undergone', or experienced. The images concentrated in this work are never reducible and their meaning is barely attributable. Almost any fragment may yield to both erotic and satirical readings, but no reading can stabilize, or need stabilize, what remains beyond category, whether it be moral, psychoanalytical or aesthetic. Liberation and exorcism constitute, precisely, a transgression of all limiting (self-)definition.

Poems such as 'Pericoloso sporgersi' ('Danger: Do Not Lean Out') (pp. 373–7) from *Rapaces* (1960), 'Wild Glee from elsewhere' (pp. 505–6), which was written in English, from *Phallus et momies* [Phalluses and Mummies] (1969), or else 'Inventaire non exhaustif de l'indécent ou le nez de la méduse' ['Incomplete inventory of the indecent or the medusa's nose'] (p. 536) from *Faire signe au machiniste* [Nodding to the Driver] (1977) give a clear picture of the humour, the arresting insight, and the provocation that Joyce Mansour's poetry can generate.

Before moving, in conclusion, to an assessment of the contemporary poetical scene, where particular attention will be paid to the work of Andrée Chedid, Jacqueline Risset, Marie-Claire Bancquart, Jeanne Hyvrard, Anne-Marie Albiach and Céline Zins, a few questions should be raised. Should contemporary women's poetry be read in the light of any particular theoretical, aesthetic, ethical, socio-political, or psychoanalytical models afforded by other contemporary French women writers? Are any such influences manifest? If so, are they avowed developments, or rather, more subtle, almost osmotically absorbed, intertextualities? Is poetry, generically, to be deemed apart, read apart from theoretical, novelistic, theatrical and other creations of other women? Is there a programmatic femininity or feminism, however defined, in contemporary French women's poetry?

It is, of course, not possible to answer in one gesture all of these questions. But they remain pertinent and may give heightened urgency and insight to both global discussion and close textual analysis. There is, however, no evidence in the work of poets in the period since 1950 of claimed allegiance to, or even vaguely systematic and identifiable adaptation of, the more philosophical or theoretical work of writers such as Simone de Beauvoir, Luce Irigaray or Julia Kristeva, or the writings of women whose creative work has been significantly oriented towards the feminine condition, such as Marguerite Duras, Violette Leduc, Hélène Cixous, Monique Wittig, Chantal Chawaf or Jeanne Hyvrard.

And yet the very feasibility of being a woman and a published poet – for all the remaining difficulties touched upon at the beginning of the chapter – rests in part on the recent, parallel and varied raising of consciousness effected by so many other women writers and thinkers. Clearly the poets of today, educated, widely read and socio-politically alert, remain ethically sensitive to the gains made and the many gains still to be made, especially in France. None of this, however – even in a work as sociologically or psychologically centred as Jeanne Hyvrard's or Andrée Chedid's – leads to an ideologization of the poetic enterprise. The principal message conveyed by other women writers would seem to be that a woman writing poetry today is free to go her own way, assume her body, her mind, her spirit, her history/herstory, her mythology.

The very earliest works published by Andrée Chedid (b. 1920) – *Textes pour une figure* [Texts for a Figure] (1949) and *Textes pour un poème* [Texts for a Poem] (1950) – are poetry and, although she has since become a distinguished novelist and dramatist, poetry remains an essential means of expression of those evolving truths that drive her writing on (as in 'La Vérité' ('Truth') (p. 259), in *Chemins à vivre* [Paths for Living])[15] beyond its conceivable prestige, to a reinsertion into the directly lived 'clartés / Profondes et périssables' ['brightness, profound and perishable'] of everyday life, as she writes in the 1983 *Épreuves du vivant* [Trials of the Living] (p. 250). *Par delà les mots* [Beyond Words] (1995) is, furthermore, the title of Andrée Chedid's latest collection and its meaning is in no sense gratuitous. If language can assist us in mapping the parameters of our meditation/analysis of being, so often 'il manque / Le Chant' (p.

248) ['The Song / is lacking'] – that which might lead us to the other side of our meanings. Poetry may thus constitute a crucial 'seeding', but it seeds plurality and offers no 'key' to itself that might reduce, limit or ideologize 'la fertile parole / Venue de l'âtre du cœur' (pp. 249–52) ['fertile speech / Come from heart's place of fire']. Song intermingles with language, especially poetry, but it is 'beyond words', synonymous with being's cosmic energy – an energy almost transcendent were it not also immanent, always available like 'l'amour / éperon du souffle' (p. 196) ['love / breath's spur'], always 'fraternal', unifying, uplifting, giving 'the proofs of a shared earth': 'malgré nos enclos, nos Babels, nos ravages, en deçà: la parole converge et nous relie' (p. 61) ['despite our enclosures, our Babels, our ravages, this side of things: speech pushes and binds us together'].

If Jacqueline Risset's (b. 1939) more recent poetry – *Sept Passages de la vie d'une femme* [Seven Stages in a Woman's Life] (1985), *L'Amour de loin* [Love from Afar] (1988) and *Petits Éléments de physique amoureuse* [Small Elements of Love Physics] (1991) – could be said to relate to Andrée Chedid's in its thematics of love, ephemerality and language, it could readily be shown to be distinctive in both the particularities of this thematics and the textual modes espoused, despite a similar reliance on fragmentation, ellipsis, repetition and pluralization of meaning. This is not surprising when one considers that her first publications, the poetic collections *Jeu* [Play] (1971) and *La Traduction commence* [Translation Begins] (1976) and the critical essays, *L'Anagramme du désir* [Anagram of Desire] (1971) and *L'Invenzione e il modello* [Invention and the Model] (1973) all testify to the influence of the *Tel Quel* group.[16] These reveal a much denser, more involuted and self-preoccupied manner, a corresponding analytical fascination with textual and mental interiority (the 1971 essay is devoted to Scève's *Délie*, for example), creative modernity and ingenuity. Whilst none of this is forgotten,[17] in *Petits Éléments de physique amoureuse* she creates a world of relative intimacy, unclutteredness and what she terms, at the close of her prefatory text, 'L'Amour de la poésie' ('The Love of Poetry'), 'jubilation de presque rien; très forte' ['jubilation from almost nothing; very powerful'].[18] The body, feeling, and a sense of the fleeting are the elements of this jubilation; but we should not overlook the curious sense that she has of just 'turning around [truth] so as not to see it and not to say it' (p. 12). And the poem, despite its 'loving crystallization', can still be deemed to be 'écran, mensonge, effet de peur' (p. 19) ['screen, lie, product of fear']. For all such doubting, many of her poems speak eloquently of what they can record and perform.

Whilst the extensive poetic work of Marie-Claire Bancquart (b. 1932) – from *Projets alternés* (1972) and *Mains dissoutes* (1975) to *Opéra des limites* [Opera of Limits] (1988), *Dans le feuilletage de la terre* [In the Flakings of the Earth] (1994) and *Énigmatiques* [Enigmatics] (1995) – may be said to represent an unfulfilled spiritual quest in which the 'angelic' and the 'divine' remain just imaginative constructs or fleeting, exploratory intuitions, it should not be assumed that her work is ethereal, purely speculative, or ungrounded. Indeed, the opposite is true. Marie-Claire Bancquart can give attention to the marvellously banal and rich phenomena flooding every so easily 'forgotten instant' as Jacqueline Risset would put it: trees, grass, the moon, plants, vegetables, smells, skin, phone boxes, puddles, pebbles, dreams, war, a woman observed. And, of course, expression, time, emotion, and death swirl in and out of a poetry that is often at once tender and tough. Desire, love and the will to distinguish and decipher propel a work that is never prepared to surrender to its avowed fragility. 'Sans cadastre' ('Unsurveyed'), from *Sans lieu sinon l'attente* [Without Place but for Waiting] (1991), exemplifies her work and the way in which it captures this fine balance of the poetic caught between the flagrantly unacceptable and an abiding sense of the more secret.

Jeanne Hyvrard (b. 1945) is perhaps better known for her early novels and other prose work, although much of the latter – *Le Corps défunt de la comédie* [The Dead Body of Comedy] (1982), *Canal de la Toussaint* [All Saints Passage] (1985) and *La Pensée corps* [Body Thought] (1989) – is highly poetical in its rhythms, its analytical or discursive ellipses, its sheer emotional intensity. It is important to note, however, that, in addition to the published poetry – *Le Silence et l'obscurité* [Silence and Darkness] (1982) and *La Baisure* [The Shafting] *suivi de Que se partagent encore les eaux* [Let the Waters Divide] (1985) – there is a great deal of poetic material, amounting to some 700 pages, that is currently awaiting publication.[19] Three things immediately strike the reader of Hyvrard's work: (i) the remarkable deconstructive power of her writing, which in its generically cross-fertilized mode is more poetical than anything else; (ii) the re-constructive, 'fusional', and simultaneously pragmatic and utopian vision that disallows stagnation and any settling for mere anger, frustration or criticism; and (iii) the vast range of inquiry and the pertinence – historically, sociologically and politically – of her poetry. *La Baisure* relentlessly exposes all that has been, and is still, so often warped and disfigured by abusive male power. Yet this hundred-page poem, whilst not achieving transcendence in its simultaneously authentic and dream-like narration, maintains a vision of continuing psychic feasibility and existential redefinability. 'Dehors la nuit était claire / L'été cardinal commençait' ['Outside the night was clear / Midsummer was begun'] are the poem's final words: night is reversible and time pivotal, a message that *Que se partagent encore les eaux* movingly develops in Hyvrard's unending drive to return beyond our originary myths to a point where they can be radically reconceived, where a new sacredness may be written, leading to a harmonization of difference within totality.

The manner, and thus the focus, of what Paul Auster has termed Anne-Marie Albiach's (b. 1937) 'sublime lyricism'[20] could hardly be further removed from those at play in Jeanne Hyvrard's writing. From *Flammigère* [Flame-bearing] (1967), through *État* [State] (1971), *Mezza Voce* and *Anawratha* (both 1984), to the recent *Travail vertical et blanc* [Vertical White Work] (1989) and *'Figure vocative'* ('Vocative Figure') (1991), Anne-Marie Albiach both meditates and performs the problematics and pleasure of the interpenetration/dissociation of earth experience and textual voice, the intertwinement of exemplary rhetoric – as each poem self-reflexively explores its very constitution as a text – and an ontological discourse that seeks to reclaim for language a lived purpose implicitly outside language. Jean-Marie Gleize has eloquently articulated the degree to which Albiach's work thus becomes the 'theatre' of its very interiority, its literality, but this 'narcissistic' lyricism is rooted in the larger question of language's form and gesture to what Bonnefoy calls 'presence': the poem is not, finally, the exclusive theatre of itself, for the 'itself' is a 'vocative figuration'.

Each of the three volumes published to date by Céline Zins (b. 1937) – *Par l'alphabet du noir* [By the Alphabet of Blackness] (1979), *Adamah* (1988) and *L'Arbre et la glycine* [The Tree and the Wysteria] (1992) – constitutes a single, if complexly articulated, long poetico-philosophical meditation. The arguably esoteric, objectified 'sublime lyricism' of Anne-Marie Albiach fades away and leaves us with a more evidently grounded discourse on the relationships experienced between self, world and word. Seeing, at once physical and non-physical, is a central preoccupation leading not to a flat inscription of things, but rather to a penetration of their interlocking blatancy and barely thinkable otherness. *L'Arbre et la glycine* generates a compelling, contemplative exploration of the interwovenness of being and nothingness; of the literal and metaphorical metamorphosis of opaqueness into light; of the interconnectedness of sight, language and space. The argument developed may be fragmented (into short textual units), elliptical, shifting in its focus, but it remains combative, patient, simultaneously self-contestatory and cumulative, undiverted by aesthetic or rhetorical narcissism, though intuitively alert to factors of clarity and unpretentious elegance. Hers is a 'simplicity', which nevertheless makes rich demands upon the reader.

We can only be grateful that women poets of the stature of Zins and Bancquart, Chedid and Albiach, Hyvrard and Risset, write and meditate the world so diversely today. This is 'l'écriture comme un grand lit nuptial' ['writing like some great nuptial bed'], as Colette Nys-Mazure describes it:[21] the poetry of women as an endless and vast new alliance and joining, as an espousal that is the Hyvrardian revelation of difference in a perception of totality.

NOTES

1 See, for example, *La Littérature française: histoire et perspectives* (1990); *Du Surréalisme à l'empire de la critique* (1984); *Twentieth-Century French Avant-Garde Poetry, 1907–1990* (1992); *La Langue la poésie* (1989); *La Poésie en France du surréalisme à nos jours* (1996); and my own *Contemporary Poetry of France* (1985).

2 See Martin Sorrell's *Elles. A Bilingual Anthology of Modern French Poetry by Women* (1995); *29 femmes*, edited by Liliane Giraudon and Henri Deluy (1994); and my own *Women's Poetry in France, 1965–1995: A Bilingual Anthology* (1997). See also my critical study *Contemporary French Women Poets* (1995) which appeared in two volumes and treats sixteen living poets.

3 By Philippe Giraudon, in Anna de Noailles, *L'Offrande* (1991), p. 7. All references in the text are to this edition.

4 Henk Vynckier, in Wilson, ed., *Encyclopedia of Continental Women Writers*.

5 In *La Vénus des aveugles* (1991), p. 7.

6 *Les Chansons et les heures, Le Rosaire des joies*, pp. 35–7. All references in the text are to this edition.

7 *Ibid.*, p. 16.

8 Lawrence Joseph, in Catherine Pozzi, *Œuvre poétique*, p. 12. All references in the text are to this edition.

9 'Through an Hour-glass lightly: Valentine Penrose and Alice Rahon Paalen', in King and McGuirk (eds.), pp. 81–112.

10 *Ibid.*

11 See *Valentine Penrose: Poems and Narrations*, trans. Roy Edwards (Manchester: Carcanet Press, 1977), p. 69. All references in the text are to this edition.

12 *Pleine marge* 4 (1986). Also quoted in Colville, pp. 96–7.

13 Preface, Louise de Vilmorin, *Poèmes*, pp. 7–16. All references in the text are to this edition.

14 Mansour, *Prose et poésie: œuvre complète*, pp. 7–8. All references are to this edition.

15 Much of Andrée Chedid's more recent poetic production has been gathered together under the title *Poèmes pour un texte (1970–91)* [Poems for a Text]. All references in the text are to this edition.

16 The *Tel Quel* group, whose literary and socio-political activities were given particular focus through the journal of the same name (1960–83), traversed various radical phases of emphasis: structuralist and formalist criticism, theory, social (communist and marxist) revolution, psychoanalysis. Philippe Sollers continues to be a central figure (now via the journal *L'Infini*) in a movement that has involved writers and philosophers including Genette, Barthes, Lacan, Derrida and Kristeva.

17 Jacqueline Risset has since written widely on Pleynet, Macchia, Biro and Dante, whom she has also translated.

18 *Petits Éléments de physique amoureuse*, p. 19.

19 Correspondence with M. Bishop. Volumes to appear include *Ton nom de végétal* [Your Plant Name] and *Le Jour de gloire* [Day of Glory], but poetry and opera also combine in some works.

20 *Random House Book of Twentieth-Century French Poetry* (New York: Random House, 1984).

21 Colette Nys-Mazure, *Le For intérieur* [Heart of Hearts] (Paris: Le Dé Bleu, 1996), p. 81.

CHAPTER ELEVEN

Voicing the feminine: French women playwrights of the twentieth century

Mary Noonan

The period 1871–1945 was a time of active acquisition of rights by women in France. The rise of militant feminism in France at the beginning of the century is paralleled by an increase in the number of women writing for the stage. French women dramatists in these early years of the century were principally writing socialist-feminist works that were read and/or produced in community halls and in Paris's *universités populaires*. The work of the bolshevik feminist, Vera Starkoff, and of the anarchist feminist Nelly Roussel (1878–1922) was produced in such Parisian locations between 1902 and 1908. In their plays they explored issues such as divorce, the woman's right to abortion and the mother's relation to authority within the family.

The first feminist theatre, the Théâtre Féministe founded in Paris in 1897 by Marya Cheliga, was emblematic of the growth of a strong feminist strand in new play-writing in France at the time. Theatre became a means for women to explore their socio-economic status and to voice their ideas in the public forum. While the more radical feminist–suffragist plays written in the early years of the century by women writers such as Séverine, Starkoff and Roussel were certainly read or performed in non-mainstream venues, by 1920 plays by women were being produced in all the main Parisian theatres.

Marie Lenéru's (1874–1918) first play, *Les Affranchis* [Free Souls] was performed at the Odéon in 1910, and she followed this success with the production of a second play, *Le Redoutable* [The Redoubtable], again at the Odéon, in 1912. Lenéru's inspiration and mentor was François de Curel, one of the founders of the school that called itself *le théâtre d'idées*, a group of writers that advocated a return to classicism in the theatre, and that prioritized theatre's civic role by staging 'pièces à thèse'. Her third play, *La Triomphatrice* [Woman Triumphant], was accepted by the Comédie Française in 1914, but was not performed there until 1918, due to the closure of Parisian theatres during the war. The play reveals the

bind in which the intellectual woman finds herself. Claude Bersier, a successful novelist, is suspected of being a 'bad mother' because she used her
talent to develop a career, to earn her own money; she is admired by her
lover for her manliness, for the maleness of her talent, yet he ultimately
rejects Claude because there is no trace in her of the woman who would
flatter the man's instinct to defend and protect. The process of the drama
highlights Claude's isolation; she is presented as a divided woman, struggling to reconcile her human needs with the social constructs of 'woman'
and 'artist/writer'. The play dramatizes the struggles of the woman in
the masculine space of intellect and writing. The woman who successfully brings her writing into the public domain must relinquish any claims
she might wish to make on the preserves of femininity or motherhood.
The play's ending presents the spectacle of the woman alone in the alien-
ating masculine space. Lenéru's sense of space and use of stage space to
suggest loss and isolation may have been influenced by her own deafness
and near-blindness. Lenéru's confident use of stage space to explore
gender relations constituted a significant advance in the use of the theatre
to stage the woman writer's exploration of her sense of self.

Rachilde (Marguerite Eymery) arrived in Paris in 1881, determined to
make her career as a writer and to join the avant-garde Symbolists, a
counter-group formed in reaction to the 'theatre of ideas'. She immediately distanced herself from the growing movement for women's rights,
seeking instead personal freedom and gender flexibility under the protection of avant-garde defiance. Her first plays, *La Voix du sang* and
Madame la Mort, were produced at the Théâtre d'Art in 1890 and 1891
respectively. Her third play to be produced, *L'Araignée de cristal*, was the
first French play to be performed at Lugné-Poe's newly-opened 'Art-
Theatre', the Théâtre de L' Œuvre, in 1894.

Set in a dimly lit drawing room opening onto a terrace brilliantly lit
by the moon, the play's focus in the open doorway, where a mother and
her son, 'l'Epouvanté', sit in the half-light; behind them, in the drawing-
room, stands a large mirror from which light appears to emanate. The
mother questions her son about his apparent malaise, and the son finally
admits to his obsessive fear of mirrors. In the description of his terror,
'l'Epouvanté' equates women with the mirrors he dreads: the mirror is
a symbol of the woman's lascivious seductiveness and her devouring sexuality. The young man is a half-dead creature next to his vibrant mother;
his voice is heavy and slow, hers is sensual. His features are described by
the author as a weak reflection of his mother's beauty; it is her mirror
that emits a disturbing light throughout the play, and it is by flinging

himself at this death-bearing mirror-woman that the protagonist seeks
his death at the play's end.

At first glance Rachilde appears to replicate negative symbolist
images of femininity in her theatre, but closer examination of her plays
reveals that they stage psychic struggles with power and sexuality from a
female perspective. Her confident use of stage space, lighting and sound
to explore aspects of the unconscious mind had a significant influence
on the emerging avant-garde theatre in France.

Many of Colette's novels were adapted to the stage from the early
1900s onwards. These adaptations were initially carried out without
Colette's direct involvement, but as her writing career progressed, she
worked directly on stage adaptations of her fiction. Her highly popular
novel, *Chéri*, was adapted for the stage by Colette and Léopold
Marchand and performed at the Théâtre Michel in 1921. This
acclaimed production featured Colette herself in the role of Léa, the
fifty-year-old retired courtesan who embarks on an affair with a man
twenty-five years her junior, and who successfully reconstructs herself as
a human being in order to survive the pain of her lover's rejection.
Colette's writing from the 1920s and 1930s, as Alex Hughes's chapter
shows, foregrounds a crisis in masculine identity in the face of female
autonomy in the post-war period, a crisis which is also reflected in the
lampooning of the 'new woman' in the French Press of the 1920s.

Régis-Leroi noted that 250 plays by women were performed in Paris
between 1920 and 1939, including eleven plays produced at the prestigious Théâtre de l'Odéon.[1] The Occupation brought theatrical activity
to a virtual standstill; however, women were writing plays in France
during this time, and a number of these works were produced in the
immediate post-war period. Marguerite Yourcenar wrote *Electre, ou la
chute des masques* (*Electra*) in 1944; the play was produced on French radio
in 1947, and was first performed in Paris at the Théâtre des Mathurins
in 1954. Although Yourcenar is best known as a writer of fiction, her six
plays constitute a significant contribution to the development of a feminine theatrical aesthetic in this century. She took as her subject matter
the legends of Greece and Italy, and the prefaces to her plays indicate
that in writing for the stage she entered consciously into dialogue with
former masters of dramatic and poetic story-telling such as Euripides,
Sophocles, Aeschylus and Dante. Yourcenar was clearly influenced by
the classical tradition, and her plays demonstrate her desire to achieve a
delicate balance of structure and characterization within the discipline
of the classical Unities of space, time and action.

Her first play, the one-act *Dialogue dans le marécage* [Dialogue in the Marsh] (1932), takes as its plot the ancient legend of Pia, a young wife incarcerated for many years by her jealous husband in a crumbling villa in the marshes outside Sienna (the tale is referred to by Dante in his *Purgatorio*). Yourcenar's play focuses on the image of the marsh, and on the ambivalent nature of the woman, Pia. As the husband, now aged, re-encounters his wife and attempts to justify his motives for having imprisoned her, the spectator is maintained in a state of uncertainty as to whether the woman he encounters is already a ghost, or a figment of his imagination or dreams. Pia's descriptions of the happiness she has felt during her years of isolation in the gloomy marshes also suggest a confusion of reality and dream; her husband receives her account of weekly visits by a lover as the ravings of a madwoman. His words reveal his fear of the woman's youth and beauty, of her potential power, of his dependence on her.

In *Dialogue*, the woman inhabits the place of hallucination, the place of primal conflict into which the man stumbles on his quest for 'goodness'. However, his attempt to control the body and feelings of the woman fails. She remains serene, rooted in the ambivalent space of uncertainty; he departs, old, bereft, alone. In the preface to this play Yourcenar stated that she was motivated in all her writing for the stage by a desire to explore the uncertainty with which human experience is imbued, and in particular the ambivalent nature of human identity.[2]

The post-1968 period is an interesting and important one in the history of women's theatre in France.[3] The 1970s in particular was a decade of intense feminist activity, with the establishment of numerous feminist groups. The period also witnessed the emergence of an unprecedented number of women playwrights in France, an increase in productions of plays by women on French stages and improved success for women directors seeking support for their work The work of women playwrights produced during the 1970s marks the appropriation of the theatre as a privileged space for the exploration of the meanings of femininity in the patriarchal context, and of the possibility of new meanings.

Simone Benmussa produced Hélène Cixous's *Portrait de Dora* [Portrait of Dora] at the Théâtre D'Orsay in Paris in February 1976; the production was a turning point in the development of women's theatre in France. Benmussa's production was an adaptation of a text that had originally been written as a radio play by Cixous, in which she had taken Freud's *Fragment of an Analysis of a Case of Hysteria*[4] as the basis for an exploration of the nature of female desire, and of the misrepresentation of that desire by the psychoanalytic profession and by logocentric discourse in general. Benmussa was interested in the text for the possibilities it offered for upsetting 'the everyday, restrictive ordering of space and time imposed on us by the powers that be . . .'[5]

The narrative content of the text enabled Benmussa to exploit the disjunction between the time frames of narrative fiction and theatrical representation. By displacing the actor's movements in relation to the spoken text – which she did by projecting film and slide images of the characters onto the set before and after the actors entered and left the stage; by generating constant movement between past and present; by using a ventriloquism effect whereby recorded voice was intercut with spoken voice, and where characters spoke each other's lines – Benmussa set up a split between narrative and representation. Writing of this production, Sharon Willis noted that 'Partially or completely untethered from character . . . voice takes on a life of its own, enters the scene as agency.'[6] This circulation of disembodied voices on the stage disturbs relations among the characters, resulting in a conflation of identities and gender.

By disrupting the spectator's desire to construct a coherent narrative, to hold the spectacle at a distance and to contain it within the representative frame, the play calls attention to the frame, and to the spectator's identification with the gaze. By foregrounding the narrative nature of Dora's story as told by Freud, and by playing on the collision between the here of theatrical representation and the elsewhere of narrative, Benmussa made it impossible for the audience to consume a unified image of the woman at the centre of the drama. In this way, she emphasized the coercive effects of a male narrative that refuses or diminishes and distorts the experience of the female subject.

In 1976, Michèle Foucher (b. 1941) created *La Table* [The Table], a feminist work which was produced the following year. Foucher wrote the piece on the basis of conversations she had with groups of working-class women in Alsace over a twelve-month period; the subject of these conversations was the meaning of the table in the women's lives. Foucher's aim was to reproduce the spoken quality of the women's speech on the stage, including their silences, hesitations, embarrassment at certain words, laughter, body language. The voices, all channeled by Foucher into a single monologue, speak of the ways in which the women relate to food, to children, to men and to work. In focusing on the spoken word and what it contains of personal history and socio-historic tradition,

Foucher's work is emblematic of a dominant trend in contemporary French women's writing for the theatre which exploits the power of the woman's voiced words to embody female experience.

Hélène Cixous's *Le Nom d'Oedipe: chant du corps interdit* [The Name of Oedipus: Song of the Forbidden Body] was successful in its exploitation of the stage's potential for exploring fluidity of identity. Originally written as the libretto for André Boucourechliev's opera, the piece was first performed at the Avignon Theatre Festival in 1978. All of the main characters are doubled, and the text is marked by disrupted syntax, silences and repetitions.[7] Cixous based her play on the Greek myth in which Oedipus unwittingly murders his father, Laius, King of Thebes, marries his mother Jocasta, and is then himself crowned King. The best known version of the myth is that told by Sophocles, who focuses on events following the oracle's pronouncement that Thebes would be freed from the plague it was suffering only when Laius's murderer was driven from the city. Sophocles charts Oedipus's resolute search for the murderer, Jocasta's suicide by hanging upon discovery of the truth, and Oedipus's self-blinding and exile. The myth has further resonance by virtue of Freud's use of it as a means of describing the development of human (principally male) sexuality in terms of a child's initial rivalry with its father for the mother's affections, and a subsequent separation from the maternal world in order to move into the world of language and the Law of the father.

The myth was undoubtedly of interest to Cixous because of the potential it offered for an exploration of the conflict between the social world, based on the laws of naming, and the private world of sexual desire. In her play, which focuses on Jocasta as a centre of vibrancy and sexual agency, Oedipus struggles and ultimately fails to cast off his role, and the name and myth that define him. In their private world, Oedipus and Jocasta exchange names and roles. The realm of naming is seen as treacherous from this intimate vantage point, where roles and identities are fluid, multiple. However, ultimately Oedipus is unable to say 'no' to his name (Cixous plays upon the homophonic nature of *non/nom* in her title). In contrast, Jocasta does not see herself as bound by the laws of conformity; she knows that their relationship is incestuous before Oedipus does, but it is not this knowledge that causes her death. Through Cixous's Jocasta, what society has proscribed finds a voice – Jocasta is the mother who exults in orgasm, an impossibility within patriarchal culture.[8] Freed from the rule of the Name, Jocasta's language attests to a profound knowledge of flesh.[9] Although she dies as a result of her failure to save Oedipus, the play ends on a positive note, with Oedipus, transformed by Jocasta's love and language, singing and speaking of a love that goes beyond the fixed sexual structures of patriarchal culture. What is most striking about the play is the sensual force of the language that frequently breaks the rules of grammar in order to give voice to a woman's desiring body.

In her 1975 text, *La Jeune Née* (*The Newly Born Woman*), Cixous comments that the woman's voice resonates with 'le premier amour sans nom' (p. 175) ['the first nameless love'], with the pleasure and violence of a relation to origin that is resistant to rupture and separation. In *Chair Chaude* (*Warmth: A Bloodsong*) (1976), Chantal Chawaf (b. 1943) dramatizes the space and time of Cixous's 'first love', the space and time prior to the acquisition of language, when the self lays claim to ideal completeness through a sense of fusion with the mother. The play voices the experience of pre-birth, birth and after-birth as lived by two characters, mother and daughter: La Mère and La Fille. The third 'character' is the heart, Le Cœur, a multiple character played by several men and women, which functions as a *chœur* or chorus. Judith Miller, who has translated the play into English, sees it as an attempt on the part of Chawaf 'to realize the potential of words to free the female unconscious, to regenerate woman's sensuality, to disintellectualize her body and to give voice to experiences rarely depicted'.[10] Chawaf emphasizes rhythm and vocal quality in an unrelenting stream of metaphors describing sensual female bodily experience. She seeks to establish female subjectivity by engaging the spectator in the rhythmical ebb and flow of acutely graphic physical (especially ventral and uterine) images. The effect is that of a fluidity of identity, as the text circulates between mother, daughter and heart; there is little characterization as such, with characters relaying the rhythmical pæan to mother–daughter love between them. Chawaf's play is an attempt to use the stage to liberate repressed biological and psychological aspects of the female psyche relating to the mother–daughter bond.

A number of plays exploring maternal desire and the mother–child bond were produced in France in the late 1970s and early 1980s. Some, such as Chawaf's *Chair Chaude* and Cixous's *Le Nom d'Oedipe*, gave voice to the woman's pleasure in her sexual body and explored the space of motherhood as space of plurality, of intersubjectivity. A number of other plays written by women playwrights during this period, however, explored the maternal as a negative space of merging with the mother.[11]

Plays such as *À Cinquante Ans elle découvrait la mer* [At Fifty, she Discovered the Sea] (1985) by Denise Chalem (b. 1953) *Loin du Grenier* [Far from the Attic] (1984) by Mona Thomas (b. 1952) or *De Si Tendres Liens* [Such Tender Bonds] (1984) by Loleh Bellon (b. 1925) explore the ambivalence at the heart of the relationship between mother and daughter. All three plays demonstrate that while the closeness of this relationship can stimulate feelings of violence, separation is associated with a sense of disaster, even death. The plays present female protagonists involved in a struggle to construct their identities in relation to the Other – mother or daughter. While these plays do not demonstrate *écriture féminine* as an exaltation of images of the maternal as spiritual nourishment, they do exploit the possibilities afforded by the theatre for the staging of the relationship between memory, narrative and female identity. What the process of each play represents is a sense of the inevitability of female continuity within the maternal, of the absence that pervades the woman's present moment, and of her compulsion to narrativize her self on the basis of fragments of memory of the (m)other.

In *Ce Sexe qui n'en est pas un* (1977), Luce Irigaray suggests that the woman's voice tells a different story to the one told by the words she is using, as do the breaks in 'articulacy' which are a feature of her speech. Ultimately, the female voice's struggle with discourse tells both of the impossibility for the female speaker of ever occupying the position of subject in the discourse of western culture, and of this voice's rootedness in a space that is not the space of the (male) subject of (patriarchal) discourse. Receptivity to this voice requires a different kind of listening, if one is to hear what it has to say about what cannot be named in the Symbolic, the order of language.

According to Claude Régy, who directed many of Marguerite Duras's works for the stage, Duras was seeking to capture what she called 'la voix de l'écriture', to hear what the text sounded like as it emerged from the unconscious, before it was set down on paper.[12] The large, empty spaces that are such a feature of Duras's later plays function as echo-chambers through which the voice of the writer's body-text echoes. The uninhabitable terrain of Duras's stage, which is also reflected in the blanks, pauses and silences of the spoken text, suggest both the source of the text and the source of the self. Paradoxically, then, Duras appears to use the very public medium of the theatre to stimulate the spectator's auditory memory and simulate the intensity of the reading experience.

In the late 1970s and early 1980s, Marguerite Duras created plays that flooded the stage with narrative text. The five plays written between 1973 and 1985 – *India Song* (1973), *Eden Cinéma* (1977), *Agatha* (1981), *Savannah Bay* (1982) and *La Musicà Deuxième* (1985) – all feature a traumatic past

event at their centre, and the retelling of that event by two or more narrators constitutes the play's 'action' in each case. There is no action in
the conventional sense – the painful dredging of past story from 'des
mémoires déformantes, créatives' [Memories that distort, that create]
(*India Song*, p. 10), is what has brought these characters into being in this
place. In *India Song* and *Eden Cinéma*, off-stage voices tell the story while
stage action consists mainly of mime. In all five of the later plays, the
spectator's attention is drawn to the fact that what is represented on stage
is already past – dramatic action took place in another time, which is
now inaccessible to both the spectator and to the voices recounting the
story.

There are long moments of absolute immobility in these plays.
Numerous stage directions indicate that the text should be voiced slowly,
and that light should increase or fade slowly. The Durassian spectator
cannot but be aware of the slow passage of time, as time weighs heavily
in this theatre. It is the time of passivity, of waiting, of receptivity to voice
and look. The text voiced in each case is at pains to point to what lies
beyond what is seen, a vast space that is inaccessible to both character
and spectator. Words, silence and sound-track (music frequently plays an
important role on Duras's stage, as do dislocated sounds such as cries of
pain and laughter, singing, the sound of rain falling, etc.) all work to link
the 'outer' space with the past, with memory and with the pain of loss
in the spectator's imagination. The scene of representation is thus
framed by the space of memory, which holds the irretrievable lost
moment of love.

The body of the woman is the threshold between these two spaces on
Duras's stage. The playing area presents the physical body of a woman,
reduced to 'appearance', bearing all the gender markings of the feminine mystique – madness, excessive passion, maternity, death drive – and
traversed by fragments of a narrative that resist coherence or closure.
This (largely silent) body at the centre of the Durassian drama is represented as an opening onto, indeed as essentially connected to, the wider
space of non-representation. Theatre provides the woman playwright
with a unique opportunity to give physical expression, principally
through the medium of the voice, and through physical severance of
voice and body, to the pain of struggling to establish contact with parts
of the self that can no longer be known.

To engage with Duras's theatre is to accept the impossibility of
knowing, of finding one's way back to the origin of the story, unless it be
by means of receptivity to the voice on her stage. For Duras interrupts

the spectator's manipulation of narrative and viewing/framing processes in order to focus her/his attention on a play of voices. In her staging directions, Duras shows herself to be concerned primarily with inducing receptivity in the reader to the physicality of voice on her stage. In signalling a space that resists representation and in taking the voice as the focus of attention in her theatre, Duras gives expression to the distressed source of her own voice within discourse.

Nathalie Sarraute (1900–99) wrote her first play – *Le Mensonge* (*The Lie*)[13] – for radio in 1964; between then and 1982, she wrote a total of six plays, all of which have been performed on the Parisian stage. In her theatrical work, she writes of voices, for voices; having worked hard to dismantle conventional notions of character in her fiction, she insisted on an obliteration of characterization and realism in the staging of her plays. The dialogue is based on a precise gauging of rhythm, pace and the minutiae of sound and breath. Sarraute has described her technique as that of 'un mécanisme minutieusement agencé où tous les rouages s'emboîtent les uns dans les autres' ['a mechanism that has been put together very meticulously, where all the parts fit into each other'].[14] The plays generally enact a conflictual dialogue sparked by what H2 in *Pour un oui ou pour un non* [Over nothing at all] refers to as 'ce qui s'appelle rien' (p. 10) ['that which is generally referred to as nothing'], an infinitesimal crack on the surface of everyday language that initiates the uncovering of a surprising world of tension and passionate struggle.

Sarraute uses small hitches in the smooth flow of banal everyday conversation in order to bring the characters, (or rather, the chorus of voices participating in what Monique Wittig has called 'l'interlocution'[15]), to the source of the word, syllable, sound or silence, to the place where naming ceases. Julia Kristeva, in *La Révolution du langage poétique* (*Revolution in Poetic Language*) (1974) writes of the subject's transition from what she calls the 'semiotic', or pre-Œdipal stage, to the symbolic stage, the space of language and the Other. According to Kristeva, 'semiotic' pleasure is pleasure derived from texts which, through their rhythms, return the reader to the rhythms, movements and sounds of the maternal body. This occurs when a writer uses language in such a way as to activate the re-emergence within discourse of 'the rhythms, intonations and echolalias of the mother–infant symbiosis'. Sarraute's theatre appears to explore the rupture between the place of semiotic fusion with the mother and the place of symbolic signification, where the ego is split and the Other is constituted through social sanction.

Monique Wittig writes of Sarraute's concern with a utopia of the word in her writing.[16] The writer's sense of exuberance in word-play, her intuitive contact with the rhythms of the semiotic contained in language and her sense of utopian space before vowels and vocables were marshalled by the judging authority of the symbolic, constitute one of the force fields on Sarraute's stage. The other is the space of 'interlocution', of the self de-centered by the language of the other. Sarraute has always resisted exploration of gender issues in her writing, and yet, it does seem that she is exploring throughout her writing, and most obviously in her stage work, the distress caused by the pull between the rhythm-based sense of completeness experienced during the pre-symbolic period, when sound was not separated from meaning, and the sensation of the fracturing of the self encountered upon entry into language.

In an article written in 1986 entitled 'Le Pays des autres' [The Country of the Other],[17] Hélène Cixous begins to develop her interpretation of theatre's civic role. What emerges from this text is a vision of theatre as a space for the staging of elemental conflict and the awakening of feelings that have atrophied as a result of the normalizing influence of western mass culture. This theatre is a place in which it is possible to regain the state of innocence; it is also the space of epic.

Cixous's *La Ville Parjure ou le réveil des Erinyes* [The Perjured City or the Awakening of the Erinyes] (1994) dramatizes *l'affaire du sang contaminé*, a court-case resulting in the conviction of a number of eminent doctors at the French national blood transfusion centre in the early 1990s for having knowingly authorized the dissemination of contaminated blood products. The play is epic in its proportions, with twenty-two scenes, a cast of some fifty actors, a running-time of eight hours and a time-scale that spans five thousand years. Its form is that of a lengthy narrative in verse, shaped in a linear sequence of scenes, most of which stage conflictual duologues. Cixous had translated Aschylus's *Eumenides* for the Théâtre du Soleil's 1992 production, *Les Atrides*. The *Eumenides* is the final part of Aeschylus's Oresteian trilogy, in which Orestes, having murdered his mother, Clytemnestra, is pursued by the Furies, or Erinyes, female spirits of vengeance. Orestes is tried by a court of the elders of Athens, at which Apollo decrees that the life of a man is more valuable than that of a woman, as the woman is but the bearer of the man's seed, and that therefore, Orestes's matricide could be absolved as an act of revenge for Clytemnestra's murder of his father, Agamemnon. Following the acquittal of Orestes, the goddess Athene appears on stage to calm the Furies and settle them in a shrine with the beneficient title of Eumenides. Aeschylus's drama was of interest to Cixous for its dramatization of the establishment of the patriarchal principle, the institution of the Law of the City, and the encryptment of maternal anger in the form of the Furies, whose banishment represents the burial of the vestiges of a primitive order.

La Ville Parjure opens with an anguished mother's cry, echoing Clytemnestra's stifled call for justice and providing a sense of continuity between the two texts. In this play, the Mother is fleeing the city, site of treachery and murder. Her two children have died at the hands of the city's medical profession, who have transfused them with contaminated blood. Cixous sets the play in a cemetery somewhere on the outskirts of an unnamed city, seeking to create a space that would be at once redolent of the Greek city, the *polis*, but which would also speak of the modern city.

La Ville Parjure reappropriates the archaic maternal territory in its initial images, and proceeds to open the way for a return to the nocturnal, dream space of the final scene, where mother and children are united with the city's other exiles in pre-Œdipal silence. As the play moves forward, what emerges is an image of two opposing economies – one rooted in the values of the marketplace and motivated by fear of loss of subjective control, the other rooted in a fearless resistance to the corruption of humanitarian values and an openness to the disruptive power of grief. However, ultimately what this text dramatizes is the tension between the poet's public and private vocations. *La Ville Parjure* resounds with the writerly dilemma of working between the two poles of poetry and polemic, of fully assuming the public responsibilities of the poet/prophet, and of answering writing's intimate imperative of a gradual uncovering of selves in the muscle, blood, breath and bone of the writing body. The conflict between the secret, intimate, and fundamentally unknowing act of creativity, and the writer's felt obligation to use the theatrical occasion to communicate an essential, ethical message, is the dynamic underpinning the play.

One of the projects of French women playwrights in this century would appear to have been the reappropriation of the myths and legends of the past. Playwrights such as Marguerite Yourcenar and Hélène Cixous have re-presented Greek mythology, the material at the origin of western theatre, in ways that foreground and undermine the binarism of sexual difference as delimited by classical theatre. A number of the playwrights mentioned here have also drawn on what Kristeva, in her essay on 'women's time', referred to as 'the time of myth' – cyclical or monumental time that is 'all-encompassing and infinite like imaginary space'.[18]

Cixous and Duras tend to use this approach to time on their stages, as do Chantal Chawaf and Catherine Anne. Catherine Anne (b. 1960) has written and directed eight plays for the French stage. The subject of her theatre to date has been youth, and more specifically, the quest of the young for identity and meaning. She combines a poetic style of writing with elements of magic realism and fairy tale in order to move beyond conventional temporal and spatial confines. Her plays – especially *Agnès; suivi de Ah! Anabelle* (1994), *Ah la la! Quelle Histoire* [Oh dear! What a Mess] (1995), and *Nuit pâle au palais* [Pale Night in the Palace] (1997) are particularly interesting for their manipulation of theatrical time and space.

Two further playwrights are significant in relation to the use of classical or mythical material and mythical time-frames in the theatre: Andrée Chedid (b. 1920) and Monique Wittig (b. 1935). Born in Cairo of Lebanese parents, Andrée Chedid has lived in Paris since 1946. Chedid's plays have been described as 'deeply-felt poetic visualizations, which although firmly anchored to the world of reality, give primacy to fantasy, suggestion, evocation'.[19] Chedid uses the stage to explore the ways in which women relate to power, taking female figures from history and legend as the focus for a conflict between the drive for power and the forces of life and love. *Bérénice d'Égypte* [Berenice of Egypt] (1968) charts the struggles of Cleopatra's younger sister to maintain democracy against the tyranny of her father, Ptolomée Aulète. In *Échec à la Reine* [Queen in Check] (1984), the queen of an anonymous kingdom rules unwillingly in her husband's absence until she is persuaded by her jester, Jok, to allow him to play the role of King, and to rule until her son's return. In a series of nine tableaux, Chedid explores a number of different attitudes to power. Character is stylized, language is highly poeticized, time and place are those of myth and legend. Chedid's use of the mythological perspective in her theatre enables her to frame history in the space of the imagination.

Monique Wittig, radical lesbian writer and activist, has written one play that has made an important contribution to the development of women's theatre in France. *Le Voyage sans fin* [The Constant Journey] was first performed in Vermont in 1984, and then in Paris in 1985. The play is a reworking of *Don Quixote*, with Quixote and Panza represented as female characters. Wittig's approach to the stage here recalls that of Marguerite Duras, in that she devised her play on the basis of complete dissociation of movement and sound in order to revitalize the spectator's attention and receptivity to both. The action is divided into fifteen short scenes; the physical movement of the actresses is accompanied by a sound-track on which voices speak a text that is not directly related to what is being performed on the stage. The sound-track also incorporates music, and the voices of actors who do not appear on the stage. Large sections of the text consist of a cataloguing of the female goddesses, heroines and warriors of history and legend; Quichotte's hundreds of books have been written by women, about women. In fact, Wittig rewrites history here as the history of female authorship, female heroism, female warring against injustice, female knight errantry.

In the 'Avant-note' to this play, Wittig comments that 'au théâtre, la présence physique des acteurs est l'événement' ['In the theatre, the physical presence of the actors is the event'], and the real thrust of the play is in the physical exuberance of the action. Wittig chose Quixote as the paradigm of the runaway warrior who is fiercely resistant to all attempts to tame her, and who is not deterred by her awareness of the fear generated by difference. In creating Quichotte, Wittig created a character who is her own legend, who emerges from nowhere and who creates herself. The audience witnesses two characters catapulted onto the stage with no text for support – the sound-track does not 'tell the story' of what happens on stage. The production emphasized physical energy and the acrobatics, juggling and other feats of the circus. In this play, Wittig has invested the physical body on the stage with some of the savagery and abrasiveness she strives to achieve in her writing, in an attempt to cut through the construct 'Woman'. Quichotte has the energy and power of an Amazon. She is fearless, wandering, free – her physical high jinks bear witness to this, and her physicality is contrasted with the critical, judgmental whisperings of the off-stage voices, who would wish to circumscribe her within convention, and who portray her as foolish or ridiculous.

Wittig differs significantly from playwrights such as Marguerite Duras, Hélène Cixous and Nathalie Sarraute in her foregrounding of the female body's joy in exuberant physical movement and her appropriation of physical power for women. Indeed, her representation of the woman's body as the space of power in relation to a dislocated narrative is unusual in the history of French women's play-writing. She does, nonetheless, parallel the work of Duras, Cixous and Sarraute in her attempt, through disjunction of voice and movement, to move the spectator to engage her auditory memory and imagination with the voiced text.

Throughout the twentieth-century women writers in France have appropriated the theatrical medium as a means of exploring their sense

of self, and of developing a female aesthetic self.[20] Theatre affords the
woman writer particular opportunities for examining her relationship
with space and time, with roles and identities, with authority and judgment. A number of the women playwrights whose work has been discussed here have used the stage to foreground the coercive nature of
representation, and the implications of conventional narrative representation for female subjectivity.

The work of a surprising number of the writers in question stages a
splitting in two of stage space: the space of representation is framed by
an 'other' space, the space of that which resists representation. This
other space would appear to be the locus of what Irigaray has described
as that part of female subjectivity which has been repressed in order to
found a logocentric order of discourse.[21] That which lies outside discourse, that which has traditionally been defined as 'madness' or 'hysteria', is represented as a utopia of the word in the theatre of Nathalie
Sarraute; as a utopia of desire in the theatre of Marguerite Duras; as a
utopia of female physicality in the theatre of Monique Wittig; and as a
utopia of intersubjectivity in the theatre of Hélène Cixous. Woman is
frequently portrayed on these stages as being in exile within the frame of
representation, journeying towards the utopian space, sometimes even
inhabiting that space.[22]

Above all, French women playwrights in the twentieth century have
undertaken a profound rethinking of the role of voice and of the auditory relationship between the spectator and the stage. Women writing
for the theatre in the post-1968 period in particular began to explore the
stage's potential for embodying the distressed source of the woman's
voice, and to develop the spectator's receptivity to a voice that gives
expression to a polyphonic disruption of narrative coherence.

NOTES

1 Régis-Leroi, 'Lorsque les femmes deviennent auteurs dramatiques: de
Marie Lenéru à Anne Mariel, elles ont abordé tous les genres' in *Minerva*,
27 June 1937.

2 Marguerite Yourcenar, *Dialogue dans le marécage* in *Théâtre* (Paris: Gallimard,
1971), vol. II, p. 177.

3 The work of women in the theatre in this period is described in some detail
in the following essays: Judith Graves Miller, 'Contemporary Women's
Voices in the French Theatre', *Modern Drama* 32 (1989), 5–19; Jane Moss,
'Women's Theatre in France', *Signs* 12 (1987), 548–67; Monique Surel-
Tupin, 'La Prise de parole des femmes au théâtre', in J. Epstein and

P. Ivernel (eds.), *Le Théâtre d'intervention depuis 1968* (Lausanne: L'Âge d'homme, 1983).

4 Sigmund Freud, *Standard Edition of the Works of Sigmund Freud* (London: Hogarth Press, 1953), vol. VII, pp. 1–22.

5 Simone Benmussa, *Benmussa Directs: Playscripts 91* (London: John Calder, 1979), pp. 10–11.

6 Willis, 'Hélène Cixous's *Portrait de Dora*.

7 See Moss, 'Women's Theatre in France', for details of the original production.

8 See Luce Irigaray, 'Le Corps à corps avec la mère' published in the collection *Sexes et parentés (Sexes and Genealogies)*.

9 See Sandra Freeman, 'Bisexuality in Cixous's *Le Nom d'Oedipe*, Theatre Research International 23, 3 (1998), 242–8.

10 Makward and Miller (eds. and trans.), *Plays by French and Francophone Women: A Critical Anthology*, p. 231

11 See Irigaray on the implications for female subjectivity of the proscription of the mother's desire and the mother–daughter bond in *Speculum. De l'autre femme (Speculum of the Other Woman)*. She further develops her thinking on the mother–daughter bond in the patriarchal context in 'Le Corps-à-corps avec la mère'.

12 Interview quoted in Papin, *L'Autre Scène*, p. 28.

13 All translations given, unless otherwise stated, are published in Nathalie Sarraute's *Collected Plays*, trans. Jolas and Wright.

14 Nathalie Sarraute, 'Le Gant Retourné', *Digraphe* 32 (1984), 51–62, at 51.

15 Monique Wittig, 'Le Lieu de l'action', *Digraphe* 32 (1984), 69–75, at 69.

16 *Ibid.*, 171.

17 Hélène Cixous, 'Le Pays des autres', reprinted under the title 'Le Lieu du Crime, Le Lieu du Pardon', in *L'Indiade ou L'Inde de leurs rêves* [The Indiad, or the India of their Dreams] (Paris: Théâtre du Soleil, 1987).

18 Julia Kristeva, 'Women's Time' in Moi (ed.), *Kristeva Reader*, pp. 188–213.

19 Knapp, *Andrée Chédid*, p. 58.

20 The younger generation of women playwrights currently writing in France is demonstrating increased confidence in the manipulation of theatrical language and form. Writers such as Noëlle Renaude (b. 1949) and Natacha de Pontcharra draw on a range of forms from different traditions in order to explore *fin-de-siècle* unease. Black comedy is emerging as the predominant mode of these writers.

21 Irigaray, *Ce sexe qui n'en est pas un*, p. 74.

22 The work of the contemporary Algerian-born playwright Fatima Gallaire (b. 1944) explores the theme of exile. Her plays stage the confluence of the pain of loss felt by the exiled woman and the repressed pain of her place of origin.

CHAPTER TWELVE

Feminist literary theory

Judith Still

The title of this chapter is misleading if it implies a coherent body of thought which might be termed 'French feminist literary theory'. Furthermore, it is not clear that feminist literary theory as such is the object of many of the leading French thinkers. Most of the key French literary theorists are men, and few are feminists as we would understand the term. Few of the French structuralists and poststructuralists[1] feel any awkwardness in using he/man language,[2] for example, despite their close attention to linguistic detail. Many influential feminists in France come from disciplines other than literary studies: for instance, Christine Delphy from sociology or Michèle Le Dœuff from philosophy. And yet French theory in the second half of the twentieth century has proved enormously influential both on feminism and, to an even greater extent, on literary theory. The influence of French theory has been felt not only in the anglophone world, where the appetite for structuralism and post-structuralism has been huge, but also in countries as diverse as Brazil, India or Japan. Although we should note that within different countries the question of the relation between elite and subaltern culture varies and this affects the purchase of particular kinds of theory. In sum, French feminist literary theory is largely practised outside France albeit under the influence of France. This chapter will focus on those French thinkers, particularly women, who have been most influential on and come closest to feminist literary theory.

There are a series of problems with terms which should be mentioned at the outset: defining 'feminist' and identifying indigenous feminist traditions, for example. At one time it was common to make an opposition between Anglo-American (or Anglo-Saxon, as the French have it) and French feminism.[3] According to the terms of the opposition, Anglo-American signalled reformist, radical or socialist feminism and French signalled poststructuralist feminism, strongly influenced by psychoanalysis.[4] It then became imperative to point out (a) that many British and

American feminists are very close to so-called French feminism; (b) that many feminists in France (albeit less well known outside France than the poststructuralist variety) are reformist or materialist, and (c) that the majority of the (feminist) world is neither French nor British nor American. In spite of that necessary corrective, I shall continue to use 'Anglo-American' and 'French' as useful shorthand to define different traditions of work.

In the Anglo-Saxon world, feminist literary theory has often been considered to have two key areas of work. The first is the critique of phallocentrism, particularly in canonical male authors (sometimes summarily referred to as Dead White Males), but also in popular culture if the definition of 'literary' is expanded as many theorists would wish it to be. The second is the rediscovery of women writers who may have been known but treated disparagingly in some respect or who may have been lost altogether. This has entailed rethinking certain conventional assumptions, for example about the relative value of different genres.

The pioneer work of Simone de Beauvoir in analysing phallocentrism in a wide range of authors (literary and non-literary), and in referring to a wide range of female authors in *Le deuxième sexe* (*The Second Sex*) has thus found more echoes abroad than in France, although Beauvoir herself has been analysed as phallocentric with respect not only to her fiction, but also to sections of *Le deuxième Sexe*.[5] In France more attention has been paid to masculine bias in psychoanalysis and philosophy (also a concern for Beauvoir of course) than in literature.[6] The work of Luce Irigaray, for instance, has proved very influential in departments of literature outside France, and yet her published work does not focus on literary texts. Two other influential writers, Hélène Cixous and Julia Kristeva, on the other hand, do focus on literature – but in ways which are not always easy to reconcile with a feminist tradition. Both pay far less attention, or rather different attention, to the biological sex of the author than the Anglo-American tradition has done. Both pay more attention to form relative to content than has typically been the case in Anglo-Saxon feminist analyses. All three writers, in common with almost all poststructuralist French thinkers,[7] are influenced (albeit to differing degrees) by the work of Freud and, in particular, by the reading of Freud found in Lacan. While that influence does not preclude a critique of the sexism in psychoanalysis (a critique which sometimes comes close to Anglo-American attacks on Freud), certain suppositions are taken for granted. These include the importance of the unconscious, the role of language in structuring both the unconscious and the social, and the ability of the subject to take up different sexed positions (so that a woman may occupy a masculine subject position or a man a feminine one[8]). The French feminist included in this chapter who is least susceptible to psychoanalysis is the radical lesbian feminist Monique Wittig – to the point where some would consider her 'Anglo-American' rather than French.

Hélène Cixous (b. 1937) is a specialist in literature: she wrote her doctorate on Joyce. As has been shown in earlier chapters, she is also a significant and prolific experimental novelist and playwright, and her work does much to explore, and sometimes creatively confuse, the boundaries between theory and practice, reading and writing.[9] Both reading and writing are celebrated in a series of bodily and passionate metaphors in her work, such as consuming, eating, loving, sleeping, gestating, giving birth, feeding, licking, lactating, sucking or suckling. Cixous's work, which should perhaps also include her pedagogical practice, has proved inspirational to a number of feminists although it is highly controversial with other feminists for reasons that should become clear. She herself has often dismissed the label 'feminist', a gesture which has a different resonance in France (where the term is sometimes very narrowly defined as a member of a bourgeois reformist movement) than it does in Britain, where a woman's refusal to be called a feminist is usually a signal of deep conservatism.

In the anglophone world her 'critical' work has received more attention than her 'creative' work, particularly two key texts written in the 1970s: *La Jeune Née* (*The Newly Born Woman*) (with Catherine Clément) and 'Le Rire de la Méduse' ('The Laugh of the Medusa'). These are often seen as defining *écriture féminine*, although Cixous's wariness about being pinned down in definitions is also often noted. Her distrust of definition has perhaps been vindicated by (or, her critics would say, has directly contributed to) the confusing mistranslation of *écriture féminine* as women's writing. The confusion arises because women's writing is understood to mean writing produced by biological females whereas *écriture féminine* can be produced by either sex. Cixous adds to the confusion herself by her profusion of feminine bodily metaphors, *and* by her assertion that women more easily produce *écriture féminine* than men do. These two facts have to be set alongside the two facts that her metaphors do not obey any conventional biological logic (children may well give birth to their mothers), and that she gives far more examples of male producers of *écriture féminine* than of women. In French, *féminin* covers both female and feminine which makes life difficult for translators of French and for English-speaking readers who are familiar with the feminist insistence on a distinction between the given of sex (female) and the social construction of gender (feminine).[10] Not only does the French language make the Anglo-American study of *gender* difficult to translate or even transport into this context, but writers such as Cixous or Irigaray (or Derrida) deliberately and polemically delight in confusing the issue. The painful struggle for the reader, who feels on safe constructionist ground momentarily and then is undercut by a flourish of what seems to be biological essentialism, is part of the pleasure or at least of the learning process. Problems arise for us partly because we are trapped in the language of our present society and political economy, and cannot simply step outside those circles into a new uncontaminated form.

Ecriture féminine could be defined as a certain style, a style which challenges the language which constructs us as certain kinds of subjects, subject to a certain kind of economy, which Cixous terms an *économie masculine* or an economy of the *proper*. This masculine economy is an economy which accepts the tenets of Aristotelian logic, the logic of non-contradiction, the mutual exclusion of opposite terms. It promotes thinking in terms of hierarchical binary oppositions (such as man versus woman), in spite of any experience or even enjoyment of the complicating or undermining evidence. Cixous is sometimes said to pay less attention to content than to style, but I would argue that she does not ignore content, and that particular representations are liberating for her at particular moments, for example Kleist's Penthesilea and Achilles,[11] or Lispector's cockroach.[12]

I shall focus briefly on the case of Lispector, the modernist novelist, as Cixous's most important *discovery* of a female practitioner of *écriture féminine*. Lispector was already well respected in Brazil, but Cixous's passionate writing and speaking about her has enhanced her reputation in Europe and North America. The best way to get a purchase on Cixous's method is to experience it; here is a sample of her writing on Lispector, whom she characteristically refers to, in a deliberate gesture of intimacy, as Clarice:

Clarice Lispector: Cette femme, notre contemporaine, brésilienne (née en Ukraine, d'origine juive), nous donne, non pas des livres, mais le vivre sauvé des livres, des récits, des constructions refoulantes. Et nous entrons, par son écriture-fenêtre, dans la terrible beauté d'apprendre à lire: en allant, à travers corps, de l'autre côté du moi. Aimer le vrai du vivant, ce qui semble *ingrat* aux yeux narcisse, le sans-prestige, le sans-actualité, aimer l'origine, s'intéresser personnellement à l'impersonnel, à l'animal, à la chose.[13]

Clarice Lispector. This woman, our contemporary, Brazilian (born in the Ukraine, of Jewish origin), gives us not books but living saved from books, from narratives, repressive constructions. And through her writing-window we enter the awesome beauty of learning to read: going, by way of the body, to the other side of the self. Loving the true of the living, what seems *ungrateful* to narcissus eyes, the nonprestigious, the nonimmediate, loving the origin, interesting oneself personally with the impersonal, with the animal, with the thing.[14]

Cixous emphasizes the living, life-giving, qualities of Lispector's work, the life which Lispector allows you to find in even the least prepossessing of creatures – such as the cockroach. Taking off from the name *Clarice*, she will emphasize the light and translucence in the writing-window. Other key words include: *aimer, donner, le vrai, la chose* and *apprendre.* In the course of lengthy detailed reading-meditations these terms take on flesh. Again in the same article:

Je me suis laissée lire selon C.L., sa passion m'a lue, et dans le courant brûlant et humide du lire, j'ai vu comme les textes familiers et étrangers, de Rilke ou de Heidegger, ou de Derrida, avaient été lus-déjà, emportés, répondus, dans l'écrire-vivre de C.L.

Ce qui suit est un moment d'une lecture de C.L.: faite dans la correspondance C.L. avec toute femme. (p. 117)

I let myself be read according to C.L., her passion read me; and in the burning and humid current of reading, I saw how familiar and strange texts, by Rilke or by Heidegger or Derrida, had been read-already, carried away, answered, in the writing-living of C.L.

What follows is a moment of a reading of C.L.: carried out in the C.L. correspondence with all women. (p. 60)

Here Cixous plays on the title of one of Lispector's works, which in French is *La Passion selon G.H.* Significantly (correspondence here meaning bond, relationship or communication) while emphasizing the correspondence of Lispector with any woman, she cites a male poet and philosophers as intertexts.[15] This slipperiness may be seen in the light of her insistent refusal of binary oppositions (for instance, in the quotations above, we find 's'intéresser personnellement à l'impersonnel' ['interesting oneself personally with the impersonal'] or 'textes familiers et étrangers' ['familiar and strange texts']).

While Cixous does not lay down the outline of a feminist theory of literature for us, what emerges from her own practice of reading Lispector is that reading should be pleasurable indeed sensual, yet also a liberating, transforming apprenticeship (which may thus include pain). Cixous savours the detail of Lispector's text, she steals a word, and uses it as an intellectual and emotional springboard, she flies with it. She allows a word to give her the experience of the thing, so *sea* will give her the taste of salt on her lips. For Cixous, Clarice enables this Heideggerian thing-ness of things, this union of the subject with what is foreign to it. She also lets Lispector's words impregnate or be impregnated by the wealth of her own personal culture, the languages she knows, the writers she has read. Thus Cixous is read by Lispector as much as the reverse. Another binary opposition, another hierarchy, is disturbed.

The highly emotional tone of Cixous's readings can irritate the Anglo-American feminist (including a number in France), who may find it 'feminine' in the conventional and derogatory sense. However, even for those who do not wish to practise this style of reading, it could be seen as a useful corrective to self-styled objective and dispassionate scholarship which too often conceals a range of prejudices which 'go without saying'.

Like Cixous, Julia Kristeva (b. 1941) is a literary specialist, and has also, more recently, written novels herself – although these have not been received with much serious critical attention. Unlike Cixous, Kristeva is a trained and practising psychoanalyst, and her own reworking of psychoanalytic theory, in particular her emphasis on the semiotic as well as the symbolic order, informs all her analyses. Crudely summarized, the semiotic derives its characteristics from psychoanalytic speculation about the pre-Œdipal relation to the mother; the symbolic order is inaugurated by the intervention of the father as Law. While the semiotic is associated with the maternal, and thus might be thought to be essentially tied to women, its rhythmical and disruptive qualities are usually located in avant-garde and poetic writing – which returns us to the predominantly, if not exclusively, male canon.

While Kristeva shares Cixous's faith in the radical potential of avant-garde poetic language, she is more inclined herself to write in a theoretical and magisterial style. That is not to say that her work is clearer than Cixous's. While Cixous's writing can be difficult for the reader because of its poetic or gnomic qualities, and some of her most creative work is highly experimental, Kristeva's densest structuralist and poststructuralist analyses have proved equally hard for readers to grasp. Both writers, indeed almost all French poststructuralists, assume a significant degree of common culture, and refer implicitly or explicitly to an impressive range of philosophical and literary intertexts. This creates problems where there is a cultural difference – which may be a question of nationality, but also of class. Consequently Anglo-American feminists, who have often been influenced by a socialist or reformist tradition which values communication and clarity, have accused Kristeva, Irigaray and Cixous of elitism and even deliberate mystification. However, all three adopt different styles in different works, depending, for example, on whether the text in question is addressed to specialists in a particular field or not – this is particularly true of Irigaray. At the same time all three are influenced by a different pedagogical perspective than the Anglo-Saxon radical one mentioned above. Most poststructuralist writing assumes that it is important for the reader to struggle, to take time, to co-produce the text creatively – this reading process should be both plea-surable and painful, just as the psychoanalytic transference[16] (a key intertext) involves both love and hate for the 'parent'.[17] While commu-nicative clarity is, importantly, acknowledged as a strategy in certain sit-uations, it is not sanctified as the only route since, it is argued, it can serve, and has so often served, as a tool of domination.

Kristeva has an eclectic range of literary reference, and has produced analyses of classical Greek plays and medieval *chansons de geste* as well as of Proust. However, her best known work focuses on the French avant-garde and modernist canon, including Lautréamont, Mallarmé and Céline. She claims that revolutionary poetic language is one necessary condition for a general revolution in thinking. While she occasionally selects for analysis a female-authored text (such as those of Duras, also admired by Cixous), she has published rather contemptuous generaliza-tions about women writers – reinforced by her analysis of the particu-lar social and psychic pressures on women in the past and still today. In spite of this justification for her position it has understandably alienated many feminist literary theorists who have little sympathy either for cel-ebrations of canonized male misogynists or for denigrations of women writers.

The work of Bataille is a useful example in that he is generally admired by French poststructuralists, including Kristeva.[18] However, Andrea Dworkin[19] would not be alone in condemning him unequivocally as a pornographer who incites sexual violence towards women; and Annie Leclerc, in *Parole de femme* [Word of a Woman] (1974) offers a French per-spective on his work which is closer to Anglo-Saxon feminist concerns (p. 127 ff.). In the case of Céline, Kristeva does not ignore his misogyny and anti-Semitism, but does see them as a side-effect of his explorations of the rocky frontier between subject and object, of his sense that identity is untenable. Rather than reading Céline as philosophical or as political ideology – and condemning him for his repulsive sentiments – she sees him as staging an abject apocalypse.[20] It is not surprising for Kristeva, as psychoanalyst, that the libidinal economy of fascism is both fascinated and repelled by the maternal and the feminine side of the self as well as by the 'other' race. She asserts:

Que 'du maternel' se trouve agir cette incertitude que j'appelle abjection, éclaire l'écriture littéraire du combat essentiel qu'un écrivain (homme ou femme) a à livrer avec ce qu'il ne nomme démoniaque que pour le signaler comme la doublure inséparable de son être même, comme l'autre (sexe) qui le travaille et le possède. Ecrit-on autrement que possédé par l'abjection, dans une catharsis indéfinie? Il n'y aura qu'un féminisme jaloux de préserver son pouvoir – dernière des idéologies revendicatrices de pouvoir – pour crier à l'usurpateur devant cet artiste qui, même s'il l'ignore, est un défaiseur de narcissme comme de toute identité imaginaire, y compris sexuelle. (*Pouvoirs de l'horreur*, p. 246)

If 'something maternal' happens to bear upon the uncertainty that I call abjection, it illuminates the literary scription of the essential struggle that a writer (man or woman) has to engage in with what he calls demonic only to call attention to it as the inseparable obverse of his very being, of the other (sex) that torments and possesses him. Does one write under any other condition than being possessed by abjection, in an indefinite catharsis? Leaving aside adherents of a feminism that is jealous of conserving its power – the last of the power-seeking ideologies – none will accuse of being a usurper the artist, who, even if he does not know it, is an undoer of narcissism and of all imaginary identity as well, sexual included. (*Powers of Horror*, p. 208)

Not surprisingly, Kristeva's sideswipes at certain kinds of feminism (often misunderstood as a dismissal of all feminism) have provoked retaliation. One critic, for example, condemns *Pouvoirs de l'horreur* (*Powers of Horror*) (1980) and presents the verdict (shared, apparently, by a group of British socialist feminists) that 'Kristeva's work is no longer in women's interests' and, more strongly, that 'Kristeva's fascist whispers . . . have [in *Powers of Horror*] become a primal scream'.[21]

A collection of translated extracts which has influenced anglophone reception of 'French feminism' is *New French Feminisms*, first published in the United States in 1980. One extract from Kristeva is entitled 'Woman Can Never Be Defined'.[22] The very title can be taken as a red rag to the bull of Anglo-American feminism, which requires the term *women* both for its analyses and for its political practice, such as the encouragement of the study of 'women's writing' as if such a category were meaningful. In fact reading the essay, rather than just the title, reveals that Kristeva is quite willing for *women* as a category to be evoked as a rallying call for specific short-term purposes such as equal pay legislation. However, she argues that 'woman' or 'the feminine' is to be understood more generally as precisely that improper slipping between fixed categories which eludes definition.

In *Des Chinoises* [*About Chinese Women*] (1974) Kristeva suggests that, rather than being trapped in a 'masculine' role, identifying with what she sums up as 'maîtrise, surmoi, parole homologuante communicative instituant un échange social stable' (p. 42) ['dominance, superego, the endorsed communicative word that institutes stable social exchange' (p. 37)] or being trapped in a stereotypical feminine role, which involves a hysterical refusal to communicate or take your place on the stage of politics and history, a woman might be able to oscillate between the pole of the father and that of the mother. She deploys this notion of *alternance* to analyse Chinese writing in a positive light. She singles out for praise, for example, the twelfth-century woman poet Li Quingzhao (pp. 99–102). However, her brief references to some of the best known western women writers such as Woolf, Tsvetaeva and Plath focus on their 'madness' and suicides ('Moi qui veut ne pas être', ['I Who Want Not To Be'] pp. 45–7). Meanwhile her interpretation of Chinese culture has been accused of Orientalism – in part because it is based on a very short period of immersion at a time when Maoism was fashionable amongst Parisian left-wing intelligentsia. Orientalism is a term coined by Edward Said in his book of that name. It includes manifest Orientalism, in the scholarly study of the Orient, and latent Orientalism, which is the body of assumptions and prejudices common in the west. The latter is more stable and unanimous than manifest Orientalism, although both share many elements (e.g., the passive, slavish, sensual and cruel Oriental). Said writes:

In the system of knowledge about the Orient, the Orient is less a place than a *topos*, a set of references, a congeries of characteristics, that seems to have its origin in a quotation, or a fragment of a text, or a citation from someone's work on the Orient, or some bit of previous imagining, or an amalgam of all these. Direct observation or circumstantial description of the Orient are the fictions presented by writing on the Orient, yet invariably these are totally secondary to systematic tasks of another sort.[23]

Kristeva's work has been considered to have elements of both manifest and latent Orientalism. Nevertheless her theory has proved enabling for some feminist literary theorists, who do not allow themselves to be put off by her sniping at 'feminism', and her belief that the revolutionary disrupting force of the 'feminine' is mostly found in male writers.

Luce Irigaray (b. 1932) has not to date published significant analyses of literature (although she wrote a doctoral thesis on Paul Valéry).

However, her analyses of psychoanalytical and philosophical texts owe much (and have given much) to the techniques of literary criticism. This is a literary criticism which is productively intertwined with psychoanalysis in its understanding and deployment of word play and word association.[24]

Irigaray's critique of the founding fathers of western phallogocentrism is sometimes close in spirit to work produced by Anglo-Americans, although the detail may well be more elliptical and dense. One example would be 'Retour sur la théorie psychanalytique' ('Psychoanalytic Theory: Another Look') in *Ce Sexe qui n'en est pas un* (*This Sex Which Is Not One*) (1977). However, she also adopts a style, closer to Cixous's way of reading, which has been termed 'amorous exchange' or 'poetic nuptials' – one example is her short work on Nietzsche, *Amante marine* [*Marine Lover of Friedrich Nietzche*]. Irigaray's work evokes a utopic horizon, and Margaret Whitford has argued that the potentially transformative experience of reading her texts may be part of the production of that dynamic utopia in the present. This assumes a reading which does not adopt a distanced and critical stance, a masculine stance which often presents itself as the only correct, objective approach and yet which is only one amongst many, and one which carries its own baggage of prejudices. Instead, a 'maternal–feminine' reading position can be adopted; this is not a totally cosy and comfortable position, but does assume a certain *giving* to the text, and a willingness to *take*, to allow the text to *give* to you. The giving to the text may involve a certain *giving up*, a willingness to lose some of the certainties to which we cling in our desperate attempts to construct ourselves as coherent and functioning subjects. While Irigaray, in common with Cixous and Kristeva, sees the importance of women functioning in the man's world in which we live (the struggle for equality characteristic of Beauvoir's work), she warns that equality, even if it could be achieved, is not enough. Difference must be fostered in a number of ways – and opening up even to textual otherness is one of the routes.

Monique Wittig (b. 1935), who considers herself a materialist, is different from the other theorists considered thus far in that her rejection of psychoanalysis is almost total. She also refuses to call herself a woman, because she is a lesbian. For Wittig, women are a social class defined in a hierarchical binary opposition with men. Lesbians, who are not dependent on and thus subordinate to men, are therefore not women. Wittig's experimental novels and her theoretical writing have been influential particularly amongst lesbian communities in the United

States – less so in France – and it has been argued that each of her books, 'by virtue of style alone, issues a profound challenge to canonized literary tradition, to the very process of reading as an exercise in community understanding'.[25] Wittig's fiction is highly and self-consciously intertextual including rewritings of works such as Dante's *Divine Comedy*, Greek myths, or The Song of Songs. It thereby suggests new strategies for reading classic texts, creative misreadings; Wittig proposes lesbianizing familiar heroes and heroines, a strategy which can be deployed in a number of contexts – including watching Hollywood movies. In common with Cixous, Kristeva and Irigaray, Wittig places enormous emphasis on language, and the need to change language in order to transform the socio-political order – a revolution in language is a necessary although far from sufficient condition. In her own writing Wittig attempts, for instance, to subvert the functioning of personal pronouns, so that, in *Les Guérillères*, for example, *elles* takes on the universal role usually played by *ils* in French.[26]

If one were to sum up the contribution made by French theory to feminist literary criticism, then it would be simultaneously a celebration and a disturbance of the term *woman* (also *feminine* or *maternal*) such that reading or writing as a woman is made both more desirable and more problematic. In the case of Wittig, I would argue, the term *lesbian* takes up the place of woman insofar as it is at once a locus of bodily pleasure and pain where impossible biological metaphors turn back on themselves, as well as a rallying call and a term which cannot be defined. The way in which Cixous or Irigaray write calls for a certain kind of reading, perhaps a utopian one, which is transformative of the reader as the reader engages with the text. The most significant development of French feminist literary theory – as much as any particular details of theory – is the incitement to the maternal-feminine reading practice.

NOTES

1 Both terms, although now heavily used, are hard to define either sociologically or conceptually. A sociological definition would point to influential groups of individuals operating mainly in Paris, in, or on the margins of, the Academy. The problem lies in the inclusivity or exclusivity of each category, and thinkers such as Barthes, Kristeva or Foucault can equally happily (or unhappily) be accommodated in either structuralism or poststructuralism. Conceptual definitions are also hard to make stick, particularly in the case of poststructuralism which is characteristically eager to challenge borders or to find leaks in apparently watertight categories. Structuralism is usually

deemed to trace its roots to the linguist Saussure who argued that meaning is produced not via nuggets of essential meaning, but via significant differences between constructed categories. Saussure's mantle is taken up by the anthropologist Lévi-Strauss who expands this argument to cover not only the spoken word but a whole range of cultural categories. Structuralism is caricaturally associated with binary oppositions, and with the privileging of synchronic formal qualities over historical change. Poststructuralism would then be associated with a questioning of the fixity of binary oppositions, and an investigation of their inevitable play of hierarchies. Feminism has, of course, always been associated with the major binary (and its attendant hierarchy) of men and women, and has also always been interested in the question of whether difference is essential or constructed. Hence, while many structuralist and poststructuralist theories ignore, and may even have been ignorant of, feminist questions, many feminists have adopted the practical strategy of applying any useful insights or methodological insights they can find.

2 This term is used by Spender, *Man Made Language*. It refers to the common practice of using specific gendered terms, such as *he* or *man* in order to refer universally to both men and women. As Spender points out, the ability of *he* to refer universally to both sexes without bias is undercut when we shift away from sentences such as 'man is a hunter: he loves to fight as well as to play' to sentences such as 'man is an animal who gives live birth and breast-feeds his young'. While women can always be referred to by the specific *she*, the apparently universal *he* allows a confusion (useful for patriarchy) as to whether it may be being used specifically or not. Are women hunters and fighters or not?

3 A good example of this is Moi's *Sexual/Textual Politics*. This has been widely read and has influenced the debate; in my view, it shows how the opposition can be a productive strategy for ordering thinking, even though the problems with accepting the schema as absolute (something Moi no doubt did not intend) have now been well rehearsed.

4 Reformist feminism aims at change in current legislation or in social practices without aiming at the overthrow of the political or economic system; it can happily exist, for instance, within established democratic political parties. Radical feminism aims at the overthrow of patriarchy. Socialist, marxist or materialist feminism aims at the overthrow of the capitalist system alongside, or as a step towards, achieving sexual equality (and can exist within revolutionary political parties or groups). Poststructuralist feminism would characterize itself as revolutionary, but would not necessarily accept the categories of, or be so optimistic about the means of bringing about radical change as, radical or socialist feminism. It usually entails an interest in (changing) the linguistic structure of the subject.

5 See, for example, Moi, *Feminist Theory and Simone de Beauvoir*.

6 There are of course exceptions to all the general rules proposed here. Annie Leclerc in *Parole de femme* analyses Malraux as well as Sartre and Bataille.

7 One of the most influential male poststructuralist thinkers with respect to feminist literary theory is Jacques Derrida. Works of his which address related issues include 'voice ii . . .', 'Choreographies', *Spurs*, and 'Women in the Beehive: a Seminar with Jacques Derrida'. For a sympathetic critique of his position see Spivak, 'Displacement and the Discourse of Women'. Spivak is concerned about a male philosopher adopting the feminine perhaps a little too easily, but she is also sceptical about the claims made for the feminine by the female poststructuralists discussed in this chapter.

8 While this particular reading of psychoanalysis sounds an admirable argument to support the notion that 'gender' does not depend on 'sex', the influence of psychoanalysis may also supply a vocabulary (if nothing more) of 'mothers' and 'fathers' which seems more conservative. Psychoanalysis (as well as cultural difference) is probably also to blame for the apparently homophobic statements in Kristeva, Irigaray and even Cixous.

9 Also that between literature–poetry and politics–history. Cixous's work is not only political in that it has implications for sexual politics, but has also been concerned with political and racial issues in Cambodia, India or South Africa. This is particularly true of her theatre and of her 'De la scène de l'Inconscient à la scène de l'Histoire: Chemin d'une écriture', in van Rossum-Guyon and Díaz-Diocaretz (eds.), pp. 15–34. However, there are also many instances of her political poeticization or mythicization of history throughout her 'prose' work; one example would be 'The Parting of the Cake', in which the writer's sensuous access to the imprisoned and separated Mandelas comes partly through the taste of almonds conjured from the name.

10 I shall leave aside the more recent work of feminist theorists such as Judith Butler who, under the influence of French poststructuralist theory as well as Queer theory, have developed the argument to show how sex is as constructed as gender.

11 In 'Extreme Fidelity', Cixous writes of warrior women in love: 'For example, Kleist's play *Penthesiliea* portrays a highly complex relationship of reversals where Achilles tries to cross over on to the side of femininity and where Penthesiliea has difficulty reconciling the obligation of being a man with the need to be a woman'. See Susan Sellars, (ed.), *Writing Differences. Readings from the Seminar of Hélène Cixous* (Milton Keynes: Open University Press, 1988) pp. 9–36 (p. 31).

12 In *The Passion according to G. H.* a middle-class woman standing in her maid's empty room is, at first, disgusted to see a cockroach, but then achieves a kind of self-transcendence by taking it into her mouth, and biting it.

13 'L'Approche de Clarice Lispector' in *Entre l'écriture*, pp. 111–38, p. 115.

14 'Clarice Lispector: The Approach', in *'Coming to Writing' and Other Essays*, p. 58. All subsequent references to this translation appear after the quotation in the body of the text.

15 *Intertext* is a term which implies a more general relationship to the work in question than *source text*, which suggests a text which has had a direct

influence on the author. Intertexts include source texts, but also texts which resonate powerfully in the reader's mind when s/he reads the work in question, even if there is no proof (or even no question) of a conscious borrowing. See Judith Still and Michael Worton, 'Introduction' in *Intertextuality: Theories and Practices* (Manchester University Press, 1990).

16 In the course of a psychoanalytic cure, it is inevitable that the patient will begin to project childhood emotions and fantasies (both positive and negative) onto the analyst, who occupies a blank parental role. Working through the transference is part of the therapeutic process.

17 The Lacanian account of the transference and counter-transference which take place between the analyst, the subject-supposed-to-know, and the analysand may also influence pedagogical theories. Shoshana Felman learns from Lacan's reading of Freud 'the imperative to learn from and through the insight which does not know its own meaning, from and through the knowledge which is not entirely in mastery – in possession – of itself'. She calls this an 'unprecedented literary lesson' transformed 'into a deliberately literary style of teaching', 'Psychoanalysis and Education: Teaching Terminable and Interminable' in *Jacques Lacan and the Adventure of Insight. Psychoanalysis in Contemporary Culture* (Cambridge, MA: Harvard University Press, 1987) pp. 68–97, p. 96. This has a particular resonance for Cixous's work as well as for Irigaray's.

18 Georges Bataille is a maverick figure in the mid-twentieth century whose works cross the boundaries between anthropology, sociology, philosophy and aesthetics. He also wrote a number of short novels which explicitly explore erotic feelings and practices, including incest, necrophilia, sado-masochism, scatology and voyeurism. Scenes of women enjoying pain, humiliation and extreme cruelty towards others are deemed by some readers to be degrading to women in general. Kristeva refers to Bataille at a number of points in almost any one of her works. With respect to abjection, see *Pouvoirs de l'horreur* (pp. 70, 79, 161, 245, 246). She has also written essays on him in Barthes *et al.*, *Bataille* (Paris: UGE, 10/18, 1973) – reprinted in *Polylogue* – and in *Histoires d'amour*.

19 Dworkin is a radical lesbian feminist who has exercised some influence, particularly in the United States and Britain, since the 1970s. In works such as *Pornography: Men Possessing Women* (New York: Perigree, 1981), she takes up the argument that while pornography is the theory, rape is the practice. She focuses on sexually explicit texts, which appear to involve some humiliation of female characters, both from 'high' culture (such as Bataille) and 'low' culture ('top-shelf' publications), linking these directly to male supremacy in general and to male violence against women in particular.

20 The abject is a slippery concept to engage with if you treat Kristeva's series of cautions and provisos seriously. Abjection is immediately defined in *Powers of Horror* as a revolt of being (as a twisted braid of affects and thoughts) a revolt against a threat from an exorbitant 'something' (not a thing) inside or outside the subject, something close but unassimilable which

both fascinates and frightens or disgusts desire. The abject is defined with a series of neither/nors which are perhaps unsurprising in a psychoanalytical and poststructuralist context, but nevertheless make it hard to conceptualize: neither subject nor object, neither within nor without . . . Thus in what may seem to be repulsive descriptions of the (maternal) body, Céline may in practice be exploding certain boundaries between oppositions which terrify the subject both as boundaries and as possible lack of boundaries. The child's relation to the maternal body is often taken as emblematic of precisely this kind of fear – being part of one's mother, indistinguishable from her, or being utterly separate(d) from her may both be frightening.

21 Jennifer Stone, 'The Horrors of Power: a Critique of "Kristeva"' in Francis Barber *et al.* (eds.), *The Politics of Theory: Proceedings of the Essex Conference on the Sociology of Literature* (Colchester: The University of Essex, 1983), pp. 38–48, at p. 42.

22 Edited by Elaine Marks and Isabelle de Courtivron, pp. 137–41.

23 *Orientalism* (Harmondsworth: Penguin, 1985), p. 177.

24 Freud's interpretation of dreams, and also of parapraxes and lapses of the tongue have also, of course, influenced the writing of Cixous – who turns them back against the master himself in her play *Dora* (1976).

25 Hélène Vivienne Wenzel, 'The Text as Body/Politics: An Appreciation of Monique Wittig's Writings in Context', *Feminist Studies* 7 (1981), p. 264. This article also serves as an example of a hostile reading of Cixous's work (and of Leclerc's), taking *écriture féminine* to entail a focus on woman as 'eternal essence'.

26 Wittig's experiments are often hard to render in translation. In *Brouillon pour une dictionnaire des amantes*, for example, all animate nouns are given in the feminine, which is shocking to the French ear and eye but which does not have an easy equivalent in English. Wittig and Zeig attempted the difficult task of translating *Brouillon* themselves, which makes it an interesting statement about translation as well as a translation of the work. (It was already an interesting statement about dictionaries as much as a dictionary.) See also Kristine J. Anderson, 'Lesbianizing English: Wittig and Zeig Translate Utopia' *Esprit créateur* 34 (1994), 90–102. Irigaray's substantial research in socio-linguistics is largely untranslated in spite of the anglophone appetite for her other work.

Bibliographies

In the bibliography, 'Women writers and their work', are arranged alphabetically, using the name by which each writer is most commonly known. Works listed in chronological order are preceded by collected works where these exist. The kind of work is indicated in parenthesis according to the following codes: autobiographical writings (a); children's literature (ch); dramatic works, including radio plays (d); essays or non-fiction (e); letters (l); novels or other fictional works (n); poetry (p); religious writings (r); short story and short prose fiction (s). In all bibliographies the place of publication, unless otherwise stated, is Paris.

1 GENERAL AND REFERENCE WORKS

Aubaud, Camille, *Lire les femmes de lettres*. Dunod, 1993.

Beach, Cecilia, *French Women Playwrights before the Twentieth Century: A Checklist*. Westport, CT: Greenwood Press, 1994.

French Women Playwrights of the Twentieth Century: A Checklist. Westport, CT: Greenwood Press, 1996).

Gelfand, Elissa and Virginia Thorndike Hules (eds.), *French Feminist Criticism: Women, Language and Literature. An Annotated Bibliography.* New York: Garland, 1985.

Larrington, Carolyne, *Women and Writing in Medieval Europe: A Sourcebook*. London: Routledge, 1995.

Resnick, Margery, and Isabelle de Courtivron, *Women Writers in Translation. An Annotated Bibliography*, 1945–1982. New York: Garland, 1984.

Sartori, Eva Martin & Dorothy Wynne Zimmerman (eds.), *French Women Writers. A Bio-Bibliographical Source Book*. Westport, CT: Greenwood Press, 1991.

Sartori, Eva (ed.), *The Feminist Companion to French Literature*. Westport, CT: Greenwood Press, forthcoming.

Wilson, Katharina M. (ed.), *An Encyclopaedia of Continental Women Writers*. 2 vols. Chicago and London: St James, 1991.

Wilwerth, Evelyne, *Visages de la littérature féminine*. Brussels: Pierre Mardaga, 1987.

2 STUDIES AND HISTORIES OF FRENCH WOMEN AND THEIR WRITING AND OF FEMINISM

Albistur, Maïté and Daniel Armogathe, *Histoire du féminisme français*. Des femmes, 1977.

Ashley, K., *et al.*, *Autobiography and Postmodernism*. Amherst, MA: University of Massachussets Press, 1994

Atack, Margaret and Phil Powrie (eds.), *Contemporary French Fiction by Women: Feminist Perspectives*. Manchester University Press, 1990.

Backer, Dorothy, *Precious Women*. New York: Basic, 1974.

Badinter, Elisabeth, *Émilie, Émilie: l'ambition féminine au XVIIIᵉ siècle*. Flammarion, 1983.

Bard, Christine, *Les Filles de Marianne. Histoire des féminismes 1914–40*. Fayard, 1995.

Beasley, Faith E., *Revising Memory: Women's Fiction and Memoirs in Seventeenth-Century France*. New Brunswick, NJ: Rutgers University Press, 1990.

Beaulieu, Jean-Philippe and Diane Desrosiers-Bonin (eds.), 'Dans le Miroir de l'écriture: La Réflexivité chez les Femmes Ecrivains d'Ancien Régime', special issue of *Paragraphes*. Université de Montréal, 1998.

Beaulieu, Jean-Philippe and Hannah Fournier (eds.), 'Femmes et textes sous l'Ancien Régime', special issue of *Atlantis: A Women's Studies Journal*, 19, 1 (Fall–Winter 1993).

Benstock, Shari (ed.), *The Private Self: The Theory and Practice of Women's Autobiography*. Chapel Hill, NC: University of North Carolina Press, 1988.

Bishop, Michael, *Contemporary French Women Poets*. 2 vols. Amsterdam: Rodopi, 1995.
  Thirty Voices in the Feminine. Amsterdam: Rodopi, 1996.

Bonnel, Roland and Catherine Rubinger, *Femmes savantes et femmes d'esprit: Women Intellectuals of the French Eighteenth Century*. New York: Peter Lang, 1994.

Bradby, David and Mary Noonan (eds.), *Women Give Voice to Women: Feminist Theory in Practice on the French Stage?*, Theatre Research International 23: 3 (Autumn 1998).

Brodski, Bella and Celeste Schenck (eds.), *Life/Lines: Theorizing Women's Autobiography*. Ithaca, NY & London: Cornell University Press, 1988.

Buck, Claire, (ed.), *The Bloomsbury Guide to Women's Literature*. New York: Prentice Hall, 1992.

Chance, Jane (ed.), *Gender and Text in the Later Middle Ages*. Gainesville, FL: University Presses of Florida, 1996.

Cherewatuk, Karen and Ulriche Wiethaus, *Dear Sister: Medieval Woman and the Epistolary Genre*. Philadelphia, PA: Pennsylvania University Press, 1993.

Colville, Georgiana and Katharine Conley (eds.), *La Femme s'entête*. Lachenal and Ritter, 1998.

DeJean, Joan, 'The Female Tradition', *L'Esprit créateur* 23: 2 (Summer 1983), 3–8. (This number is devoted exclusively to seventeenth-century French women writers.)

Tender Geographies. Women and the Origin of the Novel in France. New York: Columbia University Press, 1991.

Ancients against Moderns: Culture Wars and the Making of a Fin de Siècle. Chicago, IL: University of Chicago Press, 1997.

DeJean, Joan and Nancy K. Miller, *Displacements: Women, Tradition, Literatures in French.* Baltimore, MD: The Johns Hopkins University Press, 1991.

Desrosiers-Bonin, Diane (ed.), *Littératures* 18 (1998): 'L'Écriture des Femmes à la Renaissance Française'. Université McGill, Montréal.

Didier, Béatrice, *L'Écriture femme.* Presses universitaires de France, 1981.

Dronke, Peter, *Women Writers of the Middle Ages. A Critical Study of Texts from Perpetua (d. 203) to Marguerite Porete (d. 1310).* Cambridge University Press, 1984.

Duby, Georges and Michelle Perrot (eds.), *Histoire des femmes.* 5 vols. Plon, 1992.

Duchen, Claire, *Women's Rights and Women's Lives in France, 1944–1968.* London and New York: Routledge, 1994.

Duhet, Paule-Marie, *Les Femmes et la Révolution 1789–94.* Gallimard/Julliard, collection 'Archives', 1971.

Epstein, J. and Philippe Ivernel (eds.), *Le Théâtre d'intervention depuis 1968.* Lausanne: L'Age d'homme, 1983.

Escarpit, Denise, *La Littérature d'enfance et de jeunesse.* Presses universitaires de France, 1981.

Evans, Martha Noel, *Masks of Tradition: Women and the Politics of Writing in Twentieth Century France.* Ithaca, NY and London: Cornell University Press, 1987.

Fallaize, Elizabeth, *French Women's Writing: Recent Fiction.* Basingstoke: Macmillan, 1993.

Fauchery, Pierre, *La Destinée féminine dans le roman européen du dix-huitième siècle 1713–1807. Essai de gynécomythie romanesque.* Colin, 1972.

Ferguson, M. W., M. Quilligan and N. J. Vickers (eds.), *Rewriting the Renaissance: The Discourses of Sexual Difference in Early Modern Europe.* Chicago, IL: University of Chicago Press, 1986.

Ferrante, Joan M., *To the Glory of her Sex: Women's Roles in the Composition of Medieval Texts.* Bloomington, IN: Indiana University Press, 1997.

Fisher, Sheila and Janet E. Halley (eds.), *Seeking the Woman in Late Medieval and Renaissance Writings: Essays in French Contextual Criticism.* Knoxville, TN: University of Tennessee Press, 1989.

Garcia, Irma, *Promenade femmilière.* Des femmes, 1981.

Goldsmith, Elizabeth C., *Exclusive Conversations* (Philadelphia, PA: University of Pennsylvania Press, 1988.

Goldsmith, Elizabeth C. and Dena Goodman (eds.), *Going Public: Women and Publishing in Early Modern France,* Ithaca, NY and London, Cornell University Press 1995.

Goodman, Dena, *The Republic of Letters: A Cultural History of the French Enlightenment.* Ithaca, NY and London: Cornell University Press, 1994.

Greenberg, Wendy, *Uncanonical Women. Feminine Voice in French Poetry (1830–71).* Amsterdam and Atlanta, GA: Rodopi, 1999.

Gutwirth, Madelyn, *The Twilight of the Goddesses: Women and Representation in the French Revolutionary Era.* New Brunswick, NJ: Rutgers University Press, 1992.

Harten, Elke and Hans-Christian, *Femmes, culture et révolution.* Des femmes, 1988.

Harth, Erica, *Cartesian Women. Versions and Subversions of Rational Discourse in the Old Regime.* Ithaca, NY and London: Cornell University Press, 1992.

Hewitt, Leah, *Autobiographical Tightropes.* Lincoln, NE: University of Nebraska Press, 1990.

Hoffmann, Pierre, *La femme dans la pensée des Lumières.* Ophrys, 1977.

Holmes, Diana, *French Women's Writing 1848–1994.* London: The Athlone Press, 1996.

Hughes, Alex, and Kate Ince (eds.), *French Erotic Fiction: Women's Desiring Writing 1880–1990.* Oxford: Berg, 1996.

Jacobs, Eva, *et al.*, *Woman and Society in Eighteenth-Century France.* London: The Athlone Press, 1979.

Jardine, Alice A., and Anne M. Menke (eds.), *Shifting Scenes: Interviews on Women, Writing and Politics in Post-'68 France.* New York: Columbia University Press, 1991.

Jelinek, Estelle (ed.), *Women's Autobiography. Essays in Criticism.* Bloomington, IN: Indiana University Press, 1980.

Jensen, Katharine A., *Writing Love: Letters, Women and the Novel in France 1605–1775.* Carbondale, IL: Southern Illinois University Press, 1995.

Johnson, Penelope D., *Equal in Monastic Profession: Religious Women in Medieval France.* Chicago, IL: University of Chicago Press, 1991.

Jones, Ann. R., *The Currency of Eros: Women's Love Lyric in Europe 1540–1620.* Bloomington, IL: Indiana University Press, 1990.

Jordan, Constance, *Renaissance Feminism: Literary Texts and Political Models.* Ithaca, NY and London: Cornell University Press, 1990.

Kelly, Katherine E. (ed.), *Modern Drama by Women 1880s–1930s.* London: Routledge, 1996.

Krueger, Roberta L., *Women Readers and the Ideology of Gender in Old French Verse Romance.* Cambridge University Press, 1993.

Kuzinga, Donna and Colette Winn (eds.), *Women Writers in Pre-Revolutionary France: Strategies of Emancipation.* New York: Garland, 1997.

Lamar, Celita, *Our Voices, Ourselves: Women Writing for the French Theatre.* New York: Peter Lang, 1991.

Landes, Joan B., *Women and the Public Sphere in the Age of the French Revolution.* Ithaca, NY and London: Cornell University Press, 1988.

Larsen, Anne and Colette Winn (eds.), *Renaissance Women Writers: French Texts/American Contexts.* Detroit, IL: Wayne State University Press, 1994.
  Writing by Pre-Revolutionary French Women: From Marie de France to Elisabeth Vigée-Lebrun. New York: Garland, 1999.

Lecarme, J. and E. Lecarme-Tabone, *L'Autobiographie.* Armand Colin, 1997.

Lougee, Carolyn, *Le Paradis des femmes. Women, Salons and Social Stratification in Seventeenth-Century France.* Princeton University Press, 1976.

Maclean, Ian, *Women Triumphant (1610–1652).* Oxford University Press, 1977.

The Renaissance Notion of Woman: A Study of the Fortunes of Scholasticism and Medical Science in European Intellectual Life. Cambridge University Press, 1980.

Mathieu-Castellani, Gisèle, *La Quenoille et la lyre*. José Corti, 1998.

McCash, June Hall, *The Cultural Patronage of Medieval Women*. Athens, GA: University of Georgia Press, 1996.

McNamara, Jo Ann and John E. Halborg, *Sainted Women of the Dark Ages*. Durham, NC: Duke University Press, 1992.

Melzer, Sara E. and Leslie W. Rabine (eds.), *Rebel Daughters: Women and the French Revolution*. New York: Oxford University Press, 1992.

Miller, Judith Graves, 'Contemporary Women's Voices in French Theatre', *Modern Drama* 32 (1989), 5–19.

Miller, Nancy K, *The Poetics of Gender*. New York: Columbia University Press, 1986.

Subject to Change: Reading Feminist Writing. New York: Columbia University Press, 1988.

Milligan, Jennifer E., *The Forgotten Generation. French Women Writers of the Inter-war Period*. Oxford: Berg, 1996.

Moers, Ellen, *Literary Women. The Great Writers*. 1963. Oxford University Press, 1985.

Moi, Toril, *Sexual/Textual Politics*. London: Methuen, 1985.

Montreynaud, Florence, *Le XXe Siècle des femmes*. Nathan, 1992.

Moss, Jane, 'Women's Theatre in France', *Signs* 12 (1987), 548–67.

Moses, Claire Goldberg, *French Feminism in the Nineteenth Century*. Albany, NY: State University of New York Press, 1984.

Nativel, Colette (ed.), *Femmes savantes, savoir des femmes du crépuscule de la Renaissance à l'aube des lumières*. Geneva: Droz, 1998.

Newman, Barbara, *From Virile Women to WomanChrist: Studies in Medieval Religion and Literature*. Philadelphia, PA: Pennsylvania University Press, 1995.

Picq, Françoise, *Libération des femmes: les annéés mouvement*. Seuil, 1993.

Rabut, Marie, *Les Femmes dans la littérature française*. Vic and Amat, n.d.

Rigolot, François (ed.), 'Writing in the Feminine in the Renaissance/Écrire au féminin à la Renaissance', *L'Esprit créateur* 30: 4 (Winter 1990).

Sankovitch, Tilde, *French Women Writers and the Book: Myths of Access and Desire*. Syracuse, NY: Syracuse University Press, 1988.

Sarde, Michèle, *Regard sur les Françaises*. Stock, 1983.

Seifert, Lewis C., *Fairy Tales, Sexuality and Gender in France 1690–1715*. Cambridge University Press, 1996.

Solterer, Helen, *The Master and Minerva. Disputing Women in French Medieval Culture*. Berkeley, CA: University of California Press, 1995.

Stambolian, George and Elaine Marks (eds.), *Homosexualities and French Literature*. Ithaca, NY and London: Cornell University Press, 1990 [1977].

Stanton, Donma (ed.), *The Female Autograph*. Chicago, IL: University of Chicago Press, 1987.

'The Fiction of Préciosité and the Fear of Women', *Yale French Studies* 62 (1981), 107–34. (This number of the journal is devoted to women writers.)

Stewart, Joan Hinde, *Gynographs: French Novels by Women of the Late Eighteenth Century*. Lincoln, NE: University of Nebraska Press, 1993.

Still, Judith and Michael Worton, *Textuality and Sexuality. Reading Theories and Practices*. Manchester University Press, 1993.

Sullerot, Evelyne, *La Presse féminine en France*. Colin, 1966.

Histoire et mythologie de l'amour: huit siècles d'écrits féminins. Hachette, 1974.

Timmermans, Linda, *L'Accès des femmes à la culture, 1598–1715*. Champion, 1993.

Waelti-Walters, Jennifer, *Feminist Novelists of the Belle Epoque*. Bloomington, IN: Indiana University Press, 1990.

Wemple, Suzanne Fonay, *Women in Frankish Society: Marriage and the Cloister 500–900*. Philadelphia, PA: University of Pennsylvania Press, 1981.

Wilson, Katharina, *Women Writers of the Renaissance and Reformation*. Athens, GA: University of Georgia Press, 1987.

Wilson, Katharina (ed.), *Medieval Women Writers*. Athens, GA: University of Georgia Press, 1984.

Encyclopaedia of Continental Women Writers. New York: Garland, 1991.

Wright, E. (ed.), *Psychoanalysis and Feminism. A Critical Dictionary*. Oxford: Blackwell, 1992.

Yandell, Cathy, *Carpe Corpus: Time and Gender in Early Modern France*. Newark, DE University of Delaware Press, 1999.

ANTHOLOGIES

Bishop, Michael, *Women's Poetry in France 1965–1995: A Bilingual Anthology*. Winston Salem, NC: Wake Forest University Press, 1997.

Brécourt-Villars, Claudine (ed.). *Écrire d'amour: anthologie de textes érotiques féminins 1799–1984*. Ramsay, 1985.

Falaize, Elizabeth, *French Women's Writing: Recent Fiction*. Basingstoke: Macmillan, 1993. [Extracts.]

Makward, Christine and Judith Miller (eds. and trans.), *Plays by French and Francophone Women. A Critical Anthology*. Ann Arbor, MI: University of Michigan Press, 1994.

Moulin, Jeanine, *Huit Siècles de poésie féminine*. Seghers, 1963.

Petroff, Elizabeth Alvilda, *Medieval Women's Visionary Literature*. Oxford and New York: Oxford University Press, 1986.

Rohou, Jean (ed.), *Lettres d'amour du XVIIe siècle*. Seuil, 1994.

Sorrell, Martin, *Elles. A Bilingual Anthology of Modern French Poetry by Women*. University of Exeter Press, 1995.

Thiébaux, Marcelle, *The Writings of Medieval Women*. New York: Garland, 1987.

3 WOMEN WRITERS AND THEIR WORKS

Ackermann, Louise (1813–90), *Œuvres*. Lemerre, 1885.

Poésies philosophiques. Nice: Caisson et Mignon, 1871. (p)

Pensées d'une solitaire, précedées d'une autobiographie. Lemerre, 1882. (a)

Further reading

Greenberg, Wendy, *Uncanonical Women*, pp. 103–30, 151–60.

Jenson, Deborah, 'Gender and the aesthetic of "le mal": Louise Ackermann's *Poésies philosophiques* 1871', *Nineteenth-Century French Studies* (Fall–Winter, 1994–5), 175–193.

Adam, Juliette (1836–1936), *Le Roman de mon enfance et de ma jeunesse*. Lemerre, 1902. (a)

Mes Illusions et nos souffrances pendant le siège de Paris. Lemerre, 1906. (a)

Nos amitiés politiques avant l'abandon de la Revanche. Lemerre, 1908. (a)

L'heure vengeresse des crimes bismarckiens. Nouvelle librairie nationale, 1915. (e)

L'Angleterre en Egypt. Impr. de Cuntre, 1922. (e)

Païenne.Plon-Nourrit, n.d. (n)

Agoult, Marie d' (Daniel Stern, 1805–76), *Nélida*. Librairie d'Amyot, 1846. (n)

Essai sur la liberté considérée comme principe et fin de l'activité humaine. Amyot, 1847. (e)

Histoire de la révolution de 1848. 3 vols. G. Sandre, 1850–3. (e)

Mes Souvenirs, 1806–33. Calmann Lévy, 1877. (a)

Valentia. Calmann-Lévy, 1896. (First published in *La Presse* in 1847.) (n)

Correspondance de Liszt et de La comtesse d'Agoult, Daniel Ollivier. 2 vols. Grasset, 1933–4. (l)

Une Correspondance romantique, madame d'Agoult, Liszt, Henri Lehmann, presentée par Solange Joubert. Flammarion, 1947. (l)

Histoire de la révolution de 1848, ed. Dominique Desanti. Balland, 1985.

Nélida, ed. Ch. Dupêchez. Calmann-Lévy, 1986.

Further reading

Desanti, Dominique, *Daniel, ou le visage secret d'une comtesse romantique*. Stock, 1980.

Dupêchez, Charles, *Marie d'Agoult*. Perrin, 1989.

Albiach, Anne-Marie (b. 1937), *Flammigère*. London: Siècle à mains, 1967. (p)

État. Mercure de France, 1971. (p)

Mezza voce. Flammarion, 1984. (p)

Anawratha. Le Revest-les-Eaux: Spectres Familiers, 1984. (p)

Travail vertical et blanc. Le Revest-les-Eaux: Spectres Familiers, 1989. (p)

'Figure vocative'. Fourbis, 1991. (p)

Further reading

Bishop, Michael, *Contemporary French Women Poets*, vol. II, pp. 134–54.

Gleize, Jean-Marie, *Le Théâtre du poème. Vers Anne-Marie Albiach*. Belin, 1995.

Allart de Méritens, Hortense (1801–79), *La Femme et la démocratie de nos temps*. Delaunay, 1836. (e)

Les Enchantements de Prudence, 1872. (n)

Lettres inédites à Sainte-Beuve. Mercure de France, 1908. (l)

Ancelot, Virginie (1792–1875), "Les Honneurs et les mœurs", *Magasin théâtral*, vol. II. (d)

'Clémence', *Magasin théâtral*, vol. X. (d)

'Marie, ou, Trois époques'. *Magasin théâtral*, 1836 (d)

Les salons de Paris; foyers éteints. J. Tardieu, 1858. (e)

Un salon de Paris, 1824 à 1864. E. Dentu, 1866. (a)

Anne, Catherine (b. 1960), *Une Année sans été*. Arles: Actes-Sud Papiers, 1987. (d)

Combien de nuits faudra-t-il marcher dans la ville? Arles: Actes-Sud Papiers, 1988. (d)

Éclats. Arles: Actes-Sud Papiers, 1989. (d)

Agnès; Ah! Annabelle. Arles: Actes-Sud Papiers, 1994. (d)

Ah la la! Quelle Histoire. Arles: Actes-Sud Papiers, 1995. (d)

Nuit pâle au palais. École de loisirs, 1997. (d) And, to date, two further (unpublished) plays.

Anonymous, The 'Reponse au bestiaire d'amour de Richard de Fournival', in Richard de Fournival. *Li Bestiares d'amours di Maistre Richart de Fornival e li Response du Bestiaire*, Cesare Segre (ed.). *Documenti de Filologica* 2. Milan: Riccardo Ricciardi, 1957. (e)

Translation

Master Richard's Bestiary of Love and Response, trans. Jeanette Beer. Berkeley, CA: University of California Press, 1986.

Audouard, Olympe (1830–90), *Les Mystères du sérail et des harems turcs*. E. Dentu, 1866. (e)

La Femme dans le mariage, la séparation et le divorce. Conférence faite le 28 fevrier 1870. E. Dentu, 1870. (e)

A Travers l'Amérique; North-America. Etats-Unis: constitution, moeurs, usages, lois, institutions, sectes religieuses. Dentu, 1871. (e)

Further reading

Monicat, Bénédicte, 'Écritures de voyage et féminismes, Olympe Audouard ou le féminin en question', *French Studies* (October 1995), 24–36.

Aulnoy, Marie-Catherine Le Jumel de Barneville, comtesse d' (1650–1705), *Histoire d'Hypolite, comte de Duglas*, Paris,1690. (n & s)

Mémoires de la cour d'Espagne. 2 vols. Claude Barbin, 1690. (a, e, s)

Relations du voyage en Espagne. The Hague: Bulderen, 1691. (a, e, s)

Sentiments d'une âme pénitente. 1691. (r)

Le Retour d'une âme à Dieu. 1692. (r)

Histoire de Jean de Bourbon, Prince de Carency. 3 vols. Claude Barbin. 1692. (n)

Nouvelles espagnolles. Par Madame D***. 2 vols. Claude Barbin, 1692. (s)

Nouvelles ou mémoires historiques. Contenant ce quoi s'est passé de plus remarquable dans l'Europe, tant aux Guerres, prises de Places, & Batailles sur terre & sur mer, qu'aux divers interests des Princes et souverains qui ont agy depuis 1672 jusqu'en 1679. Par Madame D***. 2 vols. Claude Barbin. 1693. (a, e, s)

Mémoires de la Cour d'Angleterre. Par Madame D***. Claude Barbin, 1695. (a, e, s)

Les Contes des fées, 4 vols., 1697–8. (s)

Contes nouveaux ou les fées à la mode. 4 vols. Veuve de Théodore Girard, 1698. (s)

Le Comte de Warwick. Par Madame D***. Compagnie des Libraires Associez, 1703. (n)

Relations du voyage en Espagne, ed. R. Foulché-Delbosc. Klincksieck, 1926.

Contes nouveaux ou les fées à la mode. Geneva: Slatkine Reprints, 1978.

Les Contes des fées. Geneva: Slatkine Reprints, 1978.

Histoire d'Hypolite, comte de Duglas. Geneva: Slatkine Reprints, 1979.

Translations

Memoirs of the Court of Spain. 1692. Wing English Books, 1641–1700.

Travels into Spain: Being the Ingenious and Diverting Letters of the Lady ***. 1715. Intro. R. Foulché-Delbosc. New York: McBride, 1930.

The Prince of Carency. 1715, intro. Josephine Grieder. New York: Garland, 1973.

Memoirs of the Court of England in 1675, ed. George Gilbert, trans. Lucretia Arthur. London: Routledge and New York: Dutton, 1913.

The Tales of the Fairies in Three Parts. Compleat. 1715, intro. Michael Hearn. New York: Garland, 1977.

Beauties, Beasts and Enchantment: Classic French Fairy Tales, ed. Jack Zipes. Harmondsworth and New York: Penguin, 1989.

Further reading

De Graff, Amy Vanderlyn, *The Tower and the Well: A Psychological Interpretation of the Fairy Tales of Madame d'Aulnoy*. Birmingham, AL: Summa Publications, 1984.

Farrell, Michèle Longino, 'Celebration and Repression of Feminine Desire in Madame d'Aulnoy's Fairy Tale: *La Chatte Blanche*', *L'Esprit créateur* 29: 3 (1989), 52–64.

Bancquart, Marie-Claire (b. 1932), *Projets alternés*. Mortemart: Rougerie, 1972. (p)

Mains dissoutes. Mortemart: Rougerie, 1975. (p)

Mémoire d'abolie. Belfond, 1978. (p)

Voix. St Laurent du Pont: Le Verbe et l'Empreinte, 1979. (p)

Partition. Belfond, 1981. (p)

Votre Visage jusqu'à l'os. Temps actuels, 1983. (p)

Opportunité des oiseaux. Belfond, 1986. (p)

Opéra des limites. Corti, 1988. (p)

Végétales. Montereau: Les Cahiers du Confluent, 1988. (p)

Photos de famille. 1989. (n)

Sans Lieu sinon l'attente. Obsidiane, 1991. (p)

La Saveur du sel. Julliard, 1993. (n)

Further reading

Bishop, Michael, *Contemporary French Women* Poets, vol. 1, pp. 128–44.

Brunel, Pierre, and Aude Préta-de-Beaufort, *À la voix de Marie-Claire Bancquart*. Le Cherche Midi, 1996.

La Sape, special issue 'Marie-Claire Bancquart', 1999.

Baudonivia, 'The Life of the Holy Radegund'. Book II. Jo Ann McNamara and John E. Halborg (trans.), *Sainted Women of the Dark Ages*, pp. 86–105. (e)

Beauharnais, Marie-Anne-Françoise (Fanny) Mouchard de Chaban, comtesse de, *Lettres de Stéphanie*, 3 vols. 1778. (n)

L'Aveugle par amour, Amsterdam and Paris, 1781. (n)

Beauvoir, Simone de (1908–86), *L'Invitée*. Gallimard, 1943. (n)
Pyrrhus et Cinéas. Gallimard, 1944. (e)
Les Bouches inutiles. Gallimard, 1945. (d)
Le Sang des autres. Gallimard, 1945. (n)
Tous Les Hommes sont mortels. Gallimard, 1946. (n)
Pour Une Morale d'ambiguïté. Gallimard, 1947. (e)
L'Amérique au jour le jour. Morihien, 1948. (e, a)
L'Existentialisme et la sagesse des nations. Nagel, 1948. (e)
Le Deuxième sexe. 2 vols. Gallimard, 1949. (e)
Les Mandarins. Gallimard, 1954. (n)
Privilèges. Gallimard, 1954. (e)
La Longue Marche. Gallimard, 1957. (a, e)
Mémoires d'une jeune fille rangée. Gallimard, 1958. (a)
La Force de l'âge. Gallimard, 1960. (a)
La Force des choses. 2 vols. Gallimard, 1963. (a)
Une Mort très douce. Gallimard, 1964. (a)
Les Belles Images. Gallimard, 1966. (n)
La Femme rompue. Gallimard, 1967. (s)
La Vieillesse. Gallimard, 1970. (e)
Tout compte fait. Gallimard, 1972. (a)
Quand Prime Le Spirituel. Gallimard, 1979. (s)
La Cérémonie des adieux, suivi de Entretiens avec Jean-Paul Sartre, août-septembre 1974. Gallimard, 1981. (a)
Journal de guerre: septembre 1939–janvier 1941. Gallimard, 1990. (a)
Lettres à Sartre. 2 vols. Gallimard, 1990. (l)
Translations
She Came to Stay, trans. Yvonne Moyse and Roger Senhouse. 1949. London: Flamingo, 1995.
The Second Sex, trans. H. M. Parshley. 1953. Harmondsworth: Penguin, 1984.
A Very Easy Death, trans. Patrick O'Brien. 1965. Harmondsworth: Penguin, 1975.
Les Belles Images, trans. Patrick O'Brien. 1969. London: Fontana, 1982.
The Woman Destroyed, trans. Patrick O'Brien. 1969. London: Fontana, 1984.
Old Age, trans. Patrick O'Brien. 1972. Harmondsworth: Penguin, 1985.
All Said and Done, trans. Patrick O'Brien. 1974. Harmondsworth: Penguin, 1982.
The Ethics of Ambiguity, trans. Bernard Frechtman. New York: Citadel Press, 1976.
Adieux. A Farewell to Sartre, trans. Patrick O'Brien. 1983. Harmondsworth: Penguin, 1985.
When Things of the Spirit Come First, trans. Patrick O'Brien, 1983. Harmondsworth: Penguin, 1985.
Who Shall Die? trans. Claude Francis and Fernande Gontier. Mo: River Press, 1983.
The Blood of Others, trans. Yvonne Moyse and Roger Senhouse. Harmondsworth: Penguin, 1986.

The Mandarins, trans. Leonard M. Friedman. London: Fontana, 1986.
Force of Circumstance, trans. Richard Howard. Harmondsworth: Penguin, 1987.
Memoirs of a Dutiful Daughter, trans. James Kirkup. Harmondsworth: Penguin, 1987.
Letters to Sartre, trans. and ed. Quintin Hoare. 1991. London: Vintage, 1992.
All Men Are Mortal, trans. Euan Cameron, based on the original translation by Leonard M. Friedman. London: Virago, 1995.
Further reading
Angelfors, Cristina, *La Prise de conscience féminine chez Colette, Simone de Beauvoir et Marie Cardinal.* Lund: Lund University Press, 1989.
Fallaize, Elizabeth, *The Novels of Simone de Beauvoir.* London: Routledge, 1988.
Fallaize, Elizabeth, (ed.), *Simone de Beauvoir. A Critical Reader.* London: Routledge, 1998.
Holmes, Diana, *French Women's Writing 1848–1994*, pp. 147–66.
Keefe, Terry, *Simone de Beauvoir: A Study of her Writings.* London: Harrap, 1993.
Moi, Toril, *Feminist Theory and Simone de Beauvoir.* Oxford: Blackwell, 1990.
   Simone de Beauvoir: the Making of an Intellectual Woman. Oxford: Blackwell, 1994.
Belgiojoso, Cristina (1808–71), *Asie mineure et Syrie.* Michel Lévy Frères, 1858. (e)
Bellon, Loleh (b. 1925), *Les Dames du jeudi.* 1976. In *Avant-Scène-Théâtre*, 607 (1977); and *Théâtre.* Gallimard, 1986. (d)
Changement à vue. In *Avant-Scène-Théâtre*, 651 (1979); and *Théâtre.* Gallimard, 1986. (d)
Le Cœur sur la main. In *Avant-Scène-Théâtre*, 681 (1981); and *Théâtre.* Gallimard, 1986. (d)
De si tendres liens. Gallimard, 1984. (d)
L'Éloignement. Actes Sud-Papiers, 1987. (d)
Une Absence. Actes Sud-Papiers, 1988. (d)
Benoist, Françoise-Albine Puzin de la Martinière (1724–1809), *Célianne ou les amants séduits par leurs vertus.* Amsterdam and Paris, 1766. (n)
Les Erreurs d'une jolie femme ou l'Aspasie françoise. 2 vols. Brussels and Paris, 1781. (n)
Bernard, Catherine (1663–1712), *Œuvres.* Biblioteca della ricerca, Testi stranieri, 22. Fasano: Schena and Paris: Nizet, 1993–. Vol I, *Romans et nouvelles*, ed. and intro. by Franco Piva (1993).
Frédéric de Sicile. 1680. (n)
Les Malheurs de l'amour. Première nouvelle. Eléonor d'Yvrée, Paris, 1687. (n)
Le Comte d'Amboise. Nouvelle galante. 1689. (n)
Brutus. 1691. (d)
Histoire de la rupture d'Abenamar et de Fatime. 1696. (n)
Inès de Cordoue, nouvelle espagnole. 1696. (n)
Laodamie. (d)
Buffet, Marguerite, *Nouvelles observations sur la langue française.* 1668. (e)
Caesaria of Arles. 'Caesaria to Radegund and Richild', trans. Marcelle Thiébaux, *The Writings of Medieval Women*, pp. 37–42. (l)

Cardinal, Marie (b. 1920), *Écoutez la mer*, Julliard, 1962. (n)
 La Mule de corbillard, Julliard, 1963. (n)
 La Souricière, Julliard, 1965. (n)
 La Clé sur la porte. Livre de poche, 1972. (n)
 Les Mots pour le dire. Livre de poche, 1975. (n)
 Autrement dit. Livre de poche, 1977. Dialogue with Annie Leclerc. (a)
 Une vie pour deux. Livre de poche, 1978. (n)
 Cet Été-là. Livre de poche, 1979. (a)
 Au Pays de mes racines. Livre de poche, 1980. (a)
 Le Passé empiété. Livre de poche, 1983. (n)
 La Médée d'Euripide, Grasset, 1986. (Translation and preface)
 Les Grands Désordres. Livre de poche, 1987. (n)
 Comme si de rien n'était. Livre de poche, 1990. (n)
 Les Jeudis de Charles et de Lula. Livre de poche, 1993. (n)
Translations
 The Words to Say It, trans. Pat Goodheart; afterword Bruno Bettelheim. 1983.
  London: Picador, 1984.
 Devotion and Disorder, trans. Karin Montin, 1987. London: Picador, 1984.
 In Other Words, trans. Amy Cooper. Bloomington, IN: Indiana University
  Press, 1995; London: Women's Press, 1996.
Further reading
 Angelfors, Cristina, *La Prise de conscience féminine chez Colette, Simone de Beauvoir
  et Marie Cardinal.* Lund: Lund University Press, 1989.
 Cairns, Lucille, *Marie Cardinal: Motherhood and Creativity.* Glasgow: University
  of Glasgow French and German Publications, 1992.
 Fallaize, Elizabeth, *French Women's Writing*, pp. 30–50 (includes translated
  extracts).
 Hall, Colette, *Marie Cardinal.* Amsterdam: Rodopi, 1994.
Chalem, Denise (b. 1953), *A Cinquante Ans elle découvrait la mer.* 1980. *Avant-
 Scène-Théâtre* 671 (1980); Arles Actes-Sud-Papiers, 1985. (d)
 Selon toute ressemblance. Arles Actes-Sud-Papiers, 1986. (d)
 Couki et Louki sont sur un bâteau. Arles Actes-Sud-Papiers, 1987. (d)
**Charrière, Isabella (Isabelle) Agneta Elisabeth van Tuyll van
 Serooskerken de (1740–1805)**, *Œuvres complètes*, eds. J.-D. Candaux, C.
 P. Courtney, P. H. Dubois, S. Dubois-De Bruyn, P. Thompson, J.
 Vercruysse and D. M. Wood. 10 vols. Amsterdam: Van Oorschot, 1979–84.
Lettres de Mistriss Henley, Geneva, 1784. (n)
Lettres neuchâteloises. Amsterdam, 1784. (n)
Lettres écrites de Lausanne. Toulouse, 1785. (n)
Caliste, ou Suite des lettres écrites de Lausanne. Geneva and Paris, 1787. (n)
Lettres trouvées dans des porte-feuilles d'émigrés. 1793. (n)
Suite des lettres trouvées dans des porte-feuilles d'émigrés, published for the first time
 in the *Œuvres complètes.* (n)
[All the texts mentioned above appear in volume VIII of the *Œuvres complètes.*]

Caliste, ed. Claudine Hermann. Des femmes, 1979.

Lettres neuchâteloises, eds. Isabelle and Jean-Louis Vissière. La différence, 1991.

Caliste, ou Suite des lettres écrites de Lausanne, ed. Raymond Trousson. Robert Laffont, collection 'Bouquins', 1996.

Lettres de Mistriss Henley, ed. Raymond Trousson. Robert Laffont, collection 'Bouquins', 1996.

Lettres écrites de Lausanne, ed. Raymond Trousson. Robert Laffont, collection 'Bouquins', 1996.

Lettres neuchâteloises, ed. Raymond Trousson. Robert Laffont, collection 'Bouquins', 1996.

And a number of other writings.

Translations

Four Tales by Zélide, trans., S[ybil] M. S[cott]. New York: Scribner's, 1926. Reissued, Freeport, NY: Books for Libraries Press, 1970.

Further reading

Minier-Birk, Sigyn, *Madame de Charrière: les premiers romans*. Geneva: Slatkine and Paris: Champion, 1987.

Versini, Laurent, *Le Roman épistolaire*. Presses universitaires de France, 1979.

Vissière, Isabelle (ed.), *Isabelle de Charrière, une aristocrate révolutionnaire: écrits 1788–94*. Des femmes, 1988.

Châtelet, Gabrielle-Émilie Le Tonnelier de Breteuil, marquise du (1706–49), *Institutions de physique*. Prault 1740. (e)

Dissertation sur la nature et la propagation du feu. Prault, 1744. (e)

Principes mathématiques de la philosophie naturelle, par M Newton, traduits par feue Madame la Marquise du Châtelet. 1759. (e)

Lettres de la Marquise du Châtelet, ed. Theodore Besterman. 2 vols. Geneva: Institution et Musée Voltaire, 1958. (l)

Discours sur le bonheur, ed. Robert Mauzi. 1961. (e)

'Examen de la Genèse and Examen des Livres du Nouveau Testament,' MSS. 2376 & 2377, Bibliothèque de Troyes. (r) *The Fable of the Bees*, trans. Mandeville, *Essai sur l'optique* (one chapter); *Grammaire raisonnée* (three chapters), in Ira O. Wade, *Studies on Voltaire with some unpublished papers of Mme du Châtelet*. Princeton, NJ: Princeton University Press, 1947. (s, e)

Further reading

Ehrman, Esther, *Mme du Châtelet, Scientist, Philosopher and Feminist of the Enlightenment*. Leamington Spa: Berg Women's Series, 1986.

Vaillot, R., *Mme du Châtelet*. Albin Michel, 1978.

Chawaf, Chantal (b. 1943), *Retable/la Rêverie*. Des femmes, 1974. (n)

Cercœur. Mercure de France, 1975. (n)

Blé de semences. Mercure de France, 1976. (n)

Chair chaude. Mercure de France, 1976. (d)

Le Soleil et la terre. Pauvert, 1977. (n)

Rougeâtre. Pauvert, 1978. (n)

Maternité. Stock, 1979. (n)

Landes. Stock, 1980. (n)

Crépusculaires. Ramsay, 1981. (n)

Les Surfaces de l'orage. Ramsay, 1982. (n)

La Vallée incarnate. Flammarion, 1984. (n)

Elwina, le roman-fée. Flammarion, 1986. (n)

L'Intérieur des heures. Des femmes, 1987. (n)

Fées de toujours. Plon, 1988. (n)

Rédemption. Flammarion, 1988. (n)

L'Éclaircie. Flammarion, 1990. (n)

Le Corps et le verbe: la langue en sens inverse. Presses de la Renaissance, 1992.

Le Manteau noir. Flammarion, 1998. (n)

Translation

Warmth: A Bloodsong, trans. Christine P. Makward and Judith G. Miller, in *Plays by French and Francophone Women.*

Further reading

Bosshard, Marianne, *Chantal Chawaf.* Amsterdam: Rodopi, 1999.

Fallaize, Elizabeth, *French Women's Writing,* pp. 51–66 (includes some translated extracts).

Hanegan, Valerie, 'Reading as a Daughter: Chantal Chawaf Revisited', in Margaret Atack and Phil Powrie, *Contemporary French Fiction by Women,* pp. 177–91.

Chedid, Andrée (b. 1920), *Théâtre.* Flammarion, 1981. (d)

Textes pour une figure. Pré aux Clercs, 1949. (p)

Textes pour un poème (1949–70). Flammarion, 1987. (p)

Textes pour un poème. G.L.M., 1950. (p)

Textes pour le vivant. G.L.M., 1953. (p)

Textes pour la terre aimée. G.L.M., 1955. (p)

Terre et poésie. G.L.M., 1956. (p)

Terre regardée. G.L.M., 1957. (p)

Seul, le visage. G.L.M., 1960. (p)

Double-pays. G.L.M., 1965. (p)

Bérénice d'Égypte. Seuil, 1968. In *Théâtre.* (d)

Les Nombres. Seuil, 1968. In *Théâtre.* (d)

Le Personnage. In *Avant-Scène-Théâtre* 401 (15 April, 1968). (d)

Contre-chant. Flammarion, 1969. (p)

Le Montreur. Seuil, 1969. In *Théâtre.* (d)

Poèmes pour un texte (1970–91). Flammarion, 1991. (p)

Le Sixième jour. Flammarion, 1971; 1985. J'ai Lu, 1997. (n)

Visage premier. Flammarion, 1972. (p)

Fêtes et lubies. Flammarion, 1973; 1996. (p)

Le Dernier Candidat. In *Avant-Scène-Théâtre* 515 (1 April, 1973). Edn. Théâtrales Art et Comédie, 1998. (d)

Le Sommeil délivré. Flammarion, 1976; 1987. J'ai Lu, 1990. (n)

Cérémonial de la violence. Flammarion, 1976. (p)

Fraternité de la parole. Flammarion, 1976. (p)

Cavernes et soleils. Flammarion, 1979. (p)

Les Marches de sable. Flammarion, 1981; J'ai Lu, 1990. (n)

Épreuves du vivant. Flammarion, 1983. (p)

Échec à la reine. Flammarion, 1984. With *Le Personnage.* Edn. Théâtrales Art et Comédie, 1998. (d)

7 Plantes pour un herbier. (Bédée): Folle Avoine, 1985. (p)

La Maison sans racines. Flammarion, 1985. (n)

L'Enfant multiple. Flammarion, 1989; 1991, J'ai lu, 1991; 1996. (n)

La Femme en rouge, et autres nouvelles. J'ai lu, 1992; 1994. (s)

À la mort, à la vie. Flammarion, 1992. (s)

La Femme de Job. Calmann-Lévy, 1993. (n)

Par delà les mots. Flammarion, 1995. (p)

Territoires du souffle. Flammarion, 1999. (p)

And many other works.

Translations

From *Sleep Unbound*, trans. Sharon Spencer. London: Serpent's Tail, 1987.

The Sixth Day, trans. Isobel Strachey. London: Serpent's Tail, 1987.

The Return to Beirut, trans. Ros Schwartz. London: Serpent's Tail, 1989. [*La Maison sans racines*]

Selected Poems, trans. and ed. Judy Cochran. Leviston, NY and Lampeter: Edwin Mellen Press, 1995. [Parallel text.]

Further reading

Bishop, Michael, *Contemporary French Women Poets*, pp. 17–35.

Knapp, Bettina, *Andrée Chedid.* Amsterdam: Rodopi, 1984.

Villani, Sergio (ed.), *Andrée Chedid: Chantiers de l'écrit.* Woodbridge, Ontario: Albion, 1996.

Sud, special issue 94–5 (1990).

Christine de Pizan (1363–1430), *Œuvres poétiques de Christine de Pisan*, ed. Maurice Roy. 3 vols. Didot, 1886–96. (p)

Le Livre des fais et bonnes meurs du sage Roy Charles V, ed. S. Solente. 2 vols. Champion, 1936–41. (e)

Le Livre de la mutacion de Fortune, ed. S. Solente. 3 vols. A. and J. Picard, 1955. (e)

The 'Livre de la Paix' of Christine de Pisan. A Critical Edition with Introduction and Notes, ed. Charity Cannon Willard. The Hague: Mouton, 1958. (e)

Les Sept psaumes allegorisés of Christine de Pisan, a Critical Edition from the Brussels and Paris Manuscripts, ed. Ruth Ringland Rains. Washington, DC: Catholic University of American Press, 1965. (p)

'The "Livre de la Cité des dames" of Christine de Pisan: A Critical Edition', ed. Maureen C. Curnow. 4 vols. Diss. Vanderbilt University, 1975. (e, r)

Ditié de Jehanne d'Arc, eds. A. J. Kennedy and K. Varty. Medium Aevum Monographs, 9. Oxford: Society for the Study of Mediaeval Languages and Literature, 1977. (p)

L'Epistre d'Othea, ed. Halina Didycky Loukopoulos in 'Classical Mythology in the Works of Christine de Pisan, with an edition of *L'Epistre Othea* from the Manuscript Harley 4431'. Diss. Wayne State University. 1977. (l)

'La Lamentacion sur les maux de la France de Christine de Pisan', ed. A. J. Kennedy. In *Mélanges de langue et littérature françaises du Moyen Age et de la Renaissance offerts à Monsieur Charles Foulon par ses collègues, ses élèves et ses amis*. Rennes: Institut de Français, Université de Haute Bretagne, 1981, pp. 77–185. (e)

Le Livre du chemin de long estude, ed. R. Püschel. Berlin: R. Damköhler, 1881. (e)

Cent Ballades d'Amant de de Dame par Christine de Pizan, ed. Jacqueline Cerquiglini. Union Générale d'Editions, 1982. (p)

'Christine de Pizan's *Epistre à la reine* (1405)', *Revue des Langues Romanes* 92 (1988), 253–264.

Le Livre des Trois Vertus, eds. Charity Cannon Willard and Eric Hicks. Champion, 1989. (e)

Poems of Cupid, God of Love: Christine de Pizan's 'Epistre au dieu d'amours' and 'Dit de la Rose;' George Sewell's 'The Proclamation of Cupid', eds. Thelma Fenster and Mary Erler. Leiden, Brill, 1990. (p)

Le Livre du Duc des Vrais Amans, ed. Thelma S. Fenster. Binghamton, NY: Medieval and Renaissance Texts and Studies, 1995. (p)

Le Livre de L'advision-Cristine, eds. Christine Reno and Liliane Dulac. Études Christiniennes, IV. Honoré Champion, forthcoming. (a)

Le Livre du corps de policie, ed. Angus J. Kennedy. Honoré Champion, 1998. (e)

The Love Debate Poems of Christine de Pizan, ed. Barbara K. Altmann. Gainesville, FL: University of Florida Press, 1998. (p)

Translations

The Book of the City of Ladies, trans. Earl Jeffrey Richards. New York: Persea Books, 1982.

The Epistle of the Prison of Human Life, with An Epistle to the Queen of France and Lament on the Evils of Civil War, ed. and trans. Josette A. Wisman. New York: Garland, 1984.

The Treasure of the City of Ladies, or the Book of Three Virtues. Trans. Sarah Lawson. London: Penguin Books, 1985.

Le Livre de la Cité de Dames, trans. Eric Hicks and Thérèse Moreau. Stock, 1986.

Le Livre des Faits et Bonnes Moeurs du roi le Sage, trans. Eric Hicks and Thérèse Moreau. Stock, 1997.

A Medieval Woman's Mirror of Honor: The Treasury of the City of Ladies, Christine de Pizan, trans. Charity Cannon Willard. New York: Persea Books, 1989.

Christine de Pizan's 'Letter of Othea to Hector', trans. Jane Chance. The Focus Library of Medieval Women. Newburyport, MA: The Focus Information Group, 1990.

The Book of the Duke of True Lovers, transl. Thelma S. Fenster and Nadia Margolis. New York: Persea Books, 1991.

Christine's Vision, trans. Glenda K. McLeod. New York: Garland, 1993.

The Book of the Body Politic, trans. Kate Langdon Forhan. Cambridge University Press, 1994.

The Selected Writings of Christine de Pizan, eds. Renate Blumenfeld-Kosinski and Kevin Brownlee. New York: Norton, 1997.

Further feading

Dulac, Liliane and Bernard Ribémont (eds.), *Une femme de lettres au Moyen Âge: études autour de Christine de Pizan*. Orléans: Paradigme, 1995.

Richards, Earl Jeffery (ed.), *Reinterpreting Christine de Pizan*. Athens, GA: University of Georgia Press, 1992.

Willard, Charity Cannon, *Christine de Pizan: Her Life and Works*. New York: Persea Books, 1984.

Zimmermann, Margarete (ed.), *The City of Scholars: New Approaches to Christine de Pizan*. Berlin and New York: De Gruyter, 1994.

Cixous, Hélène (b. 1937), *Théâtre*. Des femmes, 1986. (d)

Dedans. Grasset, 1969. (n)

Le Troisième corps. Grasset, 1970. (n)

Les Commencements. Grasset, 1970. (n)

Un Vrai Jardin. Grasset, 1970.

Neutre. Grasset, 1972. (n)

Prénoms de personne. Seuil, 1974. (e)

La Jeune Née (with Catherine Clément). Union Générale d'Éditions, 1975. (e)

'Le Rire de la Méduse', *L'Arc* (1975), pp. 39–54. (e)

Souffles. Des femmes, 1975. (e)

LA. Gallimard, 1976. (n)

Partie. Des femmes, 1976. (n)

Portrait de Dora. Des femmes, 1976. (d)

Angst. Des femmes, 1977. (n)

La Venue à l'écriture (with Annie Leclerc and Madeleine Gagnon). UGE, 1977. (e)

Nom d'Oedipe: Chant du corps interdit. Des femmes, 1978. (d)

Préparatifs de noces au-delà de l'abîme. Des femmes, 1978. (e)

Anankè. Des femmes, 1979. (e)

Vivre l'orange/To Live the Orange. Bilingual text, trans. Ann Liddle and Sarah Cornell. Des femmes, 1979. (s)

Illa. Des femmes, 1980. (e)

With or l'art de l'innocence. Des femmes, 1981. (e)

Limonade, tout était si infini. Des femmes, 1982. (e)

Le Livre de Promethea. Gallimard, 1983. (e)

Entre l'écriture. Des femmes, 1986. (e)

l'Indiade ou l'Inde de leurs rêves. Théâtre du Soleil, 1987. (Includes the essay 'Le Pays des autres', repr. under the title 'Le Lieu du crime, le lieu du pardon'.) (d, e)

Manne. Des femmes, 1988. (e)

Jour de l'an. Des femmes, 1990. (e, a)

Akhmatova. Théâtre du Soleil, 1990. (d)

'Clarice Lispector, Marina Tsvetayeva. Autoportraits', in 'Femmes, Women, Frauen', *Avant-garde* 4 (1990). (e)

'De la Scène de l'inconscient à la scène de l'histoire', in *Hélène Cixous, chemins d'une écriture*. Amsterdam: Rodopi; Saint-Denis: Presses universitaires de Vincennes, 1990. (e)

La Ville Parjure. Théâtre du Soleil, 1994. (d)

L'Histoire (qu'on ne connaîtra jamais). Des femmes, 1994. (d)

Hélène Cixous: Photos de racines (with Mireille Caille-Gruber). Des femmes, 1994. (e, a)

Or: les lettres de mon père. Des femmes, 1997. (e/a) And many other works.

Translations

'The Laugh of the Medusa', trans. Keith Cohen and Paula Cohen. *Signs* 1 (Summer, 1976), 875–99.

Inside, trans. Carol Barko. New York: Schocken, 1986.

The Newly Born Woman, trans. Betsy Wing; intro. Sandra M. Gilbert. Minneapolis, MN: University of Minnesota Press, 1986; London: I. B. Taurus, 1996.

'The Parting of the Cake', trans. Franklin Philip, in Derrida and Tlili (eds.), *For Nelson Mandela*. Seaver Books, 1987.

'Writings on the Theatre', trans. Catherine Frank. *Qui Parle* (Spring 1989), 139–52.

Reading with Clarice Lispector, ed., trans. and intro. by Verena Andermatt Conley. Minneapolis, MN: University of Minnesota Press, 1990.

'Clarice Lispector: The Approach', in *'Coming to Writing' and Other Essays*, intro. Susan Rubin Suleiman, trans. Sarah Cornell *et al*. Cambridge, MA and London: Harvard University Press, 1991, pp. 59–77.

Rootprints: Memory and Life Writing. London: Routledge, 1997.

First Days of the Year. Minneapolis, MN: University of Minnesota Press, 1998.

Further reading

Dobson, Julia, 'The Scene of Writing: The Representation of Poetic Identity in Cixous's Recent Theatre', *Theatre Research International* 23: 3 (1998), 255–260.

Noonan, Mary, 'The Politics of Performing the Voice of Writing: Hélène Cixous's *La Ville Parjure*', *Nottingham Journal of French Studies* 31: 1 (1999).

Sellers, Susan, *Hélène Cixous: Authorship, Autobiography and Love*. Cambridge: Polity Press, 1996.

Shiach, Morag, *Hélène Cixous. A Politics of Writing*. London: Routledge, 1991.

Willis, Sharon, 'Hélène Cixous's *Portrait de Dora*: The Unseen and the Un-scene', in Sue-Ellen Case (ed.), *Performing Feminisms*. Baltimore, MD: The Johns Hopkins University Press, 1990.

Wilson, Emma, *Sexuality and the Reading Encounter: Identity and Desire in Proust, Duras, Tournier and Cixous*. Oxford: Oxford University Press, 1996, pp. 95–129.

Clemence of Barking, *The Life of St Catherine*, ed. William Macbain. Anglo-Normand Text Society. Oxford: Basil Blackwell, 1964. (e)

Translation

Virgin Lives and Holy Deaths: Two Exemplary Biographies for Anglo-Norman Women.

The Life of St Catherine. The Life of St Lawrence, trans. Jocelyn Wogan-Browne and Glyn S. Burgess. Everyman Library. London: J. M. Dent, 1996.

Further reading

Robertson, Duncan, 'Writing in the Textual Community: Clemence of Barking's Life of St Catherine', *French Forum* 21: 1 (1996), 407–30.

Wogan-Browne, Jocelyn and Glyn S. Burgess, Introduction to the translation *Virgin Lives and Holy Deaths*, xi-lxiii.

Colet, Louise (1810–76), *Fleurs du midi: poésies*. Paris: Dumont, 1836. (p)

Poésies. Typographie Lacrampe et Compagnie, 1842. (p)

Enfances célèbres. Hachette, 1858 (p)

Lui: roman contemporain. A. Bourdilliat, 1860. (n)

Translations

Lui, trans. Marilyn Gaddis Rose. Athens, G A: University of Georgia Press, 1986.

Further reading

Bellet, (ed.), *Autour de Louise Colet: Femmes de lettres au XIXᵉ siècle*. Lyons: Presses universitaires de Lyon, 1982.

Colette (Sidonie-Gabrielle Colette, 1873–1954), *Œuvres complètes*, ed. Claude Pichois. Gallimard, Bibliothèque de la Pléiade, 1984.

Théâtre. Fayard, 1989. (d)

Claudine à l'école. Ollendorf, 1900. (n)

Claudine à Paris. Ollendorf, 1901. (n)

Claudine amoureuse. Ollendorf, 1902. (n)

Claudine en ménage. Mercure de France, 1902. (n)

Les Vrilles de la vigne. 1908. In *Sido/ Les Vrilles de la vigne*. Livre de poche, 1972. (n)

Chéri. Fayard, 1920. (n)

Chéri, comédie en quatre actes. 1922. In *Théâtre*. (d)

La Maison de Claudine. Ferenczi, 1922. (n)

Le Blé en herbe. Flammarion, 1923; Garnier Flammarion, 1969. (n)

La Vagabonde. 1923. In *Théâtre*. (d)

L'Enfant et les sortilèges. 1925. In *Théâtre*. (d)

La Fin de Chéri. 1926. Flammarion, 1983.

La Naissance du jour. 1928. Garnier Flammarion, 1969. (n)

Sido. 1929. *Sido/ Les Vrilles de la vigne*. Livre de poche, 1972. (n)

Le Pur et l'impur. In *Œuvres complètes*, III.

Mes apprentissages. Ferenczi, 1936. (a)

Journal à rebours. Fayard, 1941. (a)

And many other works.

Translations

The Collected Stories of Colette, trans. Mathhew Ward; intro. Robert Phelps. 1983. Harmondsworth: Penguin, 1985.

Six Novels. London: Secker and Warburg, 1988.

The Complete Claudine, trans. Antonia White. New York: Farrar, Strauss and Giroux, 1976; London: Secker and Warburg, 1976.

Flowers and Fruit, ed. Robert Phelps; trans. Matthew Ward. London: Secker and Warburg, 1986.

My Mother's House/Sido, trans. Una Troubridge and Enid Mcleod. 1953. Harmondsworth: Penguin, 1980. *Chéri/The Last of Chéri*, trans. Roger Senhouse. Harmondsworth: Penguin, 1954; 1984.

Ripening Seed, trans. Roger Senhouse. 1959. Harmondsworth: Penguin, 1993.

The Vagabond, trans. Enid Mcleod. 1954. Harmondsworth: Penguin, 1980.

Breaking of Day, trans. Enid Mcleod. London: Women's Press, 1979.

My Apprenticeships. Harmondsworth: Secker and Warburg/Penguin, 1979.

The Pure and the Impure, trans. Herma Briffault; intro. Janet Flanner. 1967. Harmondsworth: Penguuin, 1980.

Looking Backwards, trans. David le Vay; intro. Alison Hennegan. London: The Women's Press, 1987.

Further reading

Angelfors, Cristina, *La Prise de conscience féminine chez Colette, Simone de Beauvoir et Marie Cardinal*. Lund: Lund University Press, 1989.

Callander, Margaret, *Le Blé en herbe and La Chatte*. London: Grant & Cutler, Critical Guides to French Texts, 1992.

Flieger, Jerry Aline, *Colette and the Fantom Subject of Autobiography*. Ithaca, NY: Cornell University Press, 1992.

Holmes, Diana, *Colette*. London and Basingstoke: Macmillan, 'Women Writers', 1991.

French Women's Writing 1848–1994, pp. 125–46.

Huffer, Lynne, *Another Colette: The Question of Gendered Writing*. Ann Arbor, MI: University of Michigan Press, 1992.

Ward Jouve, Nicole, *Colette*. London: Harvester Wheatsheaf, 1993.

Comtessa de Dia, see *Trobairitz*

Condorcet, Marie-Louise-Sophie de Grouchy, marquise de (1764–1822), Preface to *Esquisse d'un tableau historique des progrès de l'esprit humain, publié par P.C.F. Daunou et Mme M. L. S de Condorcet*, (her husband's, Jean-Antoine-Nicolas, marquis de Condorcet, most famous work), in Condorcet, *Œuvres complètes*. Agasse An III. (e)

Lettres sur la Sympathie, 1798. (l)

Lettres sur la Sympathie, suivies de Lettres d'amour, ed. Jean-Paul Lagrave. Montreal and Paris: L'Étincelle, 1994.

Further reading

Boissel, Thierry, *Sophie de Condorcet, femme de lumières*. Presses de la Renaissance, 1988.

Constance, epistolary poem to Baudri de Borgueil, in *Les œuvres poétiques de Baudri de Borgueil (1036–1140)*. Champion, 1926, pp. 344–9. (l)

Cottin, Sophie (1770–1807), *Œuvres complètes*, ed. J. Michaud. Corbet, 1920.

Claire d'Albe. Paris, 1799. (n)

Malvina. Maradan, 1801. (n)

Amélie Mansfield. Giguet et Michaud, 1802. (n)

Mathilde. Giguet et Michaud, 1805. (n)

Elisabeth ou les exilés de Sibérie. Giguet et Michaud, 1806. (n)

Claire d'Albe, ed. Raymond Trousson. Robert Laffont, collection 'Bouquins', 1996.

Translations

Amelia Mansfield. London: Cox and Bayliss, 1803.

Dangerous Friendship; or The Letters of Clara d'Albe. Baltimore, MD: Joseph Robinson, 1807.

Elisabeth, or The Exiles of Siberia. London: Lane, Newman & Co., 1807.

Matilda and Malek Adhel, the Saracen: A Crusade Romance. London: R. Dutton, 1809.

Malvina. London: C. Chapple, 1810.

Further reading

Cazenobe, Colette, 'Une préromantique méconnue, Madame Cottin', *Travaux de littérature* 1 (1985), 175–202.

Craven, Mme Augustus, *Lady Georgiana Fullerton.* Perrin, 1897. (e)

Crenne, Hélisenne de (1515–60), *Les Angoysses douloureuses qui procedent d'amours.* Denys Janot, 1538. (n)

Les Epistres familieres et invectives. Denys Janot, 1538. (l)

Les Œuvres de Ma Dame Helisenne de Crenne, A Sçavoir, Les angoisses douloureuses qui procedent d'amours. Les Epistres familieres & invectives. Le Songe de ladicte Dame, Le tout reveu & corrigé de nouveau par elle. Estienne Grouleau, 1560.

Œuvres. Geneva: Slatkine Reprints, 1977.

Les Angoysses douloureuses qui procedent d'amours, ed. Paule Demats. Belles Lettres, 1968.

Les Angoysses douloureuses qui procedent d'amours, ed. Jérôme Vercruysse. Lettres Modernes/Minard, 1968.

Les Angoysses douloureuses qui procedent d'amours, ed. Christine de Buzon. Champion, 1997.

Les Epistres Familieres et invectives de ma dame Helisenne, eds. Jean-Philippe Beaulieu et Hannah Fournier. Montréal: Presses de l'Université de Montréal, 1995.

Le Songe, 1541, ed. Jean-Philippe Beaulieu. Indigo et Côté-femmes éditions, 1995.

Les Epistres familieres et invectives, ed. Jerry C. Nash. Champion, 1996.

Translations

A Renaissance Woman: Helisenne's Personal and Invective Letters, trans. and eds. Marianna M. Mustacchi and Paul J. Archambault. Syracuse, NY: Syracuse University Press, 1986.

The Torments of Love, trans. and eds. Lisa Neal and Steven Rendall. Minneapolis, MN: University of Minnesota Press, 1996

Further reading

Beaulieu, Jean-Philippe, 'Didacticisme et parcours discursif dans les *Epistres* d'Helisenne de Crenne', *Renaissance and Reformation / Renaissance et Réforme* 18: 2 (1994), 31–43.

Buzon, Christine de, 'Helisenne narratrice des *Angoysses douloureuses qui procèdent d'amours'*, in A. Rivet (ed.), *La Femme au XVIe Siècle*. Le Puy en Velay: Impr. Dept., 1999.

Cotrell, Robert D., 'Female Subjectivity and Libidinal Infractions: Helisenne de Crenne's *Angoisses douloureuses* . . .', *French Forum* 16: 1 (Jan 1991), 5–19.

Nash, Jerry C., '"Exerçant œuvres viriles": Feminine Anger and Feminist (Re)Writing in Helisenne de Crenne', *L'Esprit créateur* 30: 4 (1990) 38–48.

Dacier, Anne Lefèvre (1654?–1720), *Les Poésies d'Anacréon et de Sapho*. D. Thierry, 1681. (e)

Daubié, Julie-Victoire (1824–74), *Du Progrès dans l'enseignement primaire*, 1862. (e)

La Femme pauvre au XIXe siècle. 1966–9. Avant-propos de Michelle Perrot, préface d'Agnès Thiercé. 2 vols. Côté-Femmes, 1992. (e)

L'Emancipation de la femme. (10 brochures.) 1871. (e)

Dauguet, Marie, (Julie-Marie Aubert, 1860–1942), *À travers le voile*. Léon Vannier, 1902. (p)

Par l'amour, poèmes. Mercure de France, 1904. (p)

Clartés. Sansot, 1907. (p)

Les Pastorales. Sansot, 1908. (p)

L'Essor victorieux. Sansot, 1911. (p)

Ce n'est rien, c'est la vie. Chiberre, 1924. (p)

De la Tour du Pin, marquise de, *Journal d'une femme de cinquante ans*. Chapelot, 1914. (a)

Deffand, Marie de Vichy-Chamrond, marquise du (1697–1780), *Correspondance complète de la Marquise du Deffand*. 1865. (l)

Cher Voltaire: La Correspondance de Mme du Deffand avec Voltaire, eds. Isabelle & Jean-Louis Vissière. Des femmes, 1987. (l)

Further reading

Duisit, Lionel, *Madame du Deffand, épistolière*. Geneva: Droz, 1963.

Démar, Claire (1800–33), *Textes sur l'affranchissement des femmes: 1832–33*. Payot, 1976. (e)

Deraismes, Maria (1828–94), *Ce que veulent les femmes: articles et conférences*, preface and notes by Odile Krakovitch. Syros, 1980. (e)

Eve dans l'humanité; preface by Laurence Klejman. Paris: Côté-femmes, 1990. (e)

Desbordes-Valmore, Marceline (1786–1859), *Œuvres poétiques*, 2 vols., edn. M. Bertrand. Grenoble: Presses universitaires de Grenoble, 1973.

Elegies, Marie, et romances. Francois Louis, 1819. (p)

L'Atelier d'un peintre: scenes de la vie privée. 2 vols. Charpentier, 1833. (n)

Pauvres fleurs. Dumont, 1839. (p)

Violette. Dumont, 1839. (p)

Bouquets et prières. Dumont, 1843. (p)

Correspondance intime de Marceline Desbordes-Valmore, ed. Benjamin Riviere. 2 vols. A. Lemerre, 1896. (l)

Contes, présentés par Marc Bertrand. Lyons: Presses universitaires de Lyon, 1989. (s)

Poèmes. Tchou, 1966. (p)

Poésies. Préface et choix d'Yves Bonnefoy. Gallimard, 1983. (p)

Translations

　Sainte-Beuve, Ch., *Memoirs of Madame Desbordes-Valmore, with a Selection from Her Poems*, trans. Harriet W. Preston. Boston, MA: Roberts Bros, 1873.

Further reading

　Greenberg, *Uncanonical Women*, pp. 103–19 & 131–50.

Deshoulières, Antoinette, Madame (1638–94), *Poésies de Madame Deshoulières.* (p)

Dhuoda, *Manuel pour mon fils*, ed. Pierre Riché. Sources Chrétiennes 225 and Editions du Cerf, 1975. (e)

Translation

　Handbook for William: A Carolingian Woman's Counsel for her Son, trans. Carol Neel. Lincoln, NE: University of Nebraska Press, 1991.

Further reading

　Dronke, *Women Writers of the Middle Ages*, pp. 36–54.

　Neel, Introduction to her translation of *Handbook for William*.

Djebar, Assia (b. 1936), *Les Alouettes naïves.* 1978. Arles: Actes Sud, 1997. (n)

Femmes d'Alger dans leur appartement. 1980. Des femmes, 1995. (s)

L'Amour, la fantasia. 1985. Albin Michel, 1995. (n)

Ombre sultane. J.-C. Lattes, 1987.

Loin de Médine. 1991. UGE, 1995. (n)

Filles d'Ismaël. Albin Michel, 1991. (n)

Le Blanc de l'Algérie. Albin Michel, 1995.

Vaste est la prison. Albin Michel, 1995. (n)

Les Nuits de Strasbourg. Arles: Actes Sud, 1997. (n)

Translations

　Women of Algiers in their Apartments, trans. Marjolijn de Jager. Charlottesville, VA: University Press of Virginia, 1992.

　Fantasia: An Algerian Calvacade, trans. Dorothy S. Blair. London: Quartet, 1989.

　A Sister to Scheherazade, trans. Dorothy S. Blair. London: Quartet, 1988. [*Ombre sultane*].

　Far From Medina, trans. Dorothy S. Blair. London: Quartet, 1994.

Further reading

　Donadey, A., 'Assia Djebar's Poetics of Subversion', *L'Esprit créateur* 23 (1993) 107–17.

　Marx-Scouras, M., 'Muffled Screams/Stifled Voices', *Yale French Studies* 82 (1993) 172–82.

Durand, Catherine Bédacier (d. ca. 1712), *La comtesse de Mortane.* 2 vols. Vve de C. Barlin, 1699. (n)

Histoire des amours de Grégoire VII, du cardinal de Richelieu, de la princesse de Condé, et de la marquise d'Urfé. Cologne, 1700. (n)

Les Mémoires secrets de la cour de Charles VII, roy de France. 1700. (n)

Les Belles Grecques, ou l'histoire des plus fameuses courtisanes de la Grèce. 1712. (n)

Amarante, ou le triomphe de l'amitié. Jombert, 1715. (n)

Le Triomphe de l'amitié avec plusieurs pièces de poésie. 1726. (n, p)

Duras, Claire de (1777–1828), *Ourika*. Introduction by Joan DeJean and Margaret Waller. New York: Modern Language Assocation of America, 1994. (n)

Edouard; pref. and notes Claudine Herrmann. Mercure de France, 1983. (n)

Duras, Marguerite (Marguerite Germaine M. Donnadieu, 1914–96), *Romans, cinéma, théâtre: un parcours 1943–93*. Gallimard, 1997.

Théâtre I. Gallimard, 1965. (d) [*Les Eaux et forêts; Le Square; La Musica*]

Théâtre II. Gallimard, 1968. (d) [*Suzanna Andler; Des Journées entières dans les arbres; Yes, peut-être; Le Shaga; Un Homme est venu me voir*]

Théâtre III. Gallimard, 1993. (d) [*La Bête dans la jungle; Les Papiers d'Aspern; La Danse de mort*, including Duras's French version of James Lord's stage adaptation of the story, 'The Beast in the Jungle', by Henry James (1962, revised 1981); her French version, in collaboration with Robert Antelme, of Michael Redgrave's stage adaptation of 'The Aspern Papers' by Henry James (1961); and a French adaptation of 'Dödsansen' by August Strindberg (1974).

Les Impudents. 1943. Gallimard, 1992. (n)

La Vie tranquille. Gallimard, 1944. (n)

Un barrage contre le Pacifique. Gallimard, 1950. (n)

Le Marin de Gibraltar. Gallimard, 1952. (n)

Les Petits Chevaux de Tarquinia. Gallimard, 1953. (n)

Des journées entières dans les arbres, suivi de: Le Boa, Madame Dodin, Les Chantiers. Gallimard, 1954. (s)

Le Square. Gallimard, 1955; revised 1990. (n)

Moderato cantabile. Minuit, 1958. (n)

Les Viaducs de la Seine-et-Oise. Gallimard, 1960. (d)

Hiroshima mon amour. Gallimard, 1960. (shooting script)

Dix heures et demie du soir en été. Gallimard, 1960. (n)

Une aussi longue absence (with Gérard Jarlot). Gallimard, 1961. (film script)

L'Après-midi de Monsieur Andesmas. Gallimard, 1962. (n)

Le Ravissement de Lol V. Stein. Gallimard, 1964. (n)

Le Vice-consul. Gallimard, 1966. (n)

L'Amante anglaise. Gallimard, 1967. (n)

L'Amante anglaise. Avant-Scène-Théâtre 422 (15 March 1969), 8–24. Reissued in a modified version and with a new preface as *Le Théâtre de l'amante anglaise*. Gallimard, collection 'L'Imaginaire', 1991. (d)

Détruire, dit-elle. Minuit, 1969. (n)

Abahn, Sabana, David. Gallimard, 1970. (n)

L'Amour. Gallimard, 1971. (n)

Ah! Ernesto, with illustrations by Bernard Bonhomme. Boissy Saint-Léger: François Ruy-Vidal and Harlin-Quist, 1971. (ch)

India Song. Gallimard, 1973. (d)

Nathalie Granger, suivi de: La Femme du Gange. Gallimard, 1973. (film script)

Les Parleuses. Interviews with Xavière Gauthier. Minuit, 1974.

Eden Cinéma. Mercure de France, 1977; Actes Sud-Papiers, 1988. (d)

Le Navire Night, suivi de: Césarée; Les Mains négatives; Aurélia Steiner; Aurélia Steiner; Aurélia Steiner. Mercure de France, 1979. (d, s, film script)

L'Homme assis dans le couloir. Revised version. Minuit, 1980. (s)

Véra Baxter ou les Plages de l'Atlantique. Albatros, 1980. (film script)

L'Eté 80. Minuit, 1980. (s)

Agatha. Minuit, 1981. (d)

Outside, papiers d'un jour. Pref. Yann Andréa, Albin Michel, 1981; (reissued with same pagination by P.O.L., 1984) (journalism)

L'Homme atlantique. Minuit, 1982. (s)

La Maladie de la mort. Minuit, 1982. (s)

Savannah Bay. Minuit, 1983. (d)

L'Amant. Minuit, 1984. (a)

La Mouette de Tchékhov, adapted by Marguerite Duras. Gallimard, 1985. (d)

La Musica Deuxième. Gallimard, 1985. (d)

Les Yeux bleus cheveux noirs. Minuit, 1986. (n)

La Pute de la côte normande. Minuit, 1986. (s)

La Vie matérielle. Conversations with Jérôme Beaujour. P.O.L., 1987. (s)

Emily L. Minuit, 1987. (n)

Eden cinéma, nouvelle version scénique. Actes Sud–Papiers, 1988. (d)

La Pluie d'été. P.O.L., 1990; Gallimard: folio, 1994. (n)

L'Amant de la Chine du Nord. Gallimard, 1991. (n)

Yann Andréa Steiner. P.O.L., 1992. (n)

Écrire. Gallimard, 1993. (s)

Le Monde extérieur: Outside II, ed. Christiane Blot-Labarrère. P.O.L., 1993. (journalism)

C'est tout. Minuit, 1995. (a)

La Mer écrite, Marval, 1996. (s)

Translations

Four Plays, trans. Barbara Bray. London: Oberon, 1992.

Four Novels by Marguerite Duras, trans. Richard Seaver *et al.*; intro. Germaine Brée. New York: Grove Press, 1965.

The Sea Wall, trans. Herma Briffaut. New York: Farrar, Strauss and Giroux, 1985.

The Sailor from Gibraltar, trans. Barbara Bray. New York: Riverrun, 1980.

Whole Days in the Trees, trans. Anita Barrows. London: Calder, 1984.

Hiroshima mon amour, trans. Richard Seaver. New York: Grove Press, 1966.

Ten Thirty on a Summer Night, trans. Anne Borschardt.London: Calder, 1965.

The Afternoon of Monsieur Andesmas, trans. Anne Borschardt and Barbara Bray. London: Calder, 1965.

The Ravishing of Lol V. Stein, trans. Richard Seaver. New York: Grove Press, 1966.

The Vice Consul, trans. Eillen Ellenbogen. 1968. London: Flamingo, 1990.

Suzanna Andler/La Musica/L'Amante anglaise. London: Calder, 1975.

'Destroy' She Said, trans. Barbara Bray. New York: Grove Press, 1970.

Woman to Woman, trans. Katharine A. Jensen. Lincoln, NA: University of
Nebraska Press, 1987. [*Les Parleuses*]

India Song, trans. Barbara Bray. New York: Grove Press, 1976.

Outside: Selected Writings, trans. Arthur Goldhammer. London: Flamingo,
1987.

The Malady of Death, trans. Barbara Bray. New York: Grove Press, 1985.

The Lover, trans. Barbara Bray. London: Collins, 1985; Flamingo, 1986. New
York: Pantheon, 1985.

Blue Eyes, Black Hair, trans. Barbara Bray. London: Flamingo, 1989.

Practicalities, trans. Barbara Bray. London: Flamingo, 1991.

Emily L., trans. Barbara Bray. London: Fontana, 1990.

Summer Rain, trans. Barbara Bray. London: HarperCollins, 1992; Flamingo,
1993.

The North China Lover, trans. Leigh Hafrey. London: Flamingo, 1994.

Yann Andrea Steiner, trans. Barbara Bray. London: Hodder and Stoughton,
1994; Sceptre, 1995.

Futher reading

Harvey, Robert, *Marguerite Duras: A Bio-Bibliogra*phy. Westport, CT: Greenwood
Press, 1997.

Hill, Leslie, *Marguerite Duras. Apocalyptic Desires*. London: Routledge, 1993.

Knapp, Bettina (ed.), *Critical Essays on Marguerite Duras*. New York: Hall,
1997.

Noonan, Mary, 'The Spatialization of Loss in the Theatre of Marguerite
Duras', *Theatre Research International* 23: 3 (1998) 215–24.

Taylor, Lib, 'Soundtracks: The Soundscapes of India Song', *Theatre Research
International* 23; 3 (1998), 205–214.

Vircondelet, Alain. *Duras: Biographie*. F. Bourin, 1991. Translated as *Duras. A
Biography* by Thomas Buckley, IL: Dalkey Archive Press, 1994.

Williams, James S., *The Erotics of Passage: Pleasure, Politics and Form in the Later
Works of Marguerite Duras*. Liverpool University Press, 1997.

Elie de Beaumont, Anne Louise Dumesnil-Morin (1730–83), *Lettres du
marquis de Roselle*, London and Paris, 1764. (n)

See under Tencin for details of Elie de Beaumont's completion of the
Anecdotes de la cour et du règne d'Edouard II.

Translation

The History of the Marquis de Roselle, in a Series of Letters. 2 vols. London, 1765.

**Épinay, Louise-Françoise-Pétronille Tardieu d'Esclavelles de la
Live, marquise d', (1726–83)**, *Les Conversations d'Émilie*. Leipzig, 1774.
(s)

Les Pseudo-mémoires de Mme d'Epinay. Histoire de Mme de Montbrillant, ed. Georges
Roth. 3 vols. Gallimard, 1951. (a)

Translations

The Conversations of Emily. London, 1787.

*Memoirs and Correspondence of Mme d'Epinay. Translated, with an Introduction, by
E. G. Allingham*. London, 1930.

Further reading

Weinreb, Ruth, *Eagle in a Gauze Cage: Louise d'Epinay, femme de lettres*. New York, 1993.

Ernaux, Annie (b. 1940), *Les Armoires vides*. Gallimard, 1974. (n)

Ce qu'ils disent ou rien. Gallimard, 1977. (n)

La Femme gelée. Gallimard, 1981. (n)

La Place. Gallimard, 1983. (a)

Une Femme. Gallimard, 1987. (a)

Passion simple. Gallimard, 1991. (a)

Journal du dehors. Gallimard, 1993. (a)

'Je ne suis pas sortie de ma nuit'. Gallimard, 1997. (a)

La Honte. Gallimard, 1997. (a)

Translations

Cleaned Out, trans. Carol Sanders. New York: Dalkey, 1991.

A Frozen Woman, trans. Linda Coverdale. New York: Seven Stories Press, 1996.

Positions, trans. Tanya Leslie. London: Quartet, 1991.

A Woman's Story, trans. Tanya Leslie. London: Quartet, 1990.

Passion Perfect, trans. Tanya Leslie. London: Quartet, 1993.

Exteriors. New York: Seven Stories Press, 1996.

Further reading

Day, Lorraine, *La Place/Une Femme*. Glasgow: University of Glasgow French and German Publications, 1990.

'Class, Sexuality and Subjectivity in Annie Ernaux's *Les Armoires vides*', in Margaret Atack and Phil Powrie (eds.), *Contemporary French Fiction by Women*, pp. 41–55.

Fallaize, *French Women's Writing*, pp. 67–87 (includes translated extracts).

Holmes, *French Women's Writing 1848–1994*, pp. 246–265.

Sanders, Carol, 'Stylistic Aspects of Women's Writing: The Case of Annie Ernaux', *French Cultural Studies* 4: 1/10 (February 1993), 15–30.

Sheringham, Michael, '"Invisible Presences": Fiction, Autobiography and Women's Lives', *Sites* 3 (Spring 1998).

Tondeur, Claire-Lise, *Annie Ernaux ou l'exil intérieur*. Amsterdam: Rodopi, 1996.

Espinassy, Mademoiselle d' *Essai sur l'éducation des demoiselles*, 1764. (e)

Nouvel abrégé de l'histoire de France à l'usage des jeunes gens. 7 vols. Saillant 1766–71. (ch)

Esquiros, Adèle (1819–86), *Souvenirs d'enfance*. BN cat. no. Ye676 (1849?) (a)

Etcherelli, Claire (b. 1943), *Elise ou la vraie vie*. 1967. Gallimard, 1982. (n)

À propos de Clémence. 1971. Gallimard, 1973. (n)

Un Arbre voyageur. 1978. Gallimard, 1983.

Further reading

Fallaize, *French Women's Writing*, pp. 88–108 (includes translated extracts).

Ophir, Anne, *Regards féminins: Condition féminine et création littéraire. Simone de Beauvoir, Christiane Rochefort, Claire Etcherelli*. Denoël, 1976.

Poole, Sara, *Elise ou la vraie vie*. London: Grant and Cutler (Critical Guides to French Texts), 1994.

Ferrand, Anne Bellinzani, présidente de (1657–1740), *Histoire des amours de Cléante et Belise.* Geneva: Slatkine, 1979.

Fontaines, Marie-Louise-Charlotte de Pelard de Givry, Comtesse de, *Histoire de la Comtesse de Savoye, et Histoire du comte d'Eu.* 1726. (n)
Histoire nouvelle des Amours de la jeune Bélise et de Cléante. 1689. Geneva: Slatkine, 1979. (n)
Lettres galantes de Madame. 1691. (n)

Flore, Jeanne *Les Contes Amoureux*, eds. Gabriel-A. Perouse *et al.* Lyons: Presses Universitaires de Lyon, 1980. (s)

Further reading

Bauschatz, Cathleen M., 'Parodic Didacticism in the *Contes Amoureux par Madame Jeanne Flore*', *French Forum* 20: 1 (1997) 5–21.

Longeon, Claude, 'Du nouveau sur les *Comptes Amoureux* de Madame Jeanne Flore', in *Hommes et Livres de la Renaissance.* Université Saint-Etienne: Institut Claude Logeon, 1990.

Reynolds-Cornell, Régine, 'Madame Jeanne Flore and the *Contes Amoureux*: A Pseudonym and a Paradox', *Bibliothèque d'Humanisme et Renaissance* 51 (1989), 123–33.

Foucher, Michèle (b. 1941), *La Table.* 1976. In *Avant-Scène-Théâtre* 636 (15 October 1978). (d)

Fouillée, Augustine (G. Bruno, 1833–1923), *Le Tour de France par deux enfants.* 1877. Librarie classique d'Eugène Bellin, 1977. (ch)

Gallaire, Fatima (b. 1944), *Princesses ou Ah! Vous êtes venus . . . là où il y a quelques tombes.* Paris: Quatre-Vents, 1991. (d)
Molly des sables; Au cœur, la brûlure. Avant-Scène Théâtre 954 (1994). (d)
Les Richesses de l'hiver. Avant-Scène Théâtre 991 (1996). (d)

Gautier, Judith (1845–1917), *Le Livre de jade.* Lemerre, 1867. (p)
Le Dragon impérial. Lemerre, 1869. (n)
L'Usurpateur. Albert Lacrois, 1875. (n)
Les Cruautés de l'amour. Dentu, 1879 (s)
Richard Wagner et son œuvre poétique. Charavay Frères, 1882. (e)
La Conquête du paradis. 2 vols. Frinzine, 1887. (n)
Le Collier des jours. 3 vols. Juven, 1902–9. (a)
Princesses d'amour, pièce en trois actes et 7 tableaux, musique d'Edmond Laurence. Heugel *et cie.*, 1907. (d)
Poésies. Fasquelle, 1911 (p)

Further reading

Richardson, Joanna, *Judith Gautier: A Biography.* New York: Franklin Watts, 1987.

Genlis, Stéphanie-Félicité du Crest de (1746–1830), *Œuvres*, 84 vols., Lecointe et Duray, 1825–6.
Théâtre à l'usage des jeunes personnes. Vol. I, Pancouke, 1779; vols. II, III & IV, Lambert et Baudouin, 1780. (d)
Théâtre de l'éducation (new complete edition of previous work). 5 vols. Maradan, 1813.

Adèle et Théodore, ou Lettres sur l'éducation. Lambert, 1782. (n)

Les Veillées du château ou cours de morale à l'usage des enfants. Lambert, 1784. (ch)

Discours sur l'éducation de M. le Dauphin et sur l'adoption. Onfroy, 1790. (e)

Discours sur la suppression des couvens de religieuses et l'éducation publique des femmes. Onfroy, 1790. (e)

Discours sur l'éducation publique du peuple. Onfroy, 1791. (e)

Les Vœux téméraires, ou l'enthousiasme. 2 vols. 1798. (n)

Alphonsine ou la tendresse maternelle. 2 vols. Nicolle, 1806.

Alphonse, ou le fils naturel. Maradan, 1809.

De l'Influence des femmes sur la littérature française comme protectrices des lettres et comme auteurs. Maradan, 1809. (e)

Mémoires inédits sur le 18e siècle et la Révolution française. 10 vols. Ladvocat, 1825–28. (a)

And a number of other works.

Translations

Theatre of Education. London: Cadell, 1781.

Adelaide and Theodore: or Letters on Education. 3 vols. London: Bathurst, 1783.

The Beauties of Genlis; being a collection of the most beautiful tales and other striking extracts from Adela and Theodore; the Tales of the castle; The Theatre of education and Sacred dramas. Perth 1787.

Tales of the Castle; or, Stories of Instruction and Delight, trans. Thomas Holcroft, 4 vols. Dublin: Wogan, Byrne, 1793.

Alphonsine; or, Maternal Affection. London: J. F. Hughes, 1809.

Alphonso; or, the Natural Son. London: Colburn, 1809.

Memoirs of the Countess of Genlis, Illustrative of the Eighteenth and Nineteenth Centuries. 8 vols. London: Colburn, 1825–6.

Translations of other works by Genlis not listed here also exist.

Further reading

Broglie, Gabriel de, *Madame de Genlis.* Perrin, 1985.

Plagnol-Diéval, Marie-Emmanuelle, *Madame de Genlis et le théâtre d'éducation au XVIIIe siècle.* Oxford: The Voltaire Foundation,1997.

Germain, Sylvie (b. 1954), *Le Livre des Nuits.* Gallimard, 1985. (n)

Nuit-d'Ambre. Gallimard, 1987. (n)

Jours de colère. Gallimard, 1989. (n)

Opéra muet. Gallimard, 1989. (n)

L'Enfant Méduse. Gallimard, 1991. (n)

La Pleurante des rues de Prague. Gallimard, 1992. (n)

Immensités. Gallimard, 1993. (n)

Patience et songe de lumière. Flohic, 1995. (essay on Vermeer)

Éclats de sel. Gallimard: folio, 1996. (n)

Les Échos du silence. Desclée de Brouwer, 1996. (e)

Céphalophores. Gallimard, 1997. (s)

Tobie des marais. Gallimard, 1998. (n)

L'Encre du poulpe. Gallimard-jeunesse. (ch)

Translations

The Book of Nights, trans. Christine Donougher. Sawtry: Dedalus, 1992.

*The Weeping Woman on the Streets of Prag*ue, trans. Judith Landry; interview with Elizabeth Young; intro. Emma Wilson. Sawtry: Dedalus, 1993.

The Medusa Child, trans. Liz Nash. Sawtry: Dedalus, 1994.

Night of Amber, trans. Christine Donougher. Sawtry: Dedalus, 1995.

Further reading

Viart, Dominique, *Écritures contemporaines 2*. Lettres modernes, 1999.

Girardin, Delphine Gay de (1804–55), *Essais poétiques*. Gaultier-Laguionne, 1824. (p)

Nouveaux Essais poétiques. Paris: Canel, 1826. (p)

Lady Tartuffe. Paris: Michel Lévy, 1853. (d)

Nouvelles. Paris, Michel Levy, 1853. (s)

Lettres parisiennes, biographie, bibliographie, pages choises par Charles Simond. Paris, Louis-Michaud, 1908. (e)

Translations

Lady Tartuffe. New York, Darcie and Corbyn, 1855.

Parisian Letters, trans L. Willard. Boston: Crosby & Nichols, 1851.

Further reading

Morgan, Cheryl, 'Les Chiffons de la M(éd)use: Delphine Gay de Girardin journaliste', *Romantisme* 85 (1994), 57–66.

Goll, Claire (1891–1977), *Une Allemande à Paris*. Radot, 1928. (n)

Chansons indiennes. Seghers, 1952. (p)

L'Ignifère. Librairie Saint-Germain-des-Près, 1969. (p)

Ballerine de la peur. Émile-Paul, 1971. (n)

And other writings in French and German.

Gomez Madeleine-Angélique Poisson Gabriel de (1684–1770), *Les Journées amusantes, dédiées au Roy*. 8 vols. 1722–31. (s)

Crémentine, reine de Sanga, histoire indienne. 2 vols. 1727. (n)

Les Cent nouvelles nouvelles. 19 vols. 1732–1739. (s)

Histoire du Comte d'Oxfort and of milady d'Herby, d'Eustache de Saint-Pierre et de Béatrix de Guines au Siège de la Ville de Calais, sous le Regne de Philippe de Valois en 1346 and 1347. 1737. (n)

Translations

La Belle Assemblée, or The Adventures of Six Days, trans. Eliza Hayward. London, 1724, 1725.

Select Novels (a selection of *Les Cent Nouvelles Nouvelles*). W. Shropshire, 1746.

Further Reading

Jones-Day, Shirley, 'A Woman Writer's Dilemma. Madame de Gomez and the Early Eighteenth-Century Novel in France', in Roland Bonnel and Catherine Rubinger (eds.), *Femmes savantes et femmes d'esprit*, pp. 77–98.

Gouges, Olympe de (Marie Gouze, 1708–93), *Mémoire de Madame de Valmont*, Paris, 1788 . (n)

Le Bonheur primitif de l'homme, ou les Rêveries patriotiques, 1789. (e)

Le Cri du sage, par une femme, 1789. (e)

Les Droits de la femme. 1791. (e)

Le Prince philosophe, conte oriental, 2 vols, Paris, 1792. (n)

Mémoire de Madame de Valmont, ed. Raymond Trousson. Robert Laffont, collection 'Bouquins', 1996.

Further reading

Blanc, Olivier, *Olympe de Gouges.* Syros, 1981.

Gournay, Marie de (1565–1645), *Les Advis ou les Presens de la Demoiselle de Gournay.* Toussainct Du-Bray, 1634; 1641. (e, n, p)

Les Advis, ou, les Presens de la Demoiselle de Gournay 1641, vol. 1, eds. Jean-Philippe Beaulieu and Hannah Fournier. Amsterdam: Rodopi, 1997.

L'Ombre de la Damoiselle de Gournay. Jean Libert, 1626. (e, n, p)

'Préface à l'édition des *Essais* de Montaigne'. Abel L'Angelier, 1595. François Rigolot (ed.), in *Montaigne Studies* 1 (Nov 1989), 21–60. (e)

Le Proumenoir de Monsieur de Montaigne (1594), ed. Patricia F. Cholakian. Delmar, NY: Scholars' Facsimiles and Reprints, 1985. (n)

Bouquet de Pinde, composé de fleurs diverses, ed. Maddalena Bertelà. Ravenna: Longo Editore, 1995 (p)

Egalité des hommes et des femmes; Grief des dames; suivis du Proumenoir de Monsieur de Montaigne, ed. C. Venesoen. Geneva: Droz, 1993. (e, n)

Translations

'Of the Equality of Men and Women' and 'The Complaint of the Ladies', trans. Eva M. Sartori. *Allegorica* 9 (Winter 1987), 135–64.

Preface to the 'Essays' of Michel de Montaigne by his Adoptive Daughter, Marie de Gournay, trans. Richard Hillman and Colette Quesnel. Tempe, AA: Medieval and Renaissance Texts and Studies, 1998.

Further reading

Arnould, Jean-Claude (ed.), *Marie de Gournay et l'édition de 1595 des 'Essais' de Montaigne.* Champion, 1996.

Dezon-Jones, Elayne (ed.), *Fragments d'un Discours Féminin.* José Corti, 1988.

Ilsley, Marjorie H., *A Daughter of the Renaissance: Marie le Jars de Gournay, Her Life and Works,* The Hague: Mouton, 1963.

Tetel, Marcel (ed.), 'Montaigne et Marie de Gournay', special issue of the *Journal of Medieval and Renaissance Studies* 25: 3 (1995). Reprinted by Champion, 1997.

Graffigny, Françoise d'Issembourg d'Happoncourt de (1695–1758), *Lettres d'une péruvienne.* 1747. (n)

Lettres d'une péruvienne, eds. Bernard Bray and Isabelle Landy-Houillon. Garnier-Flammarion, 1983.

Lettres d'une péruvienne, with preface by Colette Piau-Gillot. Côté-Femmes, 1990.

Lettres d'une péruvienne, ed. Raymond Trousson. Robert Laffont, collection 'Bouquins', 1996.

Further reading

Altman, Janet, 'Making Room for Peru. Graffigny's Novel Reconsidered', in C. Laforge, *Dilemmes du roman. Essays in honor of G. May.* Saratoga, CA: Anma Libri, 1989.

Gréville, Henry (Alice Durand, 1842–1902), *Dosia*. Plon, n.d. (n)
Lucie Rodey. Plon, 1880. (n)
La Fille de Dosia. Plon-Nourrit, 1899. (n)
Guérin, Eugénie de (1805–48), *Reliquiae*, eds. Jules Barbey d'Aurevilly and
   G.-S. Trebutien. Caen: Imprimerie de A. Hardel, 1855. (a)
Lettres d'Eugénie de Guérin, ed. G. Trébutien. Didier, 1865. (l)
Guette, Madame de la (1613–76), *Mémoires*. 1681. (a)
Guillet, Pernette du (1520–45), *Rymes*, ed. Victor E. Graham. Geneva:
   Droz, 1968. (p)
Rymes (with Louise Labé, *Œuvres Poétiques*), ed. Françoise Charpentier.
   Gallimard, 'Poésie', 1983.
Further reading
   Charpentier, Françoise, 'Projet poétique, travail poétique dans les *Rymes* de
      Pernette du Guillet: Autour de quatre quatrains', in François Marotin (ed.),
      Poétique et Narration. Champion, 1993.
   Cottrell, Robert, 'Pernette du Guillet and the Logic of Aggressivity', in,
      Raymond C. La Charité (ed.), *Writing the Renaissance: Essays on Sixteenth-
      Century French Literature in Honor of Floyd Gray*. Lexington, va: French Forum
      Monographs, 1992.
   Lloyd-Jones, Kenneth, 'Writing the Language of Love: Lyonnais Poetry and
      the Portrayal of Passion', *Romance Languages Annual* 7 (1995), 112–19.
Guyon, Jeanne Marie Bouvières de la Motte (1648–1717), *Moyen court
   et très facile pour l'oraison . . .* 1685. (e)
Opuscules spirituels. 1704–12. (p)
Lettres chrétiennes et spirituelles. 1717–18. (l)
L'Ame amante de son Dieu. 1717. (e, p)
La Cantique des cantiques de Salomon. 1688. (p)
Gyp (Sibylle de Mirabeau, 1850–1932), *Autour du mariage*. Calmann-Lévy,
   1883. (e)
Mademoiselle Loulou. Paris: Calmann-Lévy, 1888. (n)
L'Entrevue. Nilsson, 1899. (n)
Many other minor works, including over a hundred novels.
Further reading
   Silverman, Willa, *The Notorious Life of Gyp*. Oxford University Press, 1995.
Hardou, Citoyenne, *Projet de Règlement pour l'instruction*. 1793. (e)
Heloise (1100–63/4), 'The Personal Letters Between Abelard and Heloise',
   ed. J. T. Muckle. *Medieval Studies* 15 (1953), 47–94. (l)
'The Letter of Heloise on Religious Life and Abelard's First Reply', ed. J. T.
   Muckle. *Medieval Studies* 17 (1955), 240–81. (l)
*La Vie et les epistres: Pierre Abaelart at Heloys sa fame/ traduction attribuée à Jean de
   Meun; avec une nouvelle édition des textes latins*, ed. Eric Hicks. Geneva:
   Champion-Slatkine, 1991.
Translations
   The Letters of Abelard and Heloise, trans. Betty Radice. Harmondsworth:
      Penguin, 1974.

Further reading

> Brown, Catherine, 'Muliebriter: Doing Gender in the Letters of Heloise', in Chance (ed.), *Gender and Text in the Later Middle Ages*, pp. 25–51.
>
> Dronke, *Medieval Women Writers*, pp. 107–43.
>
> Newman, Barbara. 'Authority, Authenticity and the Repression of Heloise', in *From Virile Woman to WomanChrist*, pp. 46–75.

Héricourt, Jenny d', *La Femme affranchie*. 2 vols. Brussels: F. van Meenen, 1860. (e)

Huber, Marie, *Le Monde fou préféré au monde sage, en 24 Promenades de trois amis*. Amsterdam, 1731. (e)

> *Le Sistème des théologiens anciens et modernes, concilié par l'exposition des différens sentimens sur l'état des âmes séparées des corps, en quatorze lettres*, Amsterdam 1731 (revised and expanded editions, Amsterdam, 1733 and 'London'(?) 1739). (l)
>
> *Lettres sur la religion essentielle à l'homme, distinguée de ce qui n'en est que l'accessoire*. Amsterdam, 1738. (l)
>
> *Suite de la troisième partie sur la religion essentielle . . . en douze lettres*. 'Londres'(?) 1739. (l)

Translations

> *The World Unmasked; or the Philosopher the Greatest Cheat; in 24 Dialogues*, London 1736 (republished 1743 & 1786).
>
> *The World Unmasked; or the Philosopher the Greatest Cheat; in 24 Dialogues. The State of Souls separated from their Bodies . . . and all objections against it solved*. London, 1743.

Further reading

> Briggs, E. R., 'Marie Huber and the Campaign against Eternal Hell Torments', in Jacobs *et al.*, *Woman and Society*, pp. 218–28.

Hyvrard, Jeanne (b. 1945), *Les Prunes de Cythère*. Minuit, 1975. (n)

Mère la mort. Minuit, 1976. (n)

Les Doigts du figuier. Minuit, 1977. (p)

La Meurtritude. Minuit, 1977. (n)

Le Corps défunt de la comédie. Seuil, 1982. (e)

Le Silence et l'obscurité. Montalba, 1982. (e)

Auditions musicales certains soirs d'été. Des femmes, 1984. (s)

Canal de la Toussaint. 1985. (e)

La Baisure suivi de *Que se partagent encore les eaux*. Des femmes, 1985. (p)

La Pensée corps. 1989. (e)

La Jeune Morte en robe de dentelle. Des femmes, 1990. (n)

Translations

> *The Dead Girl in a Lace Dress*, trans. J.-P. Mentha and Jennifer Waelti-Walters. University of Edinburgh Press, 1996.
>
> *Waterweed in the Wash-Houses*, trans. Elsa Copeland. Edinburgh University Press, 1996. [*La Meurtritude*].

Further reading

> Bishop, *Contemporary French Women Poets*, vol. ii, pp. 12–31.

Cauville, Joëlle, *Mythographie hyvrardienne*. Laval, Quebec: Presses universitaires de Laval, 1996.

Fallaize, *French Women's Writing*, pp. 109–30 (includes translated extracts).

Verthuy-Williams, Mair, and Jennifer Waelti-Walters, *Jeanne Hyvrard*. Amsterdam: Rodopi, 1988.

Waelti-Walters, Jennifer, *Jeanne Hyvrard: Theorist of the Modern World*. Edinburgh University Press, 1996.

Irigaray, Luce (b. 1932), *Le Langage des déments*. The Hague: Mouton, 1973. (e)

Speculum de l'autre femme. Minuit, 1974. (e)

Ce sexe qui n'en est pas un. Minuit, 1977. (e)

Et l'une ne bouge pas sans l'autre. Minuit, 1979. (e)

Amante marine: De Friedrich Nietzsche. Minuit, 1980. (e)

Le Corps-à-corps avec la mère. Ottawa: La Pleine Lune, 1981. (e)

Passions élémentaires. Minuit, 1982. (e)

La Croyance même. Galilée, 1983. (e)

L'Oubli de l'air: Chez Martin Heidegger. Minuit, 1983. (e)

Éthique de la différence sexuelle. Minuit, 1984. (e)

Parler n'est jamais neutre. Minuit, 1985. (e)

'L'ordre sexuel du discours', *Langages* 85 (March 1987), 81–123. (e)

Sexes et parentés. Minuit, 1987. (e)

Le Temps de la différence. Livre de Poche, 1989. (e)

Je, tu, nous: pour une culture de la différence. B. Grasset, 1990. (e)

J'aime à toi: esquisse d'une félicité dans l'histoire. B. Grasset, 1992. (e)

Translations

The Irigaray Reader, ed. and intro. Margaret Whitford. Oxford: Blackwell, 1991.

Speculum of the Other Woman, trans. Gillian C. Gill. Ithaca, NY: Cornell University Press, 1985.

This Sex that is not One, trans. Catherine Porter with Carolyn Burke. Ithaca, NY: Cornell University Press, 1985.

'And the One Doesn't Stir Without the Other', trans. H. V. Wenzel. *Signs: Journal of Women in Culture and Society* 7, 1 (1981), 60–67.

Marine Lover of Friedrich Nietzsche, trans. Gillian C. Gill. New York: Columbia, 1991.

Elemental Passions, trans. Joanne Collie and Judith Still. London: The Athlone Press, 1992.

Je, tu, nous: toward a culture of difference, trans. Alison Martin. New York: Routledge, 1992.

An Ethics of Sexual Difference, trans. Carolyn Burke and Gillian C. Gill. London: The Athlone Press, 1993.

Sexes and Genealogies, trans. Gillian C. Gill. New York: Columbia University Press, 1993.

Thinking Difference, trans. Karin Mortin. London: The Athlone Press, 1994.

Further reading

Burke, Carolyn, Naomi Schor and Margaret Whitford (eds.), *Engaging with Irigaray: Feminist Philosophy and Modern European Thought*. New York: Columbia University Press, 1994.

Grosz, Elizabeth, *Sexual Subversions. Three French Feminists*. Sydney: Allen and Unwin, 1989.

Stockton, K. Bond, *God Between Their Lips. Desire Between Women in Irigaray, Brontë and Eliot*. Stanford, CA: Stanford University Press, 1994.

Whitford, Margaret, *Luce Irigaray: Philosophy in the Feminine*. London: Routledge, 1991.

Kristeva, Julia (b. 1941), *La Révolution du langage poétique: l'Avant-garde à la fin du XIXᵉ siècle. Lautréaont et Mallarmé*. Seuil, 1974. (e)

Des Chinoises. Des femmes, 1974. (e)

Polylogue. Seuil, 1977. (e)

Pouvoirs de l'horreur: essai sur l'abjection. Seuil, 1980. (e)

Histoires d'amour. Denoël, 1983. (e)

Au Commencement était l'amour: psychanalyse et foi. Hachette, 1985. (e)

Soleil noir: Dépression et mélancolie. Gallimard, 1987. (e)

Étrangers à nous-mêmes. Fayard, 1988. (e)

Les Samouraïs. Fayard, 1990. (n)

Le Vieil Homme et les loups. Fayard, 1991. (n)

Les Nouvelles Maladies de l'âme. Fayard, 1993. (e) And a number of other works.

Translations

Powers of Horror, trans. Leon S. Roudiez. New York: Columbia University Press, 1982.

Revolution in Poetic Language, trans. Margaret Waller. New York: Columbia University Press, 1984.

About Chinese Women, trans. Anita Barrows. London: Boyars, 1977; reprinted 1986.

The Kristeva Reader, ed. Toril Moi. New York: Columbia University Press, 1986.

Tales of Love, trans. Leon S. Roudiez. New York: Columbia University Press, 1987.

In the Beginning was Love: Psychoanalysis and Faith, trans, Arthur Goldhammer. New York: Columbia University Press, 1987.

Black Sun: Depression and Melancholia, trans. Leon S. Roudiez. New York: Columbia University Press, 1989.

Language, the Unknown: An Initiation into Linguistics, trans. Anne M. Menke. London: Harvester Wheatsheaf, 1989.

Strangers to Ourselves. London: Harvester Wheatsheaf, 1991.

The Samuraï: a novel, trans. Barbara Bray. New York: Columbia University Press, 1992.

The Old Man and the Wolves, trans. Barbara Bray. New York: Columbia University Press, 1994.

New Maladies of the Soul, trans. Ross Guberman. New York: Columbia University Press, 1995.

Further reading
Atack, Margaret, 'The Other Feminist', *Paragraph*, 8 (1986), 25–37.
Fletcher, John and Andrew Benjamin (eds.), *Abjection, Melancholia and Love. The Work of Julia Kristeva*. London: Routledge, 1990.
Guberman, Ross Mitchell, *Julia Kristeva. Interviews*. New York: Columbia University Press, 1996.
Lechte, John, *Julia Kristeva*. London: Routledge, 1990.
Smith, Anne-Marie, *Julia Kristeva: Speaking the Unspeakable*. London: Pluto, 1998.
Still, Judith, 'Horror in Kristeva and Bataille: Sex and Violence', *Paragraph* 20, Special number devoted to Kristeva (1997).

Krysinska, Marie (1864–1908), *Rythmes pittoresques: mirages, symboles, femmes, contes, resurrections*. Lemerre, 1890. (p)
Joies errantes: nouveaux rythmes pittoresques. Lemerre, 1894. (p)
Intermèdes. Messein, 1904.

L..., Mme, Mme, *Première lettre d'une femme sur l'éducation de son sexe. Journal des Dames*, 1791.

Labé, Louise (1520–66), *Evvres de Lovise Labé Lionnoize*. Lyons: Jean de Tournes, 1555.
Œuvres complètes, ed. Enzo Giudici. Geneva: Droz, 1981.
Œuvres complètes: Sonnets, Elégies, Débat de Folie et d'Amour, ed. François Rigolot. Flammarion, 1986. (p, e)
Œuvres poétiques (with Pernette du Guillet, *Rymes*), ed. Françoise Charpentier. Gallimard, 'Poésie', 1983. (p)

Translations
Louise Labé's Complete Works, ed. and trans. Edith R. Farrell. Troy, NY.: Whitson, 1986.
The Debate Between Follie and Love, trans. Robert Greene. London: H. Lownes, 1608.
Débat, ed. and trans. Edwin Marion Cox. London: Williams and Morgata, 1925.
Love Sonnets, trans. Frederic Prokosch. New York: New Directions, 1947.
Sonnets of Louise Labé, 'La belle cordière', trans. Alta Lind Cook. Toronto University Press, 1950.
Twenty-Four Love Sonnets, trans. Frances Lobb. London, 1950.
The Sonnets, ed. and trans. Bettina L. Knapp. Minard, 1964.
Sonnets, ed. and preface by Peter Sharratt; trans. Graham Dunstan Martin. Edinburgh Bilingual Library. Austin, TX: University of Texas, 1972.

Further reading
Baker, Deborah Lesko, *Subject of Desire: Petrarchan Poetics and the Female Voice in Louise Labé*. Purdue, IN: Purdue University Press, 1996.
Cameron, Keith. *Louise Labé: Feminist and Poet of the Renaissance*. New York: Berg Women's Series, 1990.

Demerson, Guy, *Louise Labé: les voix du lyrisme*. CNRS, 1990.

Martin, Daniel, *Signe(s) d'amante. L'agencement des œuvres de Louise Labé Lionnoize*. Champion, 1999.

Rigolot, François, *Louise Labé Lyonnaise, ou: La Renaissance au féminin*. Champion, 1997.

Lafayette, Marie Madeleine Pioche de Vergne, Comtesse de (1634–93), *Œuvres complètes*, ed. R. Duchêne. Bourin, 1990.

Romans et Nouvelles, ed. Alain Niderst, Bordas-Classiques Garnier, 1989.

La Princesse de Montpensier. 1662. Ed. Michekine Cuenin. Geneva: Droz, 1979.

Zayde. Histoire espagnole. 2 vols. Barbin, 1669 (vol. I) and 1671 (vol. II). [Zaïde] ed. Janine Anseaume Kreiter. Nizet, 1982.

La Princesse de Clèves. Barbin, 1678. Ed. Jean Mesnard. Paris: Garnier Flammarion, 1996.

Histoire de Madame Henriette d'Angleterre. Amsterdam: La Cène, 1720. With *Mémoires de la cour de France pour les années 1688 et 1689*. Mercure de France, 1969.

La Comtesse de Tende. Mercure de France, 1724.

Mémoires de la cour de France pour les années 1688 et 1689. Amsterdam: Jean-Frédéric Bernard, 1731. With *Histoire de Madame Henriette d'Angleterre*, Mercure de France, 1969.

Translations

The Princess of Montpensier. London, 1666.

Zayde. A Spanish History, trans. P. Porter. London: Milbourn, 1678.

The Princess of Clèves. London: R. Bentley and H. Magnes, 1679.

Fatal Gallantry, or, The Secret History of Henrietta Princess of England, trans. Anne Floyd. London: Clay, 1722.

The Secret History of Henrietta, Princess of England together with the Memoirs of the Court of France for the Years 1688 and 1689, trans. J. M. Shelmerdine. New York: Dutton, 1929.

The Princesse de Clèves/The Princesse de Montpensier/The Comtesse de Tende, trans., intro. and notes Terence Cave. Oxford University Press, 1992.

The Princesse de Clèves, trans. John D. Lyons. London: Norton Critical Editions, 1994.

Further reading

Beasley, Faith, *Revising Memory: Women's Fiction and Memoirs in Seventeenth-Century France*. New Brunswick, NJ: Rutgers University Press, 1990.

Beasley Faith and Katherine Ann Jensen, *Approaches to Teaching the Princess of Clèves*. New York: MLA, 1998.

Campbell, John, *Questions of Interpretation in La Princesse de Clèves*. Amsterdam and Athens, GA: Rodopi, 1996.

DeJean, Joan, 'Lafayette's Ellipses: The Privileges of Anonymity', *Publications of the Modern Language Association* (October 1984), 884–902.

Henry, Patrick (ed.), *An Inimitable Example: The Case for the Princess of Clèves*. Washington, DC: Catholic University of America Press, 1992.

Miller, Nancy K., 'Emphasis Added: Plots and Plausibilities in Women's Fiction', *Publications of the Modern Language Association* 96 (1981), 36–48.

Scott, J. W., *La Princesse de Clèves*. London: Grant and Cutler. Critical Guides to French Texts. 1983.

La Force, Charlotte-Rose de Caumont de (1646?–1724), *Histoire secrète de Bourgogne*, 2 vols. 1694. (n)

Histoire secrète de Henry IV, roy de Castille. 1695. (n)

Histoire de Marguerite de Valois, reine de Navarre, soeur de François 1. 1696. (n)

Les Contes des contes. 2 vols. 1698. (s)

Gustave Vasa, Histoire de Suède. 1697–8. (n)

Les Jeux d'Esprit, ou La promenade de la Princesse de Conti à Eu, 1701. Ed. the Marquis de La Grange. Aubry, 1862. (s)

La Roche Guilhem, Anne de (1644–1710), *Histoire des favorites, contenant ce qui s'est passé de plus remarquable sous plusieurs règnes*. 2 vols. Amsterdam, 1697. (n)

Jacqueline de Bavière, comtesse de Hainaut. Nouvelle historique, Amsterdam, 1707. (n)

Translations
   The History of Female Favorites. London, 1772.

Lambert, Anne-Thérèse de Marguenat de Courcelles, marquise de (1647–1733), *Œuvres*, ed. Robert Granderoute. Champion 1990.

Réflexions nouvelles sur les femmes. 1727. Côté-Femmes, 1989.

Avis d'une mère à son fils et à sa fille. Gannot, 1728.

Translations
   The Works of the Marchioness de Lambert. Containing thoughts on various entertaining and useful subjects, reflections on education, on the writings of Homer and on various public events of the time. London: W. Owen 1749 (further editions: 1756, 1769, J. Potts 1770, W. Owen 1781).

   Advice of a Mother to her Daughter, in *The Young Lady's Pocket Library, or Parental Monitor*, 1790. Republished, with a new introduction by Vivien Jones, Thoemmes Press, 1995.

Further reading
   Beasley, Faith E., 'Anne-Thérèse de Lambert and the Politics of Taste', *Papers on Seventeenth-Century Literature* 19: 37 (1992), 337–44.

   Hine, Ellen McNiven, 'Madame de Lambert, her sources and her circle: on the threshold of a new age', *Studies on Voltaire and the Eighteenth Century* 102. Oxford: The Voltaire Foundation, 1973, pp. 173–90.

   Marchal, Roger, *Madame de Lambert et son milieu. Studies on Voltaire and the Eighteenth Century* 289. Oxford: The Voltaire Foundation, 1991.

Langlot-Dufresnoye, Mme, *Quinze ans au Brésil, ou excursions à la Diamantine*. Bordeaux: G. Chariol, 1861. (e)

Le Boursier du Coudray, Angélique Marguerite, *Abrégé de l'art des Accouchements*. 1759 (further editions: Saintes 1769, Châlons-sur-Marne 1773, Paris 1777 & 1785, and a Flemish version, Ypres, 1775). (e)

Further reading
   Gelbart, Nina Rattner, 'Books and the Birthing Business: The Midwife

Manuals of Madame du Coudray', in Goldsmith and Goodman (eds.), *Going Public*, pp. 79–96.

Leclerc, Annie, *Parole de femme*. Grasset, 1974. (n/e)

Hommes et femmes. Grasset, 1985. (n/e)

Le Mal de mère. Grasset, 1986. (e)

Origines. Grasset, 1988. (e, a)

Clé. Grasset, 1989. (s)

Exercices de mémoire. Grasset, 1992.

And a number of other works and articles.

Further reading

Alzon, Claude, 'Le féminisme d'Annie Leclerc: *Parole de femme* ou "propos d'homme"', in *Femme mythifiée, femme mystifiée*. Presses universitaires de France, 1978, 93–101.

Fallaize, Elizabeth, *French Women's Writing*, pp. 131–59 (includes translated extracts).

Leduc, Violette (1907–72), *L'Asphyxie*. Gallimard, 1946; 1973. (n)

L'Affamée. Gallimard, 1948; 1974. (n)

Ravages. Gallimard, 1955; 1966. (n)

Thérèse et Isabelle. 1955. Gallimard, 1966. (n)

La Vieille Fille et le mort, suivi de *Les Boutons garnis*. Gallimard, 1958. (n)

Trésors à prendre. Gallimard, 1960. (n)

La Bâtarde. Gallimard, 1964. (a)

La Femme au petit renard. Gallimard, 1965. (s)

La Folie en tête. Gallimard, 1970. (a)

Le Taxi. Gallimard, 1971. (s)

La Chasse à l'amour. Gallimard, 1973. (a)

Lettres à Simone de Beauvoir. *Les Temps modernes* 495 (October 1987). (l)

Translations

La Bâtarde. An Autobiography, trans. Derek Coltman, pref. Simone de Beauvoir, intro. Anny Brackx. 1965. London: Virago, 1985.

Ravages, trans. Derek Coltman. 1966. London: Panther, 1969. [Also includes *Thérèse andt Isabelle*.

Mad in Pursuit, trans. Derek Coltman. New York: Farrar, Strauss and Giroux, 1971; London: Rupert Hart-Davis, 1971.

The Taxi, trans. Helen Weaver. New York: Farrar, Strauss and Giroux, 1972; Toronto: Doubleday, 1972.

Thérèse et Isabelle, trans. Derek Coltman. New York: Farrar, Strauss and Giroux, 1967; Dell, 1967. Also in *Ravages*.

Further reading

Courtivron, Isabelle de, *Violette Leduc*. Boston, MA: Twayne, 1984.

Hall, Colette, *Violette Leduc La Mal*. Amsterdam: Rodopi, 1999.

Hughes, Alex, *Violette Leduc: Mothers, Lovers and Language*. London: Modern Humanities Research Association, 1994.

Maclean, Marie, *The Name of the Mother: Writing Illegitimacy*. London: Routledge, 1994, pp. 164–85.

Marson, Susan, *Le Temps de l'autobiographie: Violette Leduc ou la mort avant la lettre.* Saint Denis: Presses universitaires de Vincennes, 1998.

Sheringham, Michael, *French Autobiography, Devices and Desires: Rousseau to Perec.* Oxford: Clarendon Press, 1993, pp. 148–156, 210–19.

'The Sovereignty of Solitude and the Gift of Writing in Violette Leduc's La Folie en tête', in Tery Keefe and Edmund Smythe (eds.), *Autobiography and the Existential Self: Studies in Modern French Writing.* Liverpool University Press, 1994, pp. 127–46.

Le Masson le Golft, Mlle (1749–1826), *Lettres relatives à l'éducation*, 1788. (e)

Lenéru, Marie (1874–1918), *Les Affranchis.* Hachette, 1910. (d)

Le Redoutable. Hachette, 1912. (d)

Journal. 1922. (a)

La Paix. 1921. Grasset, 1922. (d)

Le Bonheur des autres. Bloud et Gay, 'Cahiers féminins', 1925.

La Maison sur le roc. 1924. Plon, 1927.

Les Lutteurs and *La Triomphatrice*, in *Pièces de théâtre.* Figuière, 1928. (d)

Leprince de Beaumont, Marie-Jeanne (1711–80), *Lettres diverses, et critiques.* Nancy, 1750. (e)

Éducation complète. London, 1753. (e)

Le Magasin des enfants, ou Dialogue d'une sage gouvernante avec ses élèves de la première distinction. 4 vols. Lyons, 1756. The classic version of *La Belle et la Bête* appears in the first volume. (e, s)

Lettres de Madame du Montier. 2 vols. Lyons, 1756. (n)

Le Magasin des adolescentes. London, 1760. (e)

Lettres d'Emérance à Lucie. 2 vols. Lyons, 1765. (n)

Mémoires de Madame la baronne de Batteville. Lyons, 1766. (n)

Instructions pour les jeunes dames qui entrent dans le monde, se marient, leurs devoirs dans cet état et envers leurs enfans, pour servir de suite au 'Magasin des adolescentes'. J. Nourse, 1764, later published as *Le Magasin des jeunes dames.*

Le Magasin des pauvres, artisans, domestiques, et gens de la campagne. Lyons, 1768. (e)

The *magasins* went into dozens of editions right through the eighteenth century and well into the nineteenth; they were translated into English and frequently reprinted.

Le Mentor moderne. 1772. (e)

Translations

Letters from Emerance to Lucy. 2 vols. London, 1766.

The Virtuous Widow, or Memoirs of the Baroness de Batteville. Dublin, 1767.

Lespinasse, Jeanne Julie Eléanore de (1732–76), *Lettres de Mlle de Lespinasse, écrites depuis l'année 1773 jusqu'à l'année 1776, suivis de deux chapitres dans le genre du* Voyage sentimental *de Sterne, par le même auteur.* 1809. (l, s)

Lettres de Mlle de Lespinasse, précédées de 'Mlle de Lespinasse' par Sainte-Beuve. Reprint of 1893 Garnier edition with a new preface by J. N. Pascal. Plan-de-la Tour: Éditions d'Aujourd'hui, 1978. (l)

Lévesque, Louise Cavelier (1703–45), *Le Prince des Aigues marines. Le Prince invisible.* 1722. (s)

L'Héritier de Villandon, Marie-Jeanne (1664–1734), *Œuvres meslées.* 1695. (p, s)

Bigarures ingénieuses, ou Recueil de diverses pièces galantes en prose et en vers. 1696. (p, s)

La Tour ténébreuse, et Les jours lumineux, contes anglois accompagnez d'historiettes, et tirez d'une ancienne chronique composée par Richard, surnommé Cœur de Lion, roy d'Angleterre. Avec le récit de diverses avantures de ce roy. 1705. (s)

Les caprices du destin, ou Recueil d'histoires singulières et amusantes arrivées de nos jours. 1718. (s)

Lintot, Catherine Cailleau de (1728?–?), *Trois nouveaux Contes des fées, avec une préface qui n'est pas moins sérieuse.* 1735. (s)

Lubert, Mlle de, *La Princesse Lionnette et le prince Coquerico, conte*, The Hague, 1743. (s)

Sec et Noir, ou La Princesse des fleurs et le prince des Autruches, conte, avec un discours préliminaire qui contient l'apologie des contes de fées. The Hague, 1743. (s)

Lussan, Marguerite de (1682–1758), *Histoire de la Comtesse de Gondez. Ecrite par elle-même.* 2 vols. 1727. (n)

Anecdotes de la Cour de Philippe-Auguste. 6 vols in 3. 1733–6. (n)

Macé, J., *L'Arithmétique de grand-papa: Histoire de deux petits marchands de pommes.* Hetzel, 1872. (ch)

Contes du petit château. Hetzel, 1895. (ch)

Les Soirées de ma tante Rosy. Hetzel, 1895. (ch)

Mancini, Hortense (1646–99), *Mémoires.* 1676. Ed. Gérard Doscot. Mercure de France, 1987. (a)

Mancini, Marie (1639–1715), *Mémoires.* 1678. Ed. Gérard Doscot. Mercure de France, 1987. (a)

Mansour, Joyce (1928–86), *Prose et poésie: œuvre complète*, ed. Hubert Nyssen. Arles: Actes Sud, 1991 (p)

Cris. Seghers, 1953. (p)

Rapaces. Seghers, 1960. (p)

Phallus et momies. La Louvière: Daily-Bul, 1969. (p)

Ça! Le Soleil noir, 1970.

Faire signe au machiniste. Le Soleil noir, 1977.

Le Grand jamais. Maeght, 1982. (p)

Translations

Flammes immobiles. 1985. (p)

Birds of Prey, trans. Albert Herzing. (S.I.): Perivale Press, 1979. [*Rapaces*]

Screams, trans. Serge Gavronsky. Buffalo, NY: Leave Books, 1992.

Further reading

Matthews, J. H., *Joyce Mansour.* Amsterdam: Rodopi, 1985.

Marguerite de Navarre (1492–1549) *La Coche*, ed. Robert Marichal. Geneva: Droz, 1971. (p)

Correspondance avec Briçonnet, 1521–4, vols. I, II, ed. Christine Martineau. Geneva: Droz, 1975–9. (l)

Les Dernières Poésies de Marguerite de Navarre, ed. Abel Lefranc. Armand Colin, 1896. (p)

L'Heptaméron, ed. Michel François. Garnier, 1967. (s)

Les Marguerites de la Marguerite des Princesses, ed. Félix Frank, 4 vols. Jouaust, 1873. (p)

Le Miroir de l'âme pécheresse, ed. Renja Salminen. Suomalainen Tiedeakatemia, 1979. (p)

La Navire, ou Consolation du Roi François 1er à sa soeur Marguerite, ed. Robert Marichal. Champion, 1956. (p)

Les Prisons, ed. Simone Glasson. Geneva: Droz, 1978. (p)

Théâtre profane, ed. Verdun L. Saulnier. Geneva: Droz, 1963. (d)

Translations

The Heptameron, ed. and trans. P. A. Chilton. Harmondsworth: Penguin, 1984,

Further reading

Cholakian, Patricia Francis, *Rape and Writing in the Heptameron of Marguerite de Navarre*. Carbondale, IL: Southern Illinois University Press, 1991.

Cottrell, Robert D., *The Grammar of Silence. A Reading of Margerite de Navarre's Poetry*. Washington, DC: Catholic University of America Press, 1986.

Lyons, John D. and Mary B. McKinley (eds.), *Critical Tales: New Studies of the Heptameron and Early Modern Culture*. Philadelphia, PA: University of Pennsylvania Press, 1993.

Mathieu-Castellani, Gisèle, *La Conversation conteuse: les nouvelles de Marguerite de Navarre*. Presses universitaires de France, 1992.

Marguerite de Valois (1553–1615), *Correspondance 1569–1614*, ed. Eliane Viennot. Champion, 1998.

Mémoires de Marguerite de Valois, ed. Yves Cazaux. Mercure de France, 1986.

Further reading

Boucher, Jacqueline, *Deux Épouses et reines à la fin du XVIe siècle: Louise de Lorraine et Marguerite de France*. Saint-Etienne: Publications de l'Université Saint-Etienne, 1995.

Cholakian, Patricia F., 'Marguerite de Valois and the Problematics of Self-Representation', in Larsen and Winn, *Renaissance Women Writers, French Texts/American Contexts*, pp. 67–81.

Garrisson, Janine, *Marguerite de Valois*. Fayard, 1994.

Viennot, Eliane, *Marguerite de Valois, histoire d'une femme, histoire d'un mythe*. Payot, 1993.

Marie de France, *Espurgatoire S. Patrice*. In *Das Buch vom 'Espurgatoire S. Patrice' der Marie de France und seine Quelle*, ed. Karl Warnke. Halle: Max Niemeyer, 1938. (p)

Les Lais de Marie de France, ed. Karl Warnke; trans. Laurence Harf-Lancner. 'Lettres gothiques.' Livre de Poche, 1990. (p)

Les Fables. Edition critique accompagnée d'une introduction, d'une traduction, des notes et d'un glossaire. 2nd edn rev. ed. Charles Brucker. Peeters, 1998. (p)

Translations

The Lais of Marie de France, trans. Robert Hanning and Joan Ferrante. Durham, NC: The Labyrinth Press, 1982.

The Lais of Marie de France, trans. Glyn S. Burgess and Keith Busby. Harmondsworth: Penguin, 1986.

Fables, ed. and trans. Harriet Spiegel. University of Toronto Press, 1987.

Saint Patrick's Purgatory. A Poem by Marie de France, trans. Michael J. Curley. Binghamton: Medieval and Renaissance Texts and Studies, 1993.

Further reading

Bruckner, Matilda, 'Textual Identity and the Name of a Collection: Marie de France's *Lais*', in her *Shaping Romance: Interpretation, Truth and Closure in Twelfth-Century French Fictions*. Philadelphia, PA: University of Pennsylvania Press, 1993, pp. 157–206.

Dufournet, Jean (ed.), *Amour et merveille: les lais de Marie de France*. Champion, 1995.

Freeman, Michelle, 'Marie de France's Poetics of Silence: The Implications for a Feminine *Translatio*', *PMLA* 99 (1984), 860–83.

Maréchal, Chantal A., *In Quest of Marie de France: A Twelfth Century Poet*. Lewiston: Edwin Mellin Press, 1992.

Pickens, Rupert, 'Marie de France and the Body Poetic' in Chance, *Gender and Text*, pp. 135–71.

Mercœur, Elisa (1808–35), *Œuvres complètes*. 3 vols. Chez Madame Veuve Mercœur et chez Pommeret et Guenot, 1843. (p)

Poésies de Elisa Mercoeur. Crapelet, 1829. (p)

Further reading

Greenberg, Wendy, 'Elisa Mercœur: the poetics of genius and the sublime', *Ninteenth-Century French Studies* (Fall–Winter, 1995–6), 84–96.

Uncanonical Women, pp. 43–68.

Michel, Louise (1830–1905), *A travers la vie et la mort: œuvre poétique*, ed. Daniel Armogathe, with Marion V. Piper. F. Maspero, 1982. (p)

Further reading

Greenberg, *Uncanonical Women*, pp. 161–70.

Michelet, Athénaïs (1828–99), *Mémoires d'une enfant*. Flammarion, 1866. (a)

Miremont, comtesse de, *Traité de l'éducation des femmes, et cours complet d'instruction*, 1779.

Montolieu, Elisabeth Jeanne Pauline Isabelle Polier de Bottens de Crousaz, baronne de (1751–1832), *Caroline de Lichtfield*. 2 vols. London and Paris, 1786.

Montpensier, Anne-Marie d'Orléans, duchesse de, 'La Grande Mademoiselle', (1627–93), *Mémoires*. 1718, in *Collection des mémoires relatifs à l'histoire de France*. M. Petitot, vols. XL–XLII, 1825. (a)

Motteville, Françoise Bertaut de (1621–89), *Mémoires pour servir à l'histoire d'Anne d'Autriche*. 1723. Charpentier, 1867. (a)

Murat, Henriette-Julie de Castelnau, comtesse de (1670–1716), *Mémoires de Madame la comtesse de M****. 1697. (a)

Contes de Fées. 1698. (s)

Les Nouveaux Contes de Fées. 1698. (s)

Histoires sublimes et allégoriques. 1699. (s)

Voyage de campagne. 1699. (s)

Les Lutins de Château de Kernosi. 1710. (s)

Translation

Memoires of the Countess of Dunois. London, 1699.

Na Castelloza, see *Trobairitz*

NDiaye, Marie (b. 1967), *Quant au riche avenir.* Minuit, 1985. (n)

Comédie classique. P.O.L., 1987. (n)

La Femme changée en bûche. Minuit, 1989. (n)

En famille. Minuit, 1990. (n)

Un temps de saison. Minuit, 1994. (n)

La Sorcière. Minuit, 1996. (n)

Hilda. Minuit, 1999. (d)

Translation

Among Family, trans. Heather Doyal. Tunbridge Wells: Angela Royal Publishing, 1997.

Nemours, Marie d'Orléans-Longueville, duchesse de (1625–1707), *Mémoires de M.L.D.D.N.* 1709, ed. Marie-Jeanne L'Héritier deVillandon. Ed. Micheline Cuénin. Mercure de France, 1990. (a)

Noailles, Anna de (1876–1933), *Le Cœur innombrable.* 1901. Pelletan, 1918. (p)

La Domination. Calmann-Lévy, 1905. (n)

Les Vivants et les morts. Fayard, 1913.

Les Forces éternelles. Fayard, 1920. (p)

Parmi les lettres qu'on n'envoie pas. 1922. (s)

L'Honneur de souffrir. Grasset, 1927. (p)

Derniers vers et poèmes d'enfance. Grasset, 1934. (p)

Offrande. Pres. Ph. Giraudon. Orphée/La Différence, 1991.

And other works.

Further reading

Bargenda, Angela, *La Poésie d'Anna de Noailles.* Mercure de France, 1976.

La Rochefoucauld, Edmée, *Anna de Noailles.* L'Harmattan, 1995.

Perche, Louis, *Anna de Noailles.* Seghers, Poètes d'aujourd'hui, 1969.

Noël, Marie (1883–1967), *Œuvres poétiques.* Stock, 1971; 1975.

Œuvres en prose. Stock, 1977.

Contes. Stock, 1987. (s)

Chansons et les heures. Sansot, 1920. With *Le Rosaire des joies.* Gallimard, 1983. (p)

Le Rosaire des joies. Crès, 1930. With *Chansons et les heures.* Gallimard, 983. (p)

Les Chants de la merci. Crès, 1930. (p)

Chants et psaumes d'automne. Stock, 1947; 1970; 1989. (p)

L'Œuvre poétique. Stock, 1956. (p)

Notes intimes. Stock, 1959. (p)

Chants d'arrière-saison. Stock, 1961; C. de Bartillat, 1993. (p)

And other writings.

Further reading

Tharsicius, Marie, *L'Expérience poétique de Marie Noël.* Montreal: Fides, 1962.

Oingt, Marguerite d' (**1240–1310**), *Les Œuvres de Marguerite d'Oingt*, ed. Antonin Duraffour, Pierre Gardette and Paulette Durdilly. Les Belles Lettres, 1965. (r, l)

Translation

The Writings of Margaret of Oingt, Medieval Prioress and Mystic (d. 1310).

Translated from the Latin and Francoprovençal with an Introduction, Essay, and Notes, ed. Renate Blumenfeld-Kosinski. Newburyport, MA: The Focus Information Group, 1990.

Further reading

Müller, Catherine, *Marguerite Porete et Marguerite d'Oingt de l'autre côté du miroir*. New York: Peter Lang, 1999.

Newman, Barbara, *Virile Women*, pp. 136–67.

Pascal, Jacqueline (**1625–61**), *Lettres, opuscules et mémoires de Madame Périer et de Jacqueline, sœurs de Pascal, et de Marguerite Périer, sa nièce*, ed. Faugère, 1845. (p)

Penrose, Valentine (**1898–1978**), *Herbes à la lune*. GLM, 1935.

Dons des féminines. Preface, Paul Éluard. GLM, 1937

Sorts de la lueur. GLM, 1937. (p)

Poèmes. GLM, 1937. (p)

Translation

Poems and Narrations, trans. Roy Edwards. Manchester: Carcanet Press, 1977.

Further reading

Colville, Georgia, 'Through an hour-glass lightly: Valentine Penrose and Alice Rahon Paalen', in R. King and B. McGuirk, *Reconceptions: Reading Modern French Poetry*, University of Nottingham, 1986, pp. 81–112.

Porete, Marguerite (**d. 1310**), *Le Mirouer des simples âmes*, ed. Romana Guarnieri. Turnholt: Brepols, 1986. (r, p)

Translations

The Mirror of Simple Souls, trans. Ellen L. Babinsky. New York: Paulist Press, 1993.

Le Miroir des âmes simples et anéanties et qui seulement demeurent en vouloir et désir d'amour, trans. Max Huot de Longchamp. Albin Michel, 1984.

Further reading

Babinsky, Ellen L., Introduction to her translation, *The Mirror of Simple Souls*, pp. 5– 20.

Müller, Catherine, *Marguerite Porete et Marguerite d'Oingt de l'autre côté du miroir*. New York: Peter Lang, 1999.

Pozzi, Catherine (**1882–1934**), *Poèmes*. Gallimard, 1987; 1989.

Œuvre poétique, ed. Lawrence Joseph. La Différence, 1988.

Poèmes. Editions de la Revue Mesures, 1934; expanded edition published by N.R.F., 1949; 1959. (p)

Agnès. 1927. La Différence, 1988. (s)

Peau d'âme. Corréa, 1935; La Différence, 1990. (p)

Correspondance 1924–5. La Différence, 1990. (l)

Journal 1913–34. Seghers, 1990. (a)

Journal de jeunesse 1839–1906. Verdier, 1995. (a)

Further reading
> Joseph, Lawrence A., *Catherine Pozzi: une robe couleur du temps.* La Différence, 1988.

Puisieux, Madeleine de (1720–98), *Conseils à une amie,* 1749 (republished 1750, 1751, 1752, 1755, 1882). (e)
> *Les Caractères, pour servir de suite aux Conseils,* 1ère partie, London (Paris) 1750, 2ème partie, London (Paris) 1751, reprinted 1752.
> *Réflexions et avis sur les défauts et ridicules à la mode, pour servir de suite aux Conseils à une amie.* Veuve V. Brunet, 1761.
> *Conseils à une amie, Studies on Voltaire and the eighteenth century* 329, Oxford, The Voltaire Foundation 1995, pp. 419–70.

Translation
> *Characters; or, reflections on the manners of the age.* London: M. Cooper, 1751.

Further reading
> Laborde, Alice M., *Diderot et Madame de Puisieux.* Stanford French and Italian Studies, 36. Saratoga, CA: Anma Libri, 1984.

Rachilde (Marguerite Eymery, 1860–1953), *Un siècle après!* 1880, Editions du Fourneau, collection 'Juvenilia', 1985. (d)
> *Monsieur Vénus.* 1884. Flammarion, 1977. (n)
> *Nono.* 1885. Mercure de France, 1994. (n)
> *La Tour d'amour.* Mercure de France, 1899. (p)
> *La Voix du sang.* 1890. In *Contes et nouvelles, suivis du Théâtre.* Mercure de France, 1900.
> *Théâtre.* A. Savine, 1891. (d)
> *Madame la Mort.* 1891. In *Contes et nouvelles, suivis du Théâtre.* Mercure de France, 1900. (d)
> *L'Araignée de cristal. Mercure de France,* June 1892, pp. 147–55.
> *L'Animale.* 1893. Préface d'Edith Silve. Mercure de France, 1993. (n)
> *La Jongleuse.* 1900. Des femmes, 1982. (n)
> *Contes et nouvelles, suivis du Théâtre.* Mercure de France, 1900. (s, p, d)
> *Le Meneur de louves.* Mercure de France, 1905. (p)
> *Pourquoi je ne suis pas féministe.* Editions de France, 1928. (e) And a large number of other writings, including novels, memoirs, criticism and poetry.

Translations
> *Monsieur Vénus,* trans. Madeleine Boyd. New York: Covici, Friede, 1929.
> *The Juggler,* trans. Melanie Hawthorne. New Brunswick, NJ: Rutgers University Press, 1990.

Further reading
> Dauphiné, Claude, *Rachilde, femme de lettres 1900.* Périgueux: Pierre Fanlac, 1985.
> Holmes, *French Women's Writing 1848–1994,* pp. 63–82.
> 'Monstrous Women: Rachilde's Erotic Fiction', in Hughes and Ince, *Desiring Writing.*

Radegund (525–87), 'The Fall of Thuringia' and 'Letter to Artarchis', trans. Thiébaux, *The Writings of Medieval Women,* pp. 30–6.

Further reading

Karen Cherewatuk, 'Radegund and Epistolary Tradition', in Cherewatuk and Wiethaus, *Dear Sister*, pp. 20–45.

Rahon, Alice (1904–87), *À même la terre*. Editions Surréalistes, 1936. (p)

Sablier couché. Editions Sagesse, 1938. (p)

Noir animal. Mexico, Editions Dolorès de la Rue, 1941. (p)

Further reading

Colville, Georgia, 'Through an hour-glass lightly: Valentine Penrose and Alice Rahon Paalen', in R. King and B. McGuirk, *Reconceptions: Reading Modern French Poetry*, University of Nottingham, 1986, pp. 81–112.

Redonnet, Marie, (b. 1948) *Le Mort & Cie*. P.O.L., 1985. (n)

Doublures. P.O.L., 1986. (n)

Forever Valley. Minuit, 1986. (n)

Splendid Hôtel. Minuit, 1986. (n)

Rose Mélie Rose. Minuit, 1987. (n)

Tir et Lir. Minuit, 1988. (n)

Mobie-Diq. Minuit, 1989. (d)

Silsie. Gallimard, 1990. (n)

Candy Story. P.O.L., 1992. (n)

Seaside. Minuit, 1992. (n)

Le Cirque Pandor, followed by *Fort Gambo*. P.O.L., 1994. (p)

Nevermore. P.O.L., 1994. (n)

Villa Rosa. Flohic, 1996. (n)

Translations

Forever Valley, with an interview, trans. Jordan Stump. Lincoln, NE: University of Nebraska Press, 1994.

Rose Mélie Rose with the *Story of the Triptych*, trans. Jordan Stump. Lincoln, NE: University of Nebraska Press, 1994.

Splendid Hotel, trans. Jordan Stump. Lincoln, NE: University of Nebraska Press, 1994.

Further reading

Bosshard, Marianne, 'Marie Redonnet et Chantal Chawaf', in Bishop, *Thirty Voices in the Feminine*, pp. 174–82.

Fallaize, Elizabeth, 'Filling in the Blank Canvas: Memory, Identity and Inheritance in the work of Marie Redonnet', *Forum for Modern Language Studies* 28 (October 1992), 320–34.

French Women's Writing, pp. 160–175 (includes some translated extracts).
Gollopentia, Sanda, 'Ni destin, ni vocation', in Bishop, *Thirty Voices in the Feminine*, pp. 87–101.

Reyes, Alina (b. 1956), *Le Boucher*. Seuil, 1988. (n)

Lucie au long cours. Seuil, 1990. (n)

Au corset qui tue. Gallimard, 1992. (n)

Quand tu aimes, il faut partir. Gallimard, 1993. (n)

Derrière la porte. R. Laffont, 1994. (n)

Il n'y a plus que la Patagonie. Julliard, 1994. (n)

La Nuit. Losfeld, 1994. (n)

Le Chien qui voulait me manger. Gallimard, 1996. (n)

Poupée, anale animale. Zulma, 1998. (n)

Corps de femme. Zulma, 1999. (n)

Moha m'aime. Gallimard, 1999. (n)

Translations

Lucie's Long Voyage, trans. David Watson. London: Methuen, 1990; 1992.

The Butcher, trans. David Watson. 1991. London: Mandarin Paperbacks, 1992; 1993.

The Fatal Bodice, trans. David Watson. London: Methuen, 1993.

When You Love You Must Depart, trans. David Watson. London: Methuen, 1995.

*Close Encounters: An Erotic Adventure in which You are the Hero*ine (abridged edition), trans. David Watson. London: Phoenix, 1996. (Previously published as *Behind Closed Doors.* London: Wiedenfeld and Nicholson, 1995.)

Further reading

Kasper, L. R., 'L'inquiétante ambivalence de la chair', in Bishop, *Thirty Voices in the Feminine,* pp. 166–74.

Riccoboni, Marie Jeanne de Heurles de Laboras Mézières (1713–92), *Œuvres complètes.* Foucault, 1818.

Lettres de Mistriss Fanni Butlerd à Milord Charles Alfred de Caitombridge, Amsterdam and Paris. 1757. (n)

L'Histoire de M le marquis de Cressy. Amsterdam and Paris. 1758. (n)

Lettres de milady Juliette Catesby à milady Henriette Campley, son amie. Amsterdam and Paris, 1759. (n)

Lettres d'Adélaïde de Dammartin, comtesse de Sancerre et de M. le comte de Nauci, son ami, suivie d'Aloïse de Livarot. 2 vols. Paris 1766. (n)

Lettres d'Elisabeth-Sophie de Vallière à Louise-Hortense de Causeleu son amie. 2 vols. Paris 1772.

'Suite de Marianne', in Pierre Carlet de Marivaux, *La Vie de Marianne,* ed. F. Deloffre. Garnier, 1963.

Lettres de Mistriss Fanni Butlerd à Milord Charles Alfred de Caitombridge, ed. Joan Hinde Stewart. Geneva: Droz, 1979.

L'Histoire de M le marquis de Cressy, ed. by Alix S. Deguise. Des femmes, 1987.

L'Histoire de M le marquis de Cressy, ed. by Olga B. Cragg, *Studies on Voltaire and the Eighteenth Century* 266. Oxford: Voltaire Foundation, 1989.

Lettres de milady Juliette Catesby à milady Henriette Campley, son amie, with preface by Sylvain Menant. Desjonquères, 1983.

Lettres de Mistriss Fanni Butlerd à Milord Charles Alfred de Caitombridge, ed. Raymond Trousson. Robert Laffont, collection 'Bouquins', 1996.

Translations

The History of the Marquis of Cressy. London: L. Pottinger, 1759.

Letters from Juliet, Lady Catesby, to her Friend, Lady Henrietta Campley, trans. Frances Brooke. 2nd edn London: R. & J. Dodsley, 1760.

The History of Miss Jenny Salisbury. London: T. Becket and P. A. De Hondt, 1764.

The Continuation of the Life of Marianne. To Which is Added The History of Ernestina, with Letters and Other Miscellaneous Pieces. London: T. Becket and P. A. De Hondt, 1766.

Letters from the Countess de Sancerre, to Count de Nancé, her Friend. London: T. Becket and P. A. De Hondt, 1767.

Letters from Elizabeth Sophia de Valiere to Her Friend Luisa Hortensia de Canteleu, 2 vols., trans. Mr. Maceuen. Dublin: J. Potts, J. Williams, T. Walker and C. Jenkins, booksellers, 1772.

Letters from Lord Rivers to Sir Charles Cardigan, and to Other English Correspondents, While He Resided in France, trans. Percival Stockdale. London: T. Becket, 1778.

The History of Christina, Princess of Swabia; and of Eloisa de Livarot. 2 vols. London: J. Stockdale, 1784.

Further reading

Cazenobe, Colette, 'Le féminisme paradoxal de Madame Riccoboni', *Revue d'histoire littéraire de la France* 88: 1 (Jan–Feb, 1988), 23–45.

Piau, Colette, 'L'Écriture féminine? A propos de Marie-Jeanne Riccoboni', *Dix-Huitième Siècle* 16 (1984), 369–85.

Stewart, Joan Hinde, *The Novels of Madame Riccoboni.* Chapel Hill, NC: North Carolina Studies in the Romance Languages and Literatures, 1976.

Risset, Jacqueline (b. 1936), *Jeu.* Seuil, 1971. (p)

La Traduction commence. Christian Bourgeois, 1976. (p)

Sept passages de la vie d'une femme. Flammarion, 1985. (p)

Marcelin Pleynet. Seghers, 1988. (e)

L'Amour de loin. Flammarion, 1989. (p)

Petits éléments de physique amoureuse. Gallimard, 1991. (p)

L'Anagramme du désir. Rome: Bulzoni, 1971; Fourbis, 1995. (e)

Dante: une vie. Flammarion, 1995. (e)

Puissances du sommeil. Seuil, 1997.

Translations

The Translation Begins, trans. Jennifer Moxley. Providence, RI: Burning Deck, 1996.

Further reading

Bishop, Michael, *Contemporary French Women Poets,* vol. 1, pp. 83–100.

'Denise Le Dantec, Esther Tellermann, Jacqueline Risset: Figuring the Real Differently', in *Thirty Voices in the Feminine,* pp. 128–40.

Robert, Marie Anne de Roumier, *La Paysanne philosophe, ou les aventures de Madame la marquise de ***.* Amsterdam, 1762. (n)

Voyages de milord Céton dans les sept planettes, ou le nouveau mentor. The Hague and Paris, 1765–6. (n)

Rochefort, Christiane (1917–98), *Le Démon des pinceaux.* Les Œuvres Libres, 1953.

Le Fauve et le rouge-gorge. Les Œuvres Libres, 1955.

Le Repos du guerrier. Grasset, 1958.

Les Petits Enfants du siècle. Grasset, 1961; 1979.

Les Stances à Sophie. Grasset, 1966.

Une Rose pour Morrison. Grasset, 1966.
Printemps au parking. Grasset, 1969.
C'est bizarre l'écriture. Grasset, 1970.
Archaos ou le jardin étincelant. Grasset, 1972.
Encore heureux qu'on va vers l'été. Grasset, 1975.
Les Enfants d'abord. Grasset, 1976; 1978.
Ma Vie revue et corrigée par l'auteur. Stock, 1978.
Quand tu vas chez les femmes. Grasset, 1982.
Le Monde est comme deux chevaux. Grasset, 1984.
La Porte du fond. Grasset, 1988.

Translations
Warrior's Rest, trans. Lowell Bair. New York: McKay, 1959.
Children of the Century. 1961
Stanzas to Sophie, 1963

Further reading
Holmes, Diana, *French Women's Writing 1848–1994*, pp. 246–65.
'Realism, Fantasy and Feminist Meaning: the Fiction of Christiane Rochefort', in Atack and Powrie, *Contemporary French Fiction by Women*, pp. 26–40.
Ophir, Anne, *Regards féminins: Condition féminine et création littéraire. Simone de Beauvoir, Christiane Rochefort, Claire Etcherelli*. Denoël, 1976.

Roches, Madeleine (1520–87) et Catherine (1542–87) des, *Les Missives*, ed. Anne Larsen. Geneva: Droz, 1999. (l)
Les Œuvres, ed. Anne R. Larsen. Geneva: Droz, 1993. (p, e, a)
Les Secondes Œuvres, ed. Anne R. Larsen. Geneva: Droz, 1998. (p, e, a)

Further reading
Jones, Ann Rosalind, 'Contentious Readings: Urban Humanism and Gender Difference in *La Puce de Madame Des-Roches (1582)*, *Renaissance Quarterly* 48: 1 (1995), 109–28.
Larsen, Anne R., 'Catherine des Roches, the Pastoral, and Salon Poetics', in Kuzinga and Winn, *Women Writers in Pre-Revolutionary France*, pp. 227–41.
Lazard, Madeleine, 'Des Dames des Roches: une dévotion réciproque et passionnée', in 'Autour de Madame de Sévigné', ed. Roger Duchêne, special issue of *Papers on Seventeenth-Century Literature*, 1997.
Sankovitch, Tilde, 'Catherine des Roches's *Le Ravissement de Proserpine*: A Humanist/Feminist Translation', in Larsen and Winn, *Renaissance Women Writers*, pp. 55–66.

Roland de la Platière (Marie-Jeanne or Manon Phlipon, 1754–93),
Œuvres de Jeanne-Marie Phlipon Roland, ed. Luc-Antoine Champagneux. 3 vols. Baidaut, 1800.
Appel à l'impartiale postérité, Paris 1795. Later editions published as *Mémoires*. The essay for the académie de Besançon, *Comment l'éducation des femmes pourroit contribuer à rendre les hommes meilleurs*, was first published in the 1864 edition of the *Mémoires*. M. P. Faugère, 1864, vol. 11, 333–57. (a)
Voyage en Suisse 1787, ed. G. R. de Beer, Neuchâtel: La Baconnière, 1937. (e)

Une éducation bourgeoise au XVIIIe siècle (Extrait des Mémoires suivi du Discours de Besançon). UGE, 10/18, 1964. (a)

Her correspondence was also published.

Translations

Works. London: J. Johnson, 1800.

An Appeal to Impartial Posterity Written during her Confinement in the Prisons of the Abbey, and St. Pélagie, in Paris. London, 1800.

The Memoirs of Madame Roland, a Heroine of the French Revolution, trans. and ed. Evelyn Shuckburgh. Mt Kisco, NY: Meyer Bell, 1990.

Further reading

Cornevin, Marianne, *La véritable Madame Roland.* Gérard Watelet, 1989.

Roussel, Nelly (or Nelly-Roussel, Mme Henri Godet, 1878–1922),
Par la Révolte. Imprimerie L. et A. Cresson, n.d. (d)

Pourquoi elles vont á l'église. N. Roussel, *ca* 1910, in *La Mère éducatrice* 11, Nov 1923. (d)

La Faute d'Ève. In *Le Mouvement féministe* 4 (15 September 1913); and *La Libre pensée internationale* (1 June 1916). (d)

Sagan, Françoise (b. 1935), *Bonjour tristesse.* Julliard, 1954. (n)

Translations

Bonjour tristesse, trans. Irene Ash. New York: Dutton, 1955.

Sand, George (1804–76), *Indiana.* 1832. Ed. P. Salomon. Garnier, 1985. (n)

Valentine. 1832. Ed. A. Alquier. Meylan: Aurore, 1988. (n)

Lélia. 1833. Ed. B. Didier. 2 vols. Meylan: Aurore, 1987; ed. P. Reboul. Garnier, 1960. (n)

Mauprat. 1837. Ed. Cl. Sicard. Garnier-Flammarion, 1985, ed. J.-P. Lacassagne. Gallimard, 1981. (n)

Consuelo. 1842–3. *La comtesse de Rudolstadt.* 1843–4. Eds. S. Vierne and René Bourgeois. Meylan: Aurore, 1983. (n)

La Mare au diable. 1846. Eds. P. Salomon and J. Mallion. Garnier, 1981. (n)

*François le Champi.*1850. Eds. P. Salomon and J. Mallion.Garnier, 1981. (n)

*Les Maîtres sonneurs.*1853. Eds. P. Salomon and J. Mallion.Garnier, 1981; ed. M.-C. Bancquart. Gallimard, 1979. (n)

Histoire de ma vie. 1854–5. Stock, 1985. (a)

Correspondance. 6 vols. Calmann-Lévy, 1881–4. (l)

And many other works.

Translations

Indiana, trans. Sylvia Raphael; intro. Naomi Schor. Oxford University Press, World Classics, 1994.

Valentine, trans. George Burnham Ives. Chicago, IL: Academy, 1978.

Lelia, trans. Maria Espinosa. Bloomington, IN: Indiana University Press, 1978.

Mauprat, trans. Stanley Young; intro. Diane Johnson. New York: Da Capo, 1977.

Consuelo: A Romance of Venice, trans. Fayette Robinson. New York: Da Capo, 1979.

The Haunted Pool, trans. Frank H. Potter. Berkeley, CA: Shameless Hussy, 1976.

François le Champi, trans. Eirene Collis; intro. Dorothy Wynne Zimmerman. Lincoln, NA: University of Nebraska Press, 1977.

The Story of My Life, trans. Dan Hofstadter. London: Folio Society, 1984.

Correspondence, trans. Francis Steegmuller and Barbara Bray. London: Harvill, 1993.

The Master Pipers, trans. Rosemary Lloyd. Oxford University Press, World Classics, 1994.

Other works have also been translated.

Further reading

Naginski, Isabelle Hoog, *George Sand. Writing for her Life*. New Brunswick, NJ: Rutgers University Press, 1990.

Schor, Naomi, *George Sand and Idealism*. New York: Columbia University Press, 1993.

Van Rossum Guyon, Françoise (ed.), *George Sand, une œuvre multiforme: recherches nouvelles*. Amsterdam: Rodopi, 1991.

Saint-Amant, Mme, *Voyage en Californie, 1850–1*. Garnier Frères, 1851. (e)

Sarraute, Nathalie (Nathalie Tcherniak, 1900–99), *Œuvres complètes*, ed. Jean-Yves Tadié, with Viviane Forrester, Ann Jefferson, Valerie Minogue and Arnaud Rykner. Bibliothèque de la Pléiade. Gallimard, 1996.

Théâtre. Gallimard, 1982. (d)

Tropismes. Denoël, 1939. (s)

Portrait d'un inconnu. Robert Marin, 1948. (n)

Martereau. Gallimard, 1953. (n)

L'Ere du soupçon. Gallimard, 1956. (e)

Le Planétarium. Gallimard, 1959. (n)

Les Fruits d'or. Gallimard, 1963. (n)

Le Silence, followed by 'Le Mensonge'. 1964. Gallimard, 1967 and 1993. (d)

Le Mensonge. 1966. In *Théâtre*. (d)

Entre la vie et la mort. Gallimard, 1968. (n)

Isma ou ce qui s'appelle rien. 1970. Followed by 'Le Silence' and 'Le Mensonge'. Gallimard, 1970. In *Théâtre*. (d)

Vous les entendez? Gallimard, 1972. (n)

'disent les imbéciles'. Gallimard, 1976. (n)

C'est beau. Gallimard, 1978. In *Théâtre*. (d)

L'Usage de la parole. Gallimard, 1980. (n)

Pour un oui, pour un non. Gallimard, 1982. (d)

Enfance. Gallimard, 1983. (a)

Tu ne t'aimes pas. Gallimard, 1989. (n)

Ici. Gallimard, 1995.

Ouvrez. Gallimard, 1997.

Translations

Collected Plays, trans. Maria Jolas and Barbara Wright. London: Calder, 1980.

Tropisms, trans. Maria Jolas. New York: George Braziller, 1963.

Do you hear them?, trans. Maria Jolas. New York: George Braziller, 1959.

Martereau, trans. Maria Jolas. New York: George Braziller, 1959.

The Planetarium, trans. Maria Jolas. New York: George Braziller, 1960.

The Age of Suspicion, trans. Maria Jolas. New York: George Braziller, 1963.

The Golden Fruits, trans. Maria Jolas. New York: George Braziller, 1964.

Between Life and Death, trans. Maria Jolas. London: Calder and Boyars, 1975; reprinted 1984.

'fools say', trans. Maria Jolas. New York: George Braziller, 1977.

The Use of Speech, trans. Barbara Wright. London: Calder, 1983.

Childhood, trans. Barbara Wright. London: Calder, 1984.

Further reading

Barbour, Sarah, *Nathalie Sarraute and the Feminist Reader*. Lewisburg, PA: Bucknell University Press, 1993.

Gratton, J., 'Autobiography and Fragmentation: The Case of Nathalie Sarraute's *Enfance*', *Nottingham French Studies*, 34 (1995) 31–40.

Knapp, Bettina, *Nathalie Sarraute*. Amsterdam: Rodopi, 1994.

Minogue, Valerie. *Nathalie Sarraute and the War of the Words*. Edinburgh University Press, 1981.

'Fragments of a childhood: Nathalie Sarraute's *Enfance*', *Romance Studies* 9 (1986), 71–83.

Pierrot, Jean, *Nathalie Sarraute*. Corti, 1990.

Rykner, Arnaud, *Nathalie Sarraute*. Seuil, 1991.

Scudéry, Madeleine, Mademoiselle de (1607–1701), *Ibrahim ou l'Illustre Bassa*. 4 vols. Sommaville, 1641. (n)

Les Femmes illustres ou Les Harangues héroïques. Sommaville and Courbé, 1642 (Part I); Quinet and Sercy, 1644 (Part II). (s)

Artamène ou Le Grand Cyrus. 10 vols. Courbé, 1642; Geneva: Slatkine Reprints, 1972. (n)

Clélie, Histoire romaine. 10 vols. Courbé, 1654–60. Geneva: Slatkine Reprints, 1973. (n)

Célinte, Nouvelle première. Courbé, 1661. Reprinted: Nizet, 1979. (s)

Mathilde d'Aguilar. Martin and Eschart, 1667. Geneva: Slatkine Reprints, 1979. (s)

La Promenade de Versailles. Barbin, 1669. Geneva: Slatkine Reprints, 1980. (e)

Discours sur la gloire. Le Petit, 1671. (e)

Conversations sur divers sujets. 2 vols. Barbin, 1680. (e)

Conversations nouvelles sur divers sujets. 2 vols. Barbin, 1684. (e)

La Morale du monde ou conversations. 2 vols. Mortier, 1686. (e)

Entretiens de morale. 2 vols. Anisson, 1692. (e)

Translations

Ibrahim or the Illustrious Bassa, an Excellent New Romance, trans. Henry Cogan. London, 1652.

Artamenes, or the Grand Cyrus, an Excellent New Romance. London, 1653–5.

Clelia, an Excellent New Romance, trans. J. Davies and Havers. London, 1678.

An Essay upon Glory, trans. by a person of the same sex. London, 1708.

Conversations upon Several Subjects, trans. F. Spence. 2 vols. London, 1683.

Further reading

Aronson, Nicole, *Mademoiselle de Scudéry, ou, Le Voyage au pays de Tendre*. Fayard, 1986.

DeJean, *Tender Geographies.*

Goldsmith, Elizabeth C., 'Excess and Euphoria in Madeleine de Scudéry's "Conversations"', in Goldsmith and Goodman, *Exclusive Conversations*, pp. 41–75.

Greenberg, Caren, 'The World of Prose and Female Self-Inscription: Scudéry's *Les Femmes illustres*', *L'Esprit créateur* 23 (1983), 37–43.

Rathery and Boutron, *Mademoiselle de Scudéry: Sa vie et sa correspondance.* 1873. Slatkine Reprints, 1971.

Ségur, Sophie Rostopchine, Comtesse de (1799–1874), *Nouveaux Contes de fées.* 1857. Hachette, 1920. (ch)

Quel Amour d'enfant! Hachette, 1875. (ch)

Les Malheurs de Sophie. Hachette, 1886. (ch)

Un bon petit diable. Hachette, 1901. (ch)

Histoire de Blondine. Livre de poche, 1982 (ch) And many other works for children.

Translations

Fairy Tales for Little Folks, trans. Mrs Chapman – with her daughter. Philadelphia, PA: Porter and Coates, 1869.

Sophie, The Story of a Bad Little Girl, trans. Marguerite Fellowes Melcher. New York: Kopf, 1929.

There are more translations of these and other works.

Further reading

Kreyder, Laura, *L'Enfance des saints et d'autres. Essai sur la Comtesse de Ségur.* Fasano: Schena-Nizet, 1987.

Vinson, Marie-Christine, *L'Éducation des petites filles chez la Comtesse de Ségur.* Lyons: Presses universitaires de Lyon, 1987.

Serena, Carla (d. 1884), *Mon voyage, une Européenne en Perse.* Maurice Dreyfous, 1881. (e)

Séverine (1855–1929), *Line.* Crès, 1921. (n)

Sévigné, Marie de Rabutin-Chantal, marquise de (1626–96), *Correspondance*, ed. Roger Duchêne. 3 vols. Gallimard, Bibliothèque de la Pléiade, 1972–8. (l)

Lettres, ed. Émile Gérard-Gailly. 3 vols. Gallimard, Bibliothèque de la Pléiade, 1953–7. (l)

Lettres, ed Bernard Raffali. Garnier-Flammarion, 1976. (l)

Lettres. Choix, ed. Jacqueline Duchêne. Livre de poche, 1987. (l)

Translations

Selected Letters, trans. Leonard Tancock. Harmondsworth: Penguin, 1982.

Further reading

Farrell, Michèle Longino, *Performing Motherhood: The Sévigné Correspondence.* Hanover, NH: University Press of New England, 1991.

Williams, Charles G. S., *Madame de Sévigné.* Boston, MA: Twayne, 1981.

Siéfert, Louisa (1845–77), *Souvenirs rassemblés par sa mère; poésies inédites.* Paris: G. Fichbacher, 1883 (p)

Rayons perdus. Paris: Lemerre, 1869 (p)

Further reading

Greenberg, *Uncanonical Women*, pp. 69–102.

Souza, Adélaïde Marie Emilie Filleul, comtesse de Flahaut, marquise de (1761–1836), *Adèle de Sénange, ou Lettres de Lord Sydenham*, Paris, 1794. (n)

Emilie et Alphonse, ou le danger de se livrer. Paris: Pougens, 1799. (n)

Adèle de Sénange, ou Lettres de Lord Sydenham, ed. Raymond Trousson. Robert Laffont, collection 'Bouquins', 1996. (n)

Staël, Germaine Necker, Mme de (1766–1817), *Œuvres complètes de Madame la baronne de Staël-Holstein.* Geneva, Slatkine Reprints, 1967.

De la littérature, eds. Gérard Gengembre and Jean Goldzink. Flammarion, 1991. (e)

Delphine, edn. féministe, Claudine Herrmann. Des femmes, 1981; Folio, 1976; (n)

Corinne, ou, L'Italie, ed. Simone Balayé. Gallimard, 1985; Edn féministe, Claudine Herrmann. Des femmes, 1979. (n)

De l'Allemagne, ed. André Monchoux. M Didier, 1956. (e)

Considérations sur la Révolution francaise, intro. Jacques Godechot. Tallandier, 1983. (e)

Correspondance, ed., Béatrix d'Andlau. Gallimard, 1979. (l)

Correspondance générale, ed. Béatrice W. Jasinski. J.-J. Pauvert, 1960–78; Hachette, 1982–5. (l)

Correspondance: Madame de Staël, Charles de Villers, Benjamin Constant, ed. Kurt Kloocke *et al.* Frankfurt am Main and New York: P. Lang, 1993. (l)

Des Circonstances actuelles qui peuvent terminer la Révolution et des principes qui doivent fonder la République en Franc. Critical edn, Lucia Omacini. Geneva: Droz, 1979. (e)

De l'influence des passions sur le bonheur des individus et des nations. Lausanne: J. Mourer, 1796. (e)

Du Directoire au Consulat: 1er décembre 1796–15 décembre 1800, ed. Béatrice W. Jasinski. J.-J. Pauvert, 1976. (e)

Le Leman et l'Italie, 19 mai 1804–9 novembre 1805, ed. Béatrice W. Jasinski. Paris: Hachette, 1985. (e)

Lettres a Ribbing, pref. comtesse Jean de Pange, ed. Simone Balayé. Gallimard, 1960. (l)

Lettres de Mezery et de Coppet: 16 mai 1794–16 mai 1795, ed., Beatrice W. Jasinski. J.-J. Pauvert, 1968. (l)

Lettres d'une nouvelle républicaine: 17 mai 1795–fin novembre 1796, ed. Béatrice W. Jasinski. J.-J. Pauvert, 1972. (e)

Translations

An Extraordinary Woman: Selected Writings of Germaine de Staël, trans. and intro. Vivian Folkenflik. New York: Columbia University Press, 1987.

Corinne, or Italy, trans. Aviel H. Goldberger. New Brunswick, NJ: Rutgers University Press, 1987.

Further reading

Balayé, Simone, *Madame de Staël, écrire, lutter, vivre.* Geneva: Droz, 1994.

Goldberger, Auriel, Madelyn Gutwirth and Karyna Szmurlo (eds.), *Germaine de Staël: Crossing the Borders*. New Brunswick, NJ: Rutgers University Press, 1991.

Isbell, John, 'Madame de Staël, écrits retrouvés', *Cahiers staëliens* 46, (1994–5), 1–114.

Starkoff, Véra, *L'Amour libre*. PV Stock, 1902. (d)

L'Issue. PV Stock. 1903. (d)

Le Petit Verre. PV Stock, 1904. (d)

And other unpublished plays.

Tastu, Aimable (1795–1885), *Poésies*. Dupont, 1826. (p)

Tencin, Claudine-Alexandrine Guérin de (1682–1749), *Mémoires du comte de Comminge*. The Hague, 1735. (n)

Le Siège de Calais, nouvelle historique. La Haye, 1739. (n)

Les Malheurs de l'amour. 2 vols. Amsterdam and Paris, 1747. (n)

Anecdotes de la cour et du règne d'Edouard II, Roi d'Angleterre. 1776. The first two parts are by Tencin, the last one by Elie de Beaumont. (n)

Mémoires du comte de Comminge, ed. Jean de Cottignies. Lille: René Giard, 1969.

Le Siège de Calais, nouvelle historique, pref. Pierre-Jean Rémy. Desjonquères, 1983.

Mémoires du comte de Comminge. Intro. Michel Delon. Desjonquères, 1985.

Mémoires du comte de Comminge, ed. Raymond Trousson. Robert Laffont, collection 'Bouquins', 1996.

Translations

Memoirs of the Count of Comminge. London: G. Kearsley, 1774.

The Female Adventurers. 2 vols. Dublin: P. Wilson and J. Potts, 1776.

The Siege of Calais by Edward of England. An Historical Novel. 1740. New York: Garland, 1974.

Further reading

Jones-Day, Shirley, 'Madame de Tencin. An Eighteenth-Century Novelist', in Jacobs *et al.*, *Woman and Society in Eighteenth-Century France*.

Thomas, Mona (Monique, b. 1952), *Loin du grenier*, in *Avant-Scène-Théâtre* 743 (1 February, 1984). (d)

Hélène, *Avant-Scène-Théâtre* 771 (1 June 1985). (d)

Tinayre, Marcelle (1872–1948), *La Maison du péché*. Calmann-Lévy, 1902. (n)

La Rebelle. Calmann-Lévy, 1905. (n)

Hellé. Calmann-Lévy, 1913. (n)

L'Ombre de l'amour. Calmann-Lévy, 1932. (n)

Gérard et Delphine. Flammarion, 1936. (n)

Tristan, Flora (1803–44), *Les Pérégrinations d'une paria*. 1833–4. Maspéro, 1983.

Promenades dans Londres: ou, L'aristocratie et les prolétaires anglais. 1840. Ed. Francois Bedarida. Maspéro, 1978. (e)

Union ouvrière: suivie de lettres de Flora Trista. 1843. Eds. Daniel Armogathe and Jacques Grandjonc. Des femmes, 1986. (e, l)

Le Tour de France: état actuel de la classe ouvrière sous l'aspect moral, intellectuel et mate-

riel, ed. Jules-L. Puech, pref. Michel Collinet, intro. Stéphane Michaud. Seuil, 1980.(e)

Lettres, ed. Stéphane Michaud. Seuil, 1980. (l)

Translations

The London Journal of Flora Tristan or the Aristocracy and Working Classes of England, trans. Jean Hawkes. London: Virago, 1982.

The Worker's Union, trans. Beverley Livingston. Urbana, IL: University of Illinois Press, 1983.

Peregrinations of a Pariah, trans. Jean Hawkes. London: Virago, 1986.

Further reading

Michaud, Stéphane, *Flora Tristan (1803–44)*. Éditions Ouvrières, 1984.

Michaud, Stéphane (ed.), *Un Fabuleux Destin: Flora Tristan*. Dijon: Éditions –universitaires de Dijon, 1985.

Trobairitz and Female *Trouvères*, *Songs of the Woman Troudadours*, ed. and trans. Matilda Tomaryn Bruckner, Laurie Shepard and Sarah White. New York: Garland, 1995.

Songs of the Troubadours and Trouvères, eds. Samuel N. Rosenberg, Margaret Switten and Gérard Le Vot. New York: Garland, 1998.

Further reading

Bruckner, Matilda T. 'Na Castelloza, *Trobairitz* and Troubadour Lyric', *Romance Notes* 25, 3 (1985), 239–253.

Coldwell, Maria V., '*Jougleresses* and *Trobairitz*: Secular Music in Medieval France', in Jane Bowers and Judith Tick (eds.), *Women Making Music: The Western Art Tradition, 1150–1950*. Urbana, IL: University of Illinois Press, 1986, pp. 39–61.

Paden, William D., *The Voice of the Trobairitz: Perspectives on the Women Troubadours*. Philadelphia, PA: University of Pennsylvania Press, 1989.

Vichy, Diane de, *Un hiver en Provence: Lettres de Diane de Vichy à ses enfants 1767–8*, ed., Jean Noël Pascal. Centre d'Études foréziennes, 1980. (l)

Villedieu, Marie Catherine Desjardins, Madame de (1640–83), *Œuvres complètes*. Geneva: Slatkine, 1971.

Alcidamie. 2 vols. Barbin, 1661. (n)

Manlius. (d)

Lisandre, Nouvelle par Mlle des Jardins. Varbin, 1663. (n)

Recueil de poésie par Mlle des Jardins, augmenté de plusieurs pièces et lettres en cette dernière édition. Barbin, 1664. (p, s, l)

Le Favory, tragi-comédie par Mlle des Jardins. Billaine, 1666. (d)

Anaxandre, Nouvelle par Mlle des Jardins. Barbin, 1667. (n)

Carmente, Histoire grecque par Mlle des Jardins. 2 vols. Barbin, 1667. (n)

Annales galantes. 1670. Geneva: Slatkine, 1979. (n)

Lettres et billets galants. 1668. Publications de la Société d' Étude du XVIIᵉ siècle, 1975. (l)

Recueil de quelques lettres et relations galantes. Barbin, 1668. (l)

Cléonice, ou le roman galant. Barbin, 1669. Geneva: Slatkine, 1979. (n)

Le Journal amoureux. 6 vols. Barbin, 1669–70. (n)

Annales galantes. Barbin, 1670. (n)

Les Amours des grands hommes. 4 vols. Barbin, 1671. (n)

Les Exilés. 6 vols. Barbin, 1672–3. (n)

Les Galanteries grenadines. 2 vols. Barbin, 1673. (n)

Mémoires de la vie d'Henriette Sylvie de Molière. 6 vols. 1674. Tours: Université de Tours, Publication du Groupe d'Étude du xviie siècle, 1977. (n)

Les Désordres de l'amour. 1675. Geneva: Droz and Paris: Minard, 1970; Washington, DC: University Press of America, 1982. (n)

Portrait des faiblesses humaines. Barbin, 1685. (n)

Annales galantes de Grèce. 2 vols. Barbin, 1687. (n)

Le Portefeuille. 1702. Ed. J.-P. Homan. Exeter: Exeter University Press, 1979.

Correspondance, lettres et billets galants, ed. Micheline Cuénin. Publications de la Société d'Étude du xviie siècle, 19. (l)

Translations

Love Journals. London: Ratcliff and Daniel, 1671. (n)

The Loves of Sundry Philosophers and Other Great Men. 1673. (n)

The Memoirs of the Life and Rare Adventures of Henrietta Sylvia Moliere. London: W. Crooke, 1677. (n)

The Disorders of Love. London: James Magnes and Richard Bentley, 1677. (n)

Further reading

Beasley, Faith, 'Villedieu's Metamorphosis of Judicious History: *Les Désordres de l'amour*', *Biblio* 17: 37 (1987), 393–406. This number of *Biblio* has a number of other articles on Villedieu.

Cuénin, Micheline, *Roman et société sous Louis XIV: Madame de Villedieu.* 2 vols. Champion, 1979.

Lalande, Roxanne (ed.), *A Labor of Love: Critical Reflections on the Writing of Mme de Villedieu.* Westport, CT: Greenwood Press, forthcoming.

Miller, Nancy K., 'Tender Economies: Mme de Villedieu and the Costs of Indifference', *L'Esprit créateur* 23 (1983), 80–93.

Vilmorin, Louise de (1902–69), *Poèmes*, pref. André Malraux. Gallimard, 1970. (p)

Fiançailles pour rire. Gallimard, 1939.

Le Lit à colonnes. Gallimard, 1941; 1974; Livre de Poche, 1970. (n)

La Sable du sablier. Gallimard, 1945.

L'Alphabet des aveux. Gallimard, 1955. (p)

La Lettre dans un taxi. Gallimard, 1958; 1973. (n) And other writings.

Further reading

Vilmorin, Audrée de, *Essai sur Louise de Vilmorin.* Seghers, 1972.

Villeneuve, Gabrielle-Suzanne Barbot de Gallon de (1695–1755), *La Jeune Amériquaine et les contes marins.* 2 vols. 1740. (This contains the original version of *La Belle et la bête*.) (s)

La Jardinière de Vincennes, London and Paris, 1752.

Further reading

Robert, Raymonde, *Le conte de fées littéraire en France de la fin du xviie à la fin du xviiie siècle.* Presses universitaires de Nancy, 1982.

Vivien, Renée (Pauline Tarn, 1877–1909), *Poèmes de R . . . V . . . .* 2 vols. Lemerre, 1923–4.

Études et préludes. Lemerre, 1901. (p)

Cendres et poussières. Lemerre, 1902.

Brumes de fjords. Lemerre, 1902. (p)

Du vert au violet. Lemerre, 1903. (p)

Évolutions. Lemerre, 1903. (p)

La Vénus des aveugles. 1904. Éd. Luc Decaunes. La Bartavelle, 1991. (p)

A l'Heure des mains jointes. Lemerre, 1906. (p)

Chansons pour mon ombre. (Published under the name Pauline Tarn). Lemerre, 1907. (p)

Flambeaux éteints. Sansot, 1907. (p)

Dans un coin de violettes. Sansot, 1908. (p)

Sillages. Sansot, 1908. (p)

Le Vent des vaisseaux. Sansot, 1909. (p)

Haillons. Sansot, 1910. (p)

Vagabondages. Sansot, 1917. (p)

La Dame et la louve. (s)

Une femme m'apparut (n)

Anne Boleyn (n)

Translations

The Woman of the Wolf and Other Stories, trans. Karla Jay and Yvonne M. Klein. New York: Gay Presses of New York, 1983.

Further reading

Blankley, Elyse, 'Return to Mytilène: Renée Vivien and the City of Women', in Susan Squier (ed.), *Women Writers and the City: Essays in Feminist Literary Criticism.* Knoxville, TN: University of Tennessee Press, 1984, pp. 45–67.

Holmes, *French Women's Writing 1848–1994*, pp. 83–104.

Sanders, Virginie, *Vertigineusement j'allais vers les étoiles: la poésie de Renée Vivien.* Amsterdam: Rodopi, 1991.

Voilquin, Suzanne (1801–77), *Souvenirs d'une fille du peuple: La Saint-Simonienne en Égypte.* Maspéro, 1978. (a)

Wittig, Monique (b. 1935), *L'Opoponax.* Minuit, 1964.

Les Guérillères. Minuit, 1969.

Le Corps lesbien. Minuit, 1973.

Brouillon pour un dictionnaire des amantes. Grasset, 1976.

'Le Lieu de l'action', *Digraphe* 32 (1984), 69–75. (e)

Virgile, non. Minuit, 1985.

Le Voyage sans fin, in *Vlasta* 4 (suppl.), 1984; Distique, 1985. (d) And other works, including a large number of articles.

Translations

Les Guérillères, trans. David Le Vay, London: Peter Owen, 1971; New York: Avon, 1973; Boston: Beacon, 1985.

The Lesbian Body, trans. David Le Vay, London: Peter Owen, 1975; New York: Avon, 1976.

The Opoponax, trans. H. Weaver. New York: Simon and Schuster, 1976.
'The Place of Action', in *Three Decades of the New French Novel.* Urbana, IL: University of Illinois Press, 1986.
Across the Acheron, trans. Margaret Crosland and David Le Vay. London: Peter Owen, 1987. [*Virgile, non*]
The Straight Mind and Other Essays. London: Harvester Wheatsheaf, 1992.

Further reading

Lewis, Valerie Hannagan, 'Warriors and Runaways: Minique Wittig's *Le Voyage sans fin*, *Theatre Research International* 23; 3 (1998), 200–4.

Elaine Marks, 'Lesbian Intertextuality', in Marks and Stambolian, *Homosexualities*, 353–77.

Ostrovsky, Erika, *The Fiction of Monique Wittig.* Carbondale, IL: Southern Illinois University Press, 1991.

Stampanoni, Susanna, 'Un nom pour tout le monde: *L'Opoponax* de Monique Wittig', *Vlasta* 4 (1985), 89–95. This number of *Vlasta* is devoted to Wittig.

Wenzel, Hélène Vivienne., 'The Text as Body/Politics: An Appreciation of Monique Wittig's Writing in Context', *Feminist Studies* 7: 2 (1981) 264–87.

Yourcenar, Marguerite (Marguerite Antoinette Jeanne Marie Cleenwerke de Crayencourt (1903–87), *Théâtre.* 2 vols. Gallimard, 1971. (d)

Œuvres romanesques. 2 vols. Gallimard, Bibliothèque de la Pléiade, 1982
Essais et mémoires. Gallimard, Bibliothèque de la Pléiade, 1991.
Le Jardin des chimères-Icare. Perrin et Cie, 1921. (d)
Alexis; ou le Traité du vain combat. 1929; rev. 1965; with *Coup de Grâce*, Gallimard, 1978. (n)
Denier du rêve. 1934; rev. 1959; Gallimard, 1971. (n)
La Mort conduit l'attelage. Grasset, 1934. (n)
Feux. 1936; rev., Gallimard, 1974. (s/p)
Les Songes et les sorts. Grasset, 1938. ( )
Nouvelles orientales. Gallimard, 1938; rev. 1963; rev. 1975. (s)
Le Coup de grâce. Gallimard, 1939; rev. 1978, with *Alexis.* (n)
Mémoires d'Hadrien. 1951. Gallimard, 1971. (e)
Dialogue dans le marécage. 1932. Gallimard, 1988. In *Théâtre*, I. (d)
Electre ou la Chute des masques. 1947. Plon, 1957. In *Théâtre*, II. (d)
Les Charités d'Alcippe. 1956. Revised and expanded edition published by Gallimard, 1984. (p)
Sous Bénéfice d'inventaire. Gallimard, 1962; rev. 1978. (e)
Le Mystère d'Alceste, followed by *Qui n'a pas son minotaure?* Plon, 1963. (d)
L'Œuvre au noir. Gallimard, 1968. (n)
Souvenirs pieux, followed by *L'Album de Fernande.* 1973. Gallimard, 1974. [*Le Labyrinthe du monde*, I]. (a)
Archives du nord. Gallimard, 1977. [*Le Labyrinthe du monde*, II]. (a)
Mishima, ou la vision du vide. Gallimard, 1980.
Le Temps, ce grand sculpteur. Gallimard, 1983. (e)
Quoi? L'Éternité. Gallimard, 1988. Unfinished. (a)
And many other writings.

Translations

Memoirs of Hadrian, trans. Grace Frick, intro. Paul Bailey. 1963. Harmondsworth: Penguin, 1986.

Alexis, trans. Walter Kaiser. 1984. London: Black Swan, 1985.

A Coin in Nine Hands, trans. Dori Katz. 1982. London: Black Swan, 1984. [*Denier du rêve*].

Fires, trans. Dori Katz. 1981. London: Black Swan, 1985.

Oriental Tales, trans. Alberto Manguel. London: Black Swan, 1986.

Coup de grâce, trans. Grace Frick. 1983. London: Harvill, 1992.

The Alms of Alcippe, trans. Edith R. Farrell. New York: Targ, 1982.

The Dark Brain of Piranesi and Other Essays, trans. Richard Howard and Grace Frick. Henley-on-Thames: Aidan Ellis, 1985. [*Sous bénéfice d'inventaire*]

The Abyss, trans. Grace Frick. 1976. London: Black Swan, 1985. [*L'Œuvre au noir*]

That Mighty Sculptor, Time, trans. Walter Kaiser. Henley-on-Thames: Aidan Ellis, 1992.

Dear Departed, trans. Maria Louise Ascher. 1992. London: Virago, 1997. [*Souvenirs pieux*]

How Many Years, trans. Maria Louise Ascher.1995. London: Virago, 1998. [*Archives du nord*]

Further reading

Gaudin, Colette, *Marguerite Yourcenar à la surface du temps*. Amsterdam: Rodopi, 1994.

Poignault, R., *L'Antiquité dans l'oeuvre de Marguerite Yourcenar*. Brussels: Latomus, 1995.

Shurr, Georgia Hooks, *Marguerite Yourcenar: A Reader's Guide*. Lanham, MD and London: University Press of America, 1987.

Zins, Céline (b. 1937), *Par l'alphabet du noir*. C. Bourgeois, 1979. (p)

Adamah. Gallimard, 1988. (p)

L'Arbre et la glycine. Gallimard, 1991. (p)

Further reading

Bishop, *Contemporary French Women Poets*, vol. II, pp. 68–81.

Index